TESOL/TEFL Certification

 # Training Manual

OXFORD
UNIVERSITY PRESS

8 Sampson Mews, Suite 204, Don Mills, Ontario M3C 0H5
www.oupcanada.com

Oxford University Press is a department of the University of Oxford.
It furthers the University's objective of excellence in research, scholarship,
and education by publishing worldwide in

Oxford   New York

Auckland   Cape Town   Dar es Salaam   Hong Kong   Karachi
Kuala Lumpur   Madrid   Melbourne   Mexico City   Nairobi
New Delhi   Shanghai   Taipei   Toronto

With offices in

Argentina   Austria   Brazil   Chile   Czech Republic   France   Greece
Guatemala   Hungary   Italy   Japan   Poland   Portugal   Singapore
South Korea   Switzerland   Thailand   Turkey   Ukraine   Vietnam

Oxford is a trade mark of Oxford University Press
in the UK and in certain other countries

Published in Canada by Oxford University Press

ISBN 978-0-19-901268-8

Cover images: Background image © iStockphoto.com/kickers.
Small images (top row listed from left to right) © Anders Blomqvist/Lonely Planet Images/Getty Images;
© STOCK4B-RF/Stock4B/Corbis; © Kate Mitchell/Corbis; Small images
(bottom row listed from left to right) © iStock.com/mbbirdy; © STOCK4B-RF/Stock4B/Corbis;
Tony Metaxas www.fotosearch.com

Back cover image © Blue Jean Images/Corbis

Printed and bound in Canada.

2 3 – 16 15

Oxford University Press is a department of Oxford University.
Oxford University has no affiliation with Oxford Seminars.

TESOL/TEFL Certification

Training Manual

Published by **OXFORD** for Oxford Seminars
UNIVERSITY PRESS

TESOL/TEFL Certification Training Manual

Content

SECTION

Second-Language Acquisition

Content

A1 English, Asylum for the Verbally Insane

We'll begin with a box, and the plural is boxes,
But the plural of ox became oxen not oxes.
One fowl is a goose, but two are called geese,
Yet the plural of moose should never be meese.
You may find a lone mouse or a nest full of mice,
Yet the plural of house is houses, not hice.

If the plural of man is always called men,
Why shouldn't the plural of pan be called pen?
If I spoke of my foot and show you my feet,
And I give you a boot, would a pair be called beet?
If one is a tooth and a whole set are teeth,
Why shouldn't the plural of booth be called beeth?

Then one may be that, and three would be those,
Yet hat in the plural would never be hose,
And the plural of cat is cats, not cose.
We speak of a brother and also of brethren,
But though we say mother, we never say methren.
Then the masculine pronouns are he, his, and him,
But imagine the feminine, she, shis, and shim.

Let's face it—English is a crazy language.
There is no egg in eggplant nor ham in hamburger;
Neither apple nor pine in pineapple.
English muffins weren't invented in England.
We take English for granted.
But if we explore its paradoxes,
We find that quicksand can work slowly,
Boxing rings are square,
And a guinea pig is neither from Guinea nor is it a pig.

And why is it that writers write but fingers don't fing,
Grocers don't groce and hammers don't ham?
Doesn't it seem crazy that you can make amends but not one amend?
If you have a bunch of odds and ends
and get rid of all but one of them, what do you call it?

If teachers taught, why didn't preachers praught?
If a vegetarian eats vegetables, what does a humanitarian eat?
Sometimes I think all the folks who grew up speaking English should be
committed to an asylum for the verbally insane.

In what other language do people recite at a play and play at a recital?

We ship by truck but send cargo by ship.
We have noses that run and feet that smell.
And how can a slim chance and a fat chance be the same,
While a wise man and a wise guy are opposites?

You have to marvel at the unique lunacy of
A language in which your house can burn up as it burns down,
In which you fill in a form by filling it out,
And in which an alarm goes off by going on.

So if Dad is Pop, how come Mom isn't Mop?

I give up!

 ## A2 ESL Acronyms and Definitions

The following are the most common English-language-teaching acronyms. We have listed those most frequently encountered in the ESL market. There is a great deal of overlap in common usage between these terms. Where one school abroad may refer to their EFL program, another may call it an ESL program. In both cases, the essential meaning is the same, regardless of the acronym.

CALL	Computer Assisted Language Learning
CELTA	Certificate in English Language Teaching to Adults
CLL	Community Language Learning
CLT	Communicative Language Teaching
DELTA	Diploma in English Language Teaching to Adults
EAP	English for Academic Purposes
ECIS	European Council of International Schools
EIL	English as an International Language
ELICOS	English Language Intensive Courses for Overseas Students. This acronym is used in Australia to refer to ESL.
ELL	English Language Learner
ELT	English Language Teaching. This expression has come to be mainstream in the UK.
EMT	English Mother Tongue. English is your first language. This acronym is most commonly used in Europe.
EOP	English for Occupational Purposes
ESP	English for Specific Purposes. The teaching focus of ESP is related to a specific job or a special interest of the student. It can prepare them to work in a particular industry (such as food services, tourism, dentistry, etc.) and involves teaching the English vocabulary necessary to perform job functions.

FLT	Foreign Language Teaching
GTM	Grammar Translation Method
IELTS	International English Language Testing System. It measures speaking, listening, reading, and writing for people who intend to study or work in English speaking countries.
IEP	Intensive English Program. This refers to an intensive course designed to help non-English speaking students prepare for academic study at a college or university level.
L1	First Language
L2	Second Language
STT	Student Talking Time
TEFL/EFL	Teaching English as a Foreign Language/English as a Foreign Language English is taught as a foreign language to people who live in countries where English has no official status.
TESL/ESL	Teaching English as a Second Language/English as a Second Language TESL involves teaching non-native speakers in an English speaking country. In North America, the vast majority of English-language teaching is referred to as ESL. This is because of the huge demand for English among foreigners who have immigrated to North America.
TESOL	Teaching English to Speakers of Other Languages This acronym is used mostly in the United States and covers both ESL and EFL instruction.
TL	Target Language
TOEFL	Test of English as a Foreign Language A US-based standardized test administered to language learning students. More often than not, colleges and universities will require this test for non-native English speakers to study within their institution, or to be considered a competent and fluent English speaker.
TOEIC	Test of English for International Communication This test has become the standard for English Language proficiency in the global workplace and is a requirement to work in many fields.
TPR	Total Physical Response
TTT	Teacher Talking Time

ESL Educational Associations

AAIEP	American Association of Intensive English Programs is a group of college- and university-based intensive English programs.
ACELS	Advisory Council for English Language Schools in Ireland
ARELS	Association of Recognised English Language Schools in the UK

BASELT	British Association of State English Language Teaching schools in the UK
CRELS	Combined Registered English Language Schools of New Zealand
ELTAs	English Language Teacher Associations groups for teachers in Germany and Austria
IATEFL	International Association of Teachers of English as a Foreign Language, based in the UK with members around the world
JALT	Japanese Association for Language Teaching
JET	Japanese Exchange and Teaching Programme
NABE	National Association for Bilingual Education is an association that represents the interests of bilingual teachers in the US.
NEAS	National ELT Accreditation Scheme for course providers in Australia
RELSA	Recognised English Language Schools Association is an organization of independent language schools in Ireland.
TESL	Teaching English as a Second Language is a national federation of teachers and providers in Canada.
TESOL	US-based international association of teachers of English as a second or foreign language. There are regional affiliates, and many countries have their own affiliated associations.

A3 Methods and Techniques for Teaching Conversational English

Below you will find descriptions of the most popular methods and techniques you can use in the classroom to teach conversational English to speakers of other languages. These are some examples of the many methods, techniques, and activities that are available to ESL teachers. Each of these can be expanded or modified to suit the needs of your classroom. The methods that follow have been described in outline, and some examples of usage in the classroom have been provided. To further develop any particular approach, you should do some research using resources such as textbooks, the Internet, your colleagues, and fellow ESL teachers.

Conversational English is the most widely taught form of English. Conversational teaching methods relate speaking, listening, reading, and writing skills directly to English communication. Traditional teaching methods have generally relied on rote memorization and drills to reinforce specific language chunks. While these methods are effective in some circumstances, the lack of relation of the language to its broader usage restricts the relevance of the more prescriptive traditional methods.

While most of the methods and techniques described on the next few pages can be confined to specific activities, the first five approaches are broad methodologies that can influence your entire approach to the classroom. Some of these approaches/methods have fallen out of favor with contemporary language instructors, but there are elements from all that remain relevant in a modern ESL classroom. How you organize your class and which activities you choose will depend upon many factors including your personal teaching style, the dictates of the course materials and school administration, the requirements of a specific lesson, and many other influences which may come and go throughout your educational career. The best approach is a mixed approach: take what you need from the various methods and come up with a style that best suits the demands of your class.

It should be noted that some of the methods described may be labeled, defined, or described differently by other teachers or books. The title is not important; it is the underlying educational approach that matters.

Language Teaching Approaches

The following are some general language teaching approaches that you can use in your ESL classroom. Most modern language teaching is based on the Communicative Method, but other approaches are useful for comparison or in specific situations.

1. Grammar Translation Approach

The Grammar Translation Approach originated in the 1700s and was the primary method of language teaching throughout the 18th and 19th centuries. It remained the common practice for language teaching right up until the 1960s, and is still used in some school systems and in some countries. It was originally designed for teaching Greek or Latin and focused on direct translation of written texts, hence the title, "grammar translation." Grammar translation is more about teaching about the language than teaching the language itself. Little attention is given to pronunciation or the communicative function of language. Language students would be mostly reading and translating classical texts. In more modern classrooms, texts are usually provided in the students' native language and then translated into English. Each work is accompanied by an extensive vocabulary list as well as an explanation of relevant grammar. The idea is that students should be able to deduce grammar rules and understand word usage by seeing the language in context. Testing and instruction relies mainly on drill and repetition to reinforce vocabulary and grammar rules. The limitation, of course, is that spoken language is much more fluid and does not necessarily adhere to such rigid rules and defined usage.

2. Audio-Lingual Method

The Audio-Lingual Method was the first formal rebuttal to the Grammar Translation Approach. Audio-Lingualism was grounded in the understanding that the majority of communication is oral, so simple written translation is not sufficient to enable students to become proficient in another language. Also known as the Army Method because it was developed by the U.S. Army in the 1940s for a program called ASTP (Army Specialized Training Program), Audio-Lingualism relies heavily on drills and mimicry to teach students vocabulary and phrases. Grammar teaching is minimal as the focus is on correct oral response rather than formal structure. Rooted in a Behaviorist Approach to language teaching, the Audio-Lingual method makes great use of reinforcement techniques. Correct responses are quickly praised or rewarded to reinforce the behavior. All interaction between the students and teacher is conducted in the L2 to force students to use the new language to communicate.

While Audio-Lingualism is no longer the dominant method for language instruction, elements of it are still used widely in second-language classrooms. Drill and repetition, while not communicative in nature, do have their place in an ESL classroom. Pronunciation of words and phrases is best learned through practice, so even modern communicative classrooms occasionally make use of these techniques. It is important to note, however, that no classroom should rely solely on drills and mimicry. The idea is to enable students to communicate freely in the new language, so simple repetition is not sufficient to be the dominant method of instruction for an ESL class.

A

3. The Communicative Approach

The Communicative Approach is not a formal approach; rather, it is an amalgamation of popular practices used by language teachers over the course of the last few decades. Growing out of the zeitgeist of the late 1960s, the Communicative movement in applied linguistics was rooted in the idea that language teaching should be based on how language is used in the real world, and that language classes should be more responsive to the needs of students seeking to acquire a new language. This movement represented a shift away from more structural methods that emphasized drills and repetition, and towards a new emphasis on creating conditions conducive to learning. This new way of thinking was in line with the Progressive movement in education at the time.

Textbooks are used as a starting point in Communicative classrooms, but the focus is on developing functional, usable language to prepare students to interact in a variety of everyday situations. The curriculum is generally student-oriented and every effort is made to allow student needs and interests to influence course content. The Communicative Approach recognizes the myriad functions of language, from requesting information and expressing desires, to giving instructions and issuing apologies. Its purpose is to promote communicative ability, so the emphasis is on conveyance and expression of ideas and desires, rather than producing perfect grammatical structure. Classroom activities are set up to be as authentic as possible, making use of English-language newspapers, magazine articles, and numerous other genuine resources. English is the primary means of communication in the classroom and all instruction is given in the L2. The idea is to immerse students in the new language and require them to communicate in English with a focus on comprehensible expression of ideas, rather than rigid structural perfection.

4. Total Physical Response (TPR)

The Total Physical Response Method became popular in the 1970s. The underlying concept is that language must be rooted in the physical world to have concrete meaning. Developed by Dr. James J. Asher of San Jose State University, the TPR Method is based on the assumption that there is usually a long period of listening and comprehension development before a new language is put to use. This process is similar to the way that infants are exposed to language long before they are able to produce it themselves. Supported by Noam Chomsky's research on universal and generative grammar, the TPR Method relies on the notion that the human brain is biologically equipped to develop language; it just needs the right environment to promote natural language acquisition.

A typical TPR class consists of verbal commands to which the students respond physically. Games such as Simon Says and Red Light–Green Light are examples of physical responses to oral instruction. The idea is that students will begin by physically responding to the new language, and by doing so will prime the biological systems used in language acquisition. By focusing first on listening and comprehension, students will absorb significant amounts of the new language before they put it into practice; they will piece together a linguistic map of how the new language works. When they do begin speaking, they will have a ready store of vocabulary, phrases, and grammatical structures to help them to express their thoughts and ideas. Due to the physical focus of the TPR Method, it is of particular appeal to kinesthetic learners. TPR does have some drawbacks, however. It is of most use in a beginner classroom, where the focus is on vocabulary building and absorption rather than creative expression. Also, due to the physical nature of a typical TPR class, shy or timid students can be reluctant to participate.

5. The Rassias Method

Developed by Professor John Rassias of Dartmouth College, the Rassias Method aims to promote language learning by reducing inhibitions and encouraging student responses. Many second-language students are shy or conscious of making mistakes and are hesitant to practice the new language. The Rassias Method attempts to overcome this shyness through the use of a very dynamic and active classroom. Students are called upon to give responses an average of 65 times per hour. Such frequent responses do not allow the students time to become nervous about having to speak; they are speaking so frequently that they do not have time to think about what they are going to say or to worry about creating a perfect sentence. Rapid and frequent responses do not allow time for the inhibiting effects of self-consciousness. The classroom is set up as a non-competitive, non-judgmental environment to eliminate the fear of making mistakes. To allow language learning to happen, the students must be both motivated and comfortable.

According to the Rassias Method, it is also important to connect language to culture. In fact, the two cannot be disentangled. Without culture, there would be no language; without language, there could be no culture. Language should not just be spoken, it should be lived. Real-life situations should be re-created as closely as possible in the classroom to allow students to practice the language in an authentic setting. In addition to the focus on language's connection to culture, the lesson should also be tailored to the specific wants and needs of the students. With that aim, the teacher should make use of frequent, even daily, diagnostic analyses to refine and adjust the pace and approach to suit the students. If students are not learning, it is the responsibility of the teacher to make adjustments to enable them to learn. The Rassias Method is excellent for overcoming student shyness and inhibition to foster an environment conducive to language acquisition, but with that in mind, it is also a very demanding method for teachers. Teachers must be active and energetic in order to be able to hold students' attention and to maintain the rapid-fire style inherent in the Rassias Method.

Practical Techniques for Teaching Conversational English

1. Questioning Students

Questions are a common and easy way to encourage student responses and interaction in the classroom. Good questioning technique will elicit answers from the students and get them using English to express their ideas. Selecting appropriate and interesting topics is the key to a successful questioning session. It is not necessary to do all of the questioning yourself. Encourage students to ask you questions, or to question each other.

2. Dialogues

In a language-learning context, a dialogue is generally a scripted conversation between two people. Dialogues are useful in an ESL classroom because they can mimic authentic speaking situations and a written dialogue provides a clear structure to the conversation. Dialogues can be combined with role-playing or skits, or they can be simple pronunciation exercises. More advanced classes (Intermediate and above) can write their own dialogues to perform for the class.

Some tips for using dialogues:
- Keep the dialogue brief. You do not want to bore the other students while two are talking for an extended period of time.
- Ensure the speaking parts are roughly equal. If one is much longer than the other, have the students reverse roles and repeat the dialogue.

- Model the conversation for your students. It is useful for them to hear the correct pronunciation and inflection at least once before attempting it on their own.
- Discuss the scenario where the dialogue takes place. This can be done before the dialogue is performed as a sort of introduction, or it can be done after by having the students say where they think the dialogue takes place.
- Relate the dialogue to the students. Explain to them when the words and phrases in the dialogue might be heard or used. Once students are comfortable with a given dialogue, you can ask them to rephrase certain sections such as the opening or closing. For example, instead of opening the dialogue by saying, "Hello, my name is Ben. How are you today?" they could say, "Hi, how's it going? I'm Ben, nice to meet you."

3. Encouraging Conversation

The goal of an English conversation class is, of course, to converse! The teacher's role should be to facilitate and encourage a stimulating discussion among the students. This is the time for students to talk, not the teacher. It is a good idea to remember the 80/20 rule of thumb for conversation classes. That is, the students should be speaking 80 percent of the time and the teacher 20 percent (or less!).

Tips for teachers during a conversation class:
- Ensure all students are participating equally by asking direct questions or saying something like, "Let's hear what Jin thinks."
- Contribute to the conversation if it starts to fade. Inevitably, the conversation will reach a lull. You can spark debate by saying something contradictory (playing devil's advocate), or by introducing a new topic.
- Take note of common pronunciation and grammatical errors. Do not interrupt the flow of the conversation to correct these, but bring them up generally at the end. Be sure not to single out individual students when addressing errors.
- Interrupt the conversation if it is getting seriously off topic or is breaking down into an argument. Keep the discussion civil and respectful. Lively is okay, hurtful is not.

4. Group Discussions

Dividing students into small groups provides them with more opportunity to talk than do whole-class discussions. It is important to monitor the students as they are talking to ensure that everyone stays on topic and all conversation is taking place in the L2. Without careful monitoring, group discussions have a tendency to degenerate into social time.

Guidelines for successful small group discussions:
- Choose a wide variety of interesting topics to keep the discussions lively.
- Clearly explain the topics and ensure that the students understand them. You can get things started with a brief introduction or by outlining opposing points of view on a controversial topic.
- Have a concrete goal for the conversation task. Instructing students to simply "talk about X" is not a constructive activity. Have a point to the discussion, a problem for them to solve, or a debate to summarize.
- Monitor the groups to ensure all students are participating. If necessary, mix up the groups to keep stronger students from dominating the conversation.

- Rotate the group members. While familiarity can make students comfortable, it is healthy to have them exchange ideas with a variety of people in the class.
- Discuss the group conversations as a class at the end. Sum up any interesting ideas and bring up any common errors you overheard. Keep things as positive as possible. You want your students to be eager for their discussion next class! You can even give them the topic in advance to allow them to prepare their thoughts, but do not do this too often. An important skill to be developed in a conversation class is the ability to think quickly and structure thoughts in the new language without preparation time.

5. Descriptive Language Learning

The goal of this exercise is to get students to communicate descriptively with other students in the class. Students should be placed into groups of two and given a person, place, or thing to describe (or a choice from a list of alternatives). The goal is to depict the topic in descriptive physical and emotional detail so that the partner has a clear mental image of what is being described and the speaker's emotional connotation associated with it.

Follow-up tasks:

- Ask for groups willing to share their description.
- Write the topic on the board and list the descriptive terms used by the speaker. Discuss the emotional connotation of the words chosen.
- Define any words that may be new or were used in a manner different from the standard (primary) definition. Use the word lists to build vocabulary and quiz students later to ensure the words are understood.

6. Non-Structured Interaction

Non-structured interaction describes any situation where students are forced to rely on their own intellect and understanding to communicate effectively in the new language. These kinds of situations can occur spontaneously (essentially any interaction performed in English between the student and a native speaker), or they can be arranged by the teacher (such as sending a student to retrieve something from another English teacher).

By relying on what they already know and being forced to use their English skills, students take ownership over their L2 learning. Having to interact with a native English speaker for a specific task gives structure to the conversational exchange and allows students to explore what they know. In turn, this increases their ability to communicate certain needs. Often, students may know how to say or ask for something in English, but they are reluctant to try. Giving them a task to perform nudges them to move beyond their shyness and to practice the language in an authentic situation.

Non-structured interaction can take other forms as well. It is not restricted to transactional exchanges, but also can arise during the course of class conversations, in that students begin expressing themselves, arguing a point, debating, or generally communicating in English without thinking about it. The times when students "forget" they are using English because they are so focused on what they are trying to say or the point they are trying to make are pivotal moments of natural language usage. Once students see that they can do this, they will become more and more confident in their English abilities. It is important not to interrupt or disrupt their train of thought in such situations; save the corrections for later. This is the time for expression and communication, not perfect pronunciation and syntax.

7. Backward Drills

Backward drills are used to help students to learn and master long or difficult sentences. The idea behind backward drills is that students are more likely to have difficulty remembering new information than information to which they have already been exposed. By breaking a long sentence into phrases and starting at the end, the amount of immediate recall decreases as students progress through the sentence. The phrases at the end are most familiar, so students will likely have the least difficulty with them, whereas the most recently learned phrases are said first. For example, the complex sentence, "I won't be going to visit my grandparents tomorrow because I have a lot of homework to do" can be broken down and practiced as follows:

"**homework to do**."

"**a lot of** homework to do."

"**I have** a lot of homework to do."

"**because** I have a lot of homework to do."

"**visit my grandparents tomorrow** because I have a lot of homework to do."

"**be going to** visit my grandparents tomorrow because I have a lot of homework to do."

"**I won't** be going to visit my grandparents tomorrow because I have a lot of homework to do."

The new phrases are in bold. As you can see, the new phrases are always said first and the ratio of familiar information to new phrases grows as students progress through the sentence. This allows for much easier recall than if the new phrases were added at the end each time. If the new phrases are added at the end, then students have to trudge through repetition while holding the new phrase in working memory. It is much easier to forget what to say next when the least familiar phrase comes last. Using the backward drill method, the phrases become more familiar as students work through the sentence, allowing for easier memorization and better recall.

8. Micrologues and Macrologues

A micrologue is a very brief summary of a complex topic. Outlining the highlights of one's entire life is an example of a micrologue. Another example could be the history of a country or culture, a description of a recent business trip, or the life of a beloved family pet. As a micrologue should be no more than one or two minutes in length, it encourages students to find the most important points to illustrate. To be comprehensible, the micrologue must be concise and presented in an understandable and connected fashion. It should not simply be a list, but rather should contain some form of narrative structure. The gaps in the information or the jumps from place to place or era to era can often have humorous and revealing results. For example, a student's autobiographical micrologue can reveal a great deal if it details numerous sporting accomplishments but makes no mention of how he met his wife!

A macrologue is the opposite of a micrologue. A macrologue is an expanded description of an item or topic, rather than a summary. Generally, the topic of a macrologue is relatively simple, but it is expanded into its component parts. For example, a macrologue on the topic "bicycle" would dissect the bicycle into its various pieces such as the wheels, seat, brakes, pedals, etc., and would discuss their relationships and functions. Macrologues are a great way to introduce or practice related vocabulary and terms. Preparing a macrologue on a given topic gives students a comprehensive lexical understanding of all things related to that simple topic.

9. Guest Speakers

Hosting a guest speaker is a great way to liven up a class and give students something to look forward to. As with anything special, teachers should make the most of the opportunity. A guest speaker does not have to be someone famous or in a position of great importance, even another English teacher will do. Of course, the more extraordinary the occasion, the more excited the students will be, so rather than bringing in a fellow instructor from your school, try to convince a friend from another nearby school or academy to come in on her day off. Whoever the speaker is, students will be very curious to meet this new person and most will be eager to ask questions and listen to his or her answers.

How to make the most of guest speakers:

- Talk with the speaker a day or two beforehand to go over what he or she will be discussing with the class or any items he or she might be bringing in. While it is interesting for the teacher to be surprised by the guest speaker, it is better for the class if the teacher has an idea of what will transpire and can plan lead-up or follow-up activities accordingly.
- A few days in advance, tell the students that a guest speaker will be coming in. This will pique their curiosity and will also ensure full attendance when the guest speaker arrives.
- Give the students some information about the speaker and help them to formulate questions. Help them to create and structure these questions to make the Q & A period as informative and enjoyable as possible.
- If the class is small, have the students introduce themselves to the speaker. This gives them an opportunity to practice greetings and introductions and also brings the class and the speaker to a more personal level.
- Keep note on the board of any unfamiliar words the speaker uses (or jot them in a notebook if the speaker is using the board or giving a presentation). If you can do so without breaking the speaker's flow, explain the new words or phrases to the class. If that is not practical, then go over the terms after the speaker is finished. You may also want to encourage your students to take note of anything they did not understand. Take advantage of all opportunities for learning as your students will be fully engaged by this special event.

10. Field Trips

If you think back to when you were a student, you will recall that field trips were always an exciting time! Field trips offer an excellent opportunity to discuss new vocabulary and phrases as well as giving both students and teacher a chance to break the monotony of the everyday classroom routine. The key to a successful field trip is preparation. Teachers should not waste the opportunity by treating the field trip as simply a day to get out of the classroom. Planning several lessons before and after the trip to tie the excursion into the curriculum can give the students a sense of continuity and will help them to relate what they have learned to their studies.

Suggestions for a successful field trip:

- Be sure to get permission from the school administration before planning a field trip. There may be permission forms to send out, procedures to follow, or the school may simply have a no field trips policy.
- Lead up to the trip. Go over any new vocabulary, prepare some role-playing exercises, or show pictures or videos of the types of things the students might see. Students will get more out of the field trip if you do your utmost to prepare them.

- Take care when selecting a destination for the field trip. Make sure it will be interesting and relevant to your students. Taking children on a brewery tour or adults to a petting zoo might sound like a good time, but are probably not the best choices of destination.

- Help the students to formulate any questions they might want to ask on the trip. Preparing questions in advance can help them to get the most out of the trip and is valuable practice. Also be prepared to assist any students who have questions during the trip. They may feel shy or awkward asking the guide, so you can help them to use the best English possible. If you will be going on a tour, try to secure an English tour guide to make the trip as relevant as possible to your English classes.

- Take pictures and make notes of interesting things or happenings during the trip. Your students will enjoy reminiscing about the trip and it can help you with your follow-up lessons.

- Just as you spent a few lessons leading up to the trip, you should spend a few lessons to follow-up. Prepare activities that give your students an opportunity to practice any new vocabulary they may have learned. Relate what was learned on the field trip to future lessons, even if it is only to create a context or to use as an example. Chances are the field trip will be one of the most memorable experiences your students have in your class, so make the most of it!

Some possible field trip destinations:
- art gallery
- factory or other business
- fair
- farm
- museum
- park
- restaurant
- supermarket
- university
- zoo

Be creative! There are many interesting field trip options; choose something unique to the area you are teaching in, or something that particularly interests your students. Maybe you will learn something too!

11. Music

Almost everybody loves music. Music is one of the most popular forms of entertainment and is an important part of every world culture. Western pop and rock music are popular in many parts of the world and there is a good chance that your students are familiar with at least some English songs. Using music in the classroom is an enjoyable way to practice new vocabulary and colloquial phrases and to develop listening ability. English children's songs contain simple vocabulary and are intended for native speakers who are learning the language, so they are quite useful in a classroom full of young students. Other artists such as the Beatles are world famous, so your students will likely be familiar with some of their songs and may even know the words to a few!

Tips for using music in the classroom:
- Choose music with a slow beat and clear, audible lyrics. Try to find a song with a repeated chorus to reinforce that part of the song.

- Keep the songs reasonably short. While you might enjoy a 10-minute progressive-rock opus, your students will likely fail to see the point of listening to long guitar solos and musical interludes in an ESL class. Keep songs short, and keep them lyrical.
- Listen to the songs beforehand. Even if it is a song you are familiar with, sit down with the lyrics and give it a good listen. There might be innuendo or undertones that could be inappropriate for the students in your class, or verses that you have learned by heart might be very hard for an ESL student to understand.
- Tell the students the title of the song and ask them to guess what it is about. Listen to the song once with no activity or work for the students, just let them concentrate on the beat and the emotion.
- Go through the lyrics with the students. You can give them a page with the lyrics written out and blanks for them to fill in as you listen, or you can read the lyrics aloud to have them repeat after you.
- Listen to the song, but do not be afraid to pause it to allow students to catch up with writing in the blanks or to explain what was said in a certain part.
- After you have finished the activity (which may require listening a number of times), go over the lyrics again and then let the students listen uninterrupted now that they know the words. Encourage them to sing along; you can even lead the way!

12. Skits

Skits and plays are a good way to engage physical learners. These kinds of activities do require a degree of self-confidence, but with proper support from their peers and the teacher, students generally enjoy structured play-acting. Skits foster active participation and allow students to re-create authentic conversational exchanges, even if the setting of the play is fantastical.

For beginner or pre-intermediate students, it is advisable that the teacher provide a lot of support with the dialogue and stage commands. But as students become more proficient in English, they can write their own lines and maybe even create their own plays!

Allow time for the students to practice their lines and study the dialogue. With enough time and support, they should eventually be able to perform the skit in front of the class without any help from the teacher or a script. If you have time and want to be really creative, you can have them create props and costumes to really bring the performance to life. The teacher should have a copy of the script for the performance to offer any help with forgotten lines or to assist with stage direction.

13. Newspaper Articles

Newspapers are a great authentic resource to use in the classroom. They contain a variety of reading materials and, with the various sections, they are almost guaranteed to include something that interests your students. There are many activities you can do with newspaper articles. Just be sure to pre-read any articles you bring in to ensure that they are comprehensible to your students and appropriate for the class. With those considerations in mind, you can make use of just about any section of the paper, from the headlines and sports pages, to the classifieds and advertisements. Even the cartoons and comics can be put to use in an ESL class!

Some sample lesson ideas for newspaper articles:
- Divide the students into pairs or groups. Give each group a newspaper article that is about four or five paragraphs in length. Have the groups read their articles and circle the most common words. Compare the most frequent words in each article and look for any similarities and/or differences. This can lead to a discussion of the most common words in the English language.

- Divide the students into pairs. Give one member of each pair a descriptive article. Have them read the article to their partner. The partner takes notes of what the article is about, being careful to note any dates, names, or other relevant facts. The students can then compare the notes to the actual article.
- Show the class the headline or lead of a front-page article and ask them what they think the article is about. Could they write a short article based only on the headline and lead? This can be a good predictive writing activity for an intermediate or advanced class.
- Make copies of one or two comic strips, but remove the text from the speech bubbles. Have the students look at the frames and try to decide what the characters are saying. Conversely, you could cut out the speech bubbles and have the students draw the characters and what they are doing. The students can then explain what they drew and why they chose the images they did.

14. Diglot Weave

Diglot means two languages (literally, "two tongues") and the weave comes from intertwining the two languages into once piece of writing. To use this method, you will need the help of someone fluent in your students' native language(s).

Process:
1. Take an article written in the students' L1.
2. Translate some of the words in the text into English. Even if the words are unfamiliar, the context of the sentence should help the students to deduce the meaning.
3. You can either increase the number of translated words as you read farther along in the article, or you can give students subsequent articles with more and more English words in them.
4. Eventually, the students should be reading articles that are primarily in English with a handful of words in their native language.

This method can be very successful if the students are engaged by it, but some classes find it very confusing. If your students are having difficulty, discontinue this method and try again in a few months. When done well, the Diglot Weave method can rapidly enhance your students' English vocabulary. Having the context provided in their own language can help them to clearly see how the words are translated. The method does little to help with grammar or syntax, but can be quite useful as a vocabulary-building exercise.

15. Collecting Biographical Data

Biographical information about your students can be used in a number of ways. Not only is it a simple means of initiating interaction with students by asking them questions about themselves, but the information gathered can be incorporated into future lessons, games, and activities. When collecting biographical information, it is helpful to keep a record of each student's data for future reference. You can record the information on cards or pages, but be sure to keep each student's information separate. You can question students on personal information such as birth date, name, career, ethnic or family background, religion, or marital status, but you can also extend it to preferences and tastes by collecting information on your students' favorite foods, sports, recreation and leisure activities, and any number of other categories. Once you have gathered a sufficient amount of data, you can put it together in the form of a trivia game, 20 Questions activity, or another communicative task. By knowing more about your students, you can personalize your lessons and assignments which should make the activities more memorable to your students.

A4 Noam Chomsky's Theory of Generative Grammar

Language is a process of free creation; its laws and principles are fixed, but the manner in which the principles of generation are used is free and infinitely varied. Even the interpretation and use of words involves a process of free creation.

—Noam Chomsky

Any discussion of Second-Language Acquisition would be incomplete without some mention of the ground-breaking research done by Noam Chomsky. Perhaps more famous now as a political thinker, Noam Chomsky is one of the most widely read and respected intellectuals alive today. Chomsky's theory of generative grammar (first outlined in his 1957 essay titled "Syntactic Structures") revolutionized the field of linguistics and moved it into the realm of cognitive and evolutionary psychology.

According to Chomsky's theory of generative (sometimes called transformational) grammar, language consists of the surface structures we recognize in everyday communication, but underlying those surface structures are so-called deep structures that represent an innate conceptual capacity of the human brain. For example, in English, a sentence describing a boy wearing a blue shirt would be said as, "The boy wore a blue shirt." In Korean or Japanese, however, that same thought would be expressed as, "The boy a blue shirt wore." In French or Spanish it would be said, "The boy wore a shirt blue." Each of these examples relates the same basic information ("<the> boy wear [+ past tense] <a> blue shirt") and, thus, is rooted in the same deep structure, but the surface structures differ in the words used and the order in which they are placed. Stated more simply, the thought is the same; it is the translation of that thought which leads to the variety of linguistic expression in the world.

Rather than approach language as being rooted in minimal sounds arranged in degrees of complexity as the structural linguists had done, Chomsky theorized that language originated in the rudimentary or primitive sentence, and that the basis of language is the expression of thought, not merely the creation of sounds. It is from this innate grammatical base that humans can generate an infinite number of syntactic combinations (sentences) from a finite number of elements (words and punctuation). This deep structure is more abstract and conceptual and relates directly to meaning, while the surface structure is the translation of these conceptual meanings into the sounds and words we share as communicative language. Our ability to translate these deep structures in any number of ways allows for the generation of limitless surface combinations. Essentially, it is the brain's innate ability to conceptualize the abstract that allows for the linguistic translation of thought through evolved brain structures. In short, our brains are wired for language.

Generative grammar has greatly influenced the field of psycholinguistics, particularly the study of language acquisition in children. Chomsky's argument stems from the fact that children are actually exposed to very little correctly formed language. Most speech is broken and elliptical; people constantly change their minds, misspeak, interrupt and correct themselves, yet children are able to deduce the basic rules of structure which govern the language they are exposed to by identifying nouns, verbs, and modifiers, and the order in which they are placed. It is important to note that natural language acquisition in children does not come from simple copying; rather, it is a deduction of grammatical rules applied to the universal grammar in their brains. Children are then able to produce sentences and phrases that they have never heard before; they are able to develop completely novel syntactic structures based on the grammar rules they have deduced from the language they have heard.

SECTION **B**
Learning Styles

Content

B1 Views on How People Learn

Behaviorism

Behaviorism is a theory of animal and human learning that only focuses on objectively observable behaviors and discounts mental activities. Behavior theorists define learning as nothing more than the acquisition of new behavior.

Experiments by behaviorists identify conditioning as a universal learning process. There are two different types of conditioning, each yielding a different behavioral pattern:

1. Classical conditioning occurs when a natural reflex responds to a stimulus. The most popular example is Pavlov's observation that dogs salivate when they eat or even see food. Essentially, animals and people are biologically "wired" so that a certain stimulus will produce a specific response.

2. Behavioral or operant conditioning occurs when a response to a stimulus is reinforced. Basically, operant conditioning is a simple feedback system: if a reward or reinforcement follows the response to a stimulus, then the response becomes more probable in the future. For example, leading behaviorist B.F. Skinner used reinforcement techniques to teach pigeons to dance and bowl a ball in a mini-alley.

There have been many criticisms of Behaviorism, including the following:

1. Behaviorism does not account for all kinds of learning, since it disregards the activities of the mind.

2. Behaviorism does not explain some learning—such as the recognition of new language patterns by young children—for which there is no reinforcement mechanism.

3. Research has shown that animals adapt their reinforced patterns to new information. For instance, a rat can shift its behavior to respond to changes in the layout of a maze it had previously mastered through reinforcements.

How Behaviorism Impacts Learning

This theory is relatively simple to understand because it relies only on observable behavior and describes several universal laws of behavior. Its positive and negative reinforcement techniques can be very effective—both in animals, and in treatments for human disorders such as autism and antisocial behavior. Behaviorism is often used by teachers, who reward or punish student behaviors.

Constructivism

Constructivism is a philosophy of learning founded on the premise that by reflecting on our experiences, we construct our own understanding of the world we live in. Each of us generates our own rules and mental models, which we use to make sense of our experiences. Learning, therefore, is simply the process of adjusting our mental models to accommodate new experiences.

There are several guiding principles of Constructivism:

1. Learning is a search for meaning. Therefore, learning must start with the issues around which students are actively trying to construct meaning.

2. Meaning requires understanding wholes as well as parts. And parts must be understood in the context of wholes. Therefore, the learning process focuses on primary concepts, not isolated facts.

3. In order to teach well, we must understand the mental models that students use to perceive the world and the assumptions they make to support those models.

4. The purpose of learning is for an individual to construct his or her own meaning, not just memorize the right answers and regurgitate someone else's meaning. Since education is inherently interdisciplinary, the only valuable way to measure learning is to make the assessment part of the learning process, ensuring it provides students with information on the quality of their learning.

How Constructivism Impacts Learning

Curriculum—Constructivism calls for the elimination of a standardized curriculum. Instead, it promotes using curricula customized to the students' prior knowledge. Also, it emphasizes hands-on problem solving.

Instruction—Under the theory of constructivism, educators focus on making connections between facts and fostering new understanding in students. Instructors tailor their teaching strategies to student responses and encourage students to analyze, interpret, and predict information. Teachers also rely heavily on open-ended questions and promote extensive dialogue among students.

Assessment—Constructivism calls for the elimination of grades and standardized testing. Instead, assessment becomes part of the learning process so that students play a larger role in judging their own progress.

Brain-based Learning

This learning theory is based on the structure and function of the brain. As long as the brain is not prohibited from fulfilling its normal processes, learning will occur.

People often say that everyone can learn, and, in fact, everyone does learn. Every person is born with a brain that functions as an immensely powerful processor. Traditional schooling, however, often inhibits learning by discouraging, ignoring, or punishing the brain's natural learning processes.

The core principles of Brain-based Learning state that:
*   The brain can perform several activities at once, like tasting and smelling.
*   Learning engages the whole physiology.
*   The search for meaning is innate.
*   The search for meaning comes through patterning.
*   Emotions are critical to patterning.
*   The brain processes wholes and parts simultaneously.
*   Learning involves both focused attention and peripheral perception.
*   Learning involves both conscious and unconscious processes.

- We have two types of memory: spatial and rote.
- We understand best when facts are embedded in natural, spatial memory.
- Learning is enhanced by challenge and inhibited by threat.
- Each brain is unique.

The three instructional techniques associated with Brain-based Learning are:

1. Orchestrated immersion—Creating learning environments that fully immerse students in an educational experience.

2. Relaxed alertness—Trying to eliminate fear in learners, while maintaining a highly challenging environment.

3. Active processing—Allowing the learner to consolidate and internalize information by actively processing it.

How Brain-based Learning Impacts Learning

Curriculum—Teachers must design learning around student interests and make learning contextual.

Instruction—Educators let students learn in teams and use peripheral learning. Teachers structure learning around real problems, encouraging students to also learn in settings outside the classroom and the school building.

Assessment—Since all students are learning, their assessment should allow them to understand their own learning styles and preferences. This way, students monitor and enhance their own learning processes.

Control Theory

This theory of motivation proposed by William Glasser contends that behavior is never caused by a response to an outside stimulus. Instead, the Control Theory states that behavior is inspired by what a person wants most at any given time: survival, love, power, freedom, or any other basic human need.

Responding to complaints that today's students are unmotivated, Glasser attests that all living creatures control their behavior to maximize their need satisfaction. According to Glasser, if students are not motivated to do their schoolwork, it is because they view schoolwork as irrelevant to their basic human needs.

Boss teachers use rewards and punishment to coerce students to comply with rules and complete required assignments. Glasser calls this "leaning on your shovel" work. He shows how high percentages of students recognize that the work they do—even when their teachers praise them—is such low-level work.

Lead teachers, on the other hand, avoid coercion completely. Instead, they make the intrinsic rewards of doing the work clear to their students, correlating any proposed assignments to the students' basic needs. Plus, they only use grades as temporary indicators of what has and has not been learned, rather than a reward. Lead teachers will fight to protect highly engaged, deeply motivated students who are doing quality work from having to fulfill meaningless requirements.

How the Control Theory Impacts Learning

Curriculum—Teachers must negotiate both content and method with students. Students' basic needs help shape how and what they are taught.

Instruction—Teachers rely on cooperative, active learning techniques that enhance the power of the learners. Lead teachers make sure that all assignments meet some degree of their students' needs satisfaction. This secures student loyalty, which carries the class through whatever relatively meaningless tasks might be necessary to satisfy official requirements.

Assessment—Instructors only give good grades (those that certify quality work) to satisfy students' need for power. Courses for which a student does not earn a good grade are not recorded on that student's transcript. Teachers grade students using an absolute standard, rather than a relative curve.

Neuroscience

Neuroscience is the study of the human nervous system, the brain, and the biological basis of consciousness, perception, memory, and learning.

The nervous system and the brain are the physical foundation of the human learning process. Neuroscience links our observations about cognitive behavior with the actual physical processes that support such behavior. This theory is still young and is undergoing rapid, controversial development.

Some of the key findings of Neuroscience are:
- The brain has a triad structure. Our brain actually contains three brains: the lower or reptilian brain that controls basic sensory motor functions; the mammalian or limbic brain that controls emotions, memory, and biorhythms; and the neocortex or thinking brain that controls cognition, reasoning, language, and higher intelligence.
- The brain is not a computer. The structure of the brain's neuron connections is loose, flexible, webbed, overlapping, and redundant. It is impossible for such a system to function like a linear- or parallel-processing computer. Instead, the brain is better described as a self-organizing system.
- The brain changes with use, throughout our lifetime. Mental concentration and effort alters the physical structure of the brain. Our nerve cells (neurons) are connected by branches called dendrites. There are about 100 billion neurons in the brain and about 1,000 trillion connections. The number of possible combinations of connections is about $10^{1,000,000}$. As we use the brain, we strengthen certain patterns of connection, making each connection easier to create next time. This is how memory develops.

How Neuroscience Impacts Learning

When educators take Neuroscience into account, they organize a curriculum around real experiences and integrated, whole ideas. Plus, the focus is on instruction that promotes complex thinking and the growth of the brain. Neuroscience supporters advocate continued learning and intellectual development throughout adulthood.

Learning Styles

This approach to learning emphasizes the fact that individuals perceive and process information in very different ways. The Learning Styles theory implies that how much individuals learn has more to do with whether the educational experience is geared toward their particular style of learning than whether or not they are intelligent. In fact, educators should not ask, "Is this student smart?" but rather, "How is this student smart?"

The concept of Learning Styles is rooted in the classification of psychological types. The Learning Styles theory is based on research demonstrating that, as the result of heredity, upbringing, and current environmental demands, different individuals have a tendency to both perceive and process information differently. The different ways of doing so are generally classified as:

1. Concrete and abstract perceivers—Concrete perceivers absorb information through direct experience, by doing, acting, sensing, and feeling. Abstract perceivers, however, take in information through analysis, observation, and thinking.

2. Active and reflective processors—Active processors make sense of an experience by immediately using the new information. Reflective processors make sense of an experience by reflecting on and thinking about it.

Traditional schooling tends to favor abstract perceiving and reflective processing. Other kinds of learning are not rewarded and reflected in curriculum, instruction, and assessment nearly as much.

How the Learning Styles Theory Impacts Learning

Curriculum—Educators must place emphasis on intuition, feeling, sensing, and imagination, in addition to the traditional skills of analysis, reason, and sequential problem solving.

Instruction—Teachers should design their instructional methods to connect with all four learning styles, using various combinations of experience, reflection, conceptualization, and experimentation. Instructors can introduce a wide variety of experiential elements into the classroom, such as sound, music, visuals, movement, experience, and even talking.

Assessment—Teachers should employ a variety of assessment techniques, focusing on the development of whole-brain capacity and each of the different learning styles.

B2 Learning Style Preferences

Learning Style Preference Inventory

There are three basic learning styles: visual learning, auditory learning, and tactile learning. Depending on how you learn best, it may be easier for you to adopt new knowledge one way over another. This inventory will help you to understand how you learn best. Check the answers that apply to you.

	Often	Sometimes	Seldom	
I prefer written to spoken directions.	✓			
I can recall people's faces more easily than I can recall their names.	✓			
I remember what I see better than what I hear.	✓			
I can concentrate easily on visual tasks despite visual distractions around me.		✓		A
I can remember things better if I picture them in my head.	✓			
I need to picture words in my mind as I spell them.	✓			
I do well reading maps, charts, or blueprints.	✓			
I can remember the words to a song after hearing it a few times.		✓		
I remember things more easily when I repeat them aloud.			✓	
I prefer spoken to written directions.			✓	
I frequently talk to myself when I am thinking.			✓	B
I can concentrate on something despite noises around me.	✓			
I prefer listening to a story rather than telling one.	✓			
I like to have music or background noise on while I am working.		✓		
I like to write things down to remember them.		✓		
I need to take frequent stretch breaks while reading or studying.	✓			
I work well with my hands doing things such as needlework, jigsaw puzzles, or using tools.			✓	
I would rather work on a project than just read about it.	✓			C
I like to hold objects in my hands (pens, paperclips, etc.) while I study.		✓		
I am very good at sports.		✓		
I tend to use my fingers when I am counting in my head.	✓			

Scoring the Learning Style Preference Inventory

Often = 3 points   **Sometimes = 2 points**   **Seldom = 1 point**

Compare the total scores of each of the three learning style categories (A, B, and C). Your highest score reflects your preferred learning style, and offers you a window into the understanding of how you learn best. Knowledge of your learning preference will enable you to maximize your strength, and thereby enable you to become a more efficient learner. For example, if you tend to learn best a) visually, b) aurally, or c) tactile-kinesthetically, your study time can be maximized by:

A) Visual Learner
- Reading a chapter from your text before the lecture
- Taking good notes during lectures so that you can read them over later
- Reading your notes and textbook repeatedly
- Closing your eyes and visualizing what you need to remember
- Studying diagrams, charts, and tables
- Organizing, highlighting, and color-coding notes and study materials

B) Auditory Learner
- Attending all lectures, no matter what
- Taping a lecture and listening to it again later
- Reading out loud, or having text dictated to you

C) Tactile-Kinesthetic Learner
- Building models of difficult to understand concepts
- Doing things you read about
- Watching demonstrations and experiments, and then trying them yourself
- Doing math and physical problems with objects you can move
- Taking notes and drawing diagrams during lectures

If your scores are fairly equal in all three categories (an indication that you learn equally well in all three modes of learning), you can use strategies from each of the three categories to enhance your learning.

 ## Right Brain vs. Left Brain

This theory of the structure and functions of the mind suggests that the two different sides of the brain control two different modes of thinking. It also suggests that each of us prefers one mode over the other.

Experimentation has shown that the two different sides, or hemispheres, of the brain are responsible for different manners of thinking. The following table illustrates the differences between left-brain and right-brain thinking:

Left Brain	Right Brain
logical	random
sequential	intuitive
rational	holistic
analytical	synthesizing
objective	subjective
looks at parts	looks at wholes

Most individuals have a distinct preference for one of these styles of thinking. Some, however, are more whole-brained and equally adept at both modes. In general, schools tend to favor left-brain modes of thinking, while downplaying the right-brain ones. Left-brain scholastic subjects focus on logical thinking, analysis, and accuracy. Right-brained subjects, on the other hand, focus on aesthetics, feeling, and creativity.

How Right-Brain vs. Left-Brain Thinking Impacts Learning

Curriculum—In order to be more whole-brained in their orientation, schools need to give equal weight to the arts, creativity, and the skills of imagination and synthesis.

Instruction—To foster a more whole-brained scholastic experience, teachers should use instructional techniques that connect with both sides of the brain. Teachers can increase their classroom's right-brain learning activities by incorporating more patterning, metaphors, analogies, role-playing, visuals, and movement into their reading, calculation, and analytical activities.

Assessment—For a more accurate whole-brained evaluation of student learning, educators must develop new forms of assessment that honor right-brained talents and skills.

Communities of Practice

This approach views learning as an act of membership in a community of practice. The theory seeks to understand both the structure of communities and how learning occurs in them.

The Communities of Practice concept was pioneered by the Institute for Research on Learning, a spin-off of the Xerox Corporation in Palo Alto, CA. The Institute pursues a cross-disciplinary approach to learning research, involving cognitive scientists, organizational anthropologists, and traditional educators.

Communities of Practice is based on the following assumptions:
- Learning is fundamentally a social phenomenon. People organize their learning around the social communities to which they belong. Therefore, schools are only powerful learning environments for students whose social communities coincide with that school.
- Knowledge is integrated in the life of communities that share values, beliefs, languages, and ways of doing things. These are called communities of practice. Real knowledge is integrated in the doing, social relations, and expertise of these communities.

- The process of learning and membership in a community of practice are inseparable. Because learning is intertwined with community membership, it is what lets us belong to and adjust our status in the group. As we change our learning, our identity—and our relationship to the group—changes.
- Knowledge is inseparable from practice. It is not possible to know without doing. By doing, we learn.
- Empowerment, or the ability to contribute to a community, creates the potential for learning. Circumstances in which we engage, as well as our actions, have consequences for both us and our community, and create the most powerful learning environments.

How Communities of Practice Impacts Learning

This approach to learning suggests teachers understand their students' communities of practice and acknowledge the learning students do in such communities. The Communities of Practice theory also suggests educators structure learning opportunities that embed knowledge in both work practices and social relations (for example, in apprenticeships, school-based learning, service learning, and so on). Plus, educators should create opportunities for students to solve real problems with adults in real learning situations.

 ## B3 Multiple Intelligence Theory

Multiple Intelligence (MI) theory was developed in 1983 by Dr. Howard Gardner of Harvard University and has since been expanded upon by numerous psychologists and educational theorists. In his theory, Dr. Gardner outlines his belief that, rather than having a single type of intelligence, individuals may possess multiple distinct intelligences with a different aptitude in each. These intelligences determine a person's strengths and weaknesses in the classroom, the workplace, and social settings. This theory of human intelligence suggests there are several ways that people have to perceivie and understand the world.

Gardner defines **an intelligence** as a group of abilities that:
- Is somewhat autonomous from other human capacities
- Has a core set of information-processing operations
- Has a distinct history in the stages of development we each pass through
- Has plausible roots in evolutionary history

While Gardner suggests his list of intelligences may not be exhaustive, he identifies the following seven (later expanded to eight, including Naturalistic Intelligence):

1. Verbal-Linguistic—The ability to use words and language
2. Logical-Mathematical—The capacity for inductive and deductive thinking and reasoning, as well as the use of numbers and the recognition of abstract patterns
3. Visual-Spatial—The ability to visualize objects and spatial dimensions, and create internal images and pictures
4. Bodily-Kinesthetic—The wisdom of the body and the ability to control physical motion
5. Musical-Rhythmic—The ability to recognize tonal patterns and sounds, as well as a sensitivity to rhythms and beats
6. Interpersonal—The capacity for person-to-person communications and relationships
7. Intrapersonal—The capacity for understanding the spiritual, inner states of being, self-reflection, and awareness

How Multiple Intelligences Impact Learning

Curriculum—Traditional schooling heavily favors the Verbal-Linguistic and Logical-Mathematical intelligences. Gardner suggests a more balanced curriculum that incorporates the arts, self-awareness, communication, and physical education.

Instruction—Gardner advocates instructional methods that appeal to all the intelligences, including role-playing, musical performance, cooperative learning, reflection, visualization, and story telling.

Assessment—This theory calls for assessment methods that take into account the diversity of intelligences, as well as self-assessment tools that help students understand their intelligences.

B4 Getting to Know Your Intelligence Strengths

Read each statement. If it describes one of your characteristics and sounds true for the most part, answer **T** in the space provided. If it doesn't, mark an **F**. If the statement is sometimes true and sometimes false, leave the answer **blank**.

1. ___ I would rather draw a map than give someone verbal directions.

2. ___ If I am angry or happy, I usually know why.

3. ___ I can play (or used to play) a musical instrument.

4. ___ I compose rap songs and perform them.

5. ___ I can add or multiply quickly in my head.

6. ___ I help friends deal with feelings because I deal with my own feelings well.

7. ___ I like to work with calculators and computers.

8. ___ I pick up new dance steps quickly.

9. ___ It is easy for me to say what I think in an argument or debate.

10. ___ I enjoy a good lecture, speech, or sermon.

11. ___ I always know north from south no matter where I am.

12. ___ I like to gather together groups of people for parties or special events.

13. ___ I like to listen to music on the radio, CDs, or my MP3 player for much of the day.

14. ___ I always understand the drawings that come with new gadgets or appliances.

15. ___ I like to work on puzzles and play games.

16. ___ Learning to ride a bike (or to skate) is easy.

17. ___ I am irritated when I hear an argument or statement that sounds illogical.

18. ___ I can convince other people to follow my plans.

B

19. ___ I have a good sense of balance and coordination.

20. ___ I often see patterns and relationships between numbers faster than others.

21. ___ I enjoy building models (or sculpting).

22. ___ I like word games and puns.

23. ___ I can look at an object one way and see it turned backward just as easily.

24. ___ I can identify when there is a key change in a song.

25. ___ I like to work with numbers and figures.

26. ___ I like to sit quietly and reflect on my feelings.

27. ___ Just looking at shapes of buildings and structures is pleasurable to me.

28. ___ I like to hum, whistle, and sing in the shower and when I am alone.

29. ___ I am good at athletics.

30. ___ I enjoy writing detailed letters or emails to friends.

31. ___ I am usually aware of the expression on my face.

32. ___ I am sensitive to the expressions on other people's faces.

33. ___ I stay in touch with my moods. I have no trouble identifying them.

34. ___ I am sensitive to the moods of others.

35. ___ I have a good sense of what others think of me.

Put an **X** in the box for each item you marked with a **T**. Add up the number of **X**'s. A total of four **X**'s in any category indicate a strong ability.

A	9	10	17	22	30	=		William Shakespeare
B	5	7	15	20	25	=		Isaac Newton
C	1	11	14	23	27	=		Ferdinand Magellan
D	8	16	19	21	29	=		Michael Jordan
E	3	4	13	24	28	=		Johann Sebastian Bach
F	2	6	26	31	33	=		Buddha
G	12	18	32	34	35	=		Mahatma Gandhi

With whom do you share many of your strengths?

B5 Multiple Intelligences

Below are descriptions of the eight distinct intelligences outlined in current Multiple Intelligence educational theory.

Verbal-Linguistic Intelligence

The hallmark of Verbal-Linguistic intelligence is the capacity to use words effectively, whether orally (e.g., as a storyteller, orator, or politician) or in writing (e.g., as a poet, playwright, editor, or journalist). This includes the ability to manipulate the syntax or structure of language, the phonology or sounds of language, the semantics or meaning of language, and the pragmatic dimensions or practical uses of language. Some of these uses include rhetoric (using language to convince others to take a specific course of action), mnemonics (using language to remember information), explanation (using language to inform), and metalanguage (using language to talk about itself). It involves understanding the order and meaning of words in both speech and writing, and how to use the language properly, as well as understanding the sociocultural nuances of a language, including idioms, plays on words, and linguistically based humor.

Characteristics

People who are strong in Verbal-Linguistic intelligence generally have a strong aptitude for reading, speaking, and writing, whether in their native language or in a language they are learning. Some of the characteristics exhibited by people who have strong Verbal-Linguistic intelligence include the enjoyment of literature and the written word, playing word games, creating and reading poetry and stories, being involved in discussions or debates, and any other in-depth or creative use of language. Verbal-Linguistic learners' comprehension and verbalization abilities allow them to understand the structure and form of the language more deeply.

Logical-Mathematical Intelligence

Logical-Mathematical intelligence is demonstrated by the capacity to use numbers effectively (e.g., as a mathematician, tax accountant, or statistician) and to reason well (e.g., as a scientist, computer programmer, or logician). This intelligence includes sensitivity to logical patterns and relationships, statements and propositions (if–then, cause–effect), functions, and other related abstractions. This intelligence involves using numbers, math, and logic to find and understand patterns, as well as categorization, classification, inference, generalization, calculation, and hypothesis testing.

Characteristics

Those with strong Logical-Mathematical ability tend to think conceptually and abstractly and are often able to recognize patterns and relationships that may escape the casual eye. They often enjoy conducting experiments, solving puzzles, performing analyses, or asking broad questions. The ability to work with numbers and formulae and the challenge of solving complex problems often lead these students to explore grammar in great detail. Solving the code of a language can sometimes be motivation enough for strong Logical-Mathematical learners to pursue a second language.

Visual-Spatial Intelligence

Visual-Spatial intelligence includes the ability to perceive the Visual-Spatial world accurately (e.g., as a hunter, scout, or guide) and to perform transformations upon those perceptions (e.g., as an interior decorator, architect, artist, or inventor). This intelligence involves sensitivity to color, line, shape, form, space, and the relationships that exist between these elements. It includes the capacity to visualize, to graphically represent visual or spatial ideas, and to orient oneself spatially.

Characteristics

High Visual-Spatial intelligence correlates with artistic ability, but does not necessarily equate with it. People strong in this intelligence have an above-average awareness of objects, shapes, colors, textures, and patterns in the environment around them. Maps, jigsaw puzzles, games like Tetris, and matching activities tend to appeal to Visual-Spatial learners. To engage Visual-Spatial learners, try to bring flash cards or other visual media into your lessons. Tying words to pictures is useful in any vocabulary-building exercise, but the connection is especially important for Visual-Spatial learners. You can also make use of their "mind's eye" to set a scene or introduce a particular context for language.

Bodily-Kinesthetic Intelligence

Expertise in using one's whole body to express ideas and feelings (e.g., as an actor, mime, athlete, or dancer) and facility in using one's hands to produce or transform things (e.g., as a craftsperson, sculptor, mechanic, or surgeon) are both representative of Bodily-Kinesthetic intelligence. This intelligence includes specific physical skills such as coordination, balance, dexterity, strength, flexibility, and speed, as well as tactile sensitivity, the ability to manipulate objects, and the capacity to sense and to fine-tune body movement. We often talk about learning by doing. Bodily-Kinesthetic learning happens through physical movement and the actions of the body. It involves processing many different kinds of information such as how to ride a bike, drive a car, dance the waltz, catch a thrown object, play the piano, and type on a computer keyboard.

Characteristics

It may seem that Bodily-Kinesthetic intelligence is of little value in a language classroom, but this is not the case. Numerous activities involve movement or play-acting that can engage physical learners. Any physical movement, be it dance, manipulation of objects, role-playing, or elements of the Total Physical Response Method, will appeal to Bodily-Kinesthetic learners. Students with a strong aptitude in this area should be encouraged to use body language, facial expression, and pantomime to assist with communication. Conversely, those same skills can be put to use to reinforce newly learned vocabulary. If your class has a high number of Bodily-Kinesthetic learners, try to make activities as physical as possible. This does not necessarily mean that every lesson should be a physical game, but even simple vocabulary and sentence-structure activities can get students out of their seats and moving around. For example, instead of simply writing the parts of a sentence in order, create some cards that students can move around on the board to make sentences.

Musical-Rhythmic Intelligence

Also known as Auditory-Vibrational intelligence, this involves the capacity to perceive (e.g., as a music enthusiast), discriminate (e.g., as a music critic), transform (e.g., as a composer), and express (e.g., as a performer) musical forms. This intelligence includes sensitivity to the rhythm, pitch, melody, timbre, or tone of a musical piece. One can have a figural or top-down understanding of music (global, intuitive), a formal or bottom-up understanding (analytic, technical), or both. In addition to music, this intelligence deals with the whole realm of sound, tones, beats, and vibrational patterns.

Characteristics

Students who are strong in Auditory-Vibrational intelligence learn well through songs and listening activities. They are often adept at mimicking pronunciation and accents and tend to score well on dictation tasks. It is not only music that appeals to auditory-vibrational learners, but any rhythmic chant, poetry, or rap can be a good way to teach new words or structures. In addition, sounds of the natural or human world can help them to link vocabulary with concepts. Songs, beats, and rhythms can be used to help them to remember phrases and will make studying English much more enjoyable.

Interpersonal Intelligence

Interpersonal intelligence is marked by the ability to perceive and make distinctions in the moods, intentions, motivations, and feelings of other people. This can include sensitivity to facial expressions, voice, and gestures; the capacity for discriminating among many different kinds of interpersonal cues; and the ability to respond effectively to those cues in some pragmatic way (e.g., to influence a group of people to follow a certain line of action). People with strong Interpersonal intelligence work well in social settings and as part of a team, and interact well on a person-to-person basis.

Characteristics

Students with strong Interpersonal intelligence are motivated by group activities. Discussions, debates, and dialogues enable students to interact with their peers and will work to engage interpersonal learners. These students will thrive in any activity which allows them to work with others in some way. In a speaking or conversational class, it is easy to think of activities which allow your students to work together, but in a reading, writing, or grammar class, these sorts of tasks are less obvious. To integrate Interpersonal intelligence into your lessons, consider group or pair writing activities. Your students could practice reading and pronunciation by reading alternating paragraphs from a text to each other. In a grammar class, you could ask your students to check each other's answers or to work together to analyze a particular grammar point. While there is certainly a need for individual class work from time to time, there are many opportunities to allow your students to work together and to engage interpersonal learners.

Intrapersonal Intelligence

Intrapersonal intelligence can be defined as self-knowledge and the ability to act adaptively on the basis of that knowledge. This intelligence includes having an accurate picture of oneself (one's strengths and limitations), awareness of inner moods, intentions, motivations, temperaments, and desires, and the capacity for self-discipline, self-understanding, and self-esteem. The heart of this intelligence is introspection and the ability to be self-reflective; it involves emotion, value, belief, and spirituality, and is reflective of the human desire for meaning and purpose.

B

Characteristics

Intrapersonal learners enjoy activities that allow them to explore their emotions and inner thoughts. Predictive activities using facial expressions or vocal tone can allow them to consider emotions or state of mind. Journal writing and similar activities (e.g., monologues or Show and Tell) allow Intrapersonal learners to write about or discuss their thoughts and feelings. It is not just emotion and feelings which inspire those of Intrapersonal intelligence, but also any activity which allows them to express their own insights, beliefs, or values. Expressing personal opinions or being given a controversial topic to consider can engage Intrapersonal learners as effectively as journal writing or self-reflection.

Naturalistic Intelligence

Naturalistic intelligence includes the ability to discriminate and be sensitive to features of the natural world (flora, fauna, clouds, geographical configurations) and to understand the relationships found in nature. Throughout human history, this intelligence has played an important part for hunters, gatherers, and farmers. It continues to be central to disciplines such as biology, environmentalism, forestry, and resource prospecting, as well as recreational activities such as camping, hiking, or fishing. The modern consumer society uses this intelligence in the form of brand recognition for things such as makes of cars, sneakers, and so on. The pattern recognition inherent in Naturalist intelligence assists with activities from landscaping to archaeology and it involves the full range of understanding that occurs through our encounters with the natural, physical world.

Characteristics

Students with a high Naturalistic intelligence have a profound love for nature and the outdoors. They are interested in animals, plants, weather, and the natural world in general. If field trips to the great outdoors are not an option, these students can be engaged through video or pictures of animals or natural phenomena. Having Naturalistic learners visualize weather, geography, plants, or animals can spark their interest in a lesson. Rather than setting the context for a dialogue at a bus stop or checkout counter, try describing a scenario involving hikers in the woods or visitors to the zoo. There are a number of ways to bring the natural world into your lessons without ever leaving the classroom.

B6 Multiple Intelligence Planning Questions

B

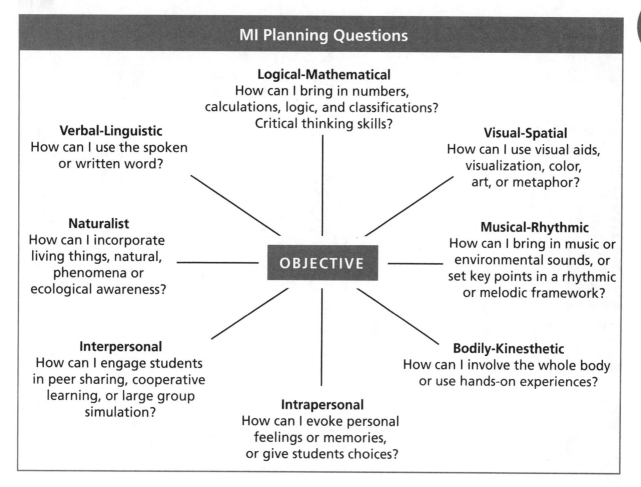

MI Planning Questions

Logical-Mathematical
How can I bring in numbers,
calculations, logic, and classifications?
Critical thinking skills?

Verbal-Linguistic
How can I use the spoken
or written word?

Visual-Spatial
How can I use visual aids,
visualization, color,
art, or metaphor?

Naturalist
How can I incorporate
living things, natural,
phenomena or
ecological awareness?

OBJECTIVE

Musical-Rhythmic
How can I bring in music or
environmental sounds, or
set key points in a rhythmic
or melodic framework?

Interpersonal
How can I engage students
in peer sharing, cooperative
learning, or large group
simulation?

Bodily-Kinesthetic
How can I involve the whole body
or use hands-on experiences?

Intrapersonal
How can I evoke personal
feelings or memories,
or give students choices?

B7 Multiple Intelligence Theory in the Classroom

Intelligence	Teaching Activities (examples)	Teaching Materials (examples)	Instructional Strategies
Verbal-Linguistic	Lectures, discussions, word games, storytelling, choral reading, journal writing	Books, CD players, computers, stamp sets, audio books	Read about it, write about it, talk about it, listen to it
Logical-Mathematical	Brain teasers, problem solving, science experiments, mental calculations, number games, critical thinking	Calculators, math manipulatives, science equipment, math games	Quantify it, think critically about it, put it in a logical framework, experiment with it
Visual-Spatial	Visual presentations, art activities, imagination games, mind-mapping, metaphors, visualization	Graphs, maps, video, LEGO sets, art materials, optical illusions, cameras, picture library	See it, draw it, visualize it, color it, mind-map it
Bodily-Kinesthetic	Hands-on learning, drama, dance, sports that teach, tactile activities, relaxation exercises	Building tools, clay, sports equipment, manipulatives, tactile learning resources	Build it, act it out, touch it, get a gut feeling about it, dance it
Musical-Rhythmic	Rhythmic learning, rapping, using songs that teach	CD players, CDs, musical instruments	Sing it, rap it, listen to it
Interpersonal	Cooperative learning, peer tutoring, community involvement, social gatherings, simulations	Board games, party supplies, props for role plays	Teach it, collaborate on it, interact with respect to it
Intrapersonal	Individualized instruction, independent study, options in course of study, self-esteem building	Self-checking materials, journals, materials for projects	Connect it to your personal life, make choices with regard to it, reflect on it
Naturalist	Nature study, ecological awareness, care of animals	Plants, animals, naturalists' tools (e.g., binoculars), gardening tools	Connect it to living things and natural phenomena

B8   The Stages of Development in Children and Youth

Age/Grade	Key Systems	Cognitive Development	Social Development	Implications
1–3 Pre-School	Family	**Preoperative stage** • Magical thinking • Circularity in thinking • Difficulty dealing with more than 1 or 2 causes • Concrete mental operations	• Emphasis on self • Oriented to parents • Needs limits, secure environment • Developing motor skills	• Build self-esteem • Support pro-social development (sharing, taking turns, asking questions) • Provide safe, caring environment
4–7 Kindergarten to 1st Grade	Family School	**Preoperative stage** • Magical thinking • Circularity in thinking • Difficulty dealing with more than 1 or 2 causes • Concrete mental operations	• Emphasis on self • Identifies with own gender • Enjoys group play • Oriented to parents	• Build self-esteem • Support pro-social development • Involve parents in activities, knowledge, social stages, and resiliency • Encourage sharing, caring behavior • Use cooperative learning groups
7–11 2nd to 5th Grade	Family School Neighborhood Peers	**Concrete operations** • Begins to think relationally and to generalize • Becomes capable of integrating several variables (causes and relationships)	• Oriented to parents • Enjoys group play and same gender peer relationships • Often competitive or has difficulties with peers • Often unaware of behavioral effect on others • Impressed by older role models • Learns behavior from parent/peer role models	• Train parents and teachers in development of resiliency • Teach collaborative skills • Use cooperative learning groups • Provide feedback on behavior • Teach decision making and problem solving
12–16 6th to 10th Grade	Family Peer group School	**Normal mental operations** • Capable of cognitive problem solving • Can think abstractly and hypothetically • Integrates multiple factors to understand concepts	• Oriented to present rather than future • Pre-occupied with self-presentation, acceptance by peer group, physical maturity • Seeks initial sexual intimacy • Seeks peer role models • Motivated by social effects of drug use • Seeks independence in decision making • Differentiates between self and environment • Feels awkward in social skills	• Oriented to peers • Teach collaborative skills • Peer role models teaching refusal skills • Use cooperative learning groups • Encourage responsible decision making • Promote peer leadership, peer helping programs • Involved in community service activities • Involved in environment
16–18 11th to 12th Grade	Peer Group School Work Family Community	**Relativistic thinking** • Capable of synthesizing wide range of relational material	• Primary concerns: individual identity, financial independence, deepening relationships, self-exploration, distancing from family, and making own decisions	• Provide opportunities for leadership • Involved in business ventures, community projects, and drug-free alternative activities • Self-directed learning, inquiry with peers, and explanation of own emerging interests

B9 The Rights of Children

When teaching children, keep in mind that every child deserves:
- the right to express herself and be listened to
- the right to make her own choices
- the right to feel safe and protected within the classroom
- the right to develop a positive sense of self
- the right to play, laugh, and have fun

B10 Youth Learning Characteristics

The following descriptions outline the general stages of learning development in children. There will be individual exceptions to these stages as well as differences across cultures, but this will give you a good idea of what children at each stage will respond to in the classroom.

3–6 years

At this stage, children are developing rapidly, both socially and cognitively. They are still developing some basic language skills in their first language. They tend to experiment with make-believe situations and will be responsive to games that encourage their creativity.

Children of this age are not particularly logical thinkers, so introducing English through a series of language rules does not make much sense. Instead, try getting them involved in discovering the language through a variety of media and real objects; learning tools should be hands-on as much as possible. Young children are concrete in their thinking, so it helps when they can physically interact with what they are learning about.

Be prepared for these students to be in constant motion. They can usually sit and listen for no more than 10 or 15 minutes at a time, so you will need to have a wide variety of activities planned for each class. Use this energy and enthusiasm to your advantage and get them to play group games and work collaboratively on simple projects. When students of this age do something well, be sure to encourage their behavior, as they respond very well to praise.

6–11 years

Children at this stage are developing more logical, organized thought processes and are better able to understand rules. They are able to use reasoning to work out a problem. This allows them to classify things into different groups or into hierarchies which can be useful when learning about word forms or vocabulary in general.

These children are getting better at cooperating with their peers to work toward a common goal. They are also more adept at trying out multiple strategies to figure out the answer to a problem. This, along with the fact that their attention spans have doubled—to 20 to 30 minutes—will allow you to create a more structured learning environment. These children are still fairly easy to motivate, since they will generally be happy to meet the expectations of a teacher who they respect and trust. Remember, however, that they are still young and will need to have variety in their lessons in order to remain interested.

11 years and older

At this stage children begin to think more abstractly. They are able to work out multiple solutions to a single problem. They are also more able to organize their thoughts and their schoolwork.

These students' maturity can open up a wide range of options in the classroom in many ways: they are able to focus their attention for a longer period of time—upwards of 30 to 40 minutes; they are more self-motivated, striving to do well for personal satisfaction; and they are becoming more diverse as people. As students' individual interests grow, allow them to take a greater role in deciding how they will learn. This may be as simple as basing class discussions on topics that interest them, or giving them increasingly open-ended assignments for which they will need to engage in self-directed learning.

 ## B11 Adults as Learners

If you teach adults, you will need to understand how they learn best. Compared to children and teens, adults have special needs and requirements as learners. Adult learning is a relatively new area of study, and the field of adult learning was pioneered by Malcolm Knowles. Knowles identified the following characteristics of adult learners:

- Adults are autonomous and self-directed. They need to be free to direct themselves. Their teachers must actively involve them in the learning process and serve as facilitators for them. Specifically, teachers must get input from students about what topics to cover and let the students work on projects that reflect their interests. Teachers should allow the students to assume responsibility for presentations and group leadership. Instructors have to be sure to act as facilitators, guiding students to their own knowledge, rather than supplying them with facts. Finally, they must show adult learners how the class will help them reach their goals (e.g., via a personal goals sheet).

- Adults have accumulated a foundation of life experiences and knowledge that may include work-related activities, family responsibilities, and previous education. They need to connect learning to this knowledge and experience base. To help accomplish this, teachers should draw out students' experience and knowledge which is relevant to the topic. Teachers must relate theories and concepts to the students and recognize the value of experience in learning.

- Adults are goal-oriented. Upon enrolling in a course, they usually know what goal they want to attain. They, therefore, appreciate an educational program that is organized and has clearly defined elements. Instructors must show students how each class will help them attain their goals. This identification of goals and course objectives must be done early in the course.

- Adults are relevancy-oriented. They must see a reason for learning something. Learning has to be applicable to their work, personal life, or other responsibilities to be of value to them. Therefore, instructors must identify objectives for adult students before the course begins. This means, also, that theories and concepts must be related to a setting familiar to participants. This need can be fulfilled by letting students choose projects that reflect their own interests.

- Adults are practical and focus on the aspects of a lesson most useful to them in their work or travels. They may not be interested in knowledge for its own sake. Teachers must tell these adults explicitly how the lesson will be useful to them.

- As do all learners, adults need to be shown respect. Instructors must acknowledge the wealth of experiences that adult participants bring to the classroom. These adults should be treated as equals in experience and knowledge and allowed to voice their opinions freely in class.

Barriers and Motivation

Unlike children and teenagers, adults have many responsibilities that they must balance against the demands of learning. Because of these responsibilities, adults have barriers against participating in learning. Some of these barriers include lack of time, money, confidence, or interest, lack of information about opportunities to learn, scheduling problems, "red tape," and problems with child care and transportation.

Motivation factors can also be a barrier. What motivates adult learners? Typical motivations include:

- Social relationships: to make new friends, to meet a need for associations and friendships.
- External expectations: to comply with instructions from someone else; to fulfill the expectations or recommendations of someone with formal authority.
- Social welfare: to improve ability and prepare to participate in community work.
- Personal advancement: to achieve higher status in a job, secure professional advancement, and stay abreast of competitors.
- Escape/Stimulation: to relieve boredom, provide a break in the routine of home or work, and provide a contrast to other life challenges.
- Cognitive interest: to learn for the sake of learning, seek knowledge for its own sake, and to satisfy an inquiring mind.

The best way to motivate adult learners is simply to enhance their reasons for enrolling and decrease the barriers. Instructors must learn why their students are enrolled (the motivators); they have to discover what is keeping them from learning. Then the instructors must plan their motivating strategies.

Adult Learning—A New Field of Study

Although adult learning is relatively new as a field of study, it is just as substantial as traditional education, and carries a potential for greater success. Of course, the heightened success requires a greater responsibility on the part of the teacher. Additionally, the students come to the course with precisely defined expectations. Unfortunately, there are barriers to their learning. The best motivators for adult learners are interest and selfish benefit. If they can be shown that the course benefits them pragmatically, they will perform better, and the benefits will be longer lasting.

B12 The Tutoring Experience

B

The most important thing to keep in mind when starting out is that you need to be sincere rather than perfect. It is natural to be a bit nervous. Do not be afraid to let your student know this. Get to know your student and let the student get to know you. In a short time you will likely become friends.

The Dos and Don'ts of Tutoring

Do ...	Don't ...
trust yourself and your common sense	try to be perfect
be committed to learning	assume that you have to be able to speak, read, and write English perfectly
be patient with yourself and your student	assume that you have to be a grammarian or linguist
learn from your mistakes	put pressure on yourself to answer every possible question right away
be creative	

Avoid Bad Tutoring Habits

People with all the best intentions can be ineffective tutors. Do not fall into any of the following bad tutoring habits.

The Woolly Tutor

The woolly tutor is someone who thinks that tutoring involves merely getting together to chat for two or three hours each week. This tutor has no clear and defined plan for what she hopes to accomplish or for what the student wants to accomplish. Without goals and a plan there is no way to evaluate progress at the end of a session. No doubt the woolly tutor and student enjoy their time together but this is not tutoring.

The Ambitious Tutor

The ambitious tutor expects too much of him- or herself and the student. The tutor tries to do too much with the student in a short time and may underrate the complexities of becoming fluent in English. The ambitious tutor works hard but may confuse the student (or at least not help much) because he or she moves too rapidly from one activity to another.

The Academic Tutor

The academic tutor will rigidly follow one pattern of teaching and will try to get the student to learn all the terms used to describe English grammar, sentence structure, and so on. While there is certainly a need to teach grammar and sometimes a need to use a few technical terms, the average student wants to **use** English, not analyze and label it. Language practice is always more important than academic discussion or linguistics.

Tutoring Tips

B

The four language skill areas are:
*   speaking (including pronunciation)
*   listening
*   reading
*   writing

Design or choose activities that involve each of the four language skills. For example, if you are teaching how to use the verb "to be," explain and practice the correct usage orally. Then ask your student to listen to several sentences containing the verb "to be" and identify the correct and incorrect sentences. Follow this up with a reading or writing exercise (such as fill in the blanks) using sentences or a longer text containing several forms of the verb.

Always Keep Broad Goals in Mind

Your goal as a tutor is to help the student become self-sufficient in English. It is easy for you or your student to become preoccupied with the smaller details of English and to lose sight of the student's survival needs, such as how to deal with emergencies, how to manage housing and income needs, etc. When you get sidetracked or when you lose your focus, think of the big picture.

Use Your Imagination and Experiment

There is no single curriculum that will suit all students who are learning English. So you will have to learn through trial and error no matter how many books you consult. Try to identify the specific problems your student has with English and design your own activities and exercises. They may not always work well, but they will teach you (and your student) things that you may never find in a textbook.

Correct Relevantly

Beginner students obviously make many more mistakes than advanced students, so the task of correcting becomes more difficult. If you stop to correct each mistake or to explain the meaning of every fourth or fifth word, you will not get through the session. More importantly, your student will go away with a patchwork of explanations rather than one or two new skills well learned.

Determine ahead of time what you both want to accomplish in the session and correct mistakes that have to do with this goal. If you are confronted by many mistakes (for example, in a piece of student writing), then focus on a few points only and correct them.

Some students want everything corrected and this may not agree with your approach. In this case, you will have to compromise. Above all, make sure your student knows when and how you will correct his or her work.

Review

To learn a particular aspect of English well, remember that it may take much more practice than you have time for in one session. Review at the beginning of each session (what was previously learned), and again at the end of each session. Periodically review what was taught over several sessions.

Use Whatever Works

There are many ESL books, games, and other resources you can use, but the best tutoring resource is usually your student. Listen carefully and really get to know him or her. Then use your common sense and whatever the world offers to help your student learn.

Set the Pace of Learning Carefully

Do not be afraid to challenge your student. He or she will be grateful for the push from someone like you. But check the student's comprehension and progress continually to make sure the pace is appropriate.

Keep Good Records

You can keep track of your sessions and the student's progress in a variety of ways. You could use a journal, a log, lesson notes collected in a binder, or copies of student work. But keep a record of everything even if it is only a note to yourself.

You can also start to collect materials that you think might be useful for future sessions. For instance, you could develop a picture library using photographs from old magazines and newspapers. Organize your pictures according to topics such as foods, the home, occupations, sports and leisure, clothing, etc. Check garage sales for word games. Make a file for these materials and share them with others at the next tutor get-together.

Keep Lessons Simple and Be Prepared for Surprises

One of the keys to tutoring is being able to break a language task down into its simplest parts and focus on these parts without referring to more complex words or aspects of the language. Occasionally, you will find that you have not prepared enough or you may discover that your student knows what you thought she did not know. So always have a back-up lesson or activity ready.

Your student may also come to a session with a problem that needs immediate attention; for example, she may need to write an official letter. Be prepared to put your lesson plan aside and work on what the student really needs at that moment.

Just as you need to allow yourself to make mistakes and experiment, you also need to allow your student to have a bad day. Sometimes you may need to simply take a break from the planned lesson and go to a cafe, a park, or a movie together.

Length of Tutoring Sessions

Shorter, more frequent tutoring sessions are more effective than longer, less frequent sessions. For example, meeting for one hour, three times per week is more effective than meeting for three hours, once per week.

Go Easy on Yourself and Have Fun

Your student will understand that you are going beyond your regular duties to assist and she will probably be thrilled to have the opportunity for a little more English practice with a native speaker. Plan and prepare, but do not be discouraged if some excellently organized lesson does not work out very well. Be honest, try something new, and enjoy.

B13 Types of Key Visuals

There are a number of ways to present information visually in the classroom. Not only will such media appeal to visual learners, but they can also be handy references for key concepts and points taught in your class.

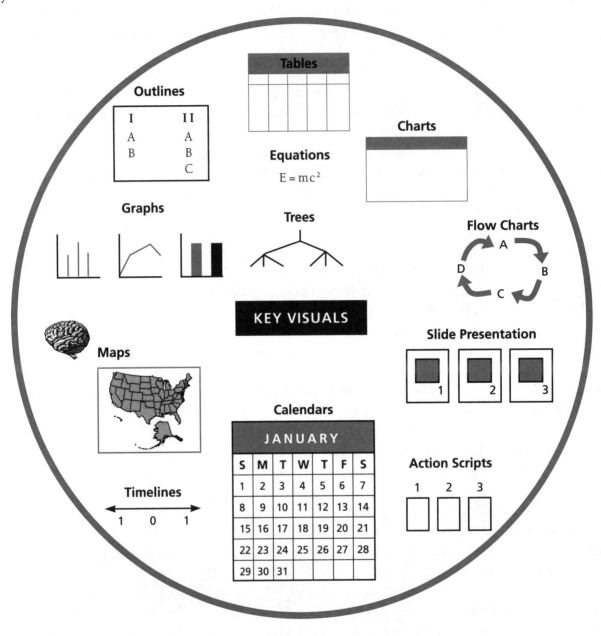

SECTION C
Teaching Practices

Content

C1 Little Teddy Stoddard

There was a story many years ago of an elementary teacher. Her name was Mrs. Thompson. As she stood in front of her 5th grade class on the very first day of school, she told the children a lie.

Like most teachers, she looked at her students and said that she loved them all the same.

But that was impossible, because there in the front row, slumped in his seat, was a little boy named Teddy Stoddard.

Mrs. Thompson had watched Teddy the year before and noticed that he did not play well with the other children, that his clothes were messy, and that he constantly needed a bath. And Teddy could be unpleasant. It got to the point where Mrs. Thompson would actually take delight in marking his papers with a broad red pen, making bold Xs and then putting a big F at the top of his papers.

At the school where Mrs. Thompson taught, she was required to review each child's past records and she put Teddy's off until last.

However, when she reviewed his file, she was in for a surprise.

Teddy's first grade teacher wrote, "Teddy is a bright child with a ready laugh. He does his work neatly and has good manners … he is a joy to be around."

His second grade teacher wrote, "Teddy is an excellent student, well liked by his classmates, but he is troubled because his mother has a terminal illness and life at home must be a struggle."

His third grade teacher wrote, "His mother's death has been hard on him. He tries to do his best but his father doesn't show much interest and his home life will soon affect him if some steps are not taken."

Teddy's fourth grade teacher wrote, "Teddy is withdrawn and doesn't show much interest in school. He doesn't have many friends and sometimes sleeps in class." By now, Mrs. Thompson had realized the problem, and she was ashamed of herself.

She felt even worse when all her students brought her Christmas presents wrapped in beautiful ribbons and bright paper except for Teddy. His present was clumsily wrapped in the heavy, brown paper that he got from a grocery bag.

Mrs. Thompson took pains to open it in the middle of the other presents. Some of the children started to laugh when she found a rhinestone bracelet with some of the stones missing, and a bottle that was one-quarter full of perfume. But she stifled the children's laughter when she exclaimed how pretty the bracelet was, put it on, and dabbed some of the perfume on her wrist.

Teddy Stoddard stayed after school that day just long enough to say, "Mrs. Thompson, today you smelled just like my Mom used to." After the children left she cried for at least an hour.

On that very day, she quit teaching reading, writing, and arithmetic. Instead, she began to teach children.

Mrs. Thompson paid particular attention to Teddy. As she worked with him, his mind seemed to come alive. The more she encouraged him, the faster he responded. By the end of the year, Teddy had become one of the smartest children in the class and, despite her lie that she would love all the children the same, Teddy became one of her "teacher's pets."

A year later, she found a note under her door, from Teddy, telling her that she was still the best teacher he ever had in his whole life.

Six years went by before she got another note from Teddy. He then wrote that he had finished high school, third in his class, and she was still the best teacher he ever had in his whole life.

Four years after that, she got another letter, saying that while things had been tough at times, he'd stayed in school, had stuck with it, and would soon graduate from college with the highest of honors. He assured Mrs. Thompson that she was still the best and favorite teacher he ever had in his whole life.

Then four more years passed and yet another letter came. This time he explained that after he got his Bachelor's Degree, he decided to go a little further. The letter explained that she was still the best and favorite teacher he ever had. But now his name was a little longer—the letter was signed, Theodore F. Stoddard, M.D.

The story doesn't end there. You see, there was yet another letter that spring. Teddy said he'd met this girl and was going to be married.

He explained that his father had died a couple of years ago and he was wondering if Mrs. Thompson might agree to sit in the place at the wedding that was usually reserved for the mother of the groom.

Of course, Mrs. Thompson did. And guess what? She wore the bracelet, the one with the several rhinestones missing. And she made sure she was wearing the perfume that Teddy remembered his mother wearing on their last Christmas together.

They hugged each other and Dr. Stoddard whispered in Mrs. Thompson's ear, "Thank you, Mrs. Thompson, for believing in me. Thank you so much for making me feel important and showing me that I could make a difference."

Mrs. Thompson, with tears in her eyes, whispered back. She said, "Teddy, You have it all wrong. You were the one who taught me that I could make a difference. I didn't know how to teach until I met you."

C2 Effective Teaching Practices

If you think about your own experiences as a student, you may be able to identify some habits or characteristics of both ineffective and effective teachers.

The Ineffective Teacher

Think about an ineffective teacher whose class you did not enjoy being in and who made learning unpleasant. Why was the teacher ineffective? Did he or she fail to engage the students in lessons or discourage students from asking questions?

List some of the ways in which this teacher was ineffective.

1. _____

2. _____

3. _____

4. _____

5. _____

Think about how this teacher responded to student misbehaviors and other disruptions in the classroom.

List some of the ways this teacher handled disruptions, being as specific as possible.

1. _____

2. _____

3. _____

4. _____

5. _____

The Effective Teacher

Think about an effective teacher you have had who made learning enjoyable, and whose lessons had a strong positive impact upon you.

List some of the ways in which this teacher was effective.

1. _____

2. _____

3. _____

4. _____

5. _____

List some of the ways this teacher handled disruptions, being as specific as possible.

1. _____

2. _____

3. _____

4. _____

5. _____

How might you use this information to shape your own teaching practices?

C

C3 Getting Started: The Basics of Teaching

The following principles apply to almost any kind of teaching. Some of these points may seem like common sense, yet these are the types of issues professional teachers spend years learning and perfecting. Many of these ideas are adapted from *Teaching by Principles: An Interactive Approach to Language Pedagogy* by H. Douglas Brown and *How To Teach English* by Jeremy Harmer.

Make Lessons Interesting

Bored students will not remember much of the lesson. Do not talk for long blocks of time. Instead, keep students involved and interacting with you and each other in English. Some may come from cultures where teachers lecture and students listen quietly. If interaction makes your students nervous, provide plenty of support by giving clear and very specific directions. For example, say, "Yuko and Yan, you work together," rather than "everyone get into pairs." Vary the types of skills you practice and activities you use, add games, and bring in real-life objects like a telephone, cookbook, or musical instrument. Vary your own dress or behavior patterns for a day. Keep in mind, though, that some degree of predictability will be appreciated by your students, fostering a feeling of safety.

Make Yourself Understandable

Simplify your vocabulary, grammar, and speaking speed to the degree necessary to be understood, and keep any instructions simple and logical. New ESL teachers frequently slow down the pace of their speech but forget to modify their vocabulary and grammar for beginner students. As your students' English ability increases, so should the complexity and speed of your English. Some of your interaction at an intermediate level, and most of it at an advanced level, can use natural grammar and speed, but make sure you slow down or repeat any highly important points. Teach your students how to ask for clarification when they need it. Try to anticipate unknown vocabulary and be prepared to explain each unknown word. Appropriate language modification gets easier with experience.

Motivate With Rewards

Students will truly want to learn when they perceive a personal reward. To boost internal motivation, remind them of the benefits that English can provide, such as English-speaking friends, better job opportunities, easier online shopping, or less stress when traveling abroad, and then teach language that will bring them closer to those benefits. Motivation can be increased externally by praise and encouragement as well as tangible rewards like prizes, certificates, or check marks on an assessment record chart. Motivation can be hindered by over-correction or teaching a topic that the student will not use in daily life.

Provide a Useful Context

Students will remember material better and take more interest in it if it has relevant contextual meaning. Arbitrary rote learning (word lists or grammar drills) may be useful in solidifying language forms, but unless there is a real-world application, sooner or later it is likely to be forgotten.

Remember that Native Language Affects English Learning

A student's native language will provide a basis for figuring out how English works. Sometimes the native language can negatively affect English production. To illustrate, the Japanese language does not use articles (a, an, the) so correct article usage is frequently difficult for Japanese students. Spanish uses idioms such as "I have thirst" or "I have sleepiness" so Spanish speakers may forget to use "I am … " with an adjective instead of a noun. Most teachers, however, have little if any understanding of their students' native language(s). While a familiarity with the native language may shed light on certain errors, it is certainly not essential. In fact, intermediate and advanced students are often able to tell you whether a specific error is related to their native language.

Do Not Assume All Errors are Bad

Native language interference contributes to a gradual process of learning in which language is refined over time to become more like natural English. For example, a student may progress through phrases such as "no I like peanuts," to "I no like peanuts," and finally to, "I don't like peanuts." Teachers must not get discouraged watching students exchange one error for another; this process is a natural part of language learning. Selectively choose errors to work on rather than trying to fix everything at once. Give priority to problems that hinder communication rather than those that are incorrect but still comprehensible. With gentle corrective feedback, students will keep improving.

Encourage Students to Think in English

Too often ESL students will get stuck in a habit of thinking in their native language and then mentally translating what they want to say or write into English. This is time-consuming and frequently leads to confusion when direct translation is not possible. Thinking in English requires students to use learned words, phrases, and language structures to express original ideas without focusing too much on language rules or translation. To illustrate, how would you change the statement "Linda ate an apple" into a question? Of course, "Did Linda eat an apple?" More than likely you did not think about adding the modal "do" (in the past tense "did" because "ate" is past tense) before the subject, changing the irregular verb "ate" to "eat" and raising your vocal intonation at the end of the sentence. While it is unreasonable to expect beginner ESL students not to rely on native language translation to some degree, one way you can minimize it is to explain new vocabulary using simple English, drawings, or gestures and allow dictionary lookups only as a last resort. You might also ask students to speak (or write if they are able) for several minutes without stopping. At some point, mental translation will become cumbersome and students should begin developing an ability to use English independently from their native language.

Build Confidence in Your Students

Students must believe in their own ability to complete a task. Without self-confidence, they are unlikely to take risks, and risk-taking is necessary in language learning. Students need to feel that it is safe to make mistakes. By trying out new or less familiar language, they may find that they are indeed capable of more communication than they thought. Try to reduce feelings of embarrassment when mistakes are made, and give far more compliments than criticisms. Make some tasks easy enough that everyone is guaranteed success.

Account for Different Learning Styles

Some people are hands-on learners; some like to watch; some like to have detailed explanations. Some people learn better visually, others audibly. Some like to work in groups, some work better individually. Language teaching should take a variety of learning styles into account through varied activities.

Know Your Students

Learn how to pronounce students' names (if need be, ask for easier nicknames) and use them. Build trust with your students by building relationships and being approachable. Make sure quiet students are included and more assertive ones do not dominate the lesson.

C4 ESL Teacher Self-Evaluation

Use the following questions as an evaluation of your performance as an ESL teacher. If there are any areas where you are unhappy with the evaluation you have given yourself, you will know that you should continue to work on improving those particular skills.

Skill 1: Feedback Opportunities
A classroom environment has been created to provide extensive academic interactions between teacher and students.
   Evaluation Questions:
- Have procedures been used to ensure that a large amount of time is allocated to academic instruction?
- Do lessons include appropriate amounts of guided practice and daily reviews?
- Is new material presented in small steps with large amounts of academic feedback?
- Depending on content, are appropriate amounts of oral and written feedback used?

Skill 2: Questioning
The questions are consistent with the instructional needs.
   Evaluation Questions:
- Are student success rates appropriate for the lesson activity?
- Do the questions support the presentation of new content in small steps?
- Are questions to individuals posed before the individual is named?
- Do questioning procedures maintain instructional momentum?

Skill 3: Student Responses
Individual responses, group responses, and written responses are used to ensure high levels of involvement from all students.
   Evaluation Questions:
- Am I blending choral and individual responses where their use is appropriate?
- Are all the students being equally involved during individual questioning?
- When appropriate, do I require written responses using the most important skills?

Skill 4: Reacting to Student Responses

Teacher reactions are consistent with student responses to questions.

Evaluation Questions:

- Does the hesitant, correct response typically receive strong praise and a quick review?
- For incorrect responses due to lack of knowledge, do I rephrase the question or re-teach?
- Do correction procedures indicate the use of rules and practical problem-solving strategies?
- Do my responses to student errors indicate an atmosphere where students are not afraid to make errors?

Skill 5: Question Clarity

Questions are clearly framed and clearly delivered.

Evaluation Questions:

- Are questions short and precise, or rambling and disjointed?
- Are questions delivered clearly and audibly?
- Are questions clearly aligned with the content focus of the lesson?
- Is student attention gained before questions are posed?

C5 Observation

Individual Work

- Does the student work well alone?
- Does the student work well in groups?
- Does the student become easily distracted from the tasks at hand?
- Does the student see work through to completion?
- Is the student able to explain ideas?
- Is the student able to organize their work?
- Does the student ask for help when needed?
- Can the student present to a group?

Group Work

- Do they become actively involved in class discussions and tasks?
- Do they work well with others?
- Are they able to share responsibility?
- Are they able to lead a group?
- Are they able to be a member of a group?
- Do they force their ideas on others?
- Do they easily succumb to pressure from others?

Groups

- Does the group easily decide on the roles of its members?
- Does the group divide up work along logical lines?
- Does the group collectively decide on a plan?

- Does the group ensure that each member understands the whole as well as their part in the task?
- Do the group members support each other in their tasks?
- Does the group use its time effectively?

C6 Methods for Evaluating Students

Listening

- Daily comprehension abilities
- Listening comprehension
- Song lyrics
- Speeches
- Stories
- True-or-false tests

Speaking

- Daily speaking abilities
- Debates
- Plays
- Student dialogues
- Teacher questioning

Reading

- Matching exercises
- Multiple-choice tests
- Reading comprehension tests
- Reading out loud

Writing

- Compositions
- Crossword puzzles
- Fill-in-the-blanks tests
- Short-answer tests

Formative evaluation is a method of judging performance while the program activities are being formed or happening. Formative evaluation focuses on the **process**.

Summative evaluation is a method of judging performance at the end of the program activities. The focus is on the **outcome**.

Note: Use both formative and summative evaluation techniques. Always give clear and precise dates and criteria for testing.

C7 A Foreigner in My Classroom

Cultural Variables and their Potential Impact on Assessment

Cooperation vs. Competition: Helping a friend is not necessarily cheating; emphasis is on feelings and attitudes rather than strictly academics.

Time: Time is treated differently in different cultures and there is not always the same emphasis on time; therefore, tests can be difficult when given time constraints.

Polychronic/Monochronic Orientation: We are accustomed to completing tasks in some kind of order—each task representing a separate or unique operation (monochronic). Other cultures do not emphasize this same "logic." Students could be assessed as not having good attention spans when it may be that they are not responsive to a particular type of instruction.

Bodily Movements: Being passive in Western classrooms is rewarded, while being active tends to be seen as a behavioral problem. Watch how your class behaves while seated as opposed to being interactive.

Proximity: What is your comfort level with regards to personal space? Try challenging that in a test situation (have someone stand right beside you).

Eye Contact: In some cultures, eye contact is a form of respect; in others, it is a sign of disrespect.

Gender: Various cultures have different accepted roles/tasks that are gender specific—you may be asking a student to complete a task that is not within his or her defined role. In addition, you may be performing a task that is outside your perceived role within the culture.

Individual vs. Family Orientation: Some students relate to themselves as part of a group—this will have an impact on your means of motivation.

Verbal/Non-Verbal Communication Norms: Not all cultures welcome children having discussions with adults. In other situations, answers may be given in class that are incorrect but the student feels a social responsibility to speak.

Fate vs. Individual Responsibility: Some cultures place responsibility on external sources such as fate, while some others place responsibility on the individual (external vs. internal locus of control).

Perceptual Style: Some cultures see a whole picture prior to seeing its components; others see individual components of a whole picture first.

Cognitive Style: In Western countries, we tend to rear children to be reflective and analytical whereas other cultures may stress relational and intuitive ways of thinking.

C8 Assessment Tools

Book Response Journals

Similar to a learning log, the book response journal is a place for students to express personal reactions and to wonder about events, themes, and ideas in a book. Students are encouraged to react to everything they read. Teachers may use these journals to respond to each student individually, sharing their questions, feelings, and ideas about literature and making suggestions for further reading or related activities. Some teachers hold individual reading conferences with their students and use these response journals as part of the conferences.

Comparison Charts

Comparison charts are one of a number of graphic organizers. They involve the examinations of similarities and differences among ideas, events, characteristics, etc. Comparison charts may take a number of forms and are an excellent way to engage students individually or in groups as they seek to focus characters, events, or themes within a single story, or to compare books, events, or properties within a given theme.

Conferences

There are many types of teacher–student conferences including reading, writing, goal setting, evaluation, and coaching. The major purposes are to collaborate, assess, and guide. These conferences do not have to be too long and they give good insight into a student's progress.

Cooperative Learning Activities

Cooperative learning involves students working together in groups (often following a teacher-presented lesson), with group goals and individual accountability. Critical to the process are two factors: 1) how to help another student without giving the answer; and 2) how to work together toward a common goal.

Demonstrations

Demonstrations transform ideas into something concrete and observable through visual, tactile, and aural stimuli such as art, drama, movement, and/or music. They could also include opportunities to demonstrate and explain procedures and strategies such as a science experiment or a solution to a non-routine math problem.

Discussions

Discussions provide safe, open forums where students are encouraged to speak, listen, and respond to opinions, feelings, and ideas regarding the designated topic.

Goal Setting

Setting goals with students provides the basis for monitoring student performance through collaboration and self-reflection.

Graffiti Walls

Graffiti walls are free-form spaces for brainstorming or communicating words, phrases, or ideas on a topic. These are often used as evolving records. A teacher may use them to facilitate brainstorming on a particular theme at the beginning of a unit, as well as to encourage students to add new words or phrases relating to the theme as the unit progresses. In addition to encouraging students to search for new and interesting words, the graffiti wall serves as a class dictionary/thesaurus as students need new words to enrich their writing.

"I learned ... " Statements

"I learned ... " statements may be in either written or oral form. Their purpose is to give students a chance to self-select one or more of the things they learned during a class session, an investigation, or a series of lessons.

Interviews

Interviews are structured or unstructured dialogues with students in which the student reports his reaction or response to a single question or a series of questions. This typically provides an opportunity for the teacher to determine the student's depth of understanding rather than whether the student can provide the correct answer. Questioning may follow a period of observation to discover if the student's perception of a situation is the same as the observer's.

KWLs

KWLs are used by teachers to assess what students know, wish to know, and have learned about a particular topic, using sheets divided into three columns labeled K, W, and L. At the beginning of a lesson, KWLs serve as written records of the students' prior knowledge (K) on the topic, and allow the opportunity for the students to note what they desire (W) to know about the topic. Following the lesson, the students can assess what they actually learned (L) about the topic.

Learning Logs

Learning logs are journals that enable students to write about the curriculum they have been studying. The major reason for using them is to encourage students to be in control of their own learning and to promote thinking through writing.

Oral Attitude Surveys

Attitude surveys provide a way in which students' self-reflections regarding group and individual performance, and affective characteristics such as effort, values, and interest are shared. Providing an oral survey allows students to share their ideas, learn from others, and deepen the way they think about the topics being discussed.

Oral Presentations

Oral presentations include speeches, storytelling, retellings, recitations, drama, videos, debates, and oral interpretations. They are evaluated according to predetermined criteria.

Peer Evaluations

Peer evaluations consist of student analysis and assessment of peer proficiency using either established or self-generated criteria. An activity must be very carefully structured if students are to receive valid feedback from their peers.

Problem-Solving Activities

In problem-solving activities, students must search for a means to find a solution to the problem. A good evaluation of the problem-solving activity requires consideration of both the thinking process and the final product.

Products

Student products represent completed student work in a variety of forms: writing, video, audiotapes, computer demonstrations, dramatic performances, bulletin boards, debates, etc. Students can demonstrate understanding, application, originality, organizational skills, growth in social and academic skills and attitudes, and success in meeting other criteria.

Response Groups

Response groups provide opportunities for small numbers of students to discuss books or events in depth with one another. Often these groups are organized and run by students themselves because they all have read the same book or experienced the same event and want to discuss it. Participating in a response group will help the teacher to gain insight into his students' thinking skills, group behaviors, and affective characteristics.

Self-Evaluations

A key concept in alternative assessment is having the student learn to recognize his own progress by taking the time to reflect. Those who are able to review their own performance, explain the reasons for choosing the processes they used, and identify the next step, develop insight, self-involvement, and self-reflection. A particularly important component of any form of assessment is the student portfolio.

C9 Lesson Plan Aids

Bringing a subject to life and providing stimulating activities can be a challenge. As always, consider your learning objective and plan the lesson around that. The more stimulating the activity, the more your students will gain from the experience. Listed below are just some of the possibilities for creative lessons. These can be combined or modified to suit nearly any component of language teaching.

advertisement
art gallery
art product
article
autobiography
banner
bibliography
blueprint
book
book jacket design
book review
bookmark
brain teaser
brochure
budget
bulletin board
calendar
cartoon
certificate
choral reading
chronology chart
classification
classroom museum
code or secret message
coins
collage
commercial
comparisons
contrast
costume
court trial
critique
debate
demonstration
diagram
diary
diorama
directory
editorial
exhibition
experiment
fable

fact file
fairy tale
family tree
flag
flannel board story
flip chart
flow chart
food labels
formula
game
glossary
greeting card
guessing game
idea checklist
illustrated story
interview
invention
inventory
jokes
journal
labeled diagram
lesson plan
letter
letterheads
machine
magazine
map
matching game
mini-center
mobile
model
montage
mosaic
movie
mural
musical instrument
newspaper
notes
oral report outline
pamphlet
panel discussion
photo album

picture book
picture dictionary
poem
portfolio
position paper
postcard
poster
prediction
puzzle
rebus story
recipe
résumé
riddle
scrapbook
seating chart
shadow box
skit or play
slide show
small database
song lyrics
sonnet
story
story problem
suitcase of artifacts
survey
tall tale
terrarium
time capsule
time line
tongue twister
totem pole
transparency
travelogue
TV script
verdict
videotape
vocabulary list
web page
word scramble
word search
wordless book

SECTION D
Lesson Planning

Content

D1 Lesson Planning Introduction

Before stepping into the classroom, you should have a good lesson plan prepared. Even if you plan to improvise much of what you will do or say during the lesson, the lesson plan will be a guide for you. If you get off track, or if things do not go as smoothly as you had anticipated, you can always refer back to your plan. If you have spent some time developing a well thought-out lesson, you should be able to take a step back and figure out how to achieve your desired outcome.

As soon as possible, find out who you will be teaching (this may be the goal of your first lesson). Who you are teaching will have a big impact upon your lesson planning. How old are the students, and what language level are they at? Is there a mix of different ages or levels in the class? What country or region are the students from? Do some research to make sure you are aware of any social or religious taboos to avoid in your lessons. Get to know the students and have them talk about their interests, accomplishments, and previous experience with English. All of this will guide you in preparing lesson plans.

You might spend a lot of time thinking about what your teaching objectives are and developing a good lesson plan, but still have an unsuccessful lesson. Try to learn from your mistakes and figure out why the lesson went wrong and how to ensure the next lesson is great!

The First Day of Class

A successful first day of class begins before the teacher and students ever meet. A placement exam may have been given to the students to determine their level of English proficiency, a textbook and other study materials have been chosen, and a trained and competent teacher has been selected to facilitate the learning environment. If any of these elements are lacking, the course may not run smoothly. If all elements are present and the teacher is prepared, the chances for success are greatly increased.

Given that the above conditions have been met, a conscientious teacher is likely to arrive with plans for teaching the first two or three lessons, probably along with some supplementary material (and ready to bring conversational situations to life), which of course is exactly the correct procedure.

Lesson Planning Guide

Your lesson plan will generally have the following three parts:
• A warm-up
• The main activity
• A follow-up

Each of these parts will need to be introduced and explained as well as wrapped up at its conclusion. They should all be focused on the lesson's learning goal and a central theme.

When planning your lesson, keep the following things in mind:
• Include activities that will appeal to students with different learning styles.
• Engage all the students as much as possible.
• Connect the lesson to a real-life situation whenever possible.
• Incorporate a variety of media.
• Plan activities that will encourage students to work cooperatively as well as competitively.
• Plan to have students work with a variety of partners or groups.

- Allow students opportunities to be creative.
- Incorporate a variety of skills into each lesson (reading, writing, speaking, listening).
- Depending on how easily the class understands the lesson, you may need to expand upon it or alter it completely.

Points to Keep in Mind

Making instructions clear for language-learning students can be a challenge. Unfortunately, there is no magic formula for giving instructions that works for all students in all situations. However, a variety of strategies applied in combination will help teachers reach a wider range of students and will serve to clarify and reinforce instructions for students as well.

Here are several practical ideas that will be helpful for both teachers and students.

1. When lesson planning, consider how you will give instructions for tasks. For each activity or assignment, think to yourself, "How can I explain this task clearly to the students?" You may want to write down in your lesson plan what you will say and what materials and visuals you will use to help clarify instructions.

2. Plan enough time in your lesson to deliver instructions thoroughly and to check students' understanding. Do not deliver instructions hurriedly while the bell is ringing and students are grabbing their books and backpacks and leaving the room.

3. Be sure you have all students' attention when giving instructions—insist on it and never make exceptions.

4. Be well prepared, not only for verbal delivery of instructions, but also with instructions written in clear, concise, simple English on the board (or on a flip chart). This additional visual will catch students whose listening skills may make it challenging to follow verbal instructions.

5. Be verbally clear and concise. Consider the following instructions:
   "Ok, everybody, listen to me. I want to tell you what we're going to do next. What we're going to do is ... I want everybody to get together with the partners you were working on the peer-editing with last week."

   > vs.

   "Please find last week's writing partner."

6. Model the task and always do an example together with the class, even for homework exercises. For in-class tasks, rather than just telling students what is expected of them, show them as well. When assigning a task, physically **do** the task yourself in front of the students. Show them with your body, gestures, and facial expression exactly what you want the task to look like when they begin doing it. With pair tasks, have the class watch while you model with another student. Check for understanding and model again if needed, or ask two students who seem to understand the task to model it together.

7. When assigning a textbook activity or exercise, ask students to open to the correct page in their textbooks and follow along as you go over the task. Use your own textbook as a prop. Point to the exercise, check that all students are following, and do the first question together as an example.

8. Repeat instructions at least once with slightly different wording, if possible.

9. Give students time to write assignments down and insist that they do.

10. Break down instructions and deliver them in steps or chunks. When instructions include a series of steps, deliver the first step, wait, check for comprehension, and then deliver the next small chunk of instructions. This gives students time to digest smaller pieces of information at a time rather than to grasp what bits and pieces they can of a lengthy explanation.

11. Use pair work. Stop in the middle and at the end of instructions, and ask students to confirm the task with a partner. This often eliminates the need for repetition by the teacher.

12. Use comprehension checks and involve students actively in the instructions process. Have students repeat assignments or instructions back to you. Ask, "Can anyone tell me what you are going to do next/for homework?" Open-ended comprehension checking questions (beginning with WH-words) such as "What is still unclear?", "What questions do you have?", and "Who has a question about that?" are much more effective than "Any questions?" The former ask for a real feedback response from students while the latter allows students to shake their heads or not respond at all.

These strategies may seem time consuming, but in reality, they are great time savers. Think of the class time spent repeating and repairing unclear instructions, the chaos created when students misunderstand a task, or the extra time added to a lesson if students fail to complete a homework assignment as a result of confusion about instructions. When added up, that is a lot of precious class time lost—time when students could be learning and teachers could be teaching.

D2 The Introductory Class

The introductory class is very important for setting the overall tone in your classroom. It is your first opportunity to get to know the students, for them to get to know you, and for them to begin working together as a group. This first class should make the students feel comfortable and excited to be in your classroom.

This is also a time to establish your expectations: tell students what the daily routine in the class will be, explain how they will be graded, and establish the rules for the classroom.

Here is a general outline of how to structure the introductory class:

1. Start with a warm-up or icebreaker activity. This will encourage students to relax and interact with as many of their classmates as possible.

2. Introduce yourself. The students will be curious about who you are, so let them know a bit about your family, hobbies, or travels. You may find that photographs are useful for this introduction.

3. Learn about the students. In a small class, you can have the students introduce themselves to everyone and talk about their interests. (Be sure to ask follow-up questions!) In larger classes, you can have students interview each other in pairs, then report what they learned about their partner to the class.

4. Play name games. This will help everyone—including you—learn each other's names.

5. Introduce the book(s) you will be using in class. This is especially important if the students will have to purchase their own materials.

6. Explain the marking scheme for the class. Show students the breakdown of their total grade: how much is based on homework, tests, participation, and projects.

7. Give the students handouts. This will help them understand what you are explaining, as well as giving them something to reference outside of class. This first handout should include your name and any contact information you wish to provide, a description of the class rules, and a breakdown of the marking scheme.

8. Establish the daily routine for your class. Explain the following basic structure of each lesson:
    a) warm-up activity
    b) review
    c) introduction of new skill or grammar point
    d) practice
    e) activity or assignment

9. Assign homework. This will get students into the routine of completing their homework after each class. The first assignment may involve having the students write a short piece about themselves or their family; this is a good way to get to know your students while assessing their writing skills.

 ## D3 Activities to Do the First Week

The first few days of class can be hard to plan. If you are unsure about your students' expectations or proficiency level, it is especially difficult. But, the first few days are also the most important. They can make or break the atmosphere in your classroom. The ideas listed below are designed to help you get to know your students (and help them get to know each other) as quickly as possible and establish a relaxed atmosphere in the classroom. Students who feel that language learning will be enjoyable and comfortable will learn the best.

   Use these activities to get you started. They can be adapted for many levels, or can be a source to spark your own creative ideas! The most important thing to remember is that your students are apprehensive and may feel uncomfortable at first. Put them at ease and, most importantly, sell yourself! Let them know that you are a good teacher and that the lessons and activities they participate in during your class will help them learn English.

*   Have students come up to the board, write their names, and tell any special meanings associated with their names. They can also write any characters from their own language, or tell why their parents gave them their names. This is a good chance to talk about the differences among cultures in name choices (i.e., some cultures are more likely to choose a family name, some will choose a name with special meaning). In a more advanced class, this can always lead into a discussion of changing one's name with marriage, how it is done in various cultures, and why.

*   Bring a world map to class and point out to the students where you live, where you or your family is from originally, and where your ancestors came from. In a low-beginner class, students can point to their home countries and say the country names. This can provide a starting point for learning country and city names. Write the names of countries and cities that the students are unfamiliar with on the board.

- Introduce yourself by showing pictures of yourself and your family. Teach the students any new vocabulary related to family (i.e., mother, father, brother, or for more advanced classes, mother-in-law, cousin, nephew). For homework, have each student bring two or three family pictures to class. Have the students talk about their pictures in pairs and prepare a short presentation (written if necessary) for the class. Then have each student show the pictures and introduce his or her family. This helps students get to know each other as well as build vocabulary. In an advanced class it can be used as an introduction and schema-building activity for writing short biographies or autobiographies.

- Later, the family picture activity can be expanded to give students practice with comparing and contrasting. Put students in pairs and have them compare and contrast the people in their pictures ("Your mother is taller than my mother"). Provide students with any vocabulary or expressions they will need beforehand. You may want to select a few pictures to point out such things as blond, fair-skinned, bald, curly hair, etc., that students may not know the words for.

- In an intermediate or advanced class, let the students interview partners and write down their partner's name, native country, and two interesting or unusual things about him or her. Then the students should make up another fact which is not true. When they introduce their partners, the class must guess which facts are true and which one is false.

- Bring construction paper, old magazines, glue, and scissors to class. Have beginner students cut out pictures that represent things they like to do and paste them on a sheet of construction paper. Have each student show his or her collage to the class, and you can provide new vocabulary words. If they are true beginners, be sure to provide a sentence model on the board for them to use, such as, "I like to _____." After all of the students have presented, have them switch collages and then explain to a partner the hobbies represented in the new pictures. This will help them practice any new vocabulary. (You may need to model this for the class before having them do it on their own.)

- Another activity to learn names is the name chain game. In this game, a student says his or her name and where he or she is from. The next student must say the first student's name and country before introducing him- or herself. The third student must say the first and second students' names and countries before making his or her own introduction. This chain continues until the students cannot remember or all of the students have introduced themselves. For more advanced classes, have each student give his or her name, country, and a hobby.

- One thing that can save you headache and frustration is to make your class rules very clear in the beginning. You want to be firm, but not overbearing, and one of the best ways to do that is by making it fun. Some of your students have never been in an ESL classroom setting and may not have the same expectations and etiquette that you expect. Try showing them a movie clip like the first few scenes of *Stand and Deliver* or the lunchroom scene at the beginning of *Lean on Me*. Both of these clips show obviously bad behavior and the students will laugh. After the clip, ask them what behaviors were unacceptable (they can all come up with at least a few!) and use this as a chance to introduce what is acceptable in your classroom. Be sure to stress that students are expected to respect their teacher and listen attentively! Another clip which shows good classroom etiquette is from *Dead Poets Society* when Robin Williams has his first class meeting with his students. This is a good clip to use to stress how differences in classroom expectations can be very positive.

The most important thing to remember in the first few days is to be confident and in control of your class and at the same time make learning English enjoyable for your students.

D4 Awareness, Continuity, and Initiative

Awareness

A good ESL teacher must always be aware of what is happening in the classroom. Listen carefully to what the students are saying to you; if you cannot understand something, take the time to figure out what the students are trying to communicate to you. This will make the current lesson, as well as future lessons, proceed more smoothly.

Be proactive in assessing whether the students understand the material as you teach. Make sure you frequently question them about the material, and invite students to give you feedback and ask you questions throughout the lesson.

Continuity

When planning each lesson, think about what students will be learning throughout the entire unit and term. Make sure each lesson builds upon what was learned previously and provides a logical lead-in to future lessons.

Also keep in mind that you may be taking over where another teacher has left off in the middle of a term. Be sure to follow the course outline that has been designed by the school or the previous teacher.

Initiative

As a teacher, you will be expected not only to present lessons to your students, but also to motivate them to learn. Use your interests and the students' interests to come up with creative ways to make the learning process active and fun. Continue to try new approaches and activities so students are always excited to step into your classroom. Remember that if you are getting bored with your lessons, so are the students.

D5 Steps to Effective Lesson Planning

Each lesson should be a complete learning experience and should teach students something new. To ensure that each lesson does this, make sure the following criteria are met:
- Think about the students.
  - Consider their age and language level.
  - What skills or knowledge have they already acquired?
  - What must they do to learn this new skill?

- Think about your teaching objectives.
  - What information are you trying to convey to the students?
  - Why should students learn this? (How does this learning fit into their learning goals for the day, unit, or term?)
  - How can you effectively convey this information to the students?

- Think about the resources that are available to you.
  - What materials do you have that could aid in the teaching process?
  - How can you most effectively use the materials to provide the students with a dynamic learning experience?
  - How can you make the best use of your teaching environment for this lesson?

- Think about the warm-up.
  - How will you capture the students' attention and motivate them to learn?
  - Make sure the warm-up is related to the overall goal of the lesson.

- Think about the main activity.
  - Decide how you will effectively make the lesson's objectives clear to the students.
  - Decide what the most appropriate method to teach the lesson will be. Will it involve a demonstration, an explanation, a group discussion, a reading, a guest speaker, or a field trip? Whatever method you choose, ensure that students will be actively involved in the learning process.
  - How will you make use of your knowledge of multiple intelligences to engage all the students?
  - How will you ensure that students are understanding any new concepts as the lesson proceeds?
  - Consider ways in which you can allow the students opportunities to practice the new skill or provide you with feedback throughout the lesson.

- Think about how you will follow up on the lesson.
  - How will you connect what the students have learned in this lesson to future lessons or to real-life situations?

- Think about how you will evaluate the students' learning.
  - How will you assess the students' understanding of new concepts?

D6 Activities for the Different Lesson Stages

The following are some suggestions for each of the three main lesson stages: Introduction, Body, and Wrap-up. You do not need to use each suggestion during every class, but remember to include a variety of techniques that will engage students in the learning process.

Introduction

- Grab the students' attention and get them interested in what they are going to be learning.
- Bring in props, stories, photos, books, videos, or songs to make the lesson more exciting.
- Pose a challenging question to the students and work it out throughout the day's lesson.
- Discuss a current news story and discuss the students' opinions about it.
- Tell the students what they will be learning that day.
- State the objective of the day's lesson.

Body

- This is the main part of the lesson. Most of your time will be spent on this; make sure things move along at a smooth pace so students do not get bored.
- Explain your main points in multiple ways. Some students will understand better by seeing, some by hearing, and some by doing, so try to facilitate all three.
- Model processes for the students; show them how you expect the work to be done.
- Have students work in pairs, in groups, and independently.
- Ask many questions throughout to ensure that students understand what is happening.
- Encourage students to ask questions.

Wrap-up

- During the wrap-up, you can make sure that students have fully understood the aims of the lesson.
- Re-state the objective of the day's lesson.
- Have students summarize what they have learned.
- Play a game or administer a brief quiz to test the students' new knowledge.
- Follow up on a question or topic discussed during the warm-up. Discuss whether or not the students now have a deeper understanding than they did before.
- Have the students write about an aspect of what they have learned in their journals.
- Connect the day's lesson to an aspect of the students' day-to-day lives so they can see its value.
- Give students a preview of the next day's lesson, explaining how it connects to what they have just learned.
- Assign homework based on the day's lesson.

D7 Objectives of Lesson Planning

When preparing your lesson plan, focus on the following three important objectives:

1. Context—Whenever possible, embed the skill you are teaching within a real-life context. Choose an appropriate theme that will make learning more interesting for the students.

2. Language—Figure out exactly which area of grammar or vocabulary you want the students to develop during the lesson. You should have specific expectations at the beginning of the lesson, so you can assess students' progress throughout the lesson.

3. Skills—Which skills do you want the students to practice during this lesson (reading, writing, listening, or speaking)? You will probably include some combination of two or more skills.

D8 Lesson Plan Outline

Objectives

- Outline the knowledge and/or skills your students should be able to demonstrate by the end of the lesson. Objectives should be narrow and achievable.
- Objectives will need to be somewhat flexible, depending upon how easily your students are able to grasp the new concepts you are teaching them.

Level

What is the English-language proficiency level of the class?

Time

How long is the lesson?

Materials

List any materials you will need to complete the lesson.

Set-up

List any preparations you will need to make in the classroom before beginning the lesson, such as special seating arrangements for the students, particularly if they are to work in groups.

Warm-up

- Describe how you will—creatively—introduce students to the day's lesson.
- The warm-up should be fun and interesting, and encourage students to begin thinking about the day's topic.

Activity

- Describe in detail how students should complete the day's lesson.
- When you are explaining the activity to the students, you should be very clear about how to complete it and, if possible, demonstrate the task yourself.
- Explain the overall purpose of the activity to the students.

Follow-up

How will the knowledge or skills acquired in this lesson be used in future lessons?

Evaluation

How will students be evaluated on what they have learned in this lesson? Possible evaluations are written tests, student presentations, or simply listening to students as they work through the day's activity. Also include some measure of self evaluation. It is important to reflect back upon a lesson and consider what went right and what went wrong. Use this information to guide your future lesson plans.

D9 Lesson Plan Templates

Lesson Plan Template 1

Class: _____	Date: _____
Time: _____	
Objectives:	
Materials:	
Set-up:	
Warm-up:	
Activity:	
Follow-up:	
Evaluation:	

Lesson Plan Template 2

Class / Level:	Date:	Time:	Topic:

Objectives:	Materials:
	Set-up:

Warm-up:

Activity:

Follow-up:	Evaluation:

D10 Reflection/Evaluation of the Lesson

Lesson Topic:	Date:

1. Learning Outcomes:

Was the instruction congruent with the objectives?

Were the intended learning behaviors and learning outcomes realized?

2. Effectiveness:

Planning/Execution of Lesson:

- Did I follow the plan? Did I keep to the schedule and start on time? Was I aware of pacing?
- Did I provide review? Did I integrate previous learning?
- Did I give students an overview of what to expect?
- Did I present with enthusiasm and motivation?
- Were directions/explanations clear?
- Were questions appropriate and challenging?
- Did I have a motivational opener?
- Was there a smooth transition from one part/lesson to the other?
- Did I summarize the lesson?

Classroom Organization/Management:

- Was the classroom physically prepared?
- Was the environment conducive to what I intended to teach?
- Were the necessary and appropriate materials present in the classroom?
- Were handout and collection procedures established or did they need adjustment?
- Was my plan for grouping of students appropriate or is there a better way?
- Was I able to get students quickly settled and on task?
- Was the dismissal technique effective?
- Were there any potential management/behavior problems that need further consideration?

3. Follow-up:

Students:

- What plan do I need to allow each student to participate at his or her appropriate level of thinking?
- How do I provide for special students; for those requiring review; for those requiring an additional challenge?

Materials/Organization:

- How could I adjust materials or add to them to enhance and strengthen learning?
- Could I organize the classroom/the students differently for greater learning opportunities?

D11 Student Evaluation of the Lesson

How did we do today?

Name of Activity: _____

Three things I liked:

_____

_____

_____

Three things to improve:

_____

_____

_____

Overall impression of activity:

_____

_____

_____

How did we do today?

Name of Activity: _____

Three things I liked:

_____

_____

_____

Three things to improve:

_____

_____

_____

Overall impression of activity:

_____

_____

D12 Weekly Schedule Template

WEEK OF:		THEME:		
MON	TUES	WED	THURS	FRI

SECTION E

Classroom Management

Content

E1 Classroom Management:
Cutting to the Heart of the Process

E2 Difficult Situations

Consider the following scenarios:

Scenario 1

You are teaching English in a small town. Although you enjoy the teaching and your students, you have concerns about your boss. Many of the statements in your contract have not been fulfilled (e.g., classroom resources are not supplied, nor is the one-bedroom apartment). Your boss has hinted that your first month's salary may be late, but when you approach the subject he does not want to discuss it.

Scenario 2

After explaining a lesson to your class, you split them into groups, but one group refuses to work together. As the other groups eagerly begin the assignment, the members of this one group sit with their arms crossed and refuse to talk.

Scenario 3

You teach in an elementary school that has 40 students in a class. The country and the school believe in corporal punishment as a way of ensuring that the large group stays focused. You have observed the teacher using a ruler to hit the hands of students that misbehave. Once the teacher leaves the room, those same students misbehave in your class. They are not responsive to your usual discipline techniques.

Scenario 4

You teach an oral communication class of 10 adults of varying levels. They are all interested and engaged in the class and communicate well on an individual basis, but during group discussions two of the more advanced students dominate the lesson.

Scenario 5

After teaching a lesson, you tell the class to do individual work. The room quickly explodes in noise. You ask them to work quietly on their own, but each time after quieting down for a minute, the room gets very noisy again.

E3 Classroom Management Techniques

Proactive Measures for Classroom Management

A proactive approach to classroom management focuses on structuring and organizing the classroom in ways that create a positive physical and emotional environment.

1. Create an inviting classroom climate.

An inviting classroom climate is one in which students and teachers treat one another with courtesy and respect; students follow rules not out of fear but because they feel ownership of them. Teachers create opportunities for students to develop and exercise control over their own behavior. Ways you can create an inviting climate include the following:

- Learn something about each student's personal interests.
- Share classroom jobs and responsibilities with students.
- Set high expectations (for behavior and achievement).
- Create classroom traditions and rituals, such as special songs and celebrations.

2. Structure a positive physical environment.

The physical environment directly influences teachers' and students' attitudes and their ability to perform. Assess your room arrangement and consider the following:

- Create enough space to move easily throughout the classroom.
- Arrange desks to support the task at hand. For example, use clusters for group work and rows for test taking.
- Create an attractive, aesthetically pleasing environment by making sure the room is clean and uncluttered.
- Put up posters, pictures, and projects that reflect students' backgrounds, activities, and accomplishments.

3. Establish clear rules and procedures.

Classroom behavior problems are least likely to occur when you carefully plan and clearly define rules and procedures that structure student behavior. Keep in mind the following guidelines:

- Phrase your rules positively. State what students should do, rather than what they should not do.
- Keep your list of rules short; choose no more than five rules. More than five is too lengthy for students to remember, and if they cannot remember the rules, they probably will not follow them.
- Plan ahead for follow-through. Consistency is essential for effective classroom management. Consider the behaviors that will result if students choose not to follow a rule, and know how you will hold students accountable for such behaviors.
- Involve students in creating classroom rules when appropriate.

4. Maintain momentum and flow.

One of your most important tasks as a proactive classroom manager is to keep the flow of instruction moving at the right pace—not too fast and not too slow. Use the following ideas to maintain momentum and flow:

- Create interesting and engaging lessons that capture students' interests.
- Have all materials readily available to avoid delays.

- Accommodate individual learning rhythms by having additional activities available for students who finish assignments early.
- Carefully plan for transition times within lessons as well as between them.

Reactive Measures for Classroom Management

You will also occasionally need to rely on reactive measures in the classroom. A reactive approach to classroom management involves reacting to misbehavior; that is, anything that is disruptive to the flow of the classroom. Here are some tips to remember:

1. Have the students describe examples of behaviors that are not appropriate and why.

2. Essentially, students misbehave for one or more of the following reasons: seeking attention, seeking power, seeking revenge, and/or seeking isolation. If you can understand why students are misbehaving, you will be better able to encourage them to change their behavior.

3. Decide how to react to misbehavior. You must decide in advance what you will react to. Choose your battles! Students will misbehave and too much intervention on your part will do more harm than good in terms of instructional flow. Make sure that your students know that what is fair is not always equal and that you will deal with each person as an individual.

4. Decide which types of intervention to use. Effective intervention will be calm, firm, direct, and immediate. However, remember that sometimes it is better to allow misbehaviors to extinguish naturally by ignoring them. Beyond that, teachers can unobtrusively discourage the behavior by doing or saying something to the student; reprimanding the student directly; making the student practice the appropriate behavior repeatedly (be careful though, this kind of overcorrection can be counterproductive if done too often or inappropriately); giving the student a time-out to isolate them from the situation and allow a cool-off period; or moving to more severe punishments as dictated by the student's behavior and the specific situation.

5. In general, the following are good guidelines for the use of punishment in the classroom:
- Use it sparingly
- Use it quickly
- Relate it directly to the misbehavior (punishment must fit the crime)
- Think about what you are doing (never react out of anger)
- Avoid complex, time-consuming punishment systems. These penalize you for punishing a student.

E4 Classroom Procedures

What types of activities should I have procedures for?
To start, you should have procedures in place telling students what to do when they enter the classroom and before they are allowed to leave the classroom. Remember to be specific and list all of your expectations.

Morning Procedures

1. Sharpen your pencil.

2. Turn in homework to appropriate tray.

3. Copy down all homework assignments.

4. Complete warm-up activity on the board.

5. When finished, wait quietly in your seat until the teacher begins class and gives instructions.

Remember:
- If you have young students, make your procedures simple to read and follow. For pre-school, Kindergarten, and 1st grade students, use a series of pictures with words to help them understand your procedures.
- You do not need to make a poster for all of your procedures such as going to the restroom, changing classes, going to lunch, walking in the hallway, etc.
- You do need to train your students on all of these types of procedures so that they understand what to do and what you expect from them.
- Take plenty of time during the first several weeks to practice these various procedures with your students so that they will remember what to do. If they do not get it right the first time, practice the procedure again and again until they do. The more time you spend on this at the beginning of the year, the less you will have to worry about it later on.

Is it worth the time it takes to practice?

Yes! If students know exactly what they are supposed to do and what is expected of them, they will be less likely to cause disruptions throughout the year. This means that you will probably have more time to teach than if you did not practice these important skills and procedures.

E5 Seven Techniques for Better Classroom Discipline

1. Focusing

Be sure you have the attention of everyone in your classroom before you start your lesson. Do not attempt to teach over the chatter of students who are not paying attention. Inexperienced teachers sometimes think that by beginning their lesson, the class will settle down. The students will see that things are underway now and it is time to go to work. Sometimes this works, but the students are also going to think that you are willing to compete with them and you do not mind talking while they talk. You are willing to speak louder so that they can finish their conversation even after you have started the lesson. They get the idea that you accept their inattention and that it is permissible to talk while you are presenting a lesson.

The focusing technique means that you will demand their attention before you begin. That way you will wait and not start until everyone has settled down. Experienced teachers know that silence on their part is very effective. They will punctuate their waiting by extending it 5 to 10 seconds after the classroom is completely quiet. Then they will begin their lesson using a quieter voice than normal. A soft-spoken teacher often has a calmer, quieter classroom than one with a stronger voice. His or her students will pay attention in order to hear what the teacher says.

2. Direct Instruction

Uncertainty increases the level of excitement in the classroom. The technique of direct instruction is to begin each class by telling the students exactly what will be happening. The teacher outlines what the class will be doing for the period. He or she may set time limits for some tasks.

An effective way to marry this technique with the first one is to include time at the end of the period for students to do activities of their choosing. The teacher may finish the description of the hour's activities with: "And I think we will have some time at the end of the period for you to chat with your friends, go to the library, or catch up on work for other classes."

The teacher is more willing to wait for class attention when he knows there is extra time to meet his goals and objectives. The students soon realize that the more time the teacher waits for their attention, the less free time they have at the end of the hour.

3. Monitoring

The key to this principle is to circulate; get up and move around the room. While your students are working, make the rounds, and check on their progress.

An effective teacher will make a pass through the whole room about two minutes after the students have started a written assignment. The teacher checks that each student has started, that the students are on the correct page, and that they have put their name on their papers. The delay is important. The teacher wants students to have a problem or two finished so that answers can be checked for whether or not they are correctly labeled or in complete sentences. Individualized instruction is provided as needed.

Students who are not yet quite on task will be quick to get going as they see the teacher approach. Those that were distracted or slow to get started can be nudged along.

The teacher does not interrupt the class or try to make general announcements unless he notices that several students have difficulty with the same thing. The teacher uses a quiet voice and the students appreciate the personal and positive attention.

4. Modeling

Values are caught, not taught. Teachers who are courteous, prompt, enthusiastic, in control, patient, and organized provide examples for their students through their own behavior. The "do as I say, not as I do" teachers send mixed messages that confuse students and invite misbehavior.

If you want students to use quiet voices in the classroom while they work, you too will use a quiet voice as you move through the room helping students.

5. Non-Verbal Cuing

A standard item in the classroom of the 1950's was the clerk's bell. A shiny nickel bell sat on the teacher's desk. With one tap of the button the teacher had everyone's attention. Teachers have shown a lot of ingenuity over the years in making use of non-verbal cues in the classroom. Some flip light switches. Others keep clickers in their pockets. Non-verbal cues can also be facial expressions, body posture, and hand signals. Care should be given in choosing the types of cues you use in the classroom. Take time to explain to your students what you want them to do when you use your cues.

6. Environmental Control

A classroom can be a warm, cheery place. Students enjoy an environment that changes periodically. Study centers with pictures and color invite enthusiasm for your subject.

Students like to know about you and your interests. Include personal items in your classroom. A family picture or a few items from a hobby or collection on your desk will trigger personal conversations with your students. As they get to know you better, you will see fewer problems with discipline.

You may need a quiet corner with few distractions for certain students. Some students will get caught up in visual exploration. For them, the splash and the color is a siren that pulls them off task. Have a place you can steer these students to. Let them get their work done first, then come back to explore and enjoy the rest of the room.

7. Positive Discipline
Use classroom rules that describe the behaviors you want instead of listing things the students cannot do. Instead of "no running in the room," use "walk when indoors." Instead of "no gum chewing," use "leave gum at home." Refer to your rules as expectations. Let your students know this is how you expect them to behave in your classroom.

Make ample use of praise. When you see good behavior, acknowledge it. This can be done verbally, of course, but it does not have to be. A nod or smile will reinforce the behavior.

E6 Characteristics of Effective Behavior Managers

Effective behavior managers
- Respect their own strengths and weaknesses as seriously as those of their students;
- Understand that social-emotional growth is a never-ending process;
- Clearly communicate rules, goals, and expectations;
- Respond to behaviors consistently and predictably;
- Discriminate between issues of responsibility and problem ownership;
- Exhibit high degrees of empathy and self-efficacy.

Behaviors teachers exhibit that contribute to successful classroom management include the following:
- Having materials organized
- Using a pleasant tone of voice
- Being aware of multiple simultaneous functions within a group
- Being able to anticipate possible problems and react quickly to avoid them

High levels of self-efficacy have a positive effect on behavior management as well as academic achievement. Teachers who exhibit high levels of self-efficacy use more positive reinforcement, prefer to work with the whole group, and persist with students who are experiencing difficulty, rather than ignoring or giving up on them. The teacher's ability to be empathetic can also be associated with student success.

Empathetic teachers report experiencing less stress and tend to be described as:
- Warm
- Caring
- Affectionate
- Friendly; frequent smiler
- Soft-spoken
- Calm
- Relaxed
- Humorous
- Analytical of behavior and motives

- Able to predict how others will act
- Sympathetic
- Not easily provoked to express anger
- Not easily depressed under difficult circumstances
- Able to subordinate their own needs and feelings for another's benefit
- Spontaneous
- Balanced in sense of self-worth and self-regard
- Encouraging
- Inspiring
- Motivating
- Adaptable to the needs of others
- Altruistic (desiring to make a personal contribution)
- Able to give positive verbal and non-verbal feedback
- Conscientious in attending to students' needs
- Not needing to be the center of attention
- Making others centrally involved
- Independent and creative
- Totally accepting of individual differences, but not focused on deviance
- Highly intuitive
- Not feeling a great need to control all people and events

E7 Classroom Management Bumps

While teaching your class, you may run into occasions when your students are misbehaving. There are numerous solutions to end misbehavior. The following material explains the different levels of action you can take—these actions are called "bumps." If you begin with bump #1 and the student does not stop, then you bump to #2, and so on and so on. Each level of action represents a more direct response to ending the undesirable behavior.

Variables Which Affect the Teacher's Decision to Respond

1. Past behavior of the student
2. Severity of the misbehavior
3. Frequency of the misbehavior
4. Time between misbehaviors
5. Importance of the lesson
6. School discipline policy
7. Student's life at home
8. Student's respect for the teacher
9. Reaction by allies

Summary Of Classroom Management Bumps

Bump #1
Low-key Responses

1. Win the students over
   - Meet them at the door
   - Show interest

2. Use a signal to begin or get attention

3. Proximity

4. Deal with the problem not the student

5. Be polite

6. Deal with the supporting cast first

7. Use minimal or non-verbal signals
   - Say student's name
   - Use gestures
   - Give the "look"
   - Pause

8. Be on alert

9. Transitions
   - Who does what by when

10. Ignore

Bump #2
Squaring Off

1. Pause or stop

2. Turn body (square off)

3. Intensify eye contact

4. Use a minimal verbal response

5. Complete interaction with a "thank you"

Bump #3
Either/Or Choices

1. Stop

2. Square off
   - Intensify eye contact

3. Give either/or statements
   - Use firm, neutral, calm voice
   - Restore social order as immediately as possible
   - Keep statement free of moral judgment
   - Deal with only the present

4. Ask for a student response

5. Listen for student's answer

6. Complete interaction with a "thank you"

Bump #4
Implied Choice

1. Follow through Bump #3.

2. Say "You've made your choice. Please … "

3. Complete interaction with a "thank you"

Bump #5
Power

1. Recognize the move to power

2. Respond by
   - Ignoring it
   - Short circuiting it
   - Describing the situation
   - Using language of attribution
   - Providing a choice
   - Asking student to leave (due to severity)

Bump #6
Informal Logical Contracts

1. Greet student and set atmosphere

2. Define problem

3. Generate alternatives

4. Agree on alternatives to try a time to begin

5. Review what has been agreed upon

6. End conference with a comment or gesture that communicates a positive feeling and tone

E8 An Effective Classroom Management Context

The following four points are fundamental to effective classroom management:

1. Know what you want and what you do not want.

2. Show and tell your students what you want.

3. When you get what you want, acknowledge (do not praise) it.

4. When you get something else, act quickly and appropriately.

Room Arrangement

While good room arrangement is not a guarantee of good behavior, poor planning in this area can create conditions that lead to problems.
*   The teacher must be able to observe all students at all times and to monitor work and behavior. The teacher should also be able to see the door from his desk.
*   Students should be able to see the teacher and presentation area without undue turning or movement.
*   Frequently used areas of the room and traffic lanes should be unobstructed and easily accessible.
*   Commonly used classroom materials (e.g., books, attendance pads, absence permits, and student reference materials) should be readily available.
*   Some degree of decoration will help add to the attractiveness of the room.

Setting Expectations for Behavior

Teachers should identify expectations for student behavior and communicate those expectations to students periodically.
*   Rules and procedures are the most common explicit expectations. A small number of general rules that emphasize appropriate behavior may be helpful. Rules should be posted in the classroom. Compliance with the rules should be monitored constantly.
*   Do not develop classroom rules you are unwilling to enforce.
*   School-wide regulations, particularly safety procedures, should be explained carefully.

Because desirable student behavior may vary depending on the activity, explicit expectations for the following procedures are helpful in creating a smoothly functioning classroom:
*   Beginning and ending the period, including attendance procedures and what students may or may not do during these times
*   Use of materials and equipment such as the pencil sharpener, storage areas, supplies, and special equipment
*   Teacher-led instruction
*   Seatwork
*   How students are to answer questions (e.g., no student answer will be recognized unless the student raises his or her hand and is called upon by the teacher)
*   Independent group work such as laboratory activities or smaller group projects

Remember, good discipline is much more likely to occur if the classroom setting and activities are structured or arranged to enhance cooperative behavior.

Managing Student Academic Work

Effective teacher-led instruction is free of:
- Ambiguous and vague terms
- Unclear sequencing
- Interruptions

Students must be held accountable for their work. The central purpose of student effort is academic tasks and learning, rather than good behavior for its own sake.

Managing Inappropriate Behavior

- Address instruction and assignments to challenge academic achievement while continuing to assure individual student success.
- Most inappropriate behavior in classrooms that is not seriously disruptive can be managed by relatively simple procedures that prevent escalation.
- Effective classroom managers practice skills that minimize misbehavior.
- Monitor students carefully and frequently so that misbehavior is detected early before it involves many students or becomes a serious disruption.
- Act to stop inappropriate behavior so as not to interrupt the instructional activity or to call excessive attention to the student by practicing the following unobtrusive strategies:
  - Move close to the offending student or students, make eye contact, and give a non-verbal signal to stop the offensive behavior.
  - Call a student's name or give a short verbal instruction to stop the behavior.
  - Redirect the student to appropriate behavior by stating what the student should be doing; cite the applicable procedure or rule. Example: "Please, look at the overhead projector and read the first line with me, I need to see everyone's eyes looking here."
- More serious, disruptive behaviors such as fighting, continuous interruption of lessons, and stealing require direct action according to school rules.
- Assertive discipline has been used by many schools, and is an effective way to manage behavior.

Appropriate Use of Consequences

- In classrooms, the most prevalent positive consequences are intrinsic student satisfaction resulting from success, accomplishment, good grades, social approval, and recognition.
- Students must be aware of the connection between tasks and grades.
- Frequent use of punishment is associated with poor classroom management and generally should be avoided.
- When used, negative consequences or punishment should be related logically to the misbehavior.
- Milder punishments are often as effective as more intense forms and do not arouse as much negative emotion.
- Misbehavior is less likely to recur if a student makes a commitment to avoid the action and to engage in more desirable alternative behaviors.
- Consistency in the application of consequences is the key factor in classroom management.

Some Principles for an ESL Classroom

- Students are not unintelligent and they can hear what is being said. They just do not necessarily understand the language, yet.
- They come from a variety of backgrounds, even in the same country.
- It is easy to misunderstand body language and certain behaviors. For example, eye contact, spitting, etc.
- Do not assume they understand something just because it seems simple to you. Simplify, boil down.
- Correct repeated patterns or mistakes.
- Good ESL strategies are good teaching strategies.

Guidelines for Effective Praise

(Applies primarily to praise associated with instruction and student performance)

Effective Praise	Ineffective Praise
1. Is delivered contingently upon student performance of desirable behaviors or genuine accomplishment.	1. Is delivered randomly and indiscriminately without specific attention to genuine accomplishment.
2. Specifies the praiseworthy aspects of the student's accomplishments.	2. Is general or global, not specifying the success.
3. Is expressed sincerely showing spontaneity, variety, and other non-verbal signs of credibility.	3. Is expressed blandly without feeling or animation, and relying on stock, perfunctory phrases.
4. Is given for genuine effort, progress, or accomplishments which are judged according to standards appropriate to individuals.	4. Is given based on comparisons with others and without regard to the effort expended or significance of the accomplishment of an individual.
5. Provides information to students about their competence or the value of their accomplishments.	5. Provides no meaningful information to the students about their accomplishments.
6. Helps students to better appreciate their thinking, problem-solving, and performance.	6. Orients students toward comparing themselves with others.
7. Attributes student success to effort and ability, implying that similar successes can be expected in the future.	7. Attributes student success to ability alone or to external factors such as luck or easy task.
8. Encourages students to appreciate their accomplishments for the effort they expend and their personal gratification.	8. Encourages students to succeed for external reasons—to please the teacher, win a competition or reward, etc.

E9 Control Techniques

General Control Techniques

On the first day of class, let students know which behaviors are acceptable and unacceptable in the classroom. This is much easier than introducing new rules later on.

Know your students' names as soon as possible, and call their names to get their attention when they misbehave.

If students are talking while you are trying to teach, stop and look them in the eye. Do not begin or resume speaking until the entire class is quiet.

Do not punish the whole class when a single student misbehaves. Allow the class to continue its work while you speak to the student privately.

If you are watching a video in class, keep the volume low so that students must listen carefully to hear it.

Younger students may respond to turning off the lights or a few claps to get their attention.

A reward system also often works for younger students. You can set daily or weekly behavioral goals; if they are met, the students are rewarded.

Specific Behaviors and Control Techniques

1. Behavior: Rambling—wandering around and off the subject; using far-fetched examples or analogies
Possible responses:
    a) Refocus attention by restating relevant point.
    b) Direct questions to the group to get them back on the subject.
    c) Ask how topic relates to current topic being discussed.
    d) Use visual aids, begin to write on board, turn on overhead projector.
    e) Say: "Would you summarize your main point please?" or "Are you asking ... ?"

2. Behavior: Shyness or Silence—lack of participation
Possible responses:
    a) Change teaching strategies from group discussion to individual written exercises, or a video-
       tape.
    b) Give strong positive reinforcement for any contribution.
    c) Involve by directly asking a student a question.
    d) Make eye contact.
    e) Appoint small-group leaders.

3. Behavior: Talkativeness—knowing everything, manipulation, chronic whining
Possible responses:
    a) Acknowledge comments made.
    b) Give limited time to express viewpoint or feelings, and then move on.
    c) Make eye contact with another participant and move toward that person.
    d) Give the person individual attention during breaks.
    e) Say: "That's an interesting point. Now let's see what other people think."

4. Behavior: Sharpshooting—trying to criticize you or encourage you to make mistakes
Possible responses:
    a) Admit that you do not know the answer and redirect the question to the group or to the individual who asked it.
    b) Acknowledge that this is a joint learning experience.
    c) Ignore the behavior.

5. Behavior: Heckling/Arguing—disagreeing with everything you say; making personal attacks
Possible responses:
    a) Redirect question to group or supportive individuals.
    b) Recognize participant's feelings and move on.
    c) Acknowledge positive points.
    d) Say: "I appreciate your comments, but I'd like to hear from others," or "It looks like we disagree."

6. Behavior: Grandstanding—getting caught up in one's own agenda or thoughts to the detriment of other students
Possible responses:
    a) Say: "You are entitled to your opinion, belief, or feelings, but now it's time we moved on to the next subject," or "Can you restate that as a question?" or "We'd like to hear more about that if there is time after the presentation."

7. Behavior: Overt Hostility/Resistance—angry, belligerent, combative behavior
Possible responses:
    a) Hostility can be a mask for fear. Reframe hostility as fear to depersonalize it.
    b) Respond to fear, not hostility.
    c) Remain calm and polite. Keep your temper in check.
    d) Do not disagree, but build on or around what has been said.
    e) Move closer to the hostile person, maintain eye contact.
    f) Always allow him or her a way to gracefully retreat from the confrontation.
    g) Say: "You seem really angry. Does anyone else feel this way?" Solicit peer pressure.
    h) Do not accept the premise or underlying assumption, if it is false or prejudicial, e.g., "If by 'queer' you mean homosexual ... "
    i) Allow the individual to solve the problem being addressed. He or she may not be able to offer solutions and will sometimes undermine his or her own position.
    j) Ignore behavior.
    k) Talk to him or her privately during a break.
    l) As a last resort, privately ask the individual to leave class for the good of the group.

8. Behavior: Griping/Complaining
Possible responses:
    a) Point out that we cannot change policy here.
    b) Validate his or her point.
    c) Indicate you will discuss the problem with the participant privately.
    d) Indicate time pressure.

9.   Behavior: Side Conversations—may be related to subject or personal
Possible responses:
   a) Do not embarrass talkers.
   b) Ask their opinion on topic being discussed.
   c) Ask talkers if they would like to share their ideas.
   d) Casually move toward those talking.
   e) Make eye contact with them.
   f) Comment on the group (but do not look at them individually).
   g) Standing near the talkers, ask a nearby participant a question so that the new discussion is near the talkers.
   h) As a last resort, stop and wait.

Keys for Managing Challenging Student Behaviors

- Instead of holding your students with an iron grip, allow them to be themselves until (and unless) their behavior distracts you or others in the class.
- When you notice unproductive behavior, try to stop it as soon as you can. Otherwise, you send a clear message to the students that it is OK for them to talk while you are talking, etc.
- Use classroom management techniques before you become irritated, impatient, or upset.
- We are much more powerful when we are centered, when we like our students, and when we view our students with fondness rather than impatience.
- Treat students with respect. When we put students down in front of others, the entire class of students will turn against us.
- Do all you can to feel good about yourself and others on a daily basis. Your attitude will come across to your students, so it is important to be in good mental and physical shape.
- If, by chance, you feel that you have spoken sharply in an attempt to manage your students, own up to it. "Wow, that sounded harsh. Forgive me!"
- Remind yourself: "If teaching were easy, everyone would be doing it." Teaching in front of a classroom full of students can be challenging, but on the other hand, very rewarding!

E10 The Four Reasons for Misbehavior in Students

The following chart demonstrates the different types of goals students possess when they are misbehaving. Study the chart to gain a better understanding of children's actions to know why they behave a certain way.

Reason for Student Misbehavior	What the Student is Saying	What the Student is Feeling	Student's Reaction to Reprimand	Some Corrective Measures
Attention	I only count when I am being noticed or served.	Annoyed. Wants to remind, coax. Delighted with label of "good" student.	Temporarily stops disturbing action when given attention.	Ignore. Answer or do the unexpected. Give attention at pleasant times.
Power	I only count when I am dominating … when you do what I want to do.	Provoked. Generally wants power. Challenged. "I will make him do it." "You cannot get away with it."	Intensifies action when reprimanded. Student wants to win, or be the boss.	Extricate self. Act—do not talk. Be friendly. Establish equality. Redirect student's efforts into constructive channels.
Revenge	I cannot be liked. I do not have power but I will count if I can hurt others, as I feel hurt by life.	Hurt, mad—"How can he do this to me?"	Wants to get even; makes him disliked.	Extricate self. Maintain order with minimum restraint. Avoid retaliation. Take time and effort to help student.
Inadequacy	I cannot do anything right so I will not try to do anything at all. I am no good.	Despair: "I give up."	No reprimand, therefore no reaction. Passive and feels there is no use in trying.	Encouragement (may take a long time). Faith in student's ability.

E11 Classroom Discipline Plan

The Classroom Discipline Plan is composed of three parts:

1. Rules that students must follow at all times.

2. Consequences that result when students choose not to follow the rules.

3. Rewards for when students do follow the rules.

Sample Elementary Discipline Plan

Classroom Rules
- Follow directions the first time they are given.
- Keep hands, feet, and objects to yourself.
- No teasing or name calling.
- Stay in your seat unless you have permission to get up.
- Raise your hand and wait to be called upon before speaking.

Consequences for Breaking a Rule
- First time: Student receives a warning
- Second time: Student is chosen last for a fun activity
- Third time: Student goes to the time-out area
- Fourth time: Teacher calls the parents
- Fifth time: Student sent to the principal
- Severe clause: Student sent to the principal

Rewards
Students who follow the rules receive:
- Praise
- Positive notes sent home
- Small rewards
- Class parties

Sample Secondary Discipline Plan

Rules

1. _____

2. _____

3. _____

4. _____

5. _____

Consequences

1st time rule is broken _____

2nd _____

3rd _____

4th _____

5th _____

Severe clause _____

Rewards

Students who follow the rules receive _____

_____

_____

E12 Discipline Record Sheet

Period: _____

Student's Name	Date	Rule Broken	Consequences Provided

E13 Behavior Assessment Summary

Student: _____

Grade: _____

Date: _____

Members present: _____

Describe inappropriate behavior(s) observed (Physical, Verbal, Other):

_____

_____

Describe what preceded the inappropriate behavior(s):

_____

_____

Target 1 or 2 behaviors to be modified:

_____

_____

Describe unsuccessful intervention approaches:

_____

_____

Brainstorm potential successful approaches:

_____

_____

Describe the new behavior goals (include consequences and reinforcement):

_____

_____

Date for Review: _____

E

E14 Monthly Positive Record

In addition to recording student misbehaviors, it is also a good idea to track positive behaviors throughout the year. This can help you to identify students with exceptional classroom etiquette and to reward those who are good throughout the year.

Month	Student	Positive Behavior	Teacher's Response
September			
October			
November			
December			
January			
February			
March			
April			
May			
June			
July			
August			

SECTION F
Teaching English Grammar

Content

F1 Parts of Speech Poem

Every name is called a noun
As "field" and "fountain," "street" and "town"

In place of noun the pronoun stands
As "he" and "she" can clap "their" hands

The adjective describes a thing
As "magic" wand or "bridal" ring

The verb means action—something done
To "read" and "write," to "jump" and "run."

How things are done the adverbs tell
As "quickly," "slowly," "badly," "well."

The preposition shows relation
As "in" the street or "at" the station

Conjunctions join in many ways
Sentences, words or phrase and phrase

The exclamation cries out "Hark, I need a very special mark!"

F2 Parts of Speech

Below are some examples of the various parts of speech for your reference. This list could be a useful resource to give to students to help them remember specific rules and/or specific phrases in the English language. They could also be useful when giving out writing assignments or when designing vocabulary and spelling tests.

Verbs

A verb is used to express action or state. It tells what is happening. It is the key element in the predicate, one of the two main parts of a sentence. Action verbs include such words as throw, sail, run, climb, read, give, take, eat, pass, fail, rise, emerge, disappear, open, build, lose, die, and feel. Verbs such as to feel, to seem, and to be, are the most frequently used verbs that express a state. A verb is also termed a simple predicate.

Active-Passive Voice Verbs
Active-passive voice verbs have two voices. In sentences using the active voice (e.g., Bill threw the ball), the subject performs the verb action. In sentences using the passive voice (e.g., The ball was thrown by Bill), the subject is the receiver of the verb action. The active voice is used for most statements and questions. The passive voice is used to emphasize the object.

Transitive Verbs

A transitive verb is any verb that acts on a direct object (e.g., She **read** the letter. He **washed** the dishes. He **manages** a small business. She **teaches** school.). A transitive verb makes no sense without an object or transitive.

Intransitive Verbs

An intransitive verb is a verb that has no direct object. Although the verb involves an action, the action is not done to anyone or anything else (e.g., He **runs** every morning. She **shopped** until she **dropped**. They **danced** until dawn). Many verbs can be transitive or intransitive depending on their use. An intransitive verb is neither a linking verb nor an auxiliary verb.

Linking Verbs

A linking verb connects a subject to its predicate without expressing action. Linking verbs describe or rename their subjects. They include the sense verbs (to feel, to look, to taste, to smell), to be, to appear, to become, to seem, and to sound. With the exception of to seem, linking verbs can be transitive or intransitive. The verb to be can be a linking verb or an auxiliary verb (e.g., he **is** the owner, she **seems** healthy, it **tastes** great, the food on the bottom shelf **smelled** terrible, it **sounds** interesting).

Auxiliary Verbs

An auxiliary verb accompanies another verb in order to help to express the person, tense, mood, voice, or condition of the latter verb. The verbs to have, to be, to do, will, can, may, and shall are commonly used auxiliary verbs. An auxiliary verb is also termed a helping verb.

Infinitive

An infinitive is a verb form that possesses characteristics of both verb and noun is usually preceded by "to" (to start, to leave, to sing). Although the preposition announces the infinitive, it does not form part of the infinitive itself.

Gerund

A gerund is the present participle of a verb that is used as a noun, or rather the verb form that ends in "ing" when used as a noun. Although the gerund is used like a noun, it retains certain characteristics of a verb, such as the ability to take an object (e.g., **Preparing** lasagna is time consuming or **Golfing** is his first love). The same word can be used as an adjective (e.g., I spied the **running** figure), or part of a verb (e.g., She was **knitting**).

Tense

The form of a verb that denotes the relationship between the action and time is called its tense. The basic tenses (present, past, future) and variations tell if an action is taking place, took place, or will take place, etc. The progressive tenses also denote action either in progress (is walking), in the past (was walking), or in the future (will be walking). The perfect tense is used for action that began in the past and continues in the present (has walked), that was completed in the past (had walked), or that will be completed in the future action (will have walked).

Conjunctions

A conjunction is a word (e.g., as, and, but, or) used to connect words or phrases and, in particular, clauses. Conjunctions are described as coordinating conjunctions, subordinating conjunctions, or correlative conjunctions.

Coordinating Conjunctions

Words that join like with like, such as a noun with another noun, an adjective with another adjective, an adverb with another adverb, etc. (e.g., a fork and a knife, hot but dry, quickly but quietly, Jack and Jill), or two independent clauses are called coordinating conjunctions. They include and, but, for, nor, or, so, and yet. The following are some examples of their use:

- The shoes **and** socks were black.
- Sonja was walking **and** talking.
- Frank spoke slowly **and** very quietly.
- Timothy worked quickly, **but** carelessly.
- Walter is not heavy, **but** Michael is.
- Tom is short, **but** Susan is not.
- I am sure that she is French, **for** I recognize her accent.
- They are well rested, **for** they went to bed early last night.
- Bill is fat, **yet** agile.
- They exercised daily, **yet** lost little weight.
- Tina was still angry, **so** she refused to attend.

Subordinating Conjunctions

Words that join subordinate clauses to main clauses are called subordinating conjunctions. They include after, although, as, because, before, even though, if, rather than, since, so that, that, though, unless, until, when, where, whether, whether or not, and while. The following are some examples of their use:

- **After** she sat down, we began dinner.
- We began dinner **after** she sat down.

- **Until** he arrives, we will not begin.
- We will not begin **until** he arrives.

- **When** the sun sets, we draw the blinds.
- We draw the blinds **when** the sun sets.

- **As** you know, we did extremely well.
- We did extremely well **as** you know.

- **Because** you like the subject, we will choose this book.
- We will choose this book **because** you like the subject.

Correlative Conjunctions

Correlative conjunctions are pairs of conjunctions used to join alternatives or equal elements. The following are some examples of their use:

- They want to visit **either** Portugal or Spain.
- They want to visit **neither** Portugal nor Spain.
- They want **not only** to visit Portugal, **but also** Spain.
- They want to visit **both** Portugal and Spain.
- They will visit Portugal **whether or not** they visit Spain.

 # F3 A Glossary of Grammatical Terms

Abbreviation

An abbreviation is a shortened version of a written word or phrase used to replace the original (e.g., ASAP, bldg., Mr., Mrs., AC). Abbreviations may be used wherever acceptable. The commonly used abbreviations vary by industry or field of study or endeavor.

Adjective

An adjective is a word that describes or modifies a noun (e.g., **tall** man). It is termed a modifier because it adds something to (modifies) a noun. An adjective can precede a noun (**black** cat) or follow it (The meal was **delicious**). An adjective is sometimes used to modify groups of words, such as noun phrases (the **astonishing** turn of events) or noun clauses (it appeared **obvious** that the contestant was drunk).

Adverb

An adverb is a word or clause that typically describes or modifies a verb (He ate **noisily**). It can also modify an adjective (She is **extremely** short) or another adverb (He sang **exceptionally** poorly). In fact, an adverb can be used to modify anything, except a noun. This includes phrases (**almost** out of sight), participles clauses (a **well**-earned vacation), and pronouns (**nearly** everyone).

Analogy

An analogy is a comparison of two things which are alike in some respects in order to explain or clarify an idea or object by showing how similar it is to something familiar. Although a simile and analogy are somewhat similar, a simile normally is more artistic, done for effect and emphasis. In contrast, the analogy serves more to explain a thought process or reasoning, or the abstract, in terms of the tangible.

Antecedent

An antecedent is the word, group of words, or clause to which a pronoun in a sentence refers. The antecedent may follow the pronoun, although it usually precedes it (e.g., **William** telephoned to say **he** would be late. They encountered **Tom** and said hello to **him**).

Antonym

An antonym is a word that has the exact opposite meaning of another (e.g., **slow** is an antonym of **fast**; **poor** is an antonym of **excellent**).

Auxiliary Verb

An auxiliary verb is a verb that accompanies another verb in order to help to express the person, tense, mood, voice, or condition of the latter verb. The verbs to have, to be, to do, can, may, and shall are commonly used auxiliary verbs. An auxiliary verb is also termed a helping verb.

Clause

A clause is a group of words that contains both a subject and a verb, but represents only part of a compound sentence or complex sentence. The clause may express a thought completely on its own (e.g., I run every morning). In this case, it is termed an independent clause. Alternatively, it may not express an idea completely without the aid of an independent or main clause (e.g., when I am in town). In this last case, it is called a subordinate clause. Adjective clauses, adverb clauses, and noun clauses are three types of subordinate clauses. An adjective clause modifies a noun or pronoun in the independent clause (e.g., The **man**, **who was also a gambler**, usually carried large amounts of cash). An adverb clause modifies a verb, adjective, or another adverb in the independent clause (e.g., **Shortly after the sun sets**, twilight begins). Finally, a noun clause acts as a noun in an independent clause (e.g., **whoever finishes first** can take the rest of the day off).

Collective Noun

A collective noun is a noun that refers to individual persons or items as a group, such as number, total, audience, or clergy. A collective noun can be considered to be singular or plural (e.g., The **number** of rejects **was** extremely high. A **number** of attendees at the convention **have** already left).

Comma

A comma is a punctuation mark (,) and is the equivalent of a brief pause. It is used to mark a division in a sentence, as may be caused by a word, phrase, or clause, particularly when accompanied by a pause. The comma also separates items in a list, designates thousands in numerals, and separates types of information in bibliographic and other data. Commas are used for clarity and to make sentences less unwieldy. Comma is derived from the Greek *komma* for segment or clause, which designated a portion of a sentence. It appeared as a full slash mark or solidus (/) in early manuscripts, but later shrank to today's size.

Complex Sentence

A complex sentence consists of one independent clause and one or more subordinate clauses (e.g., The dog quickly discovered the cat, **which had left the safety of its hiding place**). In the preceding example, the independent clause has been underlined. The subordinate clause is written in bold. See also Compound Sentence.

Compound Sentence

A compound sentence consists of two or more independent clauses and no subordinate clause. A comma and a conjunction separate the independent clauses (e.g., I finished my work for the day, and now I am ready to go out).

Compounding

Compounding is the act of joining two words to create a new word. Examples of words formed include walkout, blackout, and doghouse.

Conjunction

A conjunction is a word (e.g., and, but, or) used to connect words, phrases, or clauses. Subordinating conjunctions (e.g., whether, unless) join subordinate clauses to main clauses. Correlative conjunctions (e.g., either … or, neither … nor) are used in pairs to join alternatives or equal elements. Coordinating conjunctions are normally used to join like with like, such as a noun with another noun, an adjective with another adjective, an adverb with another adverb, etc. (e.g., a fork **and** a knife, hot **but** dry, quickly **but** quietly, Jack **and** Jill). Common coordinating conjunctions include and, but, for, or, nor, either, yet, and so.

Consonant

A consonant is, generally, a letter with a hard sound: b, c, d, f, g, h, j, k, l, m, n, p, q, r, s, t, v, w, x, y, z. That is, any letter except a, e, i, o, or u. Consonants originally were letters or letter sounds formed with the breath at least partially obstructed. They were combined with a vowel (a letter with a soft open-mouthed sound) in order to form a syllable. The consonant y sometimes acts like a vowel.

Contraction

Contraction is a term used to describe a word formed by combining two words into one and replacing the letter(s) omitted with an apostrophe (e.g., can't, don't, I'm). The three common constructions of contractions are the following:

1. A verb plus not (e.g., can't, don't, didn't, wouldn't, couldn't, wasn't)
2. A pronoun plus a verb (e.g., I'm, he's, she's, we're, you're, they're)
3. A noun plus a verb (Bill's: formed from Bill + is)

Direct Object

A direct object is a word, phrase, or clause that tells what the action of the verb acted upon or sought to accomplish. It represents the result or objective of the action (e.g., He closed **the door**. She did **whatever was asked**. "I'll see **you** later," he responded).

Double Negative

A double negative is the construction produced by using two negatives in a clause or sentence. This results from combining the negative form of a verb (e.g., can't, won't, dislike), or "not," with a negative pronoun (e.g., nobody, nothing, or nobody), a negative adverb (e.g., never, hardly, rarely), a negative conjunction (e.g., neither, nor), or "not." Some obvious examples of double negatives are: I didn't see nobody; She is not unattractive.

Ellipsis

An ellipsis is a set of three dots or periods in a row (…). They are used between two phrases or sentences to indicate that a word or phrase has been omitted. An ellipsis is also used when bits or quips of information have been taken from a long quotation or when wanting to signify a trailing off in thought or to leave it to the reader's imagination to complete. When the ellipsis appears at the end of the sentence, a period precedes it. Consequently, there are four dots instead of three.

Exclamation Point

An exclamation point is the mark (!) used in writing after an exclamation. It is often used to indicate intensity of emotion or loudness, etc. The mark evolved from the Roman habit of saying "lo" as an exclamation. In order to save time in writing, scribes wrote the two letters together, with the "l" on top and the "o" beneath it. Eventually, the "o" was filled with ink and became a dot.

Figure of Speech

A figure of speech is an expression or use of language (e.g., a metaphor, simile, personification, antithesis, etc.), in which words are used in a way other than their literal sense to create a picture or image. It is also used for other special effects and imaginative or figurative expressions.

Gerund

A gerund is the present participle of a verb that is used as a noun and ends in -ing. Although the gerund is used like a noun, it retains certain characteristics of a verb, such as the ability to take an object (e.g., **Preparing** lasagna is time consuming or **Golfing** is his first love). The same word can be used as an adjective (I spied the **running** figure) or part of a verb (She was **knitting**).

Homonym

A homonym is a word that is pronounced the same as another word, but that has a different meaning. The two words may be spelled differently. Hare and hair are examples of homonyms, as are bear and bare, and mat and matte.

Hyphen

A hyphen is a punctuation mark (-) used to join two words together, to indicate where a word has been broken between syllables at the end of a line, or to separate parts of a compound word. The normal hyphen, optional hyphen, and non-breaking hyphen are three types of hyphens. Both normal hyphens and non-breaking hyphens are visible. The normal hyphen is used as part of the usual spelling of the word. It is also termed required hyphen or hard hyphen. Non-breaking hyphens do not permit a line break. That is, the word cannot be broken into parts at the end of a line. An optional hyphen only appears if a word is split between syllables at the end of a line. It is also called a discretionary hyphen or soft hyphen.

Idiom

An idiom is an expression that cannot be concluded from the normal meanings of the words that comprise it, or from the rules of grammar of the language. Examples of idioms used in North America include **go bust** or **flat broke**, **flush**, **pushing up daisies**, and **give me a break**.

Imperative

Imperative is a term applicable to the mood or form of a verb that is used when giving command or making a request (e.g., Close the door as you leave the room. Put up your hand when you have the answer. Please be home by midnight).

Independent Clause

An independant clause is a group of words containing both a subject and a predicate that can stand alone as a complete sentence. It expresses a complete thought. In contrast, a subordinate clause is incomplete and requires an independent clause to express the idea fully (e.g., **I prefer French cuisine**, although Italian food is fine). An independent clause is also termed a main clause.

Indicative

Indicative is a term applicable to the mood or form of a verb that is used when making a conventional clear-cut statement or asking a question (e.g., The train left at noon. The old toaster no longer functions. What classes are you taking this semester?).

Indirect Object

An indirect object is a word, phrase, or clause that gives the secondary goal of the action of the verb. It typically answers the question, **To** or **for whom**, **what**, or **which**? (e.g., She gave **him** a hug. He bought **her** flowers).

Infinitive

An infinitive is a verb form that possesses characteristics of both verb and noun and is usually preceded by "to" (to start, to leave, to sing). Although the preposition announces the infinitive, it does not form part of the infinitive itself. The infinitive form of a verb is typically used in constructions that are subordinate to another verb (e.g., I forced him **to do** it).

Interrogative

Interrogative is a term applicable to a sentence or construction that asks a question. Also, a pronoun or adverb, etc., that provides a line of questioning, such as "who" in "Who was that person?" or "what" in "What did you buy?"

Intransitive Verb

An intransitive verb is a verb that has no direct object. An intransitive verb is neither an auxiliary verb nor a linking verb. Although the verb involves an action, the action is not done to anyone or anything else (e.g., He **runs** every morning. She **shopped** until she **dropped**. They **danced** until dawn). Many verbs can be transitive or intransitive depending on their use.

Irony

Irony is the use of words to express something that differs from, and is often the direct opposite of, its literal meaning; a figure of speech, or mildly sarcastic or humorous use of words, to imply the opposite of the literal meaning (e.g., Oh sure! That's what I really need).

Linking Verb

A linking verb is a verb that connects a subject to its predicate without expressing action. Linking verbs describe or rename their subjects. They include the "sense" verbs (to feel, to look, to taste, to smell), to be, to appear, to become, to seem, and to sound. With the exception of to seem, linking verbs can be transitive or intransitive. The verb to be can be a linking verb or an auxiliary verb (e.g., he **is** the owner, she **seems** healthy, it **tastes** great, the food on the bottom shelf **smelled** terrible, it **sounds** interesting).

Literal

A literal translation is one that attempts to follow the words of the original very closely and convey the exact meaning of the text, true to fact, and without exaggeration. In other words, it is the most straightforward meaning.

Metaphor

A metaphor is a figure of speech in which one idea or action is conveyed by a word or phrase that normally indicates a different idea or action. It is an unstated comparison of one thing with another. Metaphors are the most frequently used figures of speech. Unlike a simile or analogy, a metaphor asserts that one thing is another, instead of saying that it is like another (e.g., The moon was a silver coin upon the surface of the lake).

Modifier

A modifier is a word or phrase that is used to restrict or limit the meaning of another word or phrase. For example, in the phrase **green Honda**, **green** modifies **Honda**. It narrows the meaning of the phrase from all Honda vehicles to only Honda vehicles that are green in color.

Mood

The moods or modes of writing are expressed through verbs by the writer. Verbs have three possible moods. The indicative mood describes ordinary statements of fact or questions (I have only one examination remaining). The subjunctive verb is used to express a wish or something that is contrary to fact (If I graduate, you won't see me here again). The imperative mood is used for a request or a command (Bring my dinner!).

Negative

Negative refers to any word or expression that is used to assert that something is not true (e.g., he will **not** leave, the cat appears to be **un**happy, she **never** asked for assistance, he **scarcely** had enough money for bus fare). Commonly used negatives are no, never, and not. However, other words, such as hardly and scarcely, add a negative connotation. The term negative also describes words such as unhappy, unappealing, disinterested, etc.

Nonrestrictive Clause

A nonrestrictive clause refers to a subordinate clause that is not essential to assure the certainty of the word it modifies. If the subordinate clause were omitted, the meaning of the main clause would be unchanged. Commas set off the nonrestrictive clause from the rest of the sentence. (e.g., The hostess, **who was a tall blonde woman with green eyes**, led us to the drawing room.) A nonrestrictive clause is also termed a nonessential clause.

Noun

A noun is a word used to designate a person, place, thing, idea, quality, or action, such as Charles, Pittsburgh, grapefruit, privacy, durability, and arrival. Nouns may be singular or plural. A proper noun begins with a capital letter (e.g., Nashville, Nancy Drew, American Airlines), whereas a common noun begins in lowercase (e.g., city, girl, airline). Nouns are used as subjects of verbs (The **owner** prepared breakfast), direct objects (Tom painted the **fence**), objects of prepositions (The parcel was delivered to the **address**), indirect objects (The judges awarded **Bruce** first prize), predicate nouns (The employee reinvested his **stock trading profits**), objective complements (They chose Jill Burton as **Homecoming Queen**), and appositives (**Frank Smith, sales representative**).

Object

An object is a noun, noun phrase, pronoun, or clause that follows a preposition, or in which a verb acts directly or indirectly (e.g., He petted the **dog**. She gave **him** the **gift**. She did **what was asked**. They watched **television** after dinner. He opened the **curtains**). Objects may be direct or indirect. A direct object is the result of an action, whereas an indirect object tells to whom or what it happened.

Paragraph

A paragraph is a distinct portion of writing that usually contains more than one sentence, but is shorter than a chapter, and deals with a particular idea. A paragraph begins on a new line and is usually indented. It is a subsection of a larger piece, article, manuscript, book, or text.

Parentheses

Parentheses are punctuation marks which are used in pairs ( ) to set off an explanatory interjection or remark in a sentence, which is grammatically complete without it. They are also used to separate several qualities or a group of elements in a formula, equation, etc., that are to be treated as a whole.

Participle

A participle is a verb form used as an adjective (e.g., **rising** sun, **cooked** food, **broken** lamp). It may be a present participle, past participle, or perfect participle. The present participle ends in -ing (e.g., charming, rising, falling, singing). The past participle usually ends in -ed (e.g., jumped, skipped, cooked, aged, shopped). The perfect participle combines having and the past participle (e.g., having cooked, having aged, having skipped).

Period

A period is a punctuation mark (.) that signifies the completion of a sentence and the pause that should occur between sentences. This pause is longer than that required by a comma. The period is also termed a full stop. The period is also sometimes used in abbreviations, such as U.S., etc. "Period" is derived from the Greek *periodos*, which means cycle and therefore completion of a thought.

Phrase

A phrase is a group of related words that does not contain both a subject and a verb and that functions as a noun, adjective, adverb, preposition, conjunction, or verb. A phrase represents only part of a sentence. Consequently, it cannot convey a complete thought (e.g., spectacular sunrise, the old woman, in the boat, to the horizon, extending for miles, hanging at an angle, in place of, break away, in the interval, flapping in the breeze). In contrast to a phrase, a clause is a group of words that contains both a subject and a verb.

Plural

A plural word form denotes a quantity greater than one. In contrast, the singular form denotes only one. The endings of plural nouns usually differ from those of singular nouns (e.g., **cherries** plural of **cherry**, **windows** plural of **window**, **houses** plural of **house**, **mice** plural of **mouse**, **men** plural of **man**, **children** plural of **child**).

Possessive

Possessive is a form of a noun or pronoun that indicates ownership. The possessive form of a noun is usually created by adding 's to the word, or by preceding the word with the preposition of (e.g., **Cynthia**'s mother, **Bill's** wallet, a **dog's** breakfast, the **radiator's** heat, home **of Bill**, **his** hat, **her** dress, **their** gifts, **its** color).

Predicate

A predicate is one of the two principle parts of a sentence, and contains the verb and the words used to further describe or clarify what is said of the subject. It is the action segment of the sentence (e.g., All members of the graduating class **attended convocation**. The writer **received the Nobel Prize for Literature**. He **picked up his marbles and went home**).

Prefix

A prefix is an affix attached to the beginning of a word in order to modify its meaning. The prefix may be a syllable, a group of syllables, or a group of letters. Examples include in- (inadequate), im- (impossible), pre- (presorted), post-, anti-, over-, di-, un-, and pro-.

Preposition

A preposition is a word that is normally combined with a noun, pronoun, adverb, or prepositional phrase. It typically precedes what it modifies (e.g., to town, in summer, from here, outside of the home, over the table, behind the barrier). However, despite popular belief, a preposition can be used at the end of a sentence. Some prepositions are also used as conjunctions, adverbs, and other grammatical elements. Commonly used prepositions include about, above, across, after, along, among, around, as, at, before, behind, below, beneath, beside, between, by, except, for, from, in, in back of, in front of, inside, into, of, off, on, onto, out of, outside, over, past, since, through, to, toward, under, up, upon, with, within, without.

Prepositional Phrase

A prepositional phrase is a phrase that begins with a preposition and ends with a noun or pronoun. The latter serves as the object of the preposition. The prepositional phrase serves to link its noun or pronoun to the sentence (e.g., They drove **under the bridge**. His desk was **in the corner of the building**. The dog rushed **to his food dish**).

Pronoun

A pronoun is any word that can be used as a replacement for a noun, phrase, or clause and refers to something or someone. There are seven categories of pronouns:

1. A **personal pronoun** is used in place of beings and objects. It denotes person, number, and sometimes gender. They include subjects (I, you, he, she, we, they, it); objects (me, you, him, her, us, them); and possessive pronouns (my, mine, your, yours, his, her, hers, its, our, ours, their, theirs).

2. A **reflexive pronoun** is a pronoun that refers to itself. It is formed by combining a personal pronoun (my, your, him, her, them, it, our) with self or selves. The result is myself, yourself, yourselves, himself, herself, themselves, itself, ourselves. Reflexive pronouns are used to refer to the subject (He voted for himself) or for emphasis (They are newcomers themselves).

3. A **demonstrative pronoun** (this, that, these, those) points out something. It functions as an adjective (Who was **that** masked man?) or as a noun (Stop **that**!).

4. An **indefinite pronoun** refers to an unidentified person(s) or thing(s) (e.g., **Someone** must pay for this). This group of pronouns includes any, anyone, anybody, anything, all, each, every, everybody, everyone, everything, few, both, many, much, no one, nobody, none, one, other, somebody, someone, something. Many also serve as adjectives.

5. An **interrogative pronoun** is used when asking a question (who, whom, whose, which, what) (e.g., What did I hear?).

6. A **relative pronoun** is a pronoun that introduces a subordinate clause (e.g., This is the cat **that** caught the bird in our backyard). The relative pronouns are who, whoever, whom, whomever, whose, what, whatever, which, whichever, that.

7. A **reciprocal pronoun**. There are two: each other and one another.

Proper Noun

A proper noun is any noun that gives the name of a specific being or thing. Proper nouns are usually capitalized (e.g., Philadelphia, Agatha, October, Microsoft Corporation, Tuesday, Columbia University, War of the Roses).

Punctuation

Punctuation refers to the practice or act of using various conventional marks or characters, such as periods, commas, etc., in writing or printing to improve clarity. They aid comprehension by showing where to pause, slow down, etc. Also, there are various characters used such as question mark, exclamation mark, colon, semi-colon, apostrophe, hyphen, dash, parentheses, ellipsis, and quotation marks.

Question Mark

A question mark (?) denotes a question. It is used at the end of a direct question. It behaves like a period when accompanied by quotation marks. The question mark has its origin in *quaestico*, Latin for "I ask." Quaestico was shortened by space-saving scribes to become QO and later, the letter Q above the letter O. Subsequently, the Q was degraded into a squiggle and the O into a little round spot. The question mark is also called an interrogation point or interrogation mark.

Restrictive Clause

A restrictive clause is a subordinate clause that is essential to the certainty of the word it modifies. If the restrictive clause is omitted, the meaning of the main clause will differ. Commas are not used to set off a restrictive clause from the rest of the sentence (e.g., All <u>automobiles</u> **that are parked in the prohibited area in front of the school** will be towed away). A restrictive clause is also termed an essential clause.

Run-on Sentence

A run-on sentence is a sentence that consists of two or more independent clauses that are joined together without suitable punctuation. The term applies also to sentences that, although technically correct, would be easier to read if separated into shorter segments. Although a person may speak in run-on sentences, he or she uses pauses and changes in emphasis and tone. This aids listener comprehension. However, this is not possible when writing. Consequently, it is desirable to avoid the use of unnecessarily long sentences.

Semicolon

A semicolon is a punctuation mark (;) used to denote a break in continuity that is greater than that which a comma implies, but less final than that which a period creates. Semicolons are often used to separate independent clauses in a series when commas will not add sufficient clarity. More commonly, the semicolon is used in a sentence to separate the two main clauses which are not joined by a conjunction.

Sentence

A sentence refers to a group of words (or a single word) that expresses a complete thought. A sentence always contains a verb and, usually, has a subject. However, if the statement is an imperative, the subject may only be implied (e.g., Stop! Go!). Similarly, an interrogative sentence may consist of only a verb (e.g., Why? How? When?).

Simile

A simile is a figure of speech in which one thing is compared to another unlike thing in one aspect by the use of like, as, etc. (e.g., He is as slow **as** a turtle).

Slang

Slang refers to very informal vocabulary and idioms that are widely used and understood. Slang is more metaphorical, playful, and vivid than the normal language of polite usage (e.g., pinch for steal, bike for bicycle). It consists of entirely new words, as well as new meanings ascribed to existing words. With time, slang either passes into disuse or is accepted as part of standard usage.

Subject

The subject is the part of the sentence or clause about which something is said. It is a word or group of words that identifies or describes who, what is doing, or what is being done. The subject is normally the doer of the action and typically consists of a noun or pronoun. However, a phrase or gerund can also serve as the subject of a sentence (e.g., **He** ate his breakfast. **Darkness** came early. **You** and **I** must leave now. **Swimming** is his sport of choice. **What they want** is unacceptable. **Coming to work late** must stop).

Subordinate Clause

A subordinate clause is a group of words containing both a subject and a predicate that cannot stand alone as a complete sentence. It requires an independent clause to express the idea fully. A subordinate clause is also termed a dependent clause because it depends on an attached independent clause to complete the meaning. A subordinating conjunction or relative pronoun normally introduces the subordinate clause (e.g., I prefer French cuisine, <u>although</u> **Italian food is fine**).

Subordinating Conjunction

A subordinating conjunction refers to a conjunction that joins an independent clause and a subordinate (dependent) clause. Examples of subordinating conjunctions include although, because, since, until, and while (e.g., He has not visited them **since** his wife died).

Suffix

A suffix is an affix attached to the end of a word in order to modify its meaning or to change its grammatical function, as from an adjective to an adverb (e.g., from sad to sad**ly** or light to light**ly**). The suffix may be a syllable, a group of syllables, or a group of letters.

Syllable

A syllable is a segment of speech that is typically produced with a single pulse of air from the lungs. It is a word part that is pronounced as a single element. It is also a character or set of characters representing such an element of speech. A syllable consists of a vowel with (or without) one or more consonant sounds immediately before or after (e.g., fine, but, soon, that). Syllables that end in a consonant are closed syllables. Those that end in a vowel are open syllables.

Synonym

A synonym is a word that is equivalent to another word and that can be substituted for it in a particular context, although the words may not have identical meanings. For example, the verbs **to type** and **to enter** are synonyms in the context of inputting data to a personal computer. A synonym is a word accepted as another for something.

Tense

Tense describes the form of a verb that denotes the relationship between the action and time. The basic tenses (present, past, and future) and variations tell if an action is taking place, took place, or will take place, etc. The progressive tenses also denote action either in progress (is walking), in the past (was walking), or in the future (will be walking). The perfect tense is used for action that began in the past and continues in the present (has walked), that was completed in the past (had walked), or that will be completed in the future action (will have walked).

Transitive Verb

A transitive verb is any verb that acts on a direct object (e.g., She **read** the **letter**. He **washed** the **dishes**. He **manages** a small **business**. She **teaches school**).

Verb

The word or words used to express action (e.g., ride, jump, speak), occurrence (e.g., is, exists, lives, understand), or state of being (e.g., feel, seem, is, be). It tells what is happening. It is the key element in the predicate, one of the two main parts of a sentence. A verb is called intransitive if it makes sense without an object, or transitive if it requires one. A verb is also termed a simple predicate.

F4 Explaining Verb Tenses

Teaching tense can be a tricky proposition for new language teachers. While students should not have a difficult time grasping the three simple tenses (past, present, and future), English contains a total of 12 different tenses: the simple past, present, and future; the progressive or continuous past, present, and future; the perfect past, present, and future; as well as the perfect progressive past, present, and future. Using diagrams can help your students to visualize the differences and relationships between these numerous tenses. On the following pages you will find two different charts to help explain verb tense to your students.

F5 Summary Chart of Verb Tenses

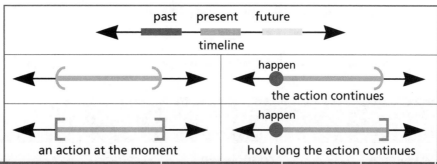

	Verb Tenses	Use	How to Form	Example	Sentence Example
Present Tenses	**Present Simple** present	to show repeated action, belief, opinion, characteristics	verb(s/es)	work works	They **work** sometimes. She **works** at Gally.
	Present Perfect already happened past · present	to show what has happened in the past and continues in the present; to show how long something has happened (often uses **for** and **since**)	have/has + past participle	have worked has worked	I **have worked** at Gallaudet for seven years. Kelly **has worked** at Gallaudet since 1993.
	Present Continuous (Progressive) present	to show an event that is going on right now	am/is/are + verb + ing	am working is working are working	Sue is **working** in the house. She and her sister **are working** at Gally now.
	Present Perfect Continuous (Progressive) already happened past · present	to show how long something has been happening and is still happening	have/has + been + verb + ing	have been working has been working	I **have been working** at Gallaudet for seven years. Kelly **has been working** at Gallaudet since 1993.

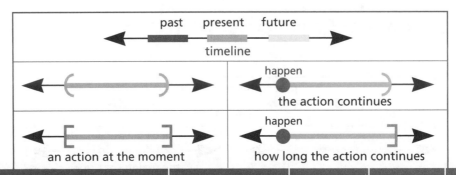

	Verb Tenses	Use	How to Form	Example	Sentence Example
Past Tenses	Past Simple — already happened — past	to show what happened at a time in the past and is finished	verb(d/ed)	worked	Yesterday Jim **worked** with Harry.
	Past Perfect — already happened — past past	to show an action in the past that happened even before another event in the past	had + past participle	had worked	The car **had worked** before the truck hit it.
	Past Continuous (Progressive) — already happened — past past	to show an event that was going on when something else happened (often uses **before, after, when**)	was/were + verb + ing	was working were working	I **was working** on the paper when my friend interrupted me. Sara and Jill **were working** at the Abbey when I stopped by.
	Past Perfect Continuous (Progressive) — already happened — past past	to show how long something had been happening before something else happened	had + been + verb + ing	had been working	The car **had been working** fine before the truck hit it.

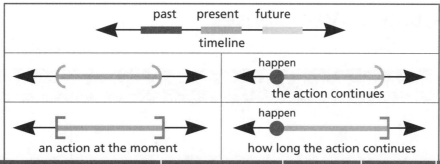

	Verb Tenses	Use	How to Form	Example	Sentence Example
Future Tenses	**Future Simple** will happen future	to show what will happen in the future	will + verb	will work	In the future I **will work** on Mars every week.
	Future Perfect will happen future future	to show something that has not yet been done but that will be done before a set time in the future	will have + past participle	will have worked	By tomorrow Steve **will have worked** on his term paper.
	Future Continuous (Progressive) will happen future future	to show an event that will be going on when something else happens	will be + verb + ing	will be working	The guard **will be working** on his project when we sneak up on him.
	Future Perfect Continuous (Progressive) will happen future future	to show how long something will have been happening by a future time	will have + been + verb + ing	will have been working	By tomorrow Steve **will have been working** for five days on his term paper.

F6 Guide to Verb Tenses

Simple Present	Present Progressive
Tom studies every day.	Tom is studying right now.
Simple Past	**Past Progressive**
Tom studied last night.	Tom was studying when they came.
Simple Future	**Future Progressive**
Tom will study tomorrow night.	Tom will be studying when they come.

Present Perfect	Present Perfect Progressive
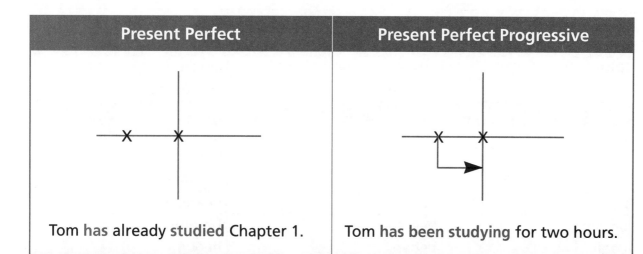 Tom **has** already **studied** Chapter 1.	Tom **has been studying** for two hours.
Past Perfect	Past Perfect Progressive
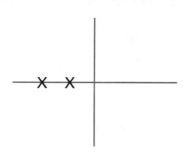 Tom **had** already **studied** chapter 1 before he began studying chapter 2.	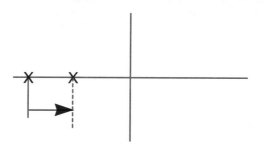 Tom **had been studying** for two hours before his friends came.
Future Perfect	Future Perfect Progressive
Tom **will** already **have studied** chapter 4 before he studies chapter 5.	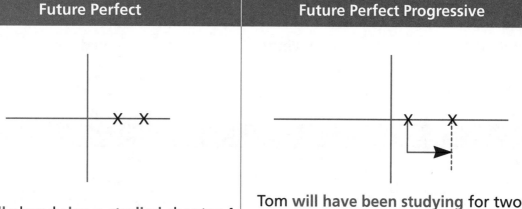 Tom **will have been studying** for two hours by the time his roommate gets home.

F7 List of Irregular Verbs

Infinitive	Simple Past	Past Participle
A		
arise	arose	arisen
awake	awakened/awoke	awakened/awoken
B		
backslide	backslid	backslidden/backslid
be	was, were	been
bear	bore	born/borne
beat	beat	beaten/beat
become	became	become
begin	began	begun
bend	bent	bent
bet	bet/betted	bet/betted
bid (farewell)	bid/bade	bidden
bid (offer amount)	bid	bid
bind	bound	bound
bite	bit	bitten
bleed	bled	bled
blow	blew	blown
break	broke	broken
breed	bred	bred
bring	brought	brought
broadcast	broadcast/broadcasted	broadcast/broadcasted
build	built	built
burn	burned/burnt	burned/burnt
burst	burst	burst
bust	busted/bust	busted/bust
buy	bought	bought
C		
cast	cast	cast
catch	caught	caught
choose	chose	chosen
cling	clung	clung
clothe	clothed/clad	clothed/clad
come	came	come
cost	cost	cost
creep	crept	crept

crossbreed	crossbred	crossbred
cut	cut	cut
D		
daydream	daydreamed/daydreamt	daydreamed/daydreamt
deal	dealt	dealt
dig	dug	dug
disprove	disproved	disproved/disproven
dive (jump head-first)	dove/dived	dived
dive (scuba diving)	dived/dove	dived
do	did	done
draw	drew	drawn
dream	dreamed/dreamt	dreamed/dreamt
drink	drank	drunk
drive	drove	driven
dwell	dwelt/dwelled	dwelt/dwelled
E		
eat	ate	eaten
F		
fall	fell	fallen
feed	fed	fed
feel	felt	felt
fight	fought	fought
find	found	found
fit (tailor, change size)	fitted/fit	fitted/fit
fit (be right size)	fit/fitted	fit/fitted
flee	fled	fled
fling	flung	flung
fly	flew	flown
forbid	forbade	forbidden
forecast	forecast	forecast
forego (also forgo)	forewent	foregone
foresee	foresaw	foreseen
foretell	foretold	foretold
forget	forgot	forgotten/forgot
forgive	forgave	forgiven
forsake	forsook	forsaken
freeze	froze	frozen
frostbite	frostbit	frostbitten
G		
get	got	gotten/got

give	gave	given
go	went	gone
grind	ground	ground
grow	grew	grown
H		
hand-feed	hand-fed	hand-fed
handwrite	handwrote	handwritten
hang	hung	hung
have	had	had
hear	heard	heard
hide	hid	hidden
hit	hit	hit
hold	held	held
hurt	hurt	hurt
I		
inbreed	inbred	inbred
inlay	inlaid	inlaid
input	input/inputted	input/inputted
interbreed	interbred	interbred
interweave	interwove/interweaved	interwoven/interweaved
interwind	interwound	interwound
J		
No irregular verbs beginning with J		
K		
keep	kept	kept
kneel	knelt/kneeled	knelt/kneeled
knit	knitted/knit	knitted/knit
know	knew	known
L		
lay	laid	laid
lead	led	led
lean	leaned/leant	leaned/leant
leap	leaped/leapt	leaped/leapt
learn	learned/learnt	learned/learnt
leave	left	left
lend	lent	lent
let	let	let
lie	lay	lain
light	lit/lighted	lit/lighted

lip-read	lip-read	lip-read
lose	lost	lost
M		
make	made	made
mean	meant	meant
meet	met	met
miscast	miscast	miscast
misdeal	misdealt	misdealt
misdo	misdid	misdone
mishear	misheard	misheard
mislay	mislaid	mislaid
mislead	misled	misled
mislearn	mislearned/mislearnt	mislearned/mislearnt
misread	misread	misread
misspeak	misspoke	misspoken
misspell	misspelled/misspelt	misspelled/misspelt
misspend	misspent	misspent
mistake	mistook	mistaken
misteach	mistaught	mistaught
misunderstand	misunderstood	misunderstood
miswrite	miswrote	miswritten
mow	mowed	mowed/mown
N		
No irregular verbs beginning with N		
O		
offset	offset	offset
outbid	outbid	outbid
outdo	outdid	outdone
outdraw	outdrew	outdrawn
outdrink	outdrank	outdrunk
outdrive	outdrove	outdriven
outfight	outfought	outfought
outgrow	outgrew	outgrown
outleap	outleaped/outleapt	outleaped/outleapt
outride	outrode	outridden
outrun	outran	outrun
outsell	outsold	outsold
outshine	outshined/outshone	outshined/outshone
outshoot	outshot	outshot
outsing	outsang	outsung

F

outsit	outsat	outsat
outsleep	outslept	outslept
outsmell	outsmelled/outsmelt	outsmelled/outsmelt
outspeak	outspoke	outspoken
outspeed	outsped	outsped
outspend	outspent	outspent
outswear	outswore	outsworn
outswim	outswam	outswum
outthink	outthought	outthought
outthrow	outthrew	outthrown
outwrite	outwrote	outwritten
overbid	overbid	overbid
overbreed	overbred	overbred
overbuild	overbuilt	overbuilt
overbuy	overbought	overbought
overcome	overcame	overcome
overdo	overdid	overdone
overdraw	overdrew	overdrawn
overdrink	overdrank	overdrunk
overeat	overate	overeaten
overfeed	overfed	overfed
overhear	overheard	overheard
overlay	overlaid	overlaid
overpay	overpaid	overpaid
override	overrode	overridden
overrun	overran	overrun
oversee	oversaw	overseen
oversell	oversold	oversold
overshoot	overshot	overshot
oversleep	overslept	overslept
overspeak	overspoke	overspoken
overspend	overspent	overspent
overspill	overspilled/overspilt	overspilled/overspilt
overtake	overtook	overtaken
overthink	overthought	overthought
overthrow	overthrew	overthrown
overwind	overwound	overwound
overwrite	overwrote	overwritten
P		
partake	partook	partaken
pay	paid	paid

plead	pleaded/pled	pleaded/pled
prebuild	prebuilt	prebuilt
predo	predid	predone
premake	premade	premade
prepay	prepaid	prepaid
presell	presold	presold
preset	preset	preset
preshrink	preshrank	preshrunk
proofread	proofread	proofread
prove	proved	proven/proved
put	put	put
Q		
quick-freeze	quick-froze	quick-frozen
quit	quit/quitted	quit/quitted
R		
read	read (sounds like "red")	read (sounds like "red")
reawake	reawoke	reawaken
rebid	rebid	rebid
rebind	rebound	rebound
rebroadcast	rebroadcast/rebroadcasted	rebroadcast/rebroadcasted
rebuild	rebuilt	rebuilt
recast	recast	recast
recut	recut	recut
redeal	redealt	redealt
redo	redid	redone
redraw	redrew	redrawn
refit (replace parts)	refit/refitted	refit/refitted
refit (re-tailor)	refitted/refit	refitted/refit
regrind	reground	reground
regrow	regrew	regrown
rehang	rehung	rehung
rehear	reheard	reheard
relay	relaid	relaid
relearn	relearned/relearnt	relearned/relearnt
relight	relit/relighted	relit/relighted
remake	remade	remade
repay	repaid	repaid
reread	reread	reread
rerun	reran	rerun
resell	resold	resold
resend	resent	resent

F

reset	reset	reset
resew	resewed	resewn/resewed
retake	retook	retaken
reteach	retaught	retaught
retear	retore	retorn
retell	retold	retold
rethink	rethought	rethought
retread	retread	retread
retrofit	retrofitted/retrofit	retrofitted/retrofit
rewake	rewoke/rewaked	rewaken/rewaked
rewear	rewore	reworn
reweave	rewove/reweaved	rewoven/reweaved
rewed	rewed/rewedded	rewed/rewedded
rewet	rewet	rewet
rewin	rewon	rewon
rewind	rewound	rewound
rewrite	rewrote	rewritten
rid	rid	rid
ride	rode	ridden
ring	rang	rung
rise	rose	risen
roughcast	roughcast	roughcast
run	ran	run
S		
saw	sawed	sawed/sawn
say	said	said
see	saw	seen
seek	sought	sought
sell	sold	sold
send	sent	sent
set	set	set
sew	sewed	sewn/sewed
shake	shook	shaken
shave	shaved	shaved/shaven
shear	sheared	sheared/shorn
shed	shed	shed
shine	shined/shone	shined/shone
shoot	shot	shot
show	showed	shown/showed
shrink	shrank/shrunk	shrunk

F

shut	shut	shut
sight-read	sight-read	sight-read
sing	sang	sung
sink	sank/sunk	sunk
sit	sat	sat
slay (kill)	slew/slayed	slain/slayed
sleep	slept	slept
slide	slid	slid
sling	slung	slung
slink	slinked/slunk	slinked/slunk
slit	slit	slit
smell	smelled/smelt	smelled/smelt
sneak	sneaked/snuck	sneaked/snuck
sow	sowed	sown/sowed
speak	spoke	spoken
speed	sped/speeded	sped/speeded
spell	spelled/spelt	spelled/spelt
spend	spent	spent
spill	spilled/spilt	spilled/spilt
spin	spun	spun
spit	spit/spat	spit/spat
split	split	split
spoil	spoiled/spoilt	spoiled/spoilt
spoon-feed	spoon-fed	spoon-fed
spread	spread	spread
spring	sprang/sprung	sprung
stand	stood	stood
steal	stole	stolen
stick	stuck	stuck
sting	stung	stung
stink	stunk/stank	stunk
strew	strewed	strewn/strewed
stride	strode	stridden
strike (delete)	struck	stricken
strike (hit)	struck	struck/stricken
string	strung	strung
strive	strove/strived	striven/strived
sublet	sublet	sublet
sunburn	sunburned/sunburnt	sunburned/sunburnt
swear	swore	sworn

F

sweat	sweat/sweated	sweat/sweated
sweep	swept	swept
swell	swelled	swollen/swelled
swim	swam	swum
swing	swung	swung
T		
take	took	taken
teach	taught	taught
tear	tore	torn
telecast	telecast	telecast
tell	told	told
test-drive	test-drove	test-driven
test-fly	test-flew	test-flown
think	thought	thought
throw	threw	thrown
thrust	thrust	thrust
tread	trod	trodden/trod
typecast	typecast	typecast
typeset	typeset	typeset
typewrite	typewrote	typewritten
U		
unbend	unbent	unbent
unbind	unbound	unbound
unclothe	unclothed	unclothed
underbid	underbid	underbid
undercut	undercut	undercut
underfeed	underfed	underfed
undergo	underwent	undergone
underlie	underlay	underlain
undersell	undersold	undersold
underspend	underspent	underspent
understand	understood	understood
undertake	undertook	undertaken
underwrite	underwrote	underwritten
undo	undid	undone
unfreeze	unfroze	unfrozen
unhang	unhung	unhung
unhide	unhid	unhidden
unlearn	unlearned	unlearned
unstick	unstuck	unstuck

unweave	unwove/unweaved	unwoven/unweaved
unwind	unwound	unwound
uphold	upheld	upheld
upset	upset	upset
V		
No commonly used irregular verbs beginning with V		
W		
wake	woke/waked	woken/waked
wear	wore	worn
weave	wove/weaved	woven/weaved
wed	wed/wedded	wed/wedded
weep	wept	wept
wet	wet	wet
win	won	won
wind	wound	wound
withdraw	withdrew	withdrawn
withhold	withheld	withheld
withstand	withstood	withstood
wring	wrung	wrung
write	wrote	written
X		
No irregular verbs beginning with X		
Y		
No irregular verbs beginning with Y		
Z		
No commonly used irregular verbs beginning with Z		

F

F8 Phrasal Verbs

In English grammar, a phrasal verb is a group of words that consists of a verb plus an adverbial or prepositional participle. If you eliminate any component of the phrasal verb you cannot interpret the intended meaning.

Example:

Most bullies will back down if confronted. ✔

Most bullies back. ✘

Most bullies down. ✘

A
act like
act up
add up (to)
ask out

B
back down
back off
back up
blow up
break down
break in
break up
bring off
bring up
bring/take back
brush up on
build up
burn down
burn up
butt in
butter up

C
call off
call on
calm down
care for
catch on
catch up
check in (to)
check off
check out
check out (of)
cheer up
chew out
chicken out
chip in

clam up
come across
come down with
come to
count on
crack down (on)
cross out
cut back

D
do in
do over
drag on
draw out
draw up
drop by
drop in (on)
drop off
drop out (of)

E
eat out
egg on
end up

F
face up to
fall through
feel up to
figure out
fill in
fill out
find out (about)

G
get across
get along (with)
get around (to)
get by
get in(to)

get off
get on
get out of
get over
get rid of
get up
give up
go out with
go with
goof off
grow up

H
hand in
hand out
hang up
have to do with
hold up

I
iron out

J
jack up
jump all over

K
keep on
kick out
knock oneself out
knock out

L
lay off
leave out
let down
let up
look back on
look down on
look forward to
look in on

look into
look like
look over
look up (to)
luck out

M
make for
make fun of
make out
make up (with)
mark down
mark up

N
nod off

P
pan out
pass away
pass out
pick on
pick out
pick up
pitch in
pull off
pull over
put away
put back
put off
put on
put out
put up (to)
put up with

R
rip off
round off
run into
run out of

S
set back
set up
show up
slip up
stand for
stand out
stand up

T
take after
take care of
take off
take up
take/bring back
tell someone off
throw away
throw out
throw up
tick off
try on
try out
try out for
turn around
turn down
turn in
turn off
turn on
turn up

W / Z
wait on
wake up
watch out for
wear out
work out
wrap up
write down
zonk out

F9 Levels of Grammar

Beginner

Beginner students have the whole of English learning in front of them, so they will progress quickly and have a great number of topics and concepts to practice, such as the following:

- familiar nouns (singular/plural, count/non-count, possessive)
- common verbs (to be, have, need, like, go, eat, buy, etc.)
- verb tenses as required for basic practical purposes (taught as fixed phrases)
- can or cannot (ability)
- familiar adjectives (including possessive, demonstrative)
- adding order of adjectives
- comparative and superlative adjectives
- familiar adverbs (especially time, frequency, manner), additional adverbs of time, frequency, and manner
- definite and indefinite articles
- imperatives (positive and negative)
- prepositions of time, location, movement, and duration
- idiomatic expressions of time, frequency, and manner
- familiar conjunctions
- pronouns (subject, object, and possessive forms)
- modal verbs for ability, possibility, necessity, suggestion, advice, permission, and promises
- collective nouns
- introduction to familiar phrasal verbs
- interrogative and possessive pronouns
- additional control over yes/no and WH-questions
- use of gerund or infinitive with familiar verbs (e.g., like, need)
- more varied exposure to verb tenses: simple present, present continuous, simple past (regular and irregular), and future (including going to)

High-Beginner

Students will build on and strengthen elements covered up to the beginner level by adding the following:
- adjective and adverb intensifiers
- adjectival comparisons with as … as, more/less … than
- adverbs of duration
- comparative and superlative adverbs
- expressions of quantity
- simple modal verbs for obligation, prohibition, degree of certainty, and habitual past action (e.g., could, should, would)
- distinction between familiar separable and non-separable phrasal verbs
- introduction to reflexive pronouns (especially as direct or indirect object)
- direct speech
- present perfect and past continuous tenses

Pre-Intermediate

Students will build on and strengthen elements covered up to the high-beginner level by adding the following:

- more separable and non-separable phrasal verbs
- reported speech
- additional verbs used with gerund or infinitive for likes, dislikes, needs, and desires
- tag questions
- more complex modal verbs for obligation, prohibition, and degree of certainty (could have, should not have, etc.)
- extended uses of reflexive pronouns (e.g., as object of preposition, or for emphasis) adverbial comparisons with as … as, more/less … than
- use of adverbial hedges (probably, perhaps, surely, etc.)

Intermediate

Students will build on and strengthen elements covered up to the pre-intermediate level by adding the following:

- adjectival use of present and past participle
- adjective clauses
- adverb clauses
- real and unreal conditionals
- additional uses of gerunds and infinitives
- transition words (therefore, next, etc.) and adverb clauses as logical markers
- relative, reciprocal, and indefinite pronouns
- embedded questions
- rejoinders (e.g., so do I, neither do I)
- extended use of past modals to express advisability
- introduction to the passive voice (present, simple past, future)
- intro to recognition/decoding of complex nouns groups, especially for reading comprehension
- past perfect tense

High-Intermediate

Students will build on and strengthen elements covered up to the intermediate level by adding the following:

- wish with the present
- past unreal conditional
- noun clauses as direct object of verbs (think, hope, etc.)
- introduction to more complex forms of the passive voice (e.g., progressive forms); prepositions of purpose
- distinction between defining and non-defining adjective clauses
- verb agreement with complex noun groups
- lexical sets
- hyponyms and superordinates

Advanced

Students will build on and strengthen elements covered up to the high-intermediate level by adding the following:
- noun clauses as subject
- noun clauses as direct object of verbs like prefer, require, wish, etc. (requiring subjunctive)
- future continuous and future perfect tenses
- parallel clause structures
- paired conjunctions (both … and, not only … but also, neither … nor, etc.)
- reduced adjective and adverb clauses
- concession (although, given/provided that …, etc.)
- consequences (so [adj.] … that, such a … that, etc.)
- exclamations with WH-words
- introduction to selection of grammatical options to reflect levels of formality (contractions, vocabulary variations, etc.)

Very Advanced/Fluent

Students will build on and strengthen elements covered up to the advanced level, principally adding increased accuracy, fluency, and effectiveness in selecting grammatical options to carry out communicative purposes.

Occasional mistakes may well persist with some basic elements (e.g., use of definite, indefinite, and zero articles, third-person singulars, or count/non-count nouns), but students' general control of English will make it possible to focus on appropriate production and comprehension of complex grammar when speaking, listening, reading, and writing. The very advanced/fluent level generally approximates the English language proficiency of an anglophone high-school graduate.

F10 Grammar Methodology—Yesterday and Today

	The Grammar Translation Method	The Communicative Method
History	Originated in the 19th century. Originally-used to teach Latin to English-speaking university students.	Originated in the late 20th century. The dominant modern approach to language teaching used the world over.
Philosophy	Through translation and copying, students will learn to read the new language.	Through practice and use, students will learn how to communicate in the new language.
Objective(s)	Students will be able to read and write in the target language.	Students will be able to communicate in the target language through speaking, listening, reading, and writing.
Direct Teaching	Central to the Grammar Translation Method. The teacher explains and gives information.	Minimal in the Communicative Method. Classes focus on interactivity and STT (student talking time).
Discovery Learning	Students are not encouraged or given the opportunity to explore language on their own. All learning is focused and structured.	Students are encouraged to explore the language and discover the rules of grammar and syntax which govern its structure.
Sample Tasks and Activities	Direct translation of passages and texts using bilingual dictionaries.	Learn about imperatives. Practice Simon Says. Read various instructions. Write recipes. Make a class cookbook. Make kimchi together.
Tools	Textbooks, dictionaries, handouts, and direct instruction from the teacher.	A variety of authentic resources including newspapers, magazines, videos, CDs, charts, and posters.

F11 How to Select Grammar Items

Grammar Items

In most cases you will be working with a school syllabus or a book where the grammar items are selected and ordered for you. In most syllabi, grammar items are carefully graded, meaning that simpler structures (e.g., This is my sister) come before more complex ones (e.g., Not having seen him for five years, I was very surprised to bump into him again).

However, students often take time to process language they have been taught before they can start using it fluently and accurately, so you will need to recycle the grammar you have taught. You can choose items to teach or practice:

- For revision
- For error correction and remedial work
- Because a grammar item is too complicated to be covered all at once, more complex items will need to be taught in small steps

F12 Sample Grammar Lessons

On the following pages you will find examples of grammar lessons for students ranging from beginner to advanced. These can offer you a starting point from which to build your own lessons. Feel free to mix and match elements of the lessons and to add your own material. It is important that teachers create and teach lessons that suit their own personal teaching style.

Sample Lesson 1: Meaning Through Action

Level: Beginner
Time: 15–25 minutes
Objective: To represent the meaning of a grammar structure through actions

Procedure
1. Perform a set of actions in front of the class, at the same time providing a running commentary on the actions.

Example
- "I am walking to the door. The door is closed. What am I going to do?
  I'm going to open the door."
- "Now, I am walking to the window. The window is open. What am I going to do? I am going to close the window."
- "Now, I am walking to the board. I am holding the chalk. What am I going to do? I am going to write on the board."

2. Repeat the activities, but this time pause before the final sentence of each sequence, and elicit the answer to the question; for example, you may say "What am I going to do?" to elicit you are going to open the door.

3. Ask individuals to perform the actions, while you provide the commentary: "Ahmed is walking to the window. What is he going to do?", etc.

4. Ask individuals to provide the commentary while first you, then another student, perform the actions.

5. Display the structure and the forms that have been used so far:

What	am I	going to	do?
	is he		

I	am	going to	open the door.
you	are		close the window.
he	is		write on the board.

Comment

This activity arises out of the Direct Method in which the new structure is associated with its meaning directly, i.e., unmediated by translation, explanation. This works well for grammar structures that can be easily enacted, such as:

- present continuous: I am walking.
- going to future: I am going to open the door.
- imperatives: Give me the book. Don't sit down.
- present perfect + just: I have just closed the window.
- possessive determiners and pronouns: This is my book. It is mine.
- demonstratives: This book is green. That book is red.
- can/can't: I can touch the floor. I can't touch the ceiling, etc.

It is less effective with more conceptually remote structures, such as past tenses and conditionals, and therefore is more appropriate for beginners or younger students.

The Structure of a Grammar Lesson

The two lessons that follow have a Presentation-Practice-Production (PPP) structure; but even when two lessons follow a similar order, there is room for a lot of variety in activities and techniques.

	Sample Lesson 2	Sample Lesson 3
Lesson Structure	PPP	PPP
Language Focus	Concept questions Timeline diagram	Students work out meaning themselves from context
Teaching Focus	Eliciting language from students to guide them towards the target language	Encouraging students to work out the rule for themselves
Materials	Flashcards Jigsaw sentence slips	"Find someone who" slips Group questionnaire
Presenting the Target Language	Dramatized situation	Reading text with task
Practice Activities	Drill Matching game Mime and guess game	Writing sentences about themselves Writing a questionnaire
Producing the Target Language	Drama activity Memory game	Using the questionnaires from the practice phase
Consolidation	Writing an account of a scene	Using a questionnaire the students have written

Sample Lesson 2: Past Continuous and Past Simple

Level: Pre-intermediate

Language: Past continuous and past simple

The past continuous gives the background to an event, e.g., I was looking for my pet hamster, when X [student] came in.

Assumed Knowledge: Present continuous, past simple

Resources: Board, flashcards (Stages 2 and 6), handout slips with two halves of sentences (Stage 7)

Preparation: Draw the flashcards (Stages 2 and 6) and make the handout slips (Stage 7).

Time: 45 minutes

Lead-in

1. Ask one student to leave the class. Tell the student she will get a surprise when she comes back in.

Comment

This creates a mystery which will engage the students' attention.

2. Create the context: tell the rest of the class to imagine they are a (big) family. They have lost their pet hamster and are looking for it everywhere (use the flashcard if hamster is a new word). Get them to begin pretending to look for the hamster, then ask the student to come back in.

Comment

This is a fun way to introduce the language point that gets all the students actively involved and provides a clear and dramatic context for an interrupted action. Other possible contexts could be a party when X arrives, doing housework when X comes in, or watching a horror movie when the lights go out.

Introduce Target Language

3. Ask the student, "What were they doing when you came in?" Get her to guess. As the student guesses, recast her language, for example:

> **S:** "They looked for something."
> **T:** "Yes ... they were looking for something." "What were they looking for?"
> "Can you guess?"

Comment

This way of drawing out the information from your students is called eliciting. It is useful for seeing how much the students know collectively, and for keeping them involved in the presentation of new language.

Check Comprehension

4. Start writing the following sentence on the board: "We were looking for a hamster when X came in" by asking the class to give you the words to make up the sentence. As the words are given, write them up in the appropriate place until the class has constructed your sentence together.

Comment

Introducing the language by asking questions is a very natural way of introducing language and keeps the students more involved than if you simply tell them the new language.

Underline <u>We were looking for a hamster</u>. Ask the class, "Did this take a long time?" Underline <u>X came in</u>. Ask the same question. Write "long" above We were looking for a hamster and "short" above X came in.

Comment

This type of question is called a concept question. It checks that students have understood the main idea behind the structure you are teaching; in this case, that a long action was interrupted by a shorter one.

You can illustrate the concept of how these verb tenses are used by drawing a timeline on the board. Recreate the timeline shown below. Ask the class what the squiggly line shows (We were looking: the long action) and what the arrow shows (when X came in: the short action which interrupted it).

To review, ask the class what represents **We were looking** (the long squiggly line), and what represents **X came in** (the arrow).

Comment

Using a timeline on the board is a useful way of illustrating the concept behind many verb tense combinations. Look for timelines in course books and other materials.

Language Focus

5. Draw a substitution table on the board (you may need to remind your students that the singular form of "you" is the same as the plural).

I He She	was			
		looking for the hamster	when	x came in
You We They	were			

Comment

A substitution table like this makes the pattern very clear to students. It draws their attention to the word forms used.

Check Comprehension

6. Show the class the first flashcard and ask them what the hamster is doing. Ask them what they think happened next. Show the second flashcard and ask them to make a sentence using "was ... -ing when". Repeat with the other pairs of cards.

Think about how the flashcards will be interpreted, and what sentences you are likely to be given.

Comment

This activity gives the students a chance to consolidate their understanding of how the "was/were ... -ing when" pattern is used and how to form more sentences using this pattern with new vocabulary. It also satisfies students' curiosity by showing how the story finished.

Practice the Language

7. Hand out slips of paper, each with one-half of a sentence written on it. Tell the class that they have to stand up and try to find the person with the other half of their sentence. If you think your students will have trouble with the words, draw pictures on the board first (snake, bee, fly, spider, etc). You can mime "swallow" if they do not know it.

I was walking in the country	when I saw a snake
I was working in the garden	when I saw a lot of bees
I was drinking a cup of tea	when I swallowed a fly
I was having a shower	when I noticed a big spider

Comment

The answers to this activity are not fixed. The students should have fun discussing which answers are possible and do not need to take it too seriously. It gives them a further opportunity to practice the new language in a controlled way.

8. When the students have found their other halves, ask them to sit together and prepare a mime of their sentence. Give them a few minutes to prepare. Put the students into small groups and then tell the pairs to perform their mimes for the group. The rest of the group should guess what happened and make a sentence using "was/were … -ing when".

Comment

This activity gives the students an opportunity to use the language to create more new sentences. The activity is fairly controlled; students can check if their sentences are correct themselves by looking at the slips of paper.

Use the Language

9. Divide students into two groups. Tell each group they were all on a street when a spaceship landed and two aliens got out. The people on the street should all be doing different things: shopping, drinking coffee, waiting for a bus, etc. Give them some time to prepare their scene for the other group. When a scene is presented, the other group should watch and try to notice what everyone is doing. Then get them to work in small groups to try to remember what everyone was doing. The following are some examples:

*   Two people were waiting for a bus. . .
*   Yes, and Pierre was eating an ice-cream cone.

Circulate to listen to what they are saying. Make notes of any problems or errors and deal with these in feedback immediately after the activity.

Consolidation

10. Get students to write an account of the scene they watched; for example: It was a sunny Saturday afternoon and the street was full of people. Two girls were looking in a shop window …, etc. They can continue the story in any way they like.

Comment

This activity gets the students to use the language more freely and to put it together with language they already know. They will use the language both in speaking—as they discuss what they remember about the scene—and in writing. Writing gives the students more time to think about the language and will help to consolidate what they have learned.

Sample Lesson 3: Superlative Adjectives

Level: Lower-intermediate

Language: Superlative adjectives (adjective + est; most + adjective):

big	biggest
sad	saddest
young	youngest
old	oldest
early	earliest
easy	easiest
careful	most careful
boring	most boring
interesting	most interesting
difficult	most difficult

Assumed Knowledge: Comparative adjectives (bigger, sadder, etc.); present perfect for life experiences.

Resources: "Find someone who" slips; group questionnaire

Preparation: Prepare the "Find someone who" slips (see Stage 1) and the questionnaire (see Stage 2).

Time: 40 minutes

Lead-in

1. Hand out slips of paper to half the class. Each slip contains a Find someone who … instruction, with a comparative adjective, for the students to use to compare themselves with each other. The following are examples:

   • **Find someone who is taller than you and sit next to them.**
   • **Find someone who has bigger feet than you and sit next to them.**
   • **Find someone who has more careful handwriting than you and sit next to them.**

Ask these students to move around the class asking questions till they find the person and then sit next to them.

Comment

This activity starts the lesson in a lively way. It also reminds the students what they know about comparatives, which will help them understand today's lesson on superlatives. A quick revision activity is a good way to start a lesson, particularly if it is done in an enjoyable format like this game.

Introduce Target Language

2. Put students into groups of 6–8. Give each group the following questionnaire:

    In your group, who
    - has the smallest feet:
    - has the biggest hands:
    - is the youngest:
    - has the most interesting hobby:
    - has the most careful handwriting:
    - takes the earliest train:
    - has the worst journey to class:
    - has the best idea for a party:

Ask them to read the questionnaire and to work out the answers for their group. Circulate while they are doing this, listening to them and helping with any problems.

Comment

Relating language to students' personal lives makes a motivating and interesting context. This questionnaire introduces the new language in written form. The students should know the adjectives (big, good, etc.) and their comparative forms (bigger, better, etc.) already, so it should not be hard for them to work out the meaning of the new language for themselves.

Check Comprehension

3. When they have finished, check that they have understood by asking each group to give you one fact about their findings.

> **T:** So, tell me one thing you found out.
> **S:** Angelika has the most brothers and sisters! Seven!

Comment

This activity has two functions: it will show you whether students have understood well enough to begin to use the new language themselves. It also rounds off the group work and brings the class back together as a whole, ready for the next activity.

Language Focus

4. Put the adjectives in the left-hand column (see Language on previous page). Then ask what the difference is between the four groups of adjectives. If they need help, tell them to think of the number of syllables in each word.

5. Put the class into pairs. Write **biggest** at the top of the right-hand column. Ask the students to fill in the rest of the column. Check the answers when they have finished.

Comment

Students can fill in some words from the words in the questionnaire. They can try to work out the others themselves.

6. Tell the pairs to look at the first two groups again and decide how they could divide them into two more groups.

7. Ask pairs at random how they have divided the words and what reason they have. Ask them if they can think of a rule for each group.

Group 1: One-syllable adjectives, e.g., young and old, add -est; sad and big end in vowel + consonant so the last consonant is doubled

Group 2: Two-syllable adjectives ending in -y, e.g., happy and funny, the **y** changes to **i** before -est

Group 3: The majority of two-syllable adjectives (except those ending in -y) take most forms, (e.g., most careful; most boring), but some can have either form (e.g., quieter/more quiet)

Group 4: Adjectives with more than two syllables take **most** form, (e.g., most interesting; most difficult)

8. Ask them to look at their questionnaire. Are there any adjectives that make a fifth group?

Group 5: Irregular adjectives (e.g., good/best; bad/worst)

Comment

Changing word endings to form the superlative is complicated. It involves a set of rules related to the number of syllables and the spelling of the adjectives. If students are given some examples and guided through the process by the teacher, they can work out the rules for themselves. Discovering grammar in this way, rather than being directly given the information, is a way of making learning more memorable.

Practice the Language

9. Write the following adjectives on the board:

bad	happy
beautiful	interesting
exciting	nice
famous	pretty
good	thin

Get students to work in pairs to discuss how to make the superlatives. Go through the words when they have finished and write the words on the board. Ask students to make a sentence about themselves using the words on the board; for example, I think Japanese food is the best.

Comment

This activity gets students to apply the rules they worked out in the previous activity and gives you the chance to check that they have understood correctly.

Use the Language

10. Write the following on the board:

What is the best book you've ever read? Why?

Collect answers from different students. Then get them to make five more questions in this pattern:

What is the _____ _____ you've ever _____? Why?

Circulate to deal with any difficulties and to give help if needed.

Comment
This is a controlled activity focusing on accuracy. Students have time to think about the adjectives they are going to use and to get the form right. However, there is also an element of creativity as students can choose what questions they will write. This makes the activity more interesting.

11. When they are ready, put students in pairs to ask and answer each other's questions. Circulate to listen to what they are saying, and to help if necessary. Make a note of any common errors so you can go through them later.

Comment
This activity gives the students the opportunity to use the new language more freely. As they answer each other's questions, they will end up discussing their experiences. In this way the new language will be integrated with language they already have.

Consolidation
12. Ask the students to write a report on their partner's choices.

F13 Grammar Poems

Because this poetic format tells the poet exactly what to do, the scaffold allows anyone to write a satisfying, well-constructed poem simply by filling in the parts of speech as required. The format is as follows:

[Title – Noun/s]
[Noun],
[Noun],
[Noun],
[Adjective noun],
[Adjective noun].
[Adjective, adjective, adjective, noun].
[Adjective, adjective, adjective, noun].
Those are just a few.
[Adjective, noun],
[Adjective, noun],
[Participle, participle, participle noun].
[Participle, participle, participle noun].
[Adjective, noun], too.
[Adjective, noun],
[Adjective, noun],
[Adjective, noun].
Don't forget [adjective noun].
Last of all—best of all—
I like [adjective noun].

F14 Whose Language Is It Anyway?

By Stephen S. Pickering

As a career language guardian, I was more than casually interested in the College Board's decision to throw out a grammar question on its PSAT after a high-school teacher pointed out that the desired answer was not technically correct. The question asked if there was a grammatical error in this sentence: "Toni Morrison's genius enables her to create novels that arise from and express the injustices African Americans have endured." The College Board thought the sentence was correct, but a journalism teacher in Maryland told the officials that the word "her" did not refer back to Toni Morrison but to "Toni Morrison's"—an error in grammar.

The teacher certainly was right on the technical question. Those who take a dark view of where the language is headed can only stare open-mouthed in disbelief that the College Board experts, specifically focused on composing a grammatically correct sentence, wrote an error into it. But as one who has always viewed American English as a sort of junk shop, stacked with bins of curious rules and tools useful mostly to journeyman quantum mechanics, I saw another way to look at the sentence. The first three words, "Toni Morrison's genius," are understood as "The genius of Toni Morrison," and thus the true antecedent of "her" is, correctly, Toni Morrison. That reading at least has some common sense on its side.

American English's genius lies in its ability to accommodate such quantum logic—to exist in two places or forms simultaneously—and, instead of imploding, actually thrive and grow. For immigrants it is surely one of the easiest languages to get by in—no genders, and easy verb forms and noun and pronoun cases. If their English is peppered with phrases and words from their mother tongues, you can bet those terms will eventually be absorbed as well.

But under all the latter-day immigrants' offerings lie Germanic foundations from the Saxon and Scandinavian eras, then layers of Latin and Greek words from those cultures' wide European influence, especially in the church, and Norman French residue dating from 1066. This jumble of liturgies makes modern English, despite its stripped-down workings, hard to learn well. Survivors of remedial classes cite, with a shiver, the insane variety of letter sounds, most infamously the supposed 22 ways E can be pronounced. But the language blunders on, and errors and misuses either get corrected or institutionalized—like the term of disdain that I first heard in an Army barracks: "I could care less," which of course means exactly its opposite.

None of this is to imply that the disputed PSAT question, or by extension good grammar, doesn't matter. It matters a lot for the transmission of precise, nuanced information; and at its best, English, with that junk-shop vocabulary thousands of words larger than those of other Western European languages, can cut and shape like a scalpel.

Having made a living for several decades trying to hone that blade as a copy editor, I ran across problems like the one in the PSAT question a dozen or more times every night. And just between us, solving them depended not so much on how many grammar rules I knew, but on determining the clearest, briefest way to get to the next sentence; that is, on good syntax and common sense.

George Orwell wrote an essay in 1946 on politics and language contending that the clarity of one's writing mirrored clarity of thought; that if a person could not state his position clearly in print, his views were probably similarly muddled. It is not a bad caution for managing this largely unmanageable language: Grammar is important—clarity is more so. Maybe that's the lesson for those PSAT students.

SECTION G
Teaching Vocabulary

Content

G1 Top 10 Ways to Introduce Vocabulary

Teachers often explain new vocabulary to students. Lexical items can include single words (house), collocations (make a bed), and longer chunks (once in a blue moon).

To illustrate meaning, our default mode is often to give a definition. With definitions, drawbacks include a lack of context, a need to use equally complex terms, and the temptation to provide other meanings of new words.

As teachers, we can add other ways of teaching lexicon to our "teaching tool belt." For students, the method we choose to illustrate is often the key to making the item meaningful and useable. Here are 10 ways to illustrate lexicon.

1. Synonyms

Using items with a similar meaning can be useful. Adjectives such as **intelligent** have several synonyms: bright, smart, clever. Phrasal verbs usually have a non-phrasal verb equivalent: go off—explode. Teachers should be wary of saying that items have the same meaning. Often, the meaning is close, but there are differences in formality, connotation, and grammatical usage.

2. Antonyms

Opposites are a common way to present and learn the meaning of new lexicon. At lower levels, items such as **rich** and **poor** are obvious examples. Again, teachers should be mindful of making generalizations. **Rich people** and **poor people** are opposites, but **rich food** and **poor food** are not. Collocations are helpful here. At higher levels, prefixes and suffixes are excellent for vocabulary building through opposites, e.g., **helpful** and **unhelpful**.

3. Drawing

The most basic sketch or stick figures can provide the perfect medium to illustrate certain vocabulary items. Some good examples include geographical terms like **estuary** or **peninsular**, statistical features of graphs like **peak**, **trough**, or **go through the roof**, and physical terms such as **back-to-back**. Artistic skills are not required!

4. Points on a Scale

A scale is an excellent way to illustrate the meaning of several gradable items at the same time. Common examples include adverbs of frequency: **never**, **rarely**, **occasionally**, **sometimes**; or adjectives of fear: **apprehensive**, **nervous**, **scared**, **terrified**. Less common items such as **petrified** can be added to the scale at higher levels. Where appropriate, teachers can add useful information such as prepositional usage on the scale, e.g., **nervous about** and **scared of**.

5. Cuisenaire Rods

These colored blocks are helpful teaching aids, and are especially useful for certain lexical areas. Key examples include prepositions of place: **on**, **under**, **between**, **among**; comparison of adjectives: **bigger than**, **the smallest**, **twice as big as**. Blocks can also represent items in a narrative to act as a visual aid to comprehension.

6. Pictures

For pre-planned teaching of lexicon, taking pictures to class can convey a great deal of lexical information very quickly. Nouns and verbs relating to specific places such as kitchens, airports, or offices work well with pictures. Parts of machines or living creatures show well in picture format, as well. Of course, having Internet access in the classroom can provide many pictures through sources like Google images.

7. Mime

Mime, often overlooked by teachers, is extremely effective for many items. Instead of defining **proud**, fold your arms as if carrying a newborn, puff out your chest and whisper, "my son." Then, ask the class how you feel and provide the word if necessary. Another useful exercise is to mime an everyday routine such as getting ready for work, driving, or preparing a meal. Ask students to write down any verbs they see. This is an excellent test of recall and a good needs-analysis activity.

8. Sound

Making the sound is a quick and easy illustration of many words: **whistle**, **groan**, **howl**, **clear one's throat**, **snap your fingers**, etc. Recordings of sound effects are an evocative way of bringing less familiar lexicon into the lesson. Listening to a sequence of sounds such as **rustling**, **scratching**, **tapping**, and **tinkling glass** provides clear illustration, an effective way of fixing the concept in the student's mind, and removes the need to describe the sound.

9. Total Physical Response (TPR)

Aspects of this approach to language learning can help students take control of new language. After illustrating physical lexicon such as **stare**, **peer**, **glance**, and **blink**, the teacher can ask students to perform the action after the words are given. This can be used for more complex items such as **peel an apple** and **change a tire**.

10. Realia

Where practical, bringing the actual item to class provides an unmistakably clear illustration of an object. This can also provide a useful stimulus to a lesson. On a slightly more ambitious scale, asking students to teach other students how to perform a task using realia can be very motivating and memorable. Examples include how to prepare a salad, how to send a text message using a particular cell phone, and how to play a card game.

This is not an exhaustive list. The most important thing is to anticipate what lexicon you might have to clarify and then choose the technique(s) that best helps to illustrate meaning.

G2 Vocabulary Cards

This is an activity that your entire class can do to practice new vocabulary words. Students can then use the cards for individual study and create new ones as they master more and more words.

Directions:

1. Cut heavy paper (such as index cards or construction paper) into rectangles about three inches long and two inches wide. Fold each rectangle in half, lengthwise.

2. On the outside of each card, write one of the vocabulary words.

3. Look up each word in a dictionary (you may also want to consult a thesaurus) and fill in the other three sides of the card with the word's definition, its synonyms, and its antonyms.

4. Use the cards to study your vocabulary words, either on your own or with a partner. As you begin to learn the words, separate them into two piles: words that you know well and words that you find difficult. As you continue studying the words, more and more of the cards will be moved to the pile of words you know well. You can then create more cards with additional vocabulary words.

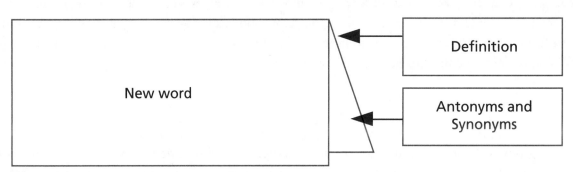

 ## G3 Word Meanings from Context

Synonyms are words that have the same or almost the same meanings. There is one word bolded in each selection. Use the context to help you identify a synonym of that word. Underline the synonym. The first selection has been done for you.

Exercise 1

1. Anne **dove** into the water so gracefully that she hardly made a splash. However, when Diego <u>plunged</u> into the pool, he sent gallons of water shooting into the air.

2. I asked 100 people to **respond** to the survey within a week. It's been six days and only 50 have bothered to reply. I hope that the others haven't decided to ignore or discard the survey.

3. I am preparing a **paper** that will explain our reasons for increasing membership dues. Once I've finished the first draft, I'll share the document with everyone on the committee.

4. We're aware of Mr. Ant's **misgivings**. Is there a way to address his doubts and convince him that our plan will work?

5. "Janet, why are you always complaining?" Cynthia asked in as calm a tone as she could manage. "Your **complaints** about the school float are the last straw. We all want more help and fewer protests from you."

6. Phil had an **inspiration**. He wouldn't just ask Donna to go to the dance with him; he would write her a poem. He figured she wouldn't turn down a romantic poetic request. He smiled as he began composing, convinced that his idea was brilliant.

Exercise 2

There is one word underlined in each sentence. Choose the word that is not a synonym of that word (in the context of the sentence) and write it on the next page. If necessary, use a dictionary or thesaurus.

1. Karen has a very <u>attractive</u> smile.
   a) appealing
   b) pleasant
   c) sticky
   d) pretty

2. I'll have to <u>revise</u> my speech before it's ready to be presented.
   a) edit
   b) change
   c) fix
   d) replace

3. That one foolish act <u>damaged</u> his reputation.
   a) harmed
   b) broke
   c) marred
   d) blemished

4. Frank has a <u>large</u> collection of rare musical instruments.
   a) extensive
   b) huge
   c) big
   d) portly

5. Please consider the probable <u>effect</u> of the actions you're about to take!
   a) change
   b) consequence
   c) result
   d) outcome

6. Let's <u>trail</u> them to see where they're going.
   a) path
   b) follow
   c) pursue
   d) stalk

1._____ 2._____ 3._____

4._____ 5._____ 6._____

Exercise 3

Create a chart like the one below with a list of words. You can construct the list by picking the important words out of a newspaper or magazine article. Fill in as many synonyms and antonyms as you can think of for each word.

Word	Synonyms	Antonyms
1. narrow	slim slender thin	broad wide
2.		
3.		
4.		
5.		
6.		
7.		
8.		

G4 Vocabulary Activities

Chains

Level: Beginner to advanced
Time: 20 minutes
Objective: To encourage students to group words in imaginative and memorable ways
Materials: One word card for each student
Preparation: Prepare a card for each student. On each card write the name of one man-made object (e.g., sweater, book, sewing machine).

Procedure:

1. Divide the class into small circles (four to five members). Give each student a word card.
2. Ask the students to look at the word on their card and to write either the name of something that went into the making of the object in front of the word, or the name of something that the object might become after the word. For example, if the word was sweater, one might write sheep before it or blanket after it.
3. Each student should then pass the card to his left-hand neighbor, who should again write a word before or after the two words now on the card, for example, grass sheep sweater.

Prototypes

Level: Beginner to advanced (the example set below is for lower-intermediate)
Time: 20–30 minutes
Objectives: To get students to consider how word sets are built up, by asking such questions as "How strongly does this word belong to its set?" and in doing so, to consider how effective such categorizations are for them in organizing and remembering vocabulary.
Preparation: Find or construct sets of words, as in the examples below.

Procedure:

1. Ask each student to take a clean sheet of paper and to write **weather** right in the middle of it.
2. They then draw five or six concentric circles round the word, the outer one reaching the edge of the paper.
3. Tell the students you are going to dictate a number of words to them to do with weather. If the students regard these as very central weather words, they put them in the inner circles. If they regard them as peripheral weather words, they put them in the outer areas.

The following is a list of words relating to weather:

rain	dawn	blow	scorching
blustery showers	overcast	breeze	flood
drought	lull	clear up	downpour
barometer	dry	low pressure	sand storm
snow	unsettled	forecast	hurricane
bright intervals	bright	force-eight wind	the sun
storm	fog	earthquake	cloud
outlook	pour	rain or shine	sky
temperature	sunshine	damp	moon

4. Check that all the words you dictated are known to at least some of the students.
5. Group the students in fours to share their placing of the vocabulary, in terms of to what degree they feel the words are related to weather. The words at the very center of their circles could be called prototypes—the members most typical of their set.

Variations

1. You can do this prototype exercise with any word set, for example:

Which males in the following list are most male?

bull	tomcat	billy goat	stallion
ogre	drake	cock	gander
dog	boar	man	cockerel
stag	ram	elephant	

Which foods in the following list are the most "foody"? Which are the least?

tapioca	lamb	cucumber	artichoke
cheese	snake	trout	banana
rice	burger	chips	flour
potatoes			

2. A role-play can also be done. Choose, or get the students to choose, a set of words such as birds, houses, or carnivores. Each student should then choose a different member of the set and be prepared to speak on its behalf. For example, if birds were the set chosen, one student might choose falcon, another pigeon, a third chicken, and so on. The students then each give a one-minute talk about the set member they have chosen, in which they try to convince the rest that their choice is prototypical of the whole set. This is done most effectively when the students give their talks in role (i.e., they might begin with "I am a falcon. I am light, powerful, and very fast" rather than "I've chosen the falcon. A falcon is light, powerful, and very fast.").

3. (Advanced) The degree of prototypicality of words may also become apparent in a text. Ask your students, in groups of three, to read the following text and underline five to eight nouns in it. Working together, they should then write down each underlined word, and next to it the name of a set to which the word might belong, followed by three or four other words that might belong to the same set. They should then read and re-read the text aloud, replacing each of the underlined words in turn by a different member of the set, and discuss the effect of their substitutions.

> Frightened people never learn, I have read. If that is so, they certainly have no right to teach. I'm not a frightened man—or no more frightened than any other man who has looked at death and knows it is for him. All the same, experience and a little pain had made me a mite too wary of the truth, even towards myself. George Smiley put that right. George was more than a mentor to me, more than a friend. Though not always present, he presided over my life. There were times when I thought of him as some kind of father to replace the one I never knew. George's visit to Sarratt gave back the dangerous edge to my memory. And now that I have the leisure to remember, that's what I mean to do for you, so that you can share my voyage and ask yourself the same questions.
>
> (John le Carré. *The Secret Pilgrim*. Hodder & Stoughton, 1991)

Try out different kinds of text: newspaper article, coursebook passage, business letter, etc. The students may also like to work with texts they have written themselves.

Using the technique with poems can also bring unexpected insights into the perceptions of both poet and reader:

Home is so sad. It stays as it was left,
Shaped to the comfort of the last to go
As if to win them back. Instead, bereft
Of anyone to please, it withers so,
Having no heart to put aside the theft
And turn again to what it started as,
A joyous shot at how things ought to be,
Long fallen wide. You can see how it was:
Look at the pictures and the cutlery,
The music in the piano stool. That vase.

(Philip Larkin. "Home is so Sad," *The Whitsun Weddings*. Faber & Faber, 1964)

G5 Vocabulary Lists

Objective: To increase vocabulary by sorting lists of related words
Directions:
Put the following words in the appropriate columns, based on the column headings. There may be more than one correct answer for some words.

eel	dog	rooster	owl
bear	hamster	whale	rabbit
horse	duck	cat	donkey
cow	lion	frog	pig
eagle	goat	bat	chicken

Animals found in a house	Animals found on a farm	Animals found in the water	Animals found in the sky	Animals found on a mountain

G

G6 100 Most Frequently Used Words

The following is a list of words that are used most frequently within the English language. Therefore, it is important to teach these words to your ESL class.

a	had	no	there
about	has	not	these
after	have	now	they
all	he	of	this
also	her	on	time
an	him	one	to
and	his	only	two
any	how	or	up
are	I	other	very
as	if	our	was
at	in	out	water
be	into	over	way
been	is	people	we
but	it	said	well
by	its	see	were
can	just	she	what
could	know	should	when
did	like	so	where
do	made	some	which
down	may	than	who
first	me	that	will
for	more	the	with
from	most	their	would
get	my	them	you
got	new	then	your

G7 Prefixes and Suffixes

How many words can you think of beginning with

tele _____   in_____   ad_____

_____   _____   _____

_____   _____   _____

ex_____   pre_____   re_____

_____   _____   _____

_____   _____   _____

Look in a dictionary for more words!

How many words can you think of ending with

_____ful   _____ing   _____ed

_____   _____   _____

_____   _____   _____

_____es   _____ly   _____y

_____   _____   _____

_____   _____   _____

G8 Labeling Pictures

Label the head:

hair	mouth
teeth	tongue
eye	lip
forehead	eyebrow
cheek	chin
ear	neck
nose	

Label the members of the family:

grandmother	baby
grandfather	mother
son	father
daughter	

Label the computer:

monitor	keyboard
printer	cable
mouse	

Label the farm animals:

cat	horse
cow	pig
chicken	sheep
goat	turkey

G

G9 Vocabulary Exercises

Exercise 1

Cross out the word in each group that is different. Then, add at least one more word to each group.

1. neighbor   sister   nephew   parent
2. concert   window   exhibit   movie
3. taxi   subway   ferry   school
4. bicycle   table   chair   desk
5. ride   like   drive   walk
6. thirsty   long   tired   interested
7. next to   between   late   under

Exercise 2

Complete the paragraph with the following verbs:

rides	gets up
works	like
watches	stays
lives	enjoy

Terry Samuels 1 _____*lives*_____ in a yurt on an island in Washington State. His life is very simple. He 2 _____ when the sun rises and he 3 _____ on his small farm. He doesn't have a car, so he 4 _____ his bicycle everywhere, and he never 5 _____ television because he doesn't have electricity! Twice a year he sees his friends in Seattle. They 6 _____ the excitement of city life. But most of the time he 7 _____ at home. "It's a peaceful life," he says. "And I 8 _____ it here."

Exercise 3

Cross out the word that doesn't work in each sentence. Can you find others that work?

1. I need a new _____ for my computer.

   keyboard   mouse   printer   shoulder

2. In yoga class we _____ a lot.

   sit   browse   stand   bend

3. Bill is a great friend. He's very _____.

   optimistic   honest   lazy   reliable

4. Jeff likes to _____ new software on his computer.

   install   win   search for   download

G

SECTION H

Teaching Pronunciation

Content

H1 English Poem

This poem is a great way to begin a lesson on pronunciation with your English students. Hand copies out to your class and have everyone read it over and then take turns saying it aloud. This is a challenging yet entertaining way to introduce non-native speakers to the common traps of English pronunciation. Unlike other languages, such as Italian, where it is possible to sound out the word to figure out how it is said, English pronunciation is a tricky thing to master!

English

I take it you already know
Of tough and bough and cough and dough?
Others may stumble, but not you
On hiccough, thorough, slough, and through?
Well done! And now you wish, perhaps
To learn of these familiar traps?

Beware of heard, a dreadful word
That looks like beard and sounds like bird.
And dead; it's said like bed; not bead;
For goodness sake, don't call it deed!
Watch out for meat and great and threat,
(They rhyme with suite and straight and debt).
A moth is not a moth in mother,
Nor both in bother, broth in brother.

And here is not a match for there,
And clear and fear for bear and pear,
And then there's dose and rose and lose—
Just look them up—and goose and choose,
And cork and work and word and sword,
And do and go, then thwart and cart,
Come, come, I've hardly made a start.

A dreadful language? Why man alive,
I'd learned to talk it when I was five,
And yet to write it, the more I tried,
I hadn't learned it at forty-five!

H2 Teaching Pronunciation

Background

Overview
- Teaching pronunciation is about teaching individual sounds as well as stress, intonation, and rhythm.
- Lately the focus has shifted from teaching the production of individual sounds to concentrating on broader, more communicative aspects of connected speech.
- Many ESL teachers are unsure as to whether teaching pronunciation should receive systemic attention in a language course.
- One problem is that many textbooks still present activities similar to the audio-lingual texts of the 1950s.

Can It Be Taught?
- Critical Period Hypothesis claims that it is impossible for adults to acquire native-like pronunciation.
- It is also believed that pronunciation is an acquired skill and that focused instruction is useless and possibly detrimental.
- Many studies have since disproved these theories.
- The general conclusion is that imitation activities are more successful with young students, while older students like a more descriptive and analytical approach.

Trends in Teaching Pronunciation
- Oldest method of teaching is elocution: imitation drills and reading aloud.
- Some studies show that students who exhibit accuracy in controlled practice fail to transfer such gains to actual communicative language use.
- Effective drills must move beyond simple identification and mimicking of decontextualized sound which ignores the usefulness of more meaningful communicative input.
- The solution is consciousness-raising activities that sensitize students to the differences between L1 and L2 systems.
- Examples of such activities are self and peer monitoring and presenting rules through discovery activities.

Issues in Teaching Pronunciation
- How do we define correct pronunciation?
- What are the social implications of teaching a standard pronunciation?
- Pronunciation expresses power and solidarity, in-group and out-group, and prestige versus stigmatization.
- Pronunciation expresses individual identity.

The Science of Pronunciation
- Speakers put language into meaning units or sense groups.
- These units give listeners signals of organization that facilitate the processing of spoken discourse.
- These chunks are called tone units or intonation groups because they are characterized by pitch change on the syllables that are perceived to be most important.
- Stressed syllables are pronounced with more energy.

- In English, stressed syllables have extra vowel length.
- When teaching pronunciation, it is best to draw on knowledge of sound systems of different languages. For example, Japanese **l** and **r** sounds: **hello** sounds like **herro**, **worry** sounds like **wolly**.
- It is also best to focus on sounds that are most important for conveying meaning.
- Voicing. For example: noun/verb meanings: advice/advise; belief/believe.

Practices for Teaching Pronunciation

Elicited Mechanical Production: Manipulation of sound patterns without apparent communicative reason and without offering students a chance to make motivated choices of sounds and stress patterns

Examples:
- Would you like to have dinner with us to**night**? Would you like to have dinner with **us** tonight?
- Tongue Twisters

Listen and Repeat: Students imitate chunks of language provided by a teacher or a recording

Discrimination Practice: Students listen for sound contrasts to train their ears

Examples:
- Reading contrasting sounds to a class and asking them to decide what has been uttered
- Bingo-like game or Yes/No game

Sounds for Meaning Contrasts: This is a variation on discrimination practice. Students try to relate linguistic form to pragmatic meaning and action. It involves a more active involvement on the part of the student.

Examples:
- He wants to buy my boat. He wants to buy my vote.
- Will you sell it? That's against the law!

Cognitive Analysis: Many students welcome some overt explanation and analysis

Examples:
- Talking about it—discussing stereotypical ideas about sloppy or correct speech
- Phonetic speech—explanations of how particular sounds are articulated
- Teaching students phonemic script—controversial but appreciated by students, especially if they use pronunciation dictionaries
- Giving rules—if they are simple, e.g., **-ed** tense marker, or **-s** inflectional ending
- Comparison of L1 and L2 sound systems—teach the system of phonemes rather than just articulation of new sounds
- Looking up pronunciation of new words in a dictionary

Right-Brain Activities: These are intended to activate the right-brain hemisphere, often involving music, poetry, guided fantasies, and relaxation techniques such as yoga.

Learning Strategies: Teaching aims to foster student autonomy and to enable students to develop strategies for coping on their own and for continuing to learn.

Examples:
- Awareness-raising questionnaires
- Student diaries
- Recording of student's productions
- Employing correction strategies such as soliciting repetition, paraphrasing, and checking feedback

The Importance of Proper Pronunciation

When we speak we reveal our interests and attitudes towards the topic being discussed and toward the people we are talking with. These messages are conveyed through the prosodic features of the language: stress and rhythm, intonation, pitch variation, and volume.

—Julie Hebert, *Methodology in Language Teaching*

Teaching Speaking: Diagnostic Profile
1. Clarity
   a) Is the student's speech clear?
   b) Are there instances where there is a breakdown in communication?
   c) What are the major problems?

2. Speed
   a) Does the student speak too quickly?
   b) Is the student's speech unintelligible because he or she speaks too quickly?

3. Loudness
   a) Does the student speak too softly?
   b) Does the lack of volume affect intelligibility?

4. Breathing
   a) Does the student speak with appropriate pauses, breaking each utterance into thought groups?

5. Fluency
   a) Does the student speak with either long silences between words or too many filled pauses (umm, ahh)?

6. Voice
   a) Is there enough variance in pitch?

7. Eye Gaze
   a) Does the student use eye-gaze behavior appropriate to the context?

8. Expressive Behavior
   a) Does the student overuse gestures?
   b) Does the facial expression match the utterance?

9. Intonation
   a) Is the student using appropriate intonation patterns in utterances?
   b) Can the student use intonation contours to signal whether utterances are statements, lists, WH-questions, or Yes/No questions?
   c) Is the student changing pitch at major stressed words?

For a full chart see Cambridge's *Methodology in Language Teaching*, pages 190–191.

Teaching Pronunciation: Some Techniques

Minimal Pairs

1. Identification

Contrast (vowels):   Contrast (consonants):
pan vs. pen   thank vs. sank
sand vs. send   thick vs. sick
land vs. lend   thumb vs. some

2. Isolation

a) bit   beat   beat   beat
b) bet   bait   bet   bet
c) tan   tan   ten   tan
d) pool pool   pool   pull

3. Sentences

a) John bit the dog.   a) Show me your bag.
b) John beat the dog.   b) Show me your back.

Influences on Pronunciation

Stress

Notice how all the responses under column B are the same. The stress in each sentence, however, is different. Mark where the stress should be in each sentence. This will be dictated by the preceding question.

A	B
1. Did he go to Paris last week?	1. No, she went to Paris last week.
2. Is Sue going to Paris?	2. No, she went to Paris last week.
3. Did Sue go to Rome last week?	3. No, she went to Paris last week.
4. Did she go last year?	3. No, she went to Paris last week.

Consonant

Consonants are sounds made by blocking the flow of air coming out from the lungs. Sounds produced without the blockage are called **vowels**. Some sounds such as those in words like **y**ellow and **w**est, are called semi-vowels. In this situation, the blockage of air may be accompanied by vibration in the vocal chords, in which case the consonant is **voiced**. If there is no vibration in the vocal chords the consonant is **unvoiced**.

Consonant Cluster

A consonant cluster is two or more consonant sounds together, for example in words like **spr**ing. There are many combinations of consonants that are not possible like the letters **ptf**. These combinations are different in different languages.

Diphthong

A diphthong is a complex vowel. It starts sounding like one vowel sound and then changes and ends sounding like another. An example is in the word rain.

Intonation

Intonation is the pattern of prominence and tone in speech. These can be compared to rhythm and melody in music. Intonation is used to convey extra meaning in speech beyond the meaning of words. For example, intonation can be used to make "How nice!" sound enthusiastic or sarcastic.

Minimal Pair

A minimal pair is a pair of words that differ only in one sound; for example, flight and fright, or cut and cat. If the speaker does not pronounce that one sound distinctly in one of the words, the listener could in theory think that the speaker said the other word. For example, if the speaker cannot distinguish between the r and l sound, he or she might say "I had a terrible flight," and may be understood to have said "I had a terrible fright." Minimal pairs are useful in teaching because they draw attention clearly on individual sounds.

Phoneme

A phoneme is a sound which is significant in language. For example, in a minimal pair, the two words differ only by one phoneme. Different languages have different phonemes. These differences can cause difficulty for students of English. Another word for phoneme is sound.

Phonetic Script

A phonetic script is an alphabet in which there is one symbol to represent each phoneme in a language. For example, the English alphabet is largely conventional, that is, words are spelled according to agreed convention rather than according to sound. A phonetic script is therefore needed to show how words are pronounced. It is a language-learning tool because it allows the student to analyze pronunciation more clearly and to refer to a dictionary for help.

Rhythm

Rhythm is the way a language sounds as a result of the pattern of stressed and unstressed syllables in speech. Rhythms differ among languages and contribute to the characteristic sound different languages have.

Syllable

A syllable is one vowel sound and any consonant sounds that are pronounced with it in a word. The vowel is the essential element, except in the case where a syllable is formed between two or more consonants (e.g., the "tt" in cotton).

Tone

Tone is the rising and falling of pitch in speech. Tone adds an extra level of meaning to what is being said. A rising sound makes it seem as if the speaker is asking a question or may not be very sure.

Vowel

A vowel is a sound produced when the flow of air from the lungs is not blocked and the vocal chords are vibrating. Changing the position of the tongue can produce different vowels. Which vowel is produced depends on the part of the tongue that is raised and how far it is raised.

Syllable Units

The syllable is the basic unit of English pronunciation. Listen to the following words and notice how some of them have two or more parts.

1 syllable	2 syllables	3 syllables
ease	easy	easily
will	willing	willingly

1. As you listen to the following words, tap your hand on the desk to count each syllable.

1	2	3	4
one	seven	eleven	identify
two	eighteen	direction	analysis
down	sentence	syllable	He wants a book.
step	working	important	We were happy.
stress	focus	emphasis	It's important.

Now read the same list aloud, tapping out the syllables while you speak.

2.   Say your name aloud, and decide how many syllables there are in it. See if the other members of the class agree. Do not worry if the class cannot agree on every name, especially where two vowels come together. You only need to have a rough sense of where the syllables come together.

3.   Words can have as few as one or two syllables or as many as seven or eight. For a challenge try and count the syllables in these long words!

interesting	vocabulary	misrepresent	rebelliousness
multipurpose	existentialism	tremendousness	theoretically
eucalyptus	dictionary	impermanence	dysfunctional
Constantinople	non-participating	antidisestablish-	geophysicist
repetition	enlightenment	mentarianism	
communication	indigestible	objectionable	
sesquipedalian	mathematical	observatory	

4. For an even greater challenge, try the longest word in the English language. It is a lung disease and it is 45 letters long!

pneumonoultramicroscopicsilicovolcanokoniosis

Pronunciation Unit /θ/ and /ð/

1. **Producing /θ/ as in <u>th</u>in, <u>th</u>irty, no<u>th</u>ing, heal<u>th</u>y, sympa<u>th</u>y, fif<u>th</u>, and tru<u>th</u>**
*   Lightly place your tongue tip between your upper and lower front teeth (not between your lips).
*   Produce the sound by forcing air out through the opening between your teeth and tongue.
*   Your vocal chords should not vibrate.
*   Hold your hand in front of your lips to feel the flow of air.

2. **Producing /ð/ as in <u>th</u>is, <u>th</u>ey, mo<u>th</u>er, fa<u>th</u>er, sou<u>th</u>ern, clo<u>th</u>e**
*   This sound is produced the same as the /θ/ except that /ð/ is voiced.
*   Lightly place your tongue tip between your upper and lower front teeth (not between your lips).
*   Produce the sound by forcing air out through the opening between your teeth and tongue.
*   Say /ð/ with less force than you use for /θ/.
*   Your vocal chords should vibrate.
*   Hold your hand in front of your lips to feel the flow of air.

3. Contrasting /θ/ and /ð/
A) Some speakers may confuse the sound /θ/ as in **thin** with the sound /ð/ as in **the**. Practice these two sounds, first normally, then with exaggeration, then normally again. Listen and repeat.

B) Now practice the sounds in words. Listen and repeat each word twice.
1. thumb /θ/
2. author /θ/
3. path /θ/
4. they /ð/
5. father /ð/θ
6. smooth /ð/
7. thick /θ/
8. those /ð/

4. Check your listening
You will hear words with the sounds /θ/ and /ð/. First, cover the words in the list with your hand. Then listen to each word. Concentrate on the sound, not the spelling. Which consonant sound do you hear? Write a check mark in the correct column.

	/θ/ as in <u>thin</u>	/ð/ as in <u>the</u>
1. this		
2. then		
3. three		
4. bath		
5. both		
6. bathe		
7. south		
8. fifth		
9. these		
10. breathe		

5. Practice the contrast: /θ/ as in <u>thin</u> with /t/ as in <u>ten</u>

Some students may confuse /θ/ as in **thin** with /t/ as in **ten**. When you pronounce /θ/, air flows out without stopping. When you pronounce /t/, the air stops, then escapes with a puff.

A) Practice these contrasting sounds.

1. taught   thought
2. team   theme
3. tree   three
4. true   through
5. tent   tenth
6. debt   death
7. boot   booth
8. mat   math

B) Now practice the contrasting sounds in sentence pairs. The first sentence of each pair has the sound /t/ and the second sentence has the sound /θ/. Listen and repeat. Notice the change in meaning.

1. a) taught   He taught a lot.
    b) thought   He thought a lot.

2. a) team   I need a team.
    b) theme   I need a theme.

3. a) tree   Which tree is it?
    b) three   Which three is it?

4. a) true   Is she true?
    b) through   Is she through?

5. a) tent   It's my tent.
    b) tenth   It's my tenth.

6. a) debt   It's not his debt.
    b) death   It's not his death.

7. a) boot   She has my boot.
    b) booth   She has my booth.

8. a) mat   It's my mat.
    b) math   It's my math.

6. Practice the contrast: /ð/ as in <u>the</u> with /d/ as in <u>day</u>

Some students may confuse /ð/ as in **the** with /d/ as in **day**. When you pronounce /ð/, the air flows out without stopping. When you pronounce /d/, the air stops, then escapes with a puff.

A) Practice these contrasting sounds.

1. day   they
2. doze   those
3. dough   though
4. dare   there
5. ladder   lather
6. loading   loathing
7. wordy   worthy
8. sued   soothe

B) Now practice the contrasting sounds in sentence pairs. The first sentence of each pair has the sound /d/ and the second sentence has the sound /ð/. Listen and repeat. Notice the change in meaning.

1. a) day   Will the day come?
    b) they   Will they come?

2. a) doze   It's not fair to doze in class.
    b) those   It's not fair to those in class.

3. a) dough   Can you spell dough?
    b) though   Can you spell though?

4. a) ladder   Look at the ladder.
    b) lather   Look at the lather.

5. a) loading   Was he loading it?
    b) loathing   Was he loathing it?

6. a) wordy   It's not wordy.
    b) worthy   It's not worthy.

7. a) sued   We sued him.
    b) soothe   We soothe him.

7. Practice other commonly confused sounds with /θ/ and /ð/

Some students may confuse /θ/ as in **thin** with /f/ as in **food**. When you pronounce /θ/ place your tongue tip between your teeth. When you pronounce /f/, touch your upper teeth with the inner part of your lower lip.

Some students may confuse /ð/ as in **the** with /v/ as in **voice**. When you pronounce /ð/, place your tongue tip between your teeth. When you pronounce /v/, touch your upper teeth with the inner part of your lower lip.

A) Practice these contrasting sounds.

1. first   thirst
2. fought   thought
3. deaf   death
4. free   three
5. vat   that
6. veil   they'll
7. vine   thine
8. lever   leather

B) Now practice the contrasting sounds in sentence pairs.

1. a) first   It's my first.
   b) thirst   It's my thirst.

2. a) fought   He fought a lot.
   b) thought   He thought a lot.

3. a) deaf   It's deaf.
   b) death   It's death.

4. a) free   Is it free?
   b) three   Is it three?

5. a) vat   It's one vat I want.
   b) that   It's one that I want.

6. a) veil   It's not "veil."
   b) they'll   It's not "they'll."

7. a) vine   Can you spell "vine"?
   b) thine   Can you spell "thine"?

8. a) lever   He held the lever.
   b) leather   He held the leather.

H3 Pronunciation Symbols

Pronunciations are given using characters based on those of the International Phonetic Alphabet (IPA). The symbols used, with their values, are as follows:

Consonants
b, d, f, h, k, 1, m, n, p, r, s, t, v, w, and z have their usual English values. Other symbols are used as follows:

g	*g*et	θ	*th*in	x	lo*ch*
j	*y*es	ð	*th*is	tʃ	*ch*ip
ʃ	*sh*e	ŋ	ri*ng*	dʒ	*j*ar
ʒ	vi*si*on				

Vowels

a	c*a*t	i	coz*y*	u:	m*oo*d
ɑr	*ar*m	i:	f*ee*d	ai	m*y*
e	b*e*d	ɒ	h*o*t	əi	p*i*pe
ɜr	h*er*	ɔr	p*o*re	au	br*ow*n
ɜ:	d*eu*x	o:	n*o*	ʌu	h*ou*se
ə	*a*go	ʌ	r*u*n	ei	d*a*y
ɪ	s*i*t	ʊ	p*u*t	ɔi	b*oy*

H4 Using Songs in the Classroom

Activity 1: Singing and Dancing Lesson Plan

The plan below is for a 55 minute lesson with up to about 14 students.

Review
- (Optional) Quick revision of language and setting up of props needed for first song.
- For example, drill colors from color word prompts and then get the students to tell you where you should put the flashcards around the class (on the door, etc.), to run and touch during songs like "Red, Yellow, Blue" or "I Can Sing a Rainbow."
- Revision of actions to get them moving
- Get the students to stand up/sit down as quickly as possible, then make the two actions random to make them listen more carefully and try to catch them out. Continue with all the actions done in the course so far (ski quickly; touch colors and classroom objects; mime animals and transport, etc.).

Song 1: Warmer Action Song
Students sit down and then get straight back up again for an easy-to-organize action song like "Red, Yellow, Blue," "Musical Statues," "YMCA," "The Wheels on the Bus," etc. If possible, this should be a song they have done at least once before—introducing new material is better left until they are more warmed up.

New language

Introduce the new language for the day, e.g., introduce a new lexical set such as toys; add more vocabulary to a topic you have introduced before, such as adding new colors; teach new phonics; teach word recognition of words they already know.

Revision

Revision of previous week's language, preferably through a fun game

Song 2: New Song

This is a good point to introduce any new songs—while students still have some concentration left! This might be, for example, a song that you want to use as the first song of next week's class, a song that practices the new or revised language above, or a song that sets you up for the language you are going to introduce next week. This and the revision stage above can be switched around if you want to use a song at the next stage.

(Optional) Song 3: Settling Down

Use a quieter song to settle the students down for bookwork, e.g., the alphabet and counting songs. Get the students moved to the table with their books and pencils ready on the table and do one of these songs before they open the books. The first thing you talk about in the book is then the thing connected to the song, e.g., asking "What is the page number?" after a counting song.

Bookwork

You can use a chant or song for opening books and closing books if you know or can make up a suitable one, or just have some quiet music in the background if you like.

Song 4: Re-energizer

Do a physical activity or a physical song they already know well to get rid of restlessness built up during bookwork.

Quieter Activity

For example, jigsaws, crafts, or story time

Song 5: Grand Finale

Finally, a rousing action song to send them off on a high. This should be a fun, physical song, but one where you are all standing around together such as "Head, Shoulders, Knees, and Toes," "Hokey Pokey," or "If You're Happy and You Know It," rather than one where students are all over the classroom like "Tables and Chairs." This being the end of the class, it is best if you use a song you can easily extend or cut short to match the available time, such as one with plenty of verses or one that can be repeated with variations.

Activity 2: Action Songs

This activity is suitable for almost any ESL class, but is particularly effective for young students at the beginner to intermediate levels. It is a great warm-up activity or end-of-day wrap-up.

Choose one of the popular children's songs from this manual, or another simple song that you are familiar with. If you have a recording of the song, you can bring it in to class, although you can easily sing the song instead (the students will probably take over the singing for you soon enough). When you introduce the song, go over the lyrics clearly so that the students understand all the words.

Demonstrate the actions that go along with the song. These may be the traditional actions that accompany the song (e.g., for "Hokey Pokey" or "Head, Shoulders, Knees, and Toes") or you may want to come up with your own actions.

After you have shown them the actions for the song, have the students follow along with you as you demonstrate again, and sing if they want to.

These are some general guidelines for doing action songs in class.

1. First, play or sing the song once or twice for the children to listen to, so that they become familiar with the tune and rhythm.

2. Then, play or sing the song again and get the students to clap the rhythm or hum the tune to the music.

3. Get the students to join in the actions with you.

4. Ask the students if they can understand what the song means from the actions. Explain anything they have not understood.

5. Play the song again. The students can perform the actions and sing along with the words if they wish.

H5 Suggested Songs for the Classroom

If You're Happy and You Know It
If you're happy and you know it, clap your hands (clap, clap)
If you're happy and you know it, clap your hands (clap, clap)
If you're happy and you know it, and you really want to show it
If you're happy and you know it, clap your hands. (clap, clap)

If you're happy and you know it, stomp your feet (stomp, stomp)
If you're happy and you know it, stomp your feet (stomp, stomp)
If you're happy and you know it, and you really want to show it
If you're happy and you know it, stomp your feet. (stomp, stomp)

Bingo
There was a farmer who had a dog,
And Bingo was his name-o.
B-I-N-G-O
B-I-N-G-O
B-I-N-G-O
And Bingo was his name-o.

There was a farmer who had a dog,
And Bingo was his name-o.
(clap)-I-N-G-O
(clap)-I-N-G-O
(clap)-I-N-G-O
And Bingo was his name-o.

(Repeat 4 more times, each time leaving out one more letter of the name and replacing it with a clap.)

Row, Row, Row your Boat
Row, row, row your boat,
Gently down the stream.
Merrily, merrily, merrily, merrily,
Life is but a dream.

Hokey Pokey
You put your right hand in,
You put your right hand out,
You put your right hand in,
And you shake it all about,
You do the hokey pokey
and you turn yourself around
That's what it's all about.

2. left hand
3. right foot
4. left foot
5. head
6. bum
7. whole self

Head, Shoulders, Knees, and Toes
Head, shoulders, knees, and toes,
Knees and toes,
Knees and toes.
Head, shoulders, knees, and toes,
Knees and toes,
Knees and toes.
And eyes, ears, mouth,
And nose.
Head, shoulders, knees, and toes,
Knees and toes
Knees and toes.

(Place both hands on parts of body as they are mentioned. On second time speed up, and get faster with each verse.)

She'll Be Coming Around the Mountain
She'll be coming around the mountain
When she comes (Toot, toot!)
She'll be coming around the mountain
When she comes (Toot, toot!)
She'll be coming around the mountain,
She'll be coming around the mountain,
She'll be coming around the mountain
When she comes (Toot, toot!)

She'll be driving six white horses
When she comes (Whoa back!)
She'll be driving six white horses
When she comes (Whoa back!)
She'll be driving six white horses,
She'll be driving six white horses,
She'll be driving six white horses
When she comes (Whoa back! Toot, toot!)

Oh, we'll all go out to meet her
When she comes (Hi babe!)
Oh, we'll all go out to meet her
When she comes (Hi babe!)
Oh, we'll all go out to meet her,
We'll all go out to meet her,
We'll all go out to meet her
When she comes (Hi babe!)
(Whoa back! Toot, toot!)

Twinkle, Twinkle
Twinkle, twinkle, little star,
How I wonder what you are.
Up above the world so high,
Like a diamond in the sky.
Twinkle, twinkle, little star,
How I wonder what you are!

This is the Way
This is the way I wash my face, wash my face, wash my face.
This is the way I wash my face, at seven o'clock in the morning.

This is the way I brush my teeth, brush my teeth, brush my teeth.
This is the way I brush my teeth, at seven o'clock in the morning.

This is the way I read my book, read my book, read my book.
This is the way I read my book, at seven o'clock in the evening.

There Were Ten in the Bed
There were ten in a bed
And the little one said
"Roll over, roll over"
So they all rolled over
And one fell out

(Repeat counting backwards from 10 to 1).

"A" You're Adorable – Perry Como

When Johnny Jones was serenading Mary,
He sure could quote a lot of poetry,
But he'd much rather tell her,
What he learned in his speller,
When they both attended PS 33!

A – You're adorable . . .
B – You're so beautiful . . .
C – You're a cutie full of charms . . .
D – You're a darling and . . .
E – You're exciting . . .
F – You're a feather in my arms . . .
G – You look good to me . . .
H – You're so heavenly . . .
I – You're the one I idolize . . .
J – We're like Jack and Jill . . .
K – You're so kiss-able . . .
L – Is the love-light in your eyes . . .
M, N, O, P . . .
You could go on all day . . .
Mmmmmmm!
Q, R, S, T . . .
Alphabetically speaking you're OK!
U – Made my life complete . . .
V – Means you're awfully sweet . . .
W, X, Y, Z . . .
It's fun to wander through,
The alphabet with you,
To tell . . . (us what?)
I mean . . . (uh huh!)
To tell you what you mean to me!
(We love you alphabetically!)

Friday, I'm In Love – The Cure

I don't care if Monday's blue
Tuesday's gray and Wednesday too
Thursday I don't care about you
It's Friday, I'm in love

Monday you can fall apart
Tuesday, Wednesday break my heart
Thursday doesn't even start
It's Friday I'm in love

Saturday, wait
And Sunday always comes too late
But Friday, never hesitate...

I don't care if Monday's black
Tuesday, Wednesday—heart attack
Thursday, never looking back
It's Friday, I'm in love
Monday, you can hold your head
Tuesday, Wednesday stay in bed
Or Thursday—watch the walls instead
It's Friday, I'm in love

Saturday, wait
And Sunday always comes too late
But Friday, never hesitate...

H6 Pronunciation Review

Exercise 1

Partner A
Dictate the following groups of words to your partner:
1. sit / seat
2. sit / set / sat
3. peak / pick
4. seek / sick
5. lick / leak
6. pet / pat / pet
7. bait / bait / bet
8. met / mat / mat

Partner B
Write down the words you hear as your partner dictates them to you.

Exercise 2

Partner B
Dictate the following sentences to your partner:
1. He bought a peck of tomatoes. / He bought a pack of tomatoes.
2. She wandered about the house. / She wondered about the house.
3. I can see three white sheets. / I can see three white sheep.

Partner A
Write down the sentences you hear as your partner dictates them to you.

H7 Common Mispronounced Words and Phrases in English

Improper	Proper	Description
A		
Acrossed	Across	It is easy to confuse across with crossed but better to keep them separate.
Affidavid	Affidavit	If your lawyer's name is David, he issues affidavits.
Old-timer's disease	Alzheimer's disease	While it is a disease of old-timers, it is named for the German neurologist, Dr. Alois Alzheimer.
Antartic	Antarctic	Just think of an arc of ants (an ant arc) and that should help you keep the /c/ in the pronunciation of this word.
Artic	Arctic	Another hard-to-see /c/, but it is there.
Aks	Ask	This mispronunciation has been around for so long (over 1,000 years) that linguist Mark Aronoff thinks we should cherish it as a part of our linguistic heritage. Most of us would give the axe to aks.
Athelete, Atheletic	Athlete, athletic	Two syllables are enough for athlete.
B		
Bob wire	Barbed wire	No, this word wasn't named for anyone named Bob; the suffix -ed, meaning having, is fading away in the US.
A blessing in the skies	A blessing in disguise	This phrase is no blessing if it comes from the skies.
C		
Calvary	Cavalry	It isn't clear why we say, Mind your Ps and Qs when we have more difficulty keeping up with our Ls and Rs.
Cannidate	Candidate	You aren't being canny to drop the /d/ in this word. Remember, it is the same as candy date. (This should help guys remember how to prepare for dates, too.)
Carpool tunnel syndrome	Carpal tunnel syndrome	This one is mispronounced and misspelled several different ways; we just picked the funniest. Carpal means pertaining to the wrist.
The Caucases	The Caucasus	Although there is more than one mountain in this chain, their name is not a plural noun.
Chomp at the bit	Champ at the bit	Chomp has probably replaced champ in the US, but we thought you might like to be reminded that the vowel should be /æ/ not /o/.

Chester drawers	Chest of drawers	The drawers of Chester is a typical way of looking at these chests down South but it misses the point.
Close	Clothes	The /th/ is a very soft sound likely to be overlooked. Show your linguistic sensitivity and always pronounce it.
Coronet	Cornet	Playing a crown (coronet) will make you about as popular as wearing a trumpet (cornet) on your head—reason enough to keep these two words straight.
D		
Dialate	Dilate	The /i/ in this word is so long there is time for another vowel but don't succumb to the temptation
Doggy-dog world	Dog-eat-dog world	The world is even worse than you think if you think it merely a doggy-dog world. Sorry to be the bearer of such bad news.
Drownd	Drown	You add the /d/ only to the past tense and past participle.
Duck tape	Duct tape	Ducks very rarely need taping though you may not know that ducts always do—to keep air from escaping through the cracks in them.
E		
Elec'toral	E'lectoral	The accent is on the second, not the third, syllable and there is no /i/ in it (not electorial).
Excape	Escape	The good news is, if you say excape, you've mastered the prefix ex- because its meaning does fit this word. The bad news is, you don't use this prefix on escape.
Expecially	Especially	Things especial are usually not expected, so don't confuse these words.
Expresso	Espresso	This word was borrowed from Italian where the Latin prefix ex- developed into es-.
Excetera	Et cetera	Latin for and (et) the rest (cetera) are actually two words that probably should be written separately.
F		
Febyuary	February	We don't like two syllables in succession with an /r/ so some of us dump the first one in this word. Most dictionaries now accept the single /r/ pronunciation, but if you have an agile tongue, you may want to shoot for the original.
Fedral	Federal	Syncopation of an unaccented vowel is fairly common in rapid speech, but in careful speech it should be avoided. (See also plute and read more about the problem here.)

Fillum	Film	We also do not like the combination /l/ + /m/. One solution is to pronounce the /l/ as /w/ (film /fiwm/, palm /pawm/) but some prefer adding a vowel in this word.
For all intensive purposes	For all intents and purposes	The younger generation is mispronouncing this phrase so intensively that it has become popular both as a mispronunciation and a misspelling.
Flounder	Founder	Since it is unlikely that a boat would founder on a flounder, we should distinguish the verb from the fish as spelling suggests.
H		
Heighth	Height	The analogy with width misleads many of us in the pronunciation of this word.
I		
In parenthesis	In parentheses	No one can enclose an expression in one parenthesis; at least two parentheses are required.
Interpretate	Interpret	This error results from the back-formation of interpretate from interpretation. But back formation is not needed; we already have interpret. (See also orientate.)
Irregardless	Regardless	-less already says without so there is no need to repeat the same sentiment with ir-.
J		
Jewlery	Jewelry	The root of this word is jewel and that doesn't change for either jeweler or jewelry.
L		
Lambast	Lambaste	Better to lambaste the lamb than to baste him— remember, the words rhyme. Bast has nothing to do with it.
Larnyx	Larynx	More metathesis. Here the /n/ and /y/ switch places. Mind your Ns and Ys as you mind your Ps and Qs.
Libel	Liable	You are liable for the damages if you are successfully sued for libel. But don't confuse these discrete words.
Libary	Library	As mentioned before, English speakers dislike two /r/ syllables in the same word. However, we have to buck up and pronounce them all.

		M
Mawv	Mauve	This word has not moved far enough away from French to assume an English pronunciation, /mawv/, and should still be pronounced /mowv/.
Mannaise	Mayonnaise	Ever wonder why the short form of a word pronounced mannaise is mayo? Well, it is because the original should be pronounced mayo-nnaise. Just remember: what would mayonnaise be without mayo?
Miniture	Miniature	Here is another word frequently syncopated. Don't leave out the third syllable, /a/.
Mis'chievous	'Mischievous	It would be mischievous not to point out the frequent misplacement of the accent on this word. Remember, it is accented the same as mischief. (Look out for the order of the /i/ and /e/ in the spelling, too.)
Mute	Moot	The definition of moot is moot (open to debate) but not the pronunciation: /mut/ and not /myut/.
		N
Nother	Other	Misanalysis is a common type of speech error based on the misperception of where to draw the line between components of a word or phrase. A whole nother comes from misanalyzing an other as a nother. Not good.
Nucular	Nuclear	The British and Australians find the North American repetition of the /u/ between the /k/ and /l/ amusing. Good reason to get it right.
Nuptual	Nuptial	Many speakers in North America add a spurious /u/ to this word, too. It should be pronounced /nêpchêl/, not /nêpchuêl/.
		O
Orientate	Orient	Another pointless back-formation. We don't need this mispronunciation from orientation when we already have orient. (See also interpretate.)
		P
Parlament	Parliament	Although some dictionaries have given up on it, there should be a /y/ after /l/: /pahr-lyê-mênt/
Prespire	Perspire	Per- has become such a regular mispronunciation of pre-, many people now correct themselves where they don't need to.
Plute	Pollute	This one, like plice (police), spose (suppose), and others, commonly result from rapid speech syncope, the loss of unaccented vowels. Just be sure you pronounce the vowel when you are speaking slowly.

Pottable	Potable	The adjective meaning drinkable rhymes with floatable and is not to be confused with the one that means capable of being potted.
Perogative	Prerogative	Even in dialects where /r/ does not always trade places with the preceding vowel (as the Texan pronunciations of differnce, vetern, etc.), the /r/ in this prefix often gets switched.
Perscription	Prescription	Same as above. It is possible that we simply confuse pre- and per- since both are legitimate prefixes.
Probly, prolly	Probably	Haplology is the dropping of one of two identical syllables such as the /ob/ and /ab/ in this word, usually the result of fast speech. Slow down and pronounce the whole word for maximum clarity and to reduce your chances of misspelling the word.
Pronounciation	Pronunciation	Just as misspelling is among the most common misspelled words, pronunciation is among the most commonly mispronounced words. Fitting, no?
R		
Reoccur	Recur	You don't have to invent a new word from occur. We already have a verb recur that does the trick.
Revelant	Relevant	Here is another word that seems to invite metathesis.
S		
Sherbert	Sherbet	Some of the same people who do not like two /r/ consonants in their words can't help repeating the one in this word.
Silicone	Silicon	Silicon is the material they make computer chips from but implants are made of silicone.
Supposably	Supposedly	Adding -ly to participles is rarely possible, so some people try to avoid it altogether. You can't avoid it here.
T		
Take for granite	Take for granted	We do tend to take granite for granted, it is so ubiquitous. But that, of course, is not the point.
Tenderhooks	Tenterhooks	Tenters are frames for stretching cloth while it dries. Hanging on tenterhooks might leave you tender but that doesn't change the pronunciation of the word.
Triathalon	Triathlon	We don't like /th/ and /l/ together, so some of us insert a spare vowel. Pronounce it right, spell it right.

U		
Upmost	Utmost	While this word does indicate that efforts are up, the word is utmost—a historical variation of outmost.
V		
Volumptuous	Voluptuous	Some voluptuous women may be lumpy, but please avoid this Freudian slip that apprises them of it.
W		
Ways	Way	"I have a ways to go" should be "I have a way to go." The article a does not fit well with a plural.
Y		
Yoke	Yolk	Another dialectal change we probably should not call an error: /l/ becomes /w/ or /u/ when not followed by a vowel. Some people just confuse these two words, though. That should be avoided.

SECTION I

Teaching Speaking/Conversation

Content

I1 Teaching Speaking/Conversation

Many ESL students will consider speaking one of the most important skills that they want to learn from you. Creating an effective and meaningful conversation lesson is much more difficult than just asking your students, "So, what do you want to talk about today?"

Including your students' interests into your speaking activities is important. This helps your lessons become more meaningful to your students. However, leaving it up to your students leaves them feeling overwhelmed and uncomfortable. As the teacher, you must teach the skills and information necessary to complete the activity, model the effective use of these skills, and provide a safe, equitable environment in which to practice these skills.

I2 Characteristics of a Successful Speaking Activity

1. Students talk a lot.
The student should be speaking for most of the activity. Unfortunately, in many classes, much of the student's time is taken up with teacher talk or pauses.

2. Participation is even.
Classroom discussion is not dominated by a minority of talkative students. All of the students should be grouped and organized to maximize the amount of student talk for each student.

3. Motivation is high.
Students are eager to speak because they are interested in the topic and they want to contribute to the achievement of a task.

4. Language is appropriate.
Students' discussions should be relevant, easily comprehensible to each other, and of an acceptable level of language accuracy.

5. Teacher monitoring and modeling.
The teacher should be walking around and monitoring conversations to ensure that the lesson is meeting its objectives and that the level of the activity is appropriate.

13 Successful Oral Fluency Practice

Of all the four skills (listening, speaking, reading, writing), speaking seems intuitively the most important: people who know a language are referred to as **speakers** of that language, implying speaking includes all other kinds of knowing; and many (if not most) foreign-language students are primarily interested in learning to speak.

Classroom activities that develop students' ability to express themselves through speech would therefore seem an important component of a language course. Yet, it is difficult to design and administer such activities—more so, in many ways, than to do so for listening, reading, or writing. The problems will be discussed presently, but first what is an **effective speaking activity**?

Also, what are some of the problems in getting students to talk in the classroom? Perhaps think back to your experiences as either a student or a teacher, or both.

 14 Problems with Speaking Activities

1. **Inhibition.** Unlike reading, writing, and listening activities, speaking requires some degree of real-time exposure to an audience. Students are often inhibited about trying to say things in a foreign language in the classroom as they are worried about making mistakes, fearful of criticism or losing face, or simply shy of the attention that their speech attracts.

2. **Nothing to say.** Even if students are not inhibited, you may often hear them complain that they cannot think of anything to say. They may have no motive to express themselves beyond the guilty feeling that they should be speaking.

3. **Low or uneven participation.** Only one participant can talk at a time if he or she is to be heard, and in a large group this means that each one will have only very little talking time. This problem is compounded by the tendency of some students to dominate, while others speak very little, or not at all.

4. **L1 use in classes where all, or a number of, the students share the same L1.** Students may tend to use it because it is easier, because it feels unnatural to speak to one another in a foreign language, and because they feel less exposed if they are speaking their mother tongue. If they are talking in small groups it can be quite difficult to get some classes—particularly the less disciplined or motivated ones—to keep to the target language.

Follow-up Discussion

Consider what you might do in the classroom in order to overcome each of the four problems described above. You may wish to supplement your ideas with the following suggestions.

15 Solutions to the Problems with Speaking Activities

1. **Use Group Work.** This increases the amount of student talk going on in a limited period of time and also lowers the inhibitions of students who are unwilling to speak in front of the full class. It is true that group work means the teacher cannot supervise all student speech; therefore, not all utterances will be correct, and students may occasionally slip into their native languages. Nevertheless, even taking into consideration occasional mistakes and L1 use, the amount of time remaining for positive, useful oral practice is still likely to be far more than in the full-class set-up.

2. **Base the Activity on Easy Language.** In general, the level of language needed for a discussion should be lower than that used in intensive language-learning activities in the same class; it should be easily recalled and produced by the participants so that they can speak fluently.

Please note: The activities in this section progress according to students' language level.

16 Beginner to Advanced Activities

Four Corners

With Four Corners you begin with a statement, an issue, or a question. Next, the students choose a corner that best captures their perspective, view, or response. They move to that corner, pair up (if there is another person with whom to pair up), and share why they made that decision. They should be prepared to share their response or their partner's if asked. Four Corners is an ideal structure for getting students to operate at more creative and evaluative levels of thinking, and is especially helpful if you are interested in getting students to debate. Of course, you can have three, five, or six corners or places where students can move to, based on their thinking or attitudes towards an issue.

Application of this Technique
Situation: You are discussing an issue, such as **Every school should provide access for wheelchairs**. You label the four corners: Strongly Agree, Agree, Strongly Disagree, Disagree. The students get time to make a decision (say 30 seconds). Then without any discussion, they move to the corner that best represents their stance. When they get to the corner, they form groups of two or three and share why they chose that corner. The teacher then randomly calls on pairs of students from each corner to identify why they made their decision.

Situation: Your grade two students have just done an investigation on organs of the body: brain, heart, stomach, and lungs. They have to decide which organ they think is the most important and why. They get time to think. Then they move to the corner that represents that organ (you may want to have a picture or word up in the corner for younger students). Now they pair up, share, and defend their ideas.

Situation: You are reading a novel or children's story. Students have to decide who was the most responsible for what happened, or what is the best solution to an emerging problem. Each corner represents one of the responses. For example, if you have the children's book *John Brown, Rose and the Midnight Cat*, the class could identify conditions under which the cat could join the family. The students could then move to the corner they believe represents the best solution, and then share and defend their answer.

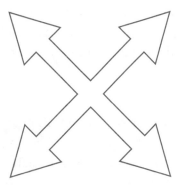

Situation: You are studying World War II. You put up each of the causes of the war in different areas of the room. Students have to make a decision as to which one they believe was the major cause and why. You could start your unit this way and then redo it at the end of the unit; students could then compare their thinking.

Situation: You are studying energy systems or pollution. Students have to decide which source of energy is the most efficient, or most costly. Or, they have to decide who is most affected by oil spills (plumbers, gill netters, cooks, bankers).

Four Corners Considerations

Encourage students to make up their own minds regarding which corner they select. Give them time to think. Then tell them not to be influenced by others—to follow their own thinking, and not to be controlled by others. If you do not encourage independent thinking, students will go to the corner that their friend(s) selects, or the most popular one, or the one the smartest person selects.

Make sure the students do not get into larger groups once they are in their corner; encourage groups of two or three. Students need to know they are accountable and responsible for thinking. In pairs, they are more accountable, and have more time to talk. For the first few times, be sticky on this one—do not let them start discussing until they all have a partner. Once this norm is set, they will follow it—unless you suggest modifications.

Four Corners Adaptations

1. If only two positions are to be taken, then the Four Corner process becomes known as a Value Line (in Jeanne Gibbs' Tribes program they call it **Putting Yourself on the Line**). Here, the students position themselves along the continuum—a line from Strongly Agree to Strongly Disagree.

Some teachers will put a piece of masking tape on the floor between the two extremes, then the students then take a stance on the tape prior to the discussion/debate, and sign their name where they are standing. After the debate, they return to the tape to stand and sign their name. They then measure the distance they shifted. You can integrate this measurement into a math activity (graphing, averages).

2. You can use a variety of themes for metaphorical thinking related to each of the corners, e.g., Song Titles, Movie Titles, and Types of Food or Animals. The theme of roads can be used to have people identify how they have experienced a situation (e.g., with teachers, how they have experienced change in their district: 1. Yellow Brick Road, 2. The Road Less Traveled, 3. Route 50, or 4. Ho Chi Min Trail).

Remember, Four Corners can be integrated or supported by other techniques and can be used for problem solving. For example, say you are having a problem with teasing in your classroom/school. You identify why students tease one another. Then you put each reason in a different location in the room. The students make a decision, then move to the area they believe is the major reason why students tease one another. Their views then become a catalyst for change.

The Game of Charades

Charades is a game of pantomimes: you have to act out a phrase without speaking, while the other members of your team try to guess what the phrase is. The objective is for your team to guess the phrase as quickly as possible. Charades is a good classroom activity that can be fun while encouraging students to think and speak quickly in English.

Equipment:
• a stopwatch or other timing device
• a notepad and pencil for scorekeeping
• blank slips of paper
• two baskets or other containers for the slips

Preparation:
Divide the players into two teams, preferably of equal size. Divide the slips of paper between the two teams. Select a neutral timekeeper/scorekeeper, or pick members from each team to take turns. Agree on how many rounds to play. Review the gestures and hand signals and invent any others you deem appropriate.

The teams temporarily go to separate rooms, or different areas within the classroom, to come up with phrases to put on their pieces of paper. These phrases may either be quotations or titles of books, movies, plays, television shows, or songs. Here are some suggested rules to prevent the phrases from being too hard to guess:
• No team should write down any phrase unless at least three people on the team have heard of it.
• No phrase should be longer than seven words.
• No phrase should consist solely of a proper name (i.e., it should also contain other words).

Once they have finished writing their phrases, the teams come back to the same room.

To Play
Each round of the game is to proceed as follows:

A player from Team A draws a phrase slip from Team B's basket. After he or she has had a short time to review the slip, the timekeeper for team B notes the time and tells the player to start. Team A then has three minutes to guess the phrase. If they figure it out, the timekeeper records how long it took. If they do not figure it out in three minutes, the timekeeper announces that the time is up, and records a time of three minutes.

A player from Team B draws a phrase slip from Team A's basket, and play proceeds as above.

Normally the game continues until every player has had a chance to act out a phrase. The score for each team is the total time that the team needed for all of the rounds. The team with the smallest score wins the game.

Gestures

To act out a phrase, one usually starts by indicating what category the phrase is in, and how many words are in the phrase. From then on, the usual procedure is to act out the words one at a time (although not necessarily in the order that they appear in the phrase). In some cases, however, it may make more sense to try to act out the entire concept of the phrase at once.

To Indicate Categories:
- **Book title:** Unfold your hands as if they were a book
- **Movie title:** Pretend to crank an old-fashioned movie camera
- **Play title:** Pretend to pull the rope that opens a theater curtain
- **Song title:** Pretend to sing
- **TV show:** Draw a rectangle to outline a TV screen
- **Quote or phrase:** Make quotation marks in the air with your fingers

To Indicate Other Things:
- **Number of words in the title:** Hold up the number of fingers
- **Which word you're working on:** Hold up the number of fingers again
- **Number of syllables in the word:** Lay the number of fingers on your arm
- **Which syllable you're working on:** Lay the number of fingers on your arm again
- **Length of word:** Make a little or big sign as if you were measuring a fish
- **The entire concept:** Sweep your arms through the air
- **On the nose/correct guess:** Point at your nose with one hand, while pointing at the person with your other hand
- **Sounds like:** Cup one hand behind an ear
- **Longer version of:** Pretend to stretch a piece of elastic
- **Shorter version of:** Do a karate chop with your hand
- **Plural:** Link your little fingers
- **Past tense:** Wave your hand over your shoulder toward your back
- **A letter of the alphabet:** Move your hand in a chopping motion toward your arm (near the top of your forearm if the letter is near the beginning of the alphabet, and near the bottom of your arm if the letter is near the end of the alphabet)

Teaching Dialogue

Lesson 1: Dialogue Role-Play
Objective: To be able to teach a dialogue in such a way that the student can enact the dialogue in a role-play with classmates.

Purpose: There are two main purposes for teaching the dialogue. First, it will provide the student with language that will help him or her perform in a particular setting (writing a check, buying a stamp, etc.).

The more specific you can be in adapting the dialogue to the students' immediate circumstances, the more meaningful the dialogue will be and the more likely it will be that the students will learn and use it.

The second purpose of the dialogue is to introduce certain high-frequency patterns of the language that will be practiced further in the dialogue expansion activities.

Note: If the students do not have text materials where they can see the written dialogue, you can write it on the board. It is usually helpful for adults to be able to see the written form. If you notice certain sounds being pronounced incorrectly because of the students' native language pronunciation, you may want to focus their attention on the letters and their correct pronunciation.

Preparation:

1. Think about the kind of situation you want the students to enact after they have finished the dialogue. Be as specific as possible.

2. Break the dialogue into pairs of lines or exchanges (these we will call cycles) and personalize it. If you want the students to be able to enact the dialogue or parts of it, it is best to break it down and personalize it; i.e., change the characters to members of the class.

For Lesson 1 the dialogue could be broken down as follows*:

a) **Roberto:** Hello, my name's *teacher's name*.
   Sara: (I'm) glad to meet you.

b) **Sara:** This is my friend, *student's name*.
   Roberto: (I'm) pleased to meet you.

c) **Roberto:** Where are you from?
   Lily: (I'm from) Thailand.

* (The words in parentheses can be omitted.)

3. Write the dialogue on a 3" x 5" card.

It is necessary for the teacher to be able to walk around and listen to and interact with each student. Having to carry a textbook around can reduce your mobility. After you have taught a few lessons you may be able to leave the book on the desk and refer to it periodically and not have to make cards.

Teaching:

1. Explain to the students using pictures, gestures, or whatever means necessary the context and purpose of the dialogue. In the case of Lesson 1 the purpose is to enable them to introduce themselves and others, and to tell where they are from.

2. As students watch and listen, enact the first line of the dialogue as you say it. (Repeat several times.)

    Hello my name's *teacher's name*.

3. Have the students repeat in chorus after the teacher until their pronunciation is fairly accurate.

Example:

    T: Hello, my name's _____ .
    S: Hello, my name's _____ .

4. Have students repeat individually personalizing the line.

    S: Hello, my name is *student's name.*

5. Repeat Steps 2 and 3, but with the next line of the dialogue:

    T: (I'm) glad to meet you. (students listen)
    T: (I'm) glad to meet you.
    S: I'm glad to meet you. (students repeat)

6. Teacher says line 1 and students respond with line 2, first in chorus and then alone.

    T: Hello, my name's *teacher's name.*
    S: (I'm) glad to meet you. My name's *student's name.*

7. Have students pair off and take turns introducing themselves while the teacher circulates, listens, and helps.

    S1: Hello, my name's _____ .
    S2: Glad to meet you. My name's _____ .

8. Repeat Steps 2 through 7 with the next two lines of the dialogue.

9. Have students enact the first four lines of the dialogue. Break students into groups of three (for the three persons) and have them enact the dialogue.

    S1: Hello, my name's _____ .
    S2: (I'm) glad to meet you. My name is _____ .
    S1: This is my friend _____ .
    S3: Pleased to meet you.

10. Repeat Steps 2 through 7 with the next two lines of the dialogue.

11. Repeat Step 9 with all of the lines of the dialogue.

Additional Activities:

1. Have students follow along in their text as the teacher reads the dialogue.

2. Have students pair off and read alternate parts of the dialogue while the teacher circulates and listens.

3. Have students pair off and show pictures of their family and tell who they are. For example: S: This is my _____ .

Lesson 2: Greetings and Introductions
Objectives: To be able to greet people, introduce yourself, introduce others, ask for information, and give information.

Dialogue:*

Robert: Hello, my name's Roberto.
Lily: (I'm) glad to meet you. My name's Lily. This is my neighbor, Sara.
Robert: (I'm) glad to meet you, Sara. Where are you from?
Sara: (I'm from) Mexico.

* (The words in parentheses can be omitted.)

Practice 1:

Hello, my name is _____. (I'm)   glad to meet you.

happy

pleased

Practice 2:

This is my   neighbor, _____. (I'm) pleased to meet you.

classmate

friend

brother

sister

mother

father

Practice 3:

His name is _____.

Her

Your

Practice 4:

I'm from   San Antonio.   He's from Texas.

Los Angeles.   She's

Mexico.   You're

Practice 5:

Where   are you from?

is he

is she

am I

Practice 6: Dictation
A) Hello my _____ Robert.
B) Glad to meet _____ . _____ name's Sara.
C) This is my _____ , Lily.
D) Pleased to _____ you, Lily. Where are you _____?
E) (I'm from) Thailand.

Practice 7: Role Play
A) _____ , this is _____ .
B) Glad to meet you. Where are you from?
A) (I'm from) _____ .

17 High-Beginner to Intermediate Activities

Making Requests

Ask your students to choose one of the boxes on the following page (or assign them a box). Each box contains three requests they need to make and three requests they can agree to. Students walk around the class to find people who will agree to the three requests listed in their box. They are to write down the name of the person who agrees to each request. They may use a person's name only once.

As students make their requests of each other, they are to agree or refuse according to what is listed in their box. Students must use **could** or **would** in a request, or the respondent does not have to agree to it. For example, students must respond positively or negatively to a request such as, "Could you tell me what time it is?" but they do not have to respond to a question such as, "What time is it?"

1. Find someone who will   NAME
    a) lend you $15   _____
    b) tell you what time the library closes   _____
    c) buy some stamps for you   _____

    You agree to
        a) exchange some money
        b) take your friend's car to the gas station to change the oil
        c) go to the jewelry store to help select a special gift

    You may not agree to any other requests!

2. Find someone who will   NAME
    a) go to the drugstore and pick up your prescription   _____
    b) explain how to use the banking machine   _____
    c) get a course catalog from the registration office for you   _____

    You agree to
        a) buy some stamps for your friend
        b) drive your friend to the airport
        c) go to the computer store to price computers

    You may not agree to any other requests!

3. Find someone who will   NAME
    a) go to the hardware store with you to get a screwdriver   _____
    b) give you change for a $10 bill   _____
    c) help you select a birthday card for your friend   _____

    You agree to
        a) tell your friend what time the library closes
        b) pick up some dry cleaning for your friend
        c) go to the butcher shop to buy some chicken for your friend

    You may not agree to any other requests!

4. Find someone who will   NAME
    a) lend you a dictionary   _____
    b) lend you some Scotch tape   _____
    c) go to the department store with you to help you pick out
       a sweater   _____

    You agree to
        a) lend your friend $15
        b) go to the shoe store with your friend to help buy dress shoes
        c) go to the bakery to buy a loaf of bread for your friend

    You may not agree to any other requests!

5. Find someone who will   NAME
a) go to the shoe store with you to help buy some dress shoes   _____
b) go to the bakery for you to buy a loaf of bread   _____
c) go to the butcher shop for you to buy some chicken   _____

You agree to
a) go to the hardware store with your friend to buy a screwdriver
b) lend your friend a dictionary
c) go to the record store with your friend to buy some CDs

You may not agree to any other requests!

6. Find someone who will   NAME
a) go to the computer store with you to price some computers   _____
b) go to the jewelry shop with you to select a special gift   _____
c) go to the music store with you to buy some CDs   _____

You agree to
a) explain to your friend how to use a bank machine
b) give your friend change for a $10 bill
c) lend your friend some Scotch tape

You may not agree to any other requests!

7. Find someone who will   NAME
a) go to the bookstore with you to buy a grammar book   _____
b) go to the antique shop with you to price coffee tables   _____
c) take your car to the gas station to change the oil   _____

You agree to
a) get a course catalog from the registration office for your friend
b) help your friend select a birthday card
c) go to the department store to help your friend pick out a sweater

You may not agree to any other requests!

8. Find someone who will   NAME
a) go to the cleaner for you to pick up your dry cleaning   _____
b) drive you to the airport on Sunday   _____
c) exchange some money for you   _____

You agree to
a) go to the bookstore to help your friend buy a grammar book
b) go to the antique shop to price coffee tables with your friend
c) go to the drugstore to pick up your friend's prescription

You may not agree to any other requests!

I

Had to … /Didn't Have to …

Work with a partner. Discuss three things you have to do and three things you do not have to do if you live with your family.

Then make a list of three things you had to do when you were younger and three things you did not have to do.

Living with Family:

Have to	Don't have to

When Younger:

Had to	Didn't have to

Ask your partner four questions about what he or she has to do now or had to do in the past. Record the answers.

1. _____

2. _____

3. _____

4. _____

_____

I8 Pre-Intermediate to High-Intermediate Activities

Best Friend/Undesirable Friend

In the following exercise, students choose which qualities would make a best friend and which qualities would make an undesirable friend. The exercise allows students to practice a number of areas: expressing opinions, comparatives and superlatives, descriptive adjectives, and reported speech. The overall concept of the lesson can easily be transferred to other subject areas such as holiday choices, choosing a school, prospective careers, etc.

Objective: To practice expressing opinions and reported speech

Outline:
Help students activate vocabulary by asking them for descriptive adjectives describing good friends and bad friends.

Distribute the worksheet to students and ask them to put the descriptive adjectives/phrases into the four categories (Very Important, Somewhat Important, Not Important, and Undesirable).

Put students into pairs and ask them to give explanations for why they chose to put the various descriptions into what category.

Ask students to pay careful attention to what their partner says and to take notes, as they will be expected to report back to a new partner.

Put students into new pairs and ask them to tell their new partner what their first partner said.

As a class, ask students about any surprises or differences of opinion they encountered during the discussions.

Extend the lesson by a follow-up discussion on what makes a good friend.

Friends

Step 1: Draw a chart titled "My Best Friend" with the following headings: Very Important, Somewhat Important, Not Important, and Undesirable.

Write each of the descriptions under one of the headings.

My Best Friend			
Very Important	Somewhat Important	Not Important	Undesirable

confident in his or her abilities

handsome or beautiful

trustworthy

outgoing

timid

punctual

intelligent

fun-loving

rich or well-off

artistic abilities

inquisitive mind

athletic abilities

well-traveled

creative

free spirit

speaks English well

interested in the same things

interested in different things

from the same social background

from different social background

loves to tell stories

reserved

ambitious

has plans for the future

happy with what he or she has

Step 2: Take notes on the preferences of your partner.

Telephone Messages

Description:
In this exercise, students practice understanding telephone conversations well enough to take an accurate phone message—a skill that requires experience and strategy.

Materials:
Toy or cardboard cutout telephones
A tape recorder (optional)
Student Handouts: Message Forms and Telephone Spelling
Teaching Materials: Telephone Message Scripts

Suggestions:
Help your students to become familiar with the layout of a standard phone message form. Distribute and discuss the Message Forms handout on page 202 to identify what information is needed and how it is generally reported. Define the vocabulary on the message form.

Read (or play a tape of yourself reading) the phone messages from the Message Scripts handout on page 204, and have students write notes—first on a practice sheet of paper, and then on the Message Forms handout.

Have each student make up his own phone message and read it to a partner to take notes.

Read the answering machine or voice mail message and response from the Message Scripts handout. If you have a tape recorder, play a tape of yourself reading the message. Then speak the response into the toy phone.

Emphasize the importance of speaking slowly and clearly. Introduce the students to phonetic spelling on the Telephone Spelling handout on page 203 to help them better understand and to be better understood when spelling aloud on the phone.

Have students make up their own answering machine message and read them to a partner, who then responds.

Message Forms

For:_____   Date:_____   Time:_____   a.m.
                                                                 p.m.

M   _____

Of   _____

Phone   _____
                  Area Code   Number   Extension

Message _____

    _____

    _____

    _____

Signed _____

	Phoned
	Returned your call
	Please call
	Will call again
	Came to see you
	Wants to see you

For:_____   Date:_____   Time:_____   a.m.
                                                                 p.m.

M   _____

Of   _____

Phone   _____
                  Area Code   Number   Extension

Message _____

    _____

    _____

    _____

Signed _____

	Phoned
	Returned your call
	Please call
	Will call again
	Came to see you
	Wants to see you

Telephone Spelling

It is often difficult to hear and understand letters when someone is spelling aloud in English, especially over the telephone. It is helpful to use phonetic alphabets to clarify what you are saying or hearing.

Examples:

Explaining: My name is Kei—K as in king, E as in Edward, I as in Ida.

Clarifying: Did you mean B as in baker or D as in David?

Two commonly used phonetic alphabets:

Alpha	Adam
Bravo	Baker
Charlie	Charlie
Delta	David
Echo	Edward
Foxtrot	Frank
Golf	George
Hotel	Henry
India	Ida
Juliet	John
Kilo	King
Lima	Lewis
Mike	Mary
November	Nancy
Oscar	Otto
Papa	Peter
Quebec	Queen
Romeo	Robert
Sierra	Susan
Tango	Thomas
Uniform	Union
Victor	Victor
Whiskey	William
X-ray	X-ray
Yankee	Young
Zulu	Zebra

Telephone Message Scripts

1.

Hello. This is Terry Brown from the Evergreen Daycare Center.

Today is Monday, April 3rd, and it's about 1:00.

This is very important. I'm calling for Sarah Dalton.

Her son Jake is not feeling well, and Sarah needs to come pick him up as soon as she can.

My number is 702-555-4359.

2.

This message is for John White.

John, this is Kim Reeves of Coastal Community College.

We have received your test scores back.

Please give me a call to set up an interview time.

Today is Thursday, August 6th, and I will be in my office all day.

My office number is 976-555-8900, extension 554.

3.

Hello. You have reached the home of Betty and Barney Rubble. We are not home right now, so please leave us a message after the tone. (Beeeeep)

This is a message for Betty. My name is Wilma and my phone number is 555-4567. I am calling on Wednesday at 2 p.m. Please call me back. Thank you.

 # 19 Intermediate Activities

Cross Cultural Survey

The Cross Cultural Survey is intended to get students thinking and talking about cultural differences. It can be modified to pertain directly to a particular culture, or it may be left general to discuss cultural differences more broadly.

Activity 1

Work in groups of three. What will people think if you do the following? How do you think their reaction might differ in other countries?

1. If you look someone directly in the eye, _____

Other countries: _____

2. If you shrug your shoulders, _____

Other countries: _____

3. If you wave, _____

Other countries: _____

4. If you keep your hands in your pockets, _____

Other countries: _____

5. If you point at someone or something, _____

Other countries: _____

6. If you make the OK gesture, _____

Other countries: _____

7. If you sit on a desk, _____

Other countries: _____

8. If you cross your fingers for good luck, _____

Other countries: _____

9. Other gestures/actions, _____

Other countries: _____

Activity 2
World Cultures
- Why do you think different groups of people develop different cultures?
- Are differences between cultures usually a result of geographical differences?
- Do you think unique traditions are an important part of a culture?
- Do you think that over time a single, common worldwide culture will evolve?
- What exactly defines a culture? Is it food, clothing, music, religion, or language? Is it something else entirely?
- Do people set out to create new traditions or do traditions naturally develop over time?

Your Experience
- How do you normally greet other people?
- What other ways have you seen people greet one another?
- Do you greet older people the same way you would greet someone your own age?
- Are there any routines or customs that you practice before, during, or after meals?
- Are there any foods that are very important to you because of the role they play in your culture?
- Are there any foods that you avoid or cannot eat because of your culture?
- Are there any particular cultures that interest you a great deal? Why?
- Are many of your friends from other cultures?
- Do you enjoy talking to other people about their cultures?

Your Culture
- What do you think is the most important aspect of your culture?
- Why is this important to you or to other individuals from your culture?
- Are there any aspects of your culture that you do not like? Why?
- Have you ever had a misunderstanding with someone from another culture because of your different cultural backgrounds? Why do you think this happened?
- Are there any common traditions in your culture that you do not fully understand?
- If you had to describe your culture to someone who is unfamiliar with it, and you had to do it in no more than five sentences, what would you say?

Class Survey

Use the following questionnaire to collect data about your classmates and their families. Work with a partner. Select one question and rewrite it as an indirect question. Ask everyone in the class your question and keep track of the answers.

When you finish, get together with three or four other pairs and pool your information. Then make a poster showing the family statistics you gathered for the students in the class.

Survey Questionnaire

1. Who comes from the biggest family?

_____

2. How many people are the oldest child? How do they feel about being the oldest?

_____

3. How many people are the youngest child? How do they feel about being the youngest?

_____

4. How many people are the middle child? How do they feel about their position?

_____

5. How many people are the only child? How do they feel about that?

_____

6. How many people were named after a relative?

_____

7. Which relative do people feel the closest to in their families?

_____

8. How many uncles and aunts does the class have all together?

_____

9. How many cousins does the class have all together?

_____

10. How many nieces and nephews does the class have all together?

_____

11. Your Question:

_____

Rephrasing Questions

Work in groups of three. Practice changing the questions below into indirect questions. Then interview each other using indirect questions. Report about the differences you discover. (Example: direct—How old are you? indirect—Could you tell me your age?)

1. What is your full name?
   What are the differences between names here and in your country?

Partner 1 _____

_____

Partner 2 _____

_____

2. Does your name have a special meaning?
   Do you know why your parents chose this name?

Partner 1 _____

_____

Partner 2 _____

_____

3. How many people were there in your family when you were growing up?

Partner 1 _____

_____

Partner 2 _____

_____

4. What were your responsibilities when you were growing up?

Partner 1 _____

_____

Partner 2 _____

_____

5. What did your parents think was important for you to learn?

Partner 1 _____

_____

Partner 2 _____

_____

6. What was your family life like when you were a teenager? What did you disagree with your parents about?

Partner 1 _____

_____

Partner 2 _____

_____

7. Do you go to anyone in your family if you have a problem? If so, who?

Partner 1 _____

_____

Partner 2 _____

_____

8. How often, and on what occasions, does your family get together?

Partner 1 _____

_____

Partner 2 _____

_____

9. What do you think the ideal family is?

Partner 1 _____

_____

Partner 2 _____

_____

I

Roommates

Read the following paragraph and list some advantages and disadvantages of living with a roommate. Compare your answers with a partner.

In North America many young people leave home as soon as they have jobs and can afford to support themselves. Some leave home because they have to attend college or university in another city. Young people want to be independent from their parents as soon as they can. They want to set up their own households, decorate according to their tastes, and live by their own rules. In some cases when they cannot afford to pay all the expenses of living on their own, they have to look for roommates to share the costs. Sharing an apartment or a house with a roommate can be an interesting, rewarding experience, or it can lead to serious problems. One thing is certain: people have to learn to compromise and to get along in these situations. Many young people are choosing to leave home and live with strangers rather than living with their families. Leaving home is an extremely important milestone in the process of becoming an independent and mature person in North America.

Advantages to having a roommate:

_____

_____

_____

_____

_____

Disadvantages to having a roommate:

_____

_____

_____

_____

_____

Get a Job!

Have students practice the following dialogue and answer the questions that follow.

Son: I'm **broke**, Dad. Can I have some money?

Dad: You are 17 years old. You are old enough to get a **part-time job** and **earn** your own **pocket money**.

Son: But I'm still a student! I don't have time to get a part-time job!

Dad: I know that you spend three hours every night playing computer games and watching TV. If you have time to waste doing that, you have time to earn money.

Son: But Dad, I don't want to work!

Dad: I know you are **lazy**. Getting a part-time job will be a good **experience** for you. If you work hard to earn money, you'll be more careful when you spend it.

1. Do you ever earn money? How do you earn it?

2. Do you know anyone who has a part-time job?

3. How do you get pocket money? What do you like to do with your pocket money?

4. What is a good age to get a part-time job?

5. Make a sentence: I am old enough to _____.

6. Make a sentence: If you _____, you'll be _____.

7. Fill in the blanks with a bolded vocabulary word from the dialogue above:

   I want to get a _____ because I think that it will be a

   good _____ for me. Plus, I want to _____ some

   _____ that I can use to buy CDs and comic books. It is better to

   work hard and have a little money than to be _____

   and _____.

Peter the Cheater

Have students practice the following dialogue and answer the questions that follow.

Friend: What's in your hand, Peter?

Peter: Shhh! Be quiet! That's my **cheat sheet**! I don't want to **get in trouble**!

Friend: You made a cheat sheet for the spelling test? You shouldn't do that. Ms. Johnson is very **sharp**. You'll never **get away with it**.

Peter: Don't worry. I won't get **caught**. If she sees me, I'll just put it in my mouth and **swallow** it.

Friend: You're silly Peter. If you would just study a little more, you could **pass** the test!

Peter: I know, but I didn't **get around** to studying because I was too busy making a cheat sheet

Friend: That's not **fair**! I studied all night for this test. I'm telling Ms. Johnson!

Peter: No!!! *Gulp*!

1. What happens if you get caught cheating?

2. What types of things can you get caught doing?

3. What things can you swallow?

4. Make a sentence: I didn't get around to _____ because I was too busy _____.

5. Fill in the blanks with a bolded vocabulary word from the dialogue above.

Peter didn't _____ studying because he was too busy making a _____. His friend told him that he won't _____ because their teacher, Ms. Johnson, is very _____. If Peter gets _____, he said he will put his cheat sheet in his mouth and _____ it.

I10 Intermediate to Advanced Activities

Three-Step Interview

Three-Step Interview is a focused way to encourage students to share their thinking, to ask questions, and to take notes. It works best with three per group, but it can be modified for groups of four.

Each student is assigned a letter, then each letter is assigned a role: A = Interviewer, B = Interviewee, C = Reporter. The roles rotate after each interview. You need to decide the length of time for each interview based on the age of your students, and their experience with this cooperative learning structure. When finished, they do a Round Robin and share the key information they recorded when they were person C.

Application of This Technique

Situation: The students have just completed a report on endangered animals or a biography on an important person. They now do a Three-Step Interview to share the key ideas in their report.

Situation: The students have just finished a Mind Map or Concept Map on a recent grammar topic. They now interview each other about the construction and conceptual flow or connections in the map.

Situation: The students have just completed a listening task on a recent political debate. They now interview each other about their thinking as they attempted to identify what opinions the speakers shared and did not share.

Situation: The school year is just starting. The students interview each other on why new teachers make them nervous or what they think are the most important classroom rules.

Situation: The students are interviewed about their thoughts and feelings concerning a book they recently read (or a chapter, article, etc.).

Situation: The students think of real-life problems such as a time when they did poorly on a test or were teased at school, or encountered problems related to specific content (e.g., paragraph writing or grammar). Students interview each other about how they solved (or could solve) the problem.

Three-Step Interview Form

Interview One: _____ (name)

_____

_____

_____

_____

_____

_____

Interview Two: _____ (name)

_____

_____

_____

_____

_____

_____

Interview Three: _____ (name)

_____

_____

_____

_____

_____

_____

Round Robin: Key Idea(s) from Interviews

_____

_____

Astronaut Survival Game

Start with this story: An asteroid is coming to hit planet Earth and all life will be destroyed. NASA is sending a spaceship to colonize and inhabit another planet. The spaceship has space for three extra people. The directors of NASA are holding interviews with possible candidates to join the new civilization.

Write down different professions of the candidates going to space on pieces of paper and distribute them to your students (do not choose obvious professions such as doctor or engineer). The most fun professions are those that make the students work on their persuasion skills. Some of the ones that work well are: baker, karate expert, gardener, English teacher, dentist. Each student will be a candidate with the given profession.

The students have a few minutes to prepare their argument as to why they should go to space, and then plead their case. The other students listen and then ask questions to the one making the presentation, such as, "What exactly is a gardener to do in space?" They can use their imagination. Perhaps they could say that aliens live on the new planet.

After all of the students have made their presentation and have answered questions, have a class vote on who they would select to go to space.

I11 High-Intermediate to Advanced Activities

Role-Play: Who Gets the Goodies

Scenario: Agatha Rich, a wealthy business woman, has just died. She did not leave any details as to who gets everything in her estate. All her friends, relatives, and basically anyone who ever knew her, are going to have a meeting with her lawyer (the teacher) to convince him or her that they should get the goodies.

Preparation:

Write up a list of what is included in Agatha's estate. You can make it as outrageous as you want. The list could include things like a cottage in the Rocky Mountains, a mink coat, a luxury yacht, a house in Spain, a pet python, a mansion, etc. Try to have at least 15–20 items on the list, depending on the size of the class.

Provide each student with a character card that shows how they know Agatha, e.g., sister, son, ex-husband #2, neighbor, magazine reporter, business partner, crazy man from down the street who is convinced Agatha loved him but just never said so, etc. You can assign the roles or the students can create their own.

Ask the students to be prepared to answer some of the following questions:

- How are you related to Agatha?
- What is your name?
- Where do you live?
- Where do you work?
- Why do you deserve the things you want from Agatha's estate?
- What did you do for Agatha in the past?
- What did you do for her recently?

They are to create a character with a whole story, and not just a name. You can allow them to write out their created information on a piece of paper and bring it to the meeting.

On the day of the meeting go over the items from the estate with the students. Have them check off three or four items that they want. The lawyer then asks the questions that the students prepared answers for, but ask some other questions that they are not expecting, e.g., How much money do you make a year? Is Agatha's sister telling the truth? The other characters can jump in any time they want to comment on what someone has said. At the end of the meeting, the lawyer will have to make a decision as to who gets what.

Expansion:

Instead of playing as individuals, have students be in groups of three or four. Each group represents a charity that Agatha supported during her lifetime. They have to present their group to the lawyer, tell why Agatha supported them, and talk about what they would do with the items in the estate if they received them. In this case, the lawyer is free to split up the estate, or give it all to one charity.

Do your best to make it seem like the real situation. If you have time, download pictures from the Internet of the items in the estate.

If you really want to get things moving, show only a few students a "picture" of what Agatha looked like during her life. During the meeting, the lawyer can ask people what they remember about Agatha. It is pretty funny when only some of them really know what the picture looks like, and leads to some great conversations!

Role-Play: The Exclusive Picture

Time: One hour, including follow-up debate

Language: As many speech acts as are possible; divergent approach

Organization: Small group

Warm-up/Preparation: Each student compiles a fictitious character profile, or merely thinks up a few ideas on what he might say in the context

Procedure: Teacher asks for volunteers, or appoints them if the students are stalling too much

Background:

The editor of a newspaper, whose sales are not going well at the moment, has just received a very graphic photo of a terrible accident involving a school bus which occurred on a nearby highway due to heavy fog. In the photo, you can see the injured and dead strewn around the crash scene. The rest is easy to imagine. The problem is whether to publish it or not. The image could shock, especially so if it is on the front page. Should the victims be left in peace and not appear on the cover of a newspaper? Then again, perhaps by publishing this photo, the editor could educate would-be careless drivers or would-be drunk drivers. Of course, why should these victims be used as free advertising? However, it is news, and nobody can fault a journalist for publishing a story and photo. Moreover, the photo may attract new customers; some people have a morbid interest in the misfortunes of others.

Roles:
- The editor, quite young
- The photographer who took the shot, single
- The accountant, married with two children
- A journalist—relative of one of the victims—in favor of publication, married (with or without children)
- A second journalist, single, who is against publication
- More journalists from various sections of the paper

(The ages and marital status may be altered as you see fit)

Facts on newspaper:
- Employs 50 workers, most with children
- Is on the verge of closure
- Respected newspaper

Follow-up:
- Teacher collects main arguments raised and writes them down in order to fully dissect what was said, and their validity and logic.
- A more open casual group debate can follow.

Variation:
Instead of a photo, it could be a damaging story about a local hero/personality.

In conclusion, when the role-playing technique is employed, it should be integrated with other language-learning activities and adapted to student needs and level. If these guidelines are followed, it can be a rewarding experience for both the students and teacher.

112 Intonation Awareness Activity

What teachers are looking for are ways to generate conversation and communication in class—and hopefully beyond. Getting students to say something—sometimes anything at all—in a conversation class is great, but it must be built upon. One way to achieve this is by sensitizing students to the conversational tactics they use naturally when talking in their native tongue: turn-taking, supporting, challenging, questioning, expanding on statements, and so on. They do not tend to use these when interacting in English.

While the students in a conversation class must be exposed to the above conversation strategies they also must be made aware that the language they use in class owes part of its impact to aspects teachers do not normally work on: tone, facial expressions, and body language. The words students employ in class often come together in sentences and the message gets across eventually, with a little help from the teacher. However, the message is very often toneless and emotionless, but nobody complains because the students are speaking. In fairness, this lack of emotion and tone is more prevalent in the lower levels, where students are still coming to terms with the new language.

When many verbal exchanges in a class seem a little too polite, perhaps because of the neutral tone employed by the speakers, try experimenting with tone by using the following conversation idea. The following activity could be used as an ice-breaker or, if developed, could form the basis for a whole lesson. It would then combine conversation with a certain amount of conscious learning.

This activity does not require much preparation and may help students to loosen up while speaking. The lesson is intended to sensitize students to the concept of tone and lessen the number of monotonous, non-expressive exchanges which occur between students. It should inject a bit of life and humor into the class and could be used as a warm-up.

Working on the assumption that some expressions or words can have many different meanings or connotations depending on how they are said, try the following activity.

Say the following in five different ways:

Goodbye
Hello
How are you?
Do we have to speak English, teacher?
I never watch TV.

(Add more expressions likely to spark several interpretations when delivered with a different tone.)

Your students may be inhibited at first, so the best thing to do is let them know what you are talking about. That is, give them a sample of how to use different tones when you want to imply different meanings. Try something like the following after the class has begun to understand the lesson:

You: John, say "Hello" to me
John: "Hello" (neutral, polite tone)
You: John, now say "Hello" to a friend
John: "Hello" (much more upbeat tone)
You: John, say "Hello" to a 6-month-old-baby!
John: "Hello" (contorted face, exaggerated fall-rise tone, etc.)

If it works, there will be laughs all around, and the point will have been made.

These expressions must be said with different settings and contexts in mind, for example:

- stopped by the police for speeding
- at a shopping check-out
- a polite meeting
- a romantic setting
- after a long separation
- Monday morning in the office
- drunk-talk
- condescending

- nervous
- an interview
- talking to a baby
- a funeral
- an exam
- ironic
- a long-lost friend

Note: Much of the extra meaning will derive from facial expressions and body language.

Examples:

When you do "I never watch TV," tell them to imagine that the sentence is being uttered by a condescending librarian to a TV addict!

When you do "How are you," tell them to imagine they know something very personal about the other person, or that they have not seen the person in 10 years, and so on.

The idea is to let the students relax a bit and actually experiment with the language they are learning to use.

I13 Conversation Starter: What to Expect at Dinnertime

Discussing the cultural differences surrounding mealtime and dinner guests can spark an interesting cultural exchange and can teach your students something about social life in Western countries.

What to Expect at Dinnertime

Hosts usually invite guests into the dining room after a brief period of socializing in the living room.

Dinner is generally served between the hours of 6:30 and 8:00 p.m. and is considered to be a family meal. The entire family, including children, will probably share the meal with guests.

The evening meal is the main meal of the day, rather than the midday meal.

Dinner may be served family-style. Dishes of food are passed from person to person for each to take a portion on their own plates. Guests who are unfamiliar with foods presented often take a small amount of each food passed to them, taking more as desired when the dishes are offered again.

Dinner may be served buffet-style. In this case, food is placed on a side table for guests to serve themselves before proceeding into the dining room or living room to eat the meal. Guests who finish their first serving and wish to take a second serving simply return to the buffet table to help themselves to more. International visitors who are unfamiliar with this form of self-service often ask to follow after another guest in order to become acquainted with the serving procedure.

Place settings at the table may include two forks, two spoons, and a knife. Guests who are not certain which food requires which piece of silverware often observe the table behavior of the host or other guests for guidance.

Some families offer a prayer of thanksgiving before beginning each meal. Saying such a prayer is referred to as **grace** and often takes place in the homes of religion-oriented families.

Guests usually refrain from beginning the meal until everyone has been served and the host has lifted his fork. An exception to this is the buffet-style meal in which guests begin eating as soon as they are seated.

Dinner may be served in two, three, or four courses: soup, salad, or fruit may be offered as a first course.

The main course or central part of the meal is usually defined by the meat, poultry, or fish served. All other foods, such as vegetables and starches (potatoes, rice, or noodles) are considered side dishes and are served in smaller portions with the meat or fish. Rice is generally not considered a main food in North America. Therefore, only a small portion may be prepared for each guest. It may be helpful to observe the hosts to see how much rice they serve themselves.

A salad of lettuce and raw vegetables or fruit may be served before, during, or after the main course.

Dessert is served at the end of the meal and may be a sweet cake or pie, fruit, ice cream, or pudding. Coffee is usually served with dessert. Guests may compliment the host on his or her cooking if they wish to do so.

Seconds, or a second helping of food, might be offered only once to a guest.

In many North American homes, the host refrains from offering the food more than a second time for fear of offending the guest by his persistence. International visitors who are accustomed to refusing the second helping a number of times should realize that the offer may be extended only once.

In North America, men and women often share in the food preparation and cleanup. At an informal dinner, for example, the host may prepare the steak, make the salad, and/or remove dishes from the table.

The traditional concept of men's work and women's work is changing in North America as more women have full-time professional careers outside the home. Household chores such as dishwashing, cleaning, and laundry are often shared on the basis of what needs to be done at the time, rather than on the basis of whether it is considered to be the man's or woman's role.

Some North Americans offer to take their international guests on a house tour. Some visitors regard this as an impolite gesture intended to allow the hosts to display their material wealth. However, North-American hosts may offer such a tour to satisfy any curiosity a visitor may have about the way North Americans live, as they themselves would be curious when visiting another country.

Additional Vocabulary

Barbecue: To cook food outdoors on a metal frame (a grill) over an open fire

Brunch: A late morning meal that is eaten instead of breakfast and lunch

Cafeteria: A type of restaurant that serves drinks and light meals

Caterer: A person or business that provides food and drinks for social events

Cuisine: A style of cooking

Drive-in: A place where you can go to eat, watch a movie, etc., in your car

Drive-through (informal: drive-thru): A part of a restaurant, bank, or other business where you can buy something or receive a service without getting out of your car

Fast food: Food that can be cooked and eaten quickly in a restaurant or taken away from the restaurant

Gourmet: A person who enjoys food and wine and knows a lot about them

Licensed restaurant: A restaurant that is allowed to serve drinks with alcohol

SECTION J

Teaching Listening

Content

J1 Listening Skills Development

Introduction

The primary form of linguistic communication is speech; therefore, listening is the most important receptive (and learning) skill for foreign language students. An ability to listen and interpret many shades of meaning from what is heard is a fundamental communicative ability. Teaching listening involves training in some enabling skills such as perception of sounds, stress, intonation patterns, accents, attitudes, and so on, as well as listening comprehension practice.

Organizing Listening Comprehension Activities

As in reading comprehension, there should always be a purpose in listening. In most cases, this will be some form of comprehension. You should establish regular procedures for listening activities in which students will develop from a gist of what is being said to specific comprehension through repeated listening.

- **Understanding the setting:** After the first listening, students should be able to understand the setting of the recording: where the speakers are, how many speakers there are, the ages, roles, professions, moods of the speakers, etc. As well, students should have a general idea as to what they are talking about. A good question to ask is "Are they standing or sitting?" This encourages students to think about the setting so that they can go on to speculate about the content of what the speakers are saying. The first listening also allows the students to get accustomed to the voices.

- **Pre-teach difficult vocabulary:** Teaching isolated and unconnected lists of words and phrases is probably not a good idea. Teachers may choose to introduce the setting before the students listen. This provides an opportunity to elicit or introduce and explain the sort of language that might be heard in the setting. This language can be listed on the board and students can listen and note what they actually hear.

- **Focused listening:** Listening tasks give the students a reason for listening and focus their attention. The purpose of the listening tasks should be clearly explained before the students listen. They are for practicing listening, not testing the students' memory!

- **Graded listening tasks:** Listening is taught by building comprehension from general understanding to identification of specific information. Listening tasks can be graded from easy to more difficult by the forms of questions used. The simplest task is T/F (True/False) statements (e.g., The librarian asked for a book. T/F), sometimes extended to T/F/DK (True/False/Don't Know). The next stages are Either/Or questions (Did the librarian ask for a book or a letter?) followed by Multiple Choice (The librarian asked for a _____. a) book b) pencil c) letter d) stapler). Open Questions (Who, What, When, Where, Why, and How) require more in-depth understanding of the listening material (What book did the librarian ask for?). Tasks become more difficult as the information given in each question is reduced.

  Here is a rhyme you can teach to introduce WH-questions:

  > I keep six honest serving-men
  > (They taught me all I knew);
  > Their names are What and Why and When
  > And How and Where and Who.
  > —Rudyard Kipling

- **Sharing listening tasks:** In large classes you will probably have students of differing proficiency. All of the students do not need to work on the same task. For example, a group of students can be given questions 1–5, another group questions 6–10, and so on. After, students can share their answers.

- **Delaying the teacher's answer:** When the teacher gives the answer to a question, the students stop thinking. After listening, let students share their answers but do not give your answers. Let them listen again to check their answers. Checking work on their own is very valuable for students.

- **Keep the listening short:** Intensive listening requires intense concentration. Students find it difficult to maintain this level of concentration for more than one or two minutes. If the recording is longer, split it into smaller sections.

- **After comprehension, analysis:** After students have understood the gist and some important details of a recording, analyze it in more detail and investigate the way in which speakers have expressed their ideas. Have they revealed their mood, their opinions, their relationship, and so on? Analyze the speed and style of speech, the use of hesitation, repetition, false starts, paraphrasing, etc.

J2 The Teacher is a CD Player (Intermediate)

Age Group: 8–14
Time: 20 minutes
Objectives:
- Linguistic: listening and writing
- Other: to encourage a sense of responsibility among the students

Description: This is a dictation with a difference: the teacher acts as a CD player which responds to spoken commands
Preparation: Choose a short text to work with, perhaps from your course book

In Class:
1. Ask the students what buttons you find on a CD player.

As they tell you, write the English names on the board like the following:

PLAY   **STOP**   **FAST FORWARD**   **REWIND**

2. Tell the students that you are going to give them a dictation that is rather unusual. Explain that you are a CD player and that when they say the commands on the board, you do what they say. They have to write down what the CD player says. The CD player cannot do anything without a command in English. Check that the students understand by asking, "What do you say to make me start?"

3. Say, "We're ready to start" and wait until someone says "Play."

4. Start to read the text at a normal speaking pace and keep going until someone (usually in desperation) says "Stop."

   At first, it will probably be chaotic. Be patient, and resist the temptation to interfere, to speak more slowly, or to stop—it is very important for the success of the activity that you are a machine that only obeys their commands.

5. Continue like this until the end of the text.

6. When you reach the end of the text, ask the students to check what they have written in pairs, and to look for mistakes. Then go through the text with the whole class.

Follow-up:
This is an activity where feedback can be very fruitful as it gives the students a chance to reflect on what they have done. Ask them if they liked the activity. Why or why not? How could they do it better next time? Write down what they say, and the next time you do this kind of dictation, review their comments before you start.

Comments:
This dictation has the advantage of handing the control over to the class. They can go back and forwards as often as they like. It is important to remember that a CD player has no mind of its own and no speed control, and that the speed of the dictation should be a normal speaking pace.

J3 The Frog Family (Beginner to Lower Intermediate)

Age Group: 5–10
Time: 30 minutes
Objectives:
- Linguistic: listening for the gist, relating words and actions, family vocabulary
- Other: to involve the students in storytelling

Description: The teacher tells a story about the Frog family and the students act out the parts of the characters
Preparation: Flashcards or board drawings of the Frog family, chalk or string, paper for lily pads
In-Class Preparation:
1. Practice telling the story. Include very explicit actions that the students will be able to imitate.

2. Prepare pictures of the Frog family.

3. Draw a large lily pad and make an area of floor into a pond with chalk or string.

In Class:

1. Tell the students that you are going to tell them a story about the Frog family. Then, either draw the frogs or put up pictures on the board. Check that they know who is who.

2. Ask the students questions like "Have you ever seen a frog?", "Where do frogs live?", "What do they sit on?", "Do they like to be hot or cold?", and "How can they get cool?" Then show them the outline of the pond on the floor and the big lily pad in it.

3. Tell them the story, remembering to use lots of gestures to make the meaning very clear.

4. Tell the students you are going to tell the story again, but this time five of them are going to be the Frog family. Ask for volunteers and line them up by the edge of the pond.

5. Tell the story again, and as each student hears their character they put up their hand. Encourage them to do the gestures with you as you tell the story.

6. All the students will want to participate in acting out the story. Once they have heard it several times you can divide the class into several ponds and tell the story with several Frog families at a time.

Story Outline

This is the most basic version of the story. You can add details like names and sizes if you want to, though they should always be things that you can illustrate with mime or pictures.

The Frog Family

Story	Actions
This is a story about Daddy Frog, Mommy Frog, Sister Frog, Brother Frog, and Baby Frog.	Point to the pictures as you name the frogs.
It was hot—very, very hot.	Wipe your forehead, and make hot gestures.
And Daddy Frog went jump, jump, jump, and sat on a leaf in the pond.	Point to the picture of Daddy Frog and squat down beside the pond. Jump three times and sit on the leaf in the pond.
Mommy Frog was hot—very, very hot. So Daddy Frog said, "Come here!"	Point to Mommy Frog, squat by the pond, and make hot gestures. Point to Daddy Frog, return to the leaf, and beckon to Mommy Frog.
Mommy Frog went jump, jump, jump, and sat on the leaf in the pond.	Point to Mommy Frog, squat by the pond, and jump three times to sit on the leaf by Daddy Frog.
Sister Frog was hot—very, very hot. So Mommy Frog said, "Come here!"	Point to Sister Frog, squat by the pond, and make hot gestures. Point to Mommy Frog, return to the and beckon to Sister Frog.

Sister Frog went jump, jump, jump and sat on the leaf in the pond.	Point to Sister Frog, squat by the pond and jump three times to sit on the leaf by Mommy Frog.
Brother Frog was hot—very, very hot. So Sister Frog said, "Come here!"	Point to Brother Frog, squat by the pond, and make hot gestures. Point to Sister Frog, return to the leaf and beckon to Brother Frog.
Brother Frog went jump, jump, jump and sat on the leaf in the pond.	Point to Brother Frog, squat by the pond and jump three times to sit on the leaf by Sister Frog.
Baby Frog was hot—very, very hot. So Brother Frog said, "Come here!"	Point to Baby Frog, squat by the pond, and make hot gestures. Point to Brother Frog, return to the leaf and beckon to Baby Frog.
Baby Frog went jump, jump, jump and sat on the leaf in the pond.	Point to Baby Frog, squat by the pond and jump three times to sit on the leaf by Brother Frog.
And then—SPLASH—they all fell into the water!	Start to move backward and forward as if you were losing your balance and fall into the pond.

Follow-up 1:
Ask the students to draw a picture of the Frog family.

Follow-up 2:
The students can make masks for the characters.

J4 Paper Fortune-Teller Activity (Beginner to Lower Intermediate)

Age Group: 7–13
Time: 20 minutes
Objectives:
- Reviewing colors and numbers
- Practicing simple statements

Supplies Needed:
- Construction paper
- Scissors
- Pen or pencil

Description:
While students in your class are finishing up another in-class assignment or activity, give the half of your class that has already finished the following written illustrations and have them create a paper fortune-teller by following your verbal instructions. Once finished, each student who completed the project should tell another person how to make a paper fortune-teller, without showing them the written instructions.

Paper Fortune-Teller

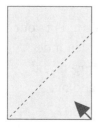

Start by making a square piece of paper. To start making the square, fold one corner of a piece of paper over to the adjacent side.

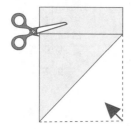

To finish making the square, cut off the small rectangle, forming a square (which is already folded into a triangle).

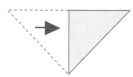

Flip the triangle over and fold the two opposite ends of the triangle together, forming a smaller triangle.

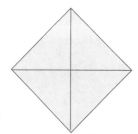

Open the paper up (unfolding all the folds).

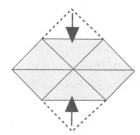

Fold a corner into the central point. Repeat with the opposite corner.
Repeat with the other two corners. You'll end up with a square.

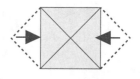

Flip the paper over.
Fold a corner over into the center. Repeat with the opposite corner.
Fold over the two remaining corners. You'll end up with a smaller square.

Fold the square in half. Unfold and fold in half the other way.

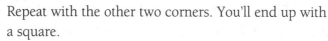

Lift your folded square. Open up each of the four square flaps underneath. Put your right index finger and thumb in the two flaps on the right and put your left index finger and thumb in the two flaps on the left. Gently push your index fingers and thumbs together. You will be able to move the four parts around—up and out.

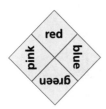

Write any four colors on the four outside flaps.
Flip the fortune teller over, and write eight numbers on the triangular flaps.

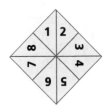

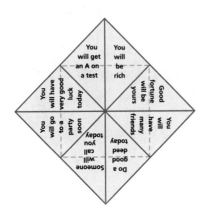

Write eight fortunes inside the flaps (underneath the numbers). Some examples of fortunes include:

- You will get an A on a test.
- You will be rich.
- Good fortune will be yours.
- You will have many friends.
- Do a good deed today.
- Someone will call you today.
- You will go to a party soon.
- Be careful on Tuesday.
- You will have very good luck today.

You can now be a fortune-teller. Have someone choose one of the four colors.
Spell that color out, while moving the fortune-teller up and out
(e.g, RED= R up, E out, D up).
Then have the person choose one of the numbers that is showing.
Move the fortune-teller up and out the corresponding number of times.
When you finish, have the person choose one of the four visible numbers.
Open up the flap she chooses, and read her fortune.

J5 Listening Activities and Approaches in the Classroom

1. Variety is important when planning classroom activities. Here is a list of potential listening activities to engage your students.

Back-to-Back: Ask students to carry on a conversation or pass information to one another while sitting back-to-back so they cannot see body language or facial expressions. This helps mimic the difficulties associated with talking on the telephone.

Numbers and Dates: Students often have trouble hearing and reproducing numbers, particularly large numbers. Dictate a quick series of numbers (large numbers, decimals, and fractions for advanced students) and ask students to write what they hear. These can be in the form of telephone numbers, serial numbers, or even an ISBN from a book, to give a few examples.

Rhyming: The teacher reads a series of rhyming words (three or four of each series, e.g., tree, three, see, me) and students write them in the correct order.

Guessing Definitions: Read definitions of words to your students and ask them to listen and guess the words that you are defining.

Intonation and Stress: Read a conversation or short passage in an exaggerated and theatrical way. Give your students the text you are reading and ask them to mark changes in stress or intonation in your speech. Ask students to reproduce what they have heard afterwards.

Paraphrasing/Translating: Ask your students to rewrite the listening text either in their own words or in another language.

Summarizing: Students listen to a brief passage and then summarize what they hear.

Songs: You may either bring recorded material into the class or encourage students to learn and sing a song together as a group.

Cloze: Provide the text of a listening activity with certain key words or lines missing. Listeners are to fill in the missing information.

Film/Theater/Video: If resources are available, provide a video or a film for your students to watch, analyze, and discuss.

Dictation: Ask students to write down the exact words of a recording of some material, or of you reading the material aloud.

Telephone: Form your students into two lines or rows and whisper a sentence to the end of each of the lines. Students should continue whispering the repeated sentence to one another down the lines. Ask students at the other end to say or write what they heard. It will likely not be the same!

Detecting Mistakes: Tell a story that the students are familiar with, but deliberately change some of the facts in the story. Listeners should try to identify the mistakes.

Obeying Instructions: Give clear instructions (stand up, sit down, draw, etc.) for the students to follow in class. You can extend this into a game such as Simon Says for younger students.

Note Taking: Give or present a lecture on a fixed topic in a structured and orderly way, and ask students to take notes on the lecture. Discuss the content as a class afterwards.

2. **Multitasking is a good way to engage the more advanced students in a mixed-level class.**

Teachers of large multilevel classes often struggle with how to engage and challenge the advanced students while at the same time teaching to the rest of the class. Multitasking is one possible solution to this problem. Multitasking with language is something that most native speakers do well, but it often presents a challenge for non-native speakers.

Multitasking refers to the ability to do two or more tasks at one time. For example, most people can have a conversation with a friend in a café and also simultaneously hear some of what is being said in their native language at a table behind them. They might even be reading the menu too!

There are a variety of ways to practice this in the classroom, but keep in mind that the activities need to be presented in a way that does not distract the lower-level students who will only be focused on a single task. One idea is to hand out a brief reading passage that is to be completed at the same time as a listening activity. For example, if an instructor is working with a song in class, they might hand out a story or anecdote about the band to some advanced students and ask them to read it during the class. Another idea is to group your advanced students together for the listening activity and then approach them for a quiet conversation during the listening. They will be confused at first, but with repetition students will begin to see the value of multitasking activities of this nature.

3. **Focused and intensive listening activities are valuable but they are also tiring and stressful; plan your lessons accordingly.**

There is a good chance that students will need to take listening exams at some point in their lives. Practicing the stressful and intensive atmosphere of a listening exam in your class is an excellent way to help students prepare and to learn about their own strengths and weaknesses.

Teachers will find, however, that after activities like this, their students will be drained and the classroom atmosphere may be generally tired and quiet. This is the time when good lesson planning is important. Particularly long, intensive, or difficult listening activities need to be followed by something physically active and entertaining for students. This may be a favorite game of the class or a competitive speaking activity of some kind, but the teacher will need to do something to change the mood in the classroom from dull and depressed back to excited and engaged.

A listening exercise can also take the form of listening to a student or a teacher read aloud in class. Different people—students and teachers—react differently to the task of reading aloud. It can be useful and effective, however, so for teachers who are considering it, here are a few things they should remember.

*   One student reading and 49 listening is not a good use of class time because the one reading can be nervous and the other 49 listening are easily distracted.
*   Divide large classes into groups for reading aloud activities.
*   Encourage the One Book Open method of reading aloud. The only book open is to be that of the reader. Students who are listening must close their books and focus on the speaker. This means that students who are not reading aloud will be more likely to listen attentively, and less likely to interrupt the reader with corrections.
*   Do not ask students to read something that they are unfamiliar with. Always allow time for them to prepare and familiarize themselves with the material first.
*   Correct students on their pronunciation after they have finished reading so you do not interrupt their flow and concentration.

- More passive students need a listening option so try to design activities that do not require everyone to read aloud; however, it is also important for them to gain the pronunciation practice the others have had while reading aloud, so design activities to also get them speaking.

4. **Students often come to teachers with the question of how to improve their listening ability. Here are some tips that you can give them.**

- Listening closely to your classmates will help you improve your listening. Many classmates have pronunciation problems so if you can understand them, then you will certainly be able to understand native speakers easily.
- Listen carefully to your favorite English songs and try to write down the words. If you have any problems, check the lyrics online or bring them to class and ask the teacher for help.
- Before you do a listening activity in class, you should make guesses and predictions about what you will hear. This will help you to prepare for listening and should help you focus on key points or words that will, in turn, improve your listening comprehension.
- Watch DVDs in English with the subtitles on. Subtitles do not hurt your listening ability; you will still be listening while reading the subtitles and they will help you fill in the parts that you miss or do not hear clearly.
- The radio is one of the greatest listening challenges available because you do not have the benefit of body language or facial expressions from the speaker. Listen to the radio to practice your global listening skills; this works particularly well when trying to understand the content of a news broadcast or report.
- You need to be responsible for your own listening. Try to identify your strengths and weaknesses as a listener and work on ways to improve. Ask your teacher for advice if you want to practice a particular aspect of listening.

J6 Songs

Using songs and music in the classroom can work for all levels and it has a number of benefits in terms of language learning.

There are three main reasons why teachers should make use of song in the classroom. The first is that almost everyone can recall certain lines of songs that they listened to years ago. Why is this? It seems that our brains are especially attuned to recall words in the form of song. Secondly, songs are fun. Songs can bring an entertaining and lively atmosphere to the classroom and help to relax students and lower their anxiety. This helps to create a positive learning environment in the class. Lastly, by varying the presentation format, teachers can effectively use songs with a multilevel class.

Here is a typical and effective format to follow for using music in an ESL class.

Choose: Choosing the correct material is important. Songs selected for class need to be both reasonably comprehensible and interesting for the students. Try to find material that is currently popular and appealing with your group of students, as well as age-appropriate.

Preview: Once you have selected the material, preview it to your class before you listen. Tell them who the artist is, what the song is called, and any particular meaning that the song may have. This will help students to listen actively and enthusiastically.

Pre-Listen: Allow the students at least one opportunity to relax and listen to the music without asking them to complete any tasks. Repeat this step if time allows.

Intensive-Listen: Here you should choose one particular verse of the song and ask students to copy down the exact words to that verse. The teacher will need to replay this verse multiple times, but this task will challenge even the most advanced students in your class.

Cloze-Listen: Hand out the lyrics to the song with certain words, groups of words, or lines missing and ask the students to fill in what they hear. This will allow lower-level students the opportunity to contribute and will maintain the focused listening of the entire class.

Post-Listen: After you have completed all the listening exercises associated with the song, the students should be asked some questions or given an opportunity to discuss their interpretation of the meaning of the song. This completes the activity nicely and allows for analysis and critical thinking. Music and songs contain a great deal of emotion, so you can ask the students to discuss how the song made them feel or what mood they think the songwriter was in.

Songs are an enjoyable way to practice listening skills. Probably the most common way to make use of songs in a listening class is to give the students a copy of the lyrics with some words and phrases removed. As they listen, they can fill in the blanks to complete the lyrics. Before beginning the activity, it is helpful to play the song while the students just close their eyes and listen. After they have heard the song once, then you can play it again and have them fill in the blanks. You should play the song at least twice as they fill in the spaces, then once they are finished, play it again so they can listen and read or sing along with the words.

"If I Had $1,000,000" by the Barenaked Ladies

A) Fill in the blanks as you listen. Each blank is one word.

If I had a million dollars (If I had a million dollars)

I'd buy you a _____ (I ____ buy you a house)

If I had a million dollars (repeat)

I'd buy you _____ for your house (maybe a nice chesterfield or an ottoman)

If I had a million dollars (repeat)

I'd buy you a _____ (a nice Reliant _____)

If I had a million dollars, I'd buy your love.

If I had a million dollars _____ _____ a tree fort in our yard

If I had a million dollars you could help, it _____ _____ _____ _____

If I had a million dollars maybe we could put a little tiny _____ in there somewhere

(You know, we just could go up there and hang out. Like open the fridge and stuff …)

If I had a million dollars (repeat)

I'd buy you a _____ _____ (but not a real _____ _____, that's cruel)

If I had a million dollars (repeat)

I'd buy you an _____ _____ (yep, like a llama or an emu)

If I had a million dollars (repeat)

I'd buy you John Merrick's remains (oh all them crazy elephant bones)

If I had a million dollars, I'd buy _____ _____

If I had a million dollars we _____ _____ ____ _____ ____ _____ _____

If I had a million dollars we'd take a limousine 'cause it costs more

If I had a million dollars we wouldn't have to _____ Kraft dinner

(But we would eat Kraft dinner. Of course we would, we'd _____ _____ _____ …)

If I had a million dollars (repeat)

I'd buy you a _____ _____ (but not a real _____ _____, that's cruel)

If I had a million dollars (repeat)

I'd buy you _____ _____ (a Picasso or a Garfunkel)

If I had a million dollars (repeat)

I'd buy you a monkey (_____ _____ _____ _____ ___ _____?)

If I had a million dollars, I'd buy _____ _____

If I had a million dollars; if I had a million dollars

If I had a million dollars; if I had a million dollars

If I had a million dollars … I'd be rich!

J

B) Discuss these questions with your partner:

1. Does the singer have a million dollars?

2. What would he buy if he had a million dollars?

3. What is the cost of the things that the singer would buy?

4. What questions do you have about the song?

5. What things would you buy if you had a million dollars?

"Heavenly" by Harry Connick, Jr.

A) Fill in the blanks as you listen. Each blank is one word.

He's always smiling

He never looks mean

Even when _____ _____ _____ in between

The _____ _____ _____ _____ is smiling

'Cause he's in love

The _____ _____ _____ _____ is smiling

'Cause he's in love with the _____ _____ _____ _____

She's there in the evening

She never comes late

All day she spins around

But _____ _____ _____ _____

The _____ _____ _____ _____ is smiling

'Cause she's in love

The _____ _____ _____ _____ is smiling

'Cause she's in love with the _____ _____ _____ _____

When two heavenly bodies glow

All the stars agree

_____ _____ might be born

Maybe even a _____

And in the morning

They don't say goodbye

But with a kiss

They blend _____ _____ _____

Oh, they're smiling

'Cause they're in love

The man in the moon is smiling

'Cause he's in love with the girl in the world

The man in the moon is smiling

'Cause he's in love with the girl in the world

Heavenly!

B) Listen and answer the following questions:

1. Who is "he" _____? Who is "she" _____?

2. Who might be born to them? _____ or _____

J

J7 TV or Movie Listening Exercise (Intermediate to Advanced)

The Set-up:

- Choose a scene from a sitcom or a movie that students can easily relate to (i.e., similar jobs, life-styles, or age-group).
- Watch the selection with the class and prompt conversation on what happened to the characters. Try to elicit the use of new vocabulary learned from the selection.
- Try to connect the new vocabulary brought up by students to specific scenes, settings, and moods in the scene.
- Finally, try to compare the selection's situations to real situations in your students' lives.
- After class, let your students borrow the video or DVD, or lead them to link(s) online, and tell them to listen to the dialogue, noting new vocabulary—especially new phrases.

Reasoning and goals:

By viewing the situations in the selection and comparing them to real-life situations, students can see how particular phrases and collocations are used in their proper context. By having students studying the selection at home, they can extend their exposure to the scenes and dialogues which can help them to pick up more subtle language cues and uses, and also to practice the tone and inflection present in the selection.

Further ideas and continued practice:

- Turn this activity into an ongoing practice throughout the course.
- Recommend that your students concentrate on just one sitcom or scenes from a single movie time after time to help them follow the rhythm and collocations of the conversations and to help familiarize them with the accents of the characters.
- Suggest that students focus their attention on a particular character in the selection as this can help them better understand the emotion and feeling of the dialogue and helps them to concentrate on one aspect of the selection. After a time, have them watch and focus on a different character.
- Make sure to give clear instructions on how to continue the exercise at home and follow up in subsequent lessons. You want your students to get as much as possible out of this exercise and to have the opportunity to activate any new knowledge they gain.

J8 A New Twist on Listening Exercises

Listening is one of the most challenging skills to improve, simply because the students cannot work at their own pace. They might read at a slower pace, or work out the meaning of a sentence on paper before moving on, which is simply impossible and impractical in a conversation.

Always try to include an element of listening in each lesson, and not just with an activity prepared beforehand. Any activity can be adjusted to incorporate listening, which also helps put a new twist on the usual exercises. Try one of the following:

1. A word search in which you dictate some or all of the words to find first, then check the spelling as a class. The students then complete the word search (in class or as homework).

2. Follow the instructions of a worksheet, but do several of the exercises, sentences, etc., aloud as a class. You can have the students work alone or in pairs. With smaller classes, you can ask additional questions not on the worksheet to encourage participation from everyone.

3. Extend an activity with a listening and speaking exercise. For example, after completing a worksheet on the future tense, give three or four new, original sentences about your plans for the weekend. Students listen, and then work in pairs to ask an appropriate follow-up question. You can then have the students do the same: tell, ask, and answer in pairs or groups.

J

SECTION K
Teaching Reading

Content

K1 Types of Reading Skills

Ask the students this question: When you read a schedule, summary, or other outlining document written in your own language, do you read every word?

The answer is most definitely: No! Point out to them that this should be true when they read English, just as it is when they read their native language. This means that it is not always necessary to read and understand each and every word when reading English. Ask them to remember that reading skills in their native language and English are basically the same.

Here is a quick overview of the four types of reading skills used in every language.

- Skimming—used to understand the gist or main idea
- Scanning—used to find a particular piece of information
- Intensive reading—accurate reading for detailed understanding
- Extensive reading—used for pleasure and general understanding

Skimming

Skimming is used to quickly gather the most important information, or gist. This is done by running your eyes over the text, noting important information. Use skimming, for example, to quickly get up to speed on a current business situation. It is not essential to understand every word when skimming.

Examples of skimming:
- Newspapers (to get the general news of the day quickly)
- Magazines (to discover which articles you would like to read in more detail quickly)
- Business and travel brochures (to get informed quickly)

Scanning

Scanning is used to find a particular piece of information. This is done by running your eyes over the text looking for the specific piece of information you need. Use scanning on schedules, meeting plans, etc., in order to find the specific details you require. If you see words or phrases that you do not understand, do not worry when scanning.

Examples of scanning:
- The TV listings section of your newspaper
- A train/airplane schedule
- A conference guide

Intensive Reading

Intensive reading is used on shorter texts in order to extract specific information. It is a very close accurate reading for detail. Use intensive reading skills to grasp the details of a specific situation. In this case, it is important that you understand each word, number, or fact.

Examples of intensive reading:
- A bookkeeping report
- An insurance claim
- A contract

Extensive Reading

Extensive reading is used to obtain a general understanding of a subject and includes reading longer texts for pleasure, as well as textbooks. Use extensive reading skills to improve your general knowledge of, for example, business procedures. Do not worry about whether you understand every word.

Examples of extensive reading:
*   The latest marketing strategy book
*   A novel you read before going to bed
*   Magazine articles that interest you

K2 Good ESL Reading Habits

1. Read the entire text or section on your first time through it—even if you do not understand some of the words. On your second read-through, you can look up any difficult vocabulary.

2. If you are using your finger to guide your eyes along, be sure to keep it ahead of your eyes.

3. Read the text in small chunks; try to read phrases or sentences rather than single words in isolation.

4. Do not engage in timed reading activities unless they are followed by comprehension activities.

5. Always keep reading—both in class and at home.

K3 The Reader as a Detective

A reader is very much like a detective. The job of a detective is to find the solution to a problem or mystery. A good detective knows what to look for. A good detective is sensitive to the things around him or her and is able to ask intelligent and probing questions. He or she knows which clues and information in a case are important and which are not. A detective knows how to use and interpret these important clues to find a solution.

A reader has a similar job to do. A reader is also presented with information, much of it new and unfamiliar, and is expected to understand and interpret what is being read. A good reader, like a good detective, knows what to look for. A good reader is able to ask intelligent and thoughtful questions before actually beginning to read. A good reader uses the title and subtitle of an article to form questions, which he or she then tries to answer while reading. A good reader can tell the important ideas from the less important ones and is able to see the relationship between them.

To understand an author's ideas, the reader must also be able to understand the vocabulary an author uses. A reader will often encounter unfamiliar words while reading. Here again, the good reader learns to identify which words are essential to understanding the writer's ideas and which words are not. The good reader also knows different ways to solve the mystery of an unfamiliar word.

There are three basic strategies that a reader can use to understand the meaning of an unfamiliar word:

1. Identify the structure of the word; that is, analyze the different parts of the word (its prefix, suffix, and root).
2. Look up the word in a dictionary.
3. Use the context of the word to understand its meaning; this is perhaps the most important and most useful way to discern the meaning of an unfamiliar word.

Context is the sentence or paragraph in which a word appears. Often, the sentence or sentences around the unfamiliar word will offer an indication of, or clue to, the word's meaning. These indications or clues are referred to as context clues.

Types of Context Clues to Look For

The following list shows some of the different kinds of context clues authors provide in their writing. After each kind of clue, you will find a brief explanation and some examples.

1.   Synonym or Restatement Clues

Authors sometimes use another word in the same sentence or a neighboring sentence that has the same meaning as the unfamiliar word.

Do you know the meaning of these words: **plight**, **emulate**, **cocksure**? Read each sentence in the following list. Find another word or words with the same meaning as the bolded word.

a) The woman found herself in a difficult situation. In fact, her **plight** was so serious that she decided to get help.

b) Children often try to **emulate** or copy the behavior that they see on television.

c) Mr. Kelada was incredibly **cocksure**. It was this excessive self-confidence that made Sara want to prove him wrong whenever he gave an opinion.

2.   Comparison/Contrast Clues

A sentence may contain a word that has the opposite meaning from the unfamiliar word. Authors sometimes use words such as **on the other hand**, **however**, **although**, **unlike**, **yet**, and **but** to alert the reader to the fact that a word with an opposite meaning is being used.

Do you know the meaning of these words: **stroll**, **slip**, **deprecating**? Read each sentence in the following list. Find a word or words with an opposite meaning from the bolded word. What word is used to indicate an opposite meaning?

a) Some people like to walk quickly home after work, but I prefer to **stroll** home and look at the store windows along the way.

b) Although the doctor usually performed the operation perfectly, the nurse knew he had **slipped** when she saw the patient's blood pressure suddenly rise.

c) When I was a child, my mother seemed to approve of almost everything I wanted to do. My father, however, always seemed to have a **deprecating** reaction to whatever I did.

K

3. Example Clues

Authors sometimes provide specific examples to illustrate or explain the meaning of a word.

Do you know the meaning of these words: **detachment**, **demeanor**, **loquacious**? Use the examples in each sentence below to identify the meaning of the bolded word.

a) There was a kind of **detachment** about the old man's behavior. It appeared as if he didn't care what you were saying to him, as if what you were saying was of no interest to him.

b) In a battle situation, he always appeared calm and relaxed. It was that calm **demeanor** that earned him the respect and admiration of the other soldiers.

c) Mr. Kalada was the most **loquacious** man I'd ever met. He talked with everyone on the ship, and he always had something to say, no matter what the topic.

4. Direct Explanation Clues

Sometimes a writer may directly explain the meaning of a word. The author may indicate a direct explanation by using commas or parentheses. A third way may simply be to use a phrase that explains a word's meaning.

Do you know the meaning of these words: **imperceptible**, **phial**, **siren**? Find the explanation for each bolded word below.

a) The powerful poison was **imperceptible** when mixed in liquid: that is, it could not be tasted, seen, or smelled.

b) From the shelf above him, the old man took down a **phial**, a small glass bottle used to keep liquids, and he placed it on the table in front of him.

c) According to ancient mythology many sailors met their deaths at sea at the hands of **sirens**, beautiful creatures who were part woman and part bird and who were able to seduce men with their singing.

5. Experience or Situation Clues

Some words can be understood simply by the circumstance or situation in which they are used. The reader may be able to understand a word's meaning because the situation described is similar to the reader's own experience.

Do you know the meaning of these words: **creak**, **apprehensive**, **berth**? Use the situation described in each sentence below to identify the meaning of the bolded word.

a) Alan found himself on the first floor of an old, seemingly abandoned building. As he walked up to the second floor, he could hear the old wooden stairs **creak** with each step he took.

b) It was the first time Nancy had been in a big city. She felt a little **apprehensive** as she walked out onto the street, with so many strange faces staring at her.

c) It was our first night on the ship. Feeling tired after a long, uneventful day at sea, I returned to my cabin, lay down on my **berth**, and quickly fell asleep.

Take a moment to review the different kinds of context clues. Learn to recognize context clues when you read. Do not be afraid to use them to help you guess the meaning of unfamiliar vocabulary. Become a good word detective. Use context clues to solve the mystery of new words.

K4 Reading Skills Development

Skills Needed for Reading

1. Prediction
   a) Use anticipation questions; i.e., give a title such as "Women in Africa" and ask students to anticipate the questions they think the article may answer
   b) Analyze a book using the index, chapter, and paragraph headings (read topic sentences) to predict the topic of the book
   c) Ask students to complete sentences; i.e., It was a lovely day so/but …

2. Coherence
   Understand the ways in which the idea(s) in the reading selection are linked and developed

3. Inference and Interpretation
   Apply knowledge of the real world to what is stated, as well as to what is implied (but not stated)

Rules to Bear in Mind When Planning the Teaching Program

1. **The law of experience:** Doing something makes it likely you will remember it. First impressions are the most lasting.

2. **The law of frequency:** The more often you do something, the more likely you are to remember it.

3. **The law of recency:** The more recently you have done something, the more likely you are to recall it.

4. **The law of enjoyment:** Your students know what they want to learn and why. The problem is that they do not know how. A teacher's job is to produce an interesting lesson respecting the maturity level of the students. Note: many reading schemes fail to interest adults.

Reading Approaches Applied to Tasks

Both the text and the reader's motivation dictate **how** he or she will read. As discussed in the section Types of Reading Skills, we skim to get the gist of the passage, scan for specific information, and read intensively for more detailed information. There is also an extensive approach when reading for pleasure or global understanding.

Creating and Using Tasks

Tasks should be kept to two or three in number, and simple language should be used. The students should know the task for each stage in the reading before they start. Allow time for a quick feedback session after the tasks have been completed.

Some examples of tasks:

a) **For preparation (doing this helps build context and activates schemata for the situation present in the text):**
    - Brainstorm on the topic
    - Discuss visuals, headlines, or phrases from the text
    - Predict what will be in the text

b) **For skimming:**
    - Answer questions about gist
    - Identify the main ideas of the text
    - Select the best summary
    - Match the subtitles with the correct paragraph
    - Create titles or headlines for the passage

c) **For scanning:**
    - Answer questions
    - Fill in charts
    - Locate specified elements in the text

d) **For intensive:**
    - Find meaning of vocabulary from context
    - Answer detailed questions
    - Answer inferential questions

Remember: Be sure the questions you assign are not directly taken from the text. Try to rephrase and use different language so students have to really understand and report their own ideas.

A Word on Context

Rarely is there a time when we, as native speakers, approach a written text without any idea of where it came from or what it may contain. Almost always there exists some sort of visual or written clue as to its origin, genre, and content. These clues activate the appropriate schema, through which we interpret the incoming information. Allow your students the same opportunity when presenting them with a reading skills lesson. Any authentic text should (if possible) be kept in its original form, as the color, print type, headline, and even the paper's texture offer appropriate schema-activating information for the reader.

K5 Forty-Five Games to Improve Reading Comprehension

Here are 45 classroom-tested activities that can help you improve your students' reading comprehension.

Emotional Outlet

Ask each student to choose a main character from a story and write a list of feelings or emotions expressed by that character. All items on the list must start with the initial letter of the character's first name. When the students have finished their lists, have them share their choices with class-mates, describing the circumstances in the story that led them to select those words.

Hold Up the Card

Give each student a set of cards on which you have printed the names of the central characters in a particular story—one character per card. Then read some descriptive sentences about these char-acters and their functions in the story. Students are to identify the character being described and hold up the appropriately labeled card.

Quiz Bowl

Divide your class into small groups and have each group present a quiz program based on several dif-ferent stories found in the reading text. The stories should be divided into categories, such as travel, sports, nature, etc. The groups may use additional sources of information, such as almanacs, encyclo-pedias, or travel brochures, to form questions deal-ing with designated categories. Then the groups can take turns presenting their quiz programs, with the rest of the class acting as contestants.

Fishbowl Fun

Have your students write questions about stories they have read on small slips of paper, making sure to include the title of the story and the author's name. Fasten a paper clip to each slip and place them together in a fishbowl. Then make a fishing pole from a pencil, string, and a small magnet. Let the students fish for questions and attempt to answer them orally.

Story Notebooks

Ask each student to keep a small notebook titled Stories I Have Read. After they have read a new story, have them answer the following questions in their notebooks:

a) What is the name of the story?
b) Who wrote it?
c) Who are the main characters?
d) Which character do you like the best?
e) Why do you like this character?
f) What part of the story do you like the best?
g) Why do you like this part?

You might also want the students to illustrate a major scene from each story on the page(s) oppo-site their answers.

Secret Identities

Have each student write a description of a famous character from literature—making sure not to divulge that character's name, for example:

I am brown and furry.
I love honey.
Christopher Robin is my best friend.
Who am I? (Winnie the Pooh)

The students should take turns reading their descriptions aloud while the rest of the class tries to guess the characters' identities.

Story Rolls

Have your students choose their favorite stories and list the main events in sequence. Then let them illustrate the incidents, in order, on long sheets of butcher paper. When the drawings are finished, give each student two cardboard tubes (paper tow-els or aluminum foil rolls work best) and have each student roll his or her illustrations from the first tube to the second, and narrate the story for the rest of the class. A second student may need to assist in the rolling of the illustrations.

How Would You Feel?

You can help your students recognize tone and feeling with this exercise, which is unrelated to any particular story. Start by listing the following questions on the board under the heading "Would you feel sad or glad if … "

a) You could solve a mystery?
b) Your bicycle was stolen?
c) Your kite blew away?

Discuss these questions and the feelings they evoke with your class. Continue the exercise by changing the initial adjectives to playful, serious, calm, nervous, etc.; the questions may have to change as well.

Rewrites

Have students choose the final paragraph of a story they have read recently and use it as the starting point for original stories of their own. Or, you might want them to rewrite the last few paragraphs of a favorite story to give it a different ending. Have the students share their version with classmates, asking them to supply new titles for the rewritten stories.

True or False?

Start by preparing several statements about a particular story—some true and some false. Then give each student two cards: one labeled **true** and the other labeled **false**. As you read each statement aloud, instruct the students to hold up the appropriate card.

Mix-up

Print the major events of a story on paper strips and place the strips in improper order on your board ledge. Ask students to put the strips in the correct order, according to the sequence of events in the story. Repeat the procedure for several different stories.

Recorded Dialogue

Divide the class into pairs and have each pair choose a few paragraphs from a story with a lot of two-person dialogue. They should practice reading the passage orally, and then record their reading. Make sure each pair tapes a summary of the events leading up to the paragraphs of dialogue first. Keep the recordings available for classmates to listen to in their leisure time.

Recall Sessions

Divide the class into small groups and assign each group a different story to read. When everyone has finished reading, ask the students to position themselves in a circle for this comprehension exercise. Lead off by stating the first main event in the story, then ask the student on your left to state the next event, and so on around the circle.

Fortune Cookie Forecasts

Have your students make fortune cookies from construction paper. Now instruct the students to choose books or stories they have recently read as a class and select one main character to focus on for this activity. Based on the actual events of the story, they are to make a prediction that might happen to the chosen character. Let each student put his or her prediction inside a fortune cookie and tape it shut. Place them all together in a large jar. Students are to take turns picking fortune cookies from the jar and guessing which character and story the prediction refers to. As a follow-up activity, you might also want the students to write new endings to the stories, based on the predictions they have chosen.

Why Did It Happen?

Write the following sentences on your board and ask your students to suggest possible reasons for each event. This exercise will help students improve their ability to make inferences and draw conclusions.

- **It was a foggy day and a bird flew into the building.**

- **Mark brought a bowl of hot chicken soup over to his friend's house.**

Rate It

Encourage students to react critically to the stories they read through a numerical rating system. With your guidance, have students establish their own criteria for rating stories, from poor to excellent. Then instruct them to fill in a chart with information about each story they read, including the date, title, main character, main idea, and the numerical rating.

Taping Sessions

Cut out several short stories from discarded basal readers, staple them together, and give one to each student in your class. Ask the students to read and summarize their stories; then let them record these summaries along with three comprehension questions. (Answers to these questions should be printed on an answer key.) Invite students to listen to their classmates' recordings, answer the comprehension questions, and then check their responses against the answer key.

Scrambled Sentences

Help students reinforce sequencing skills with this exercise. Start by writing the following sentences on your board:

- Anita handed the salesperson $10.
- Anita decided to buy a new pair of shoes.
- Anita went to the large store's shoe department.
- The salesperson said the shoes cost $7.
- Anita selected a pair of black shoes.

Have the students number the sentences in their proper order, rewrite them in paragraph or math-problem form, and then compose a comprehension question to accompany it. In this case, the most logical question would be: How much change did Anita receive?

Act It Out

Isolate particular episodes or events from several stories your class has recently read. Describe these events on small slips of paper and put them together in a jar. The students should take turns drawing slips from the jar and acting the events out in charade style. The rest of the class must guess which episode is being acted out and in which story it took place.

Paragraph Swap

Ask the students to write descriptive paragraphs about a character or an event appearing in their reading text. Then divide the class into pairs and have the students read their paragraphs aloud to their partners. The listener must identify the character described and the name of the story in which the character appeared.

Character Predictions

Ask each student to choose a recently read story from the reading text, and to write a sentence predicting a future event in the life of one of its main characters. One by one, have the students identify their characters for the rest of the class and attempt to convey their predictions using gestures only.

Story Mobiles

Have your students make decorative hanging mobiles to illustrate major events in stories from their reading texts. They will need wire coat hangers, string, scissors, crayons, and paste. Have them begin by writing the titles and authors of the stories they have chosen on long strips of tag board. Each student should punch one hole at the top of this strip and fasten it with string to the bottom of the hanger. Next, have the students punch several holes along the bottom of the title strip. From these holes, the students should hang pictures from magazines and newspapers, or original drawings that illustrate major events. These pictures should be mounted on construction paper and hung from the title strip in sequential order. The last hanging piece should be labeled with the student's name.

Problem Solving for Fun

Choose student volunteers to form a panel to discuss the problems that major characters in recently read books or stories encounter. Try the following questions:

a) What major problem did the main character or characters face?

b) How was this problem solved?

c) Would you have done something different to solve the problem?

Key Words

Have students underline the important words in a paragraph. They should then list these words in order of appearance and orally reconstruct the paragraph for classmates.

What Happened Next?

Write the following statements on your board:

• Sarah was riding very fast on her bike. She did not see the hole in the road. What happened next?

• Chuck came home from school early. His head felt hot and his throat hurt. What happened next?

Ask the students to explain what they think happened next, making sure they can defend their answers.

Story Chart

Draw a large chart on your board with the headings Scene, Characters, Location, and Action. Choose a few stories your students have recently read and ask for volunteers to fill in the chart you have drawn. This will reinforce your students' sequencing skills and ability to summarize events.

Favorite Scenes

Have students construct scenes from their favorite books or short stories using *papier mâché,* pieces of fabric, colored construction paper, string, or any other materials that would visually enhance the scene. Then let each student share his or her creation with the rest of the class, making sure to describe the events that led up to, and followed, the chosen scene.

Who Said It?

To help students infer from a sentence more than what is actually stated, write the following sentence on the board: It will cost $400 to paint your house. Ask students who said this—a doctor, painter, or salesperson. After doing this with other, similar sentences (We will be cruising at 35,000 feet—pilot, baker, or engineer?) have students work in teams to construct their own Who Said It? sentences.

Classified Advertisements

Have the students select particular situations from stories in their reading texts and use them as starting points for written classified advertisements. For instance, a story about a man who moves from Alaska to Florida could be the start of an ad selling a used snow blower.

Scrambled Words

Put the following scrambled words on the board: tesak, plpae, and oatomt. Tell students that all three are things we can eat, and ask them to unscramble each word and write its correct spelling (steak, apple, tomato). Then have students write their own scrambled words that belong to a certain category and exchange them with classmates, who will then unscramble them.

Reactions

Make sets of cards with a word expressing a feeling, such as angry, tired, excited, or disappointed on each card. Give each student a set. Then read a short passage in which one or more of the words on the cards would be a correct response. For example: Tony spent many hours building a snowman on the front lawn. When he went inside, a big branch broke and fell on the snowman, smashing it to pieces. Ask students, "How would Tony feel? Hold up the card or cards that tell me." Encourage students to defend their answers.

Absurd Sentences

Read sentences such as the following to students and ask them to tell you which word makes each sentence absurd. Then ask them to tell you what more appropriate word could be substituted.

- The room was hot, so Jim decided to open a football.
- For our vacation, we drove across the country in a wastebasket.
- After the first snowfall, Linda ran outside and started to build a meatball.
- Bill ate a tank of spaghetti.

Hidden Clues

Discuss with students the fact that sometimes we have to analyze sentences to find their hidden clues or facts. Then read the following sentence: Mr. Jefferson took the rake from the cellar and walked out to the lawn. Lead students to infer the fact that the statement describes an incident that happened during the fall. Discuss similar sentences, such as John came in the house and took off his wet raincoat, and which inferences can be made.

Detect the Bias

Explain that a biased sentence will express a personal judgment rather than state an observable fact. Find three advertisements from newspaper or magazines and write these on the board, along with a non-biased sentence (such as It is beginning to rain) and have students indicate which three are biased.

Comic Strips

Collect as many comic strips as you have students in your class, and cut off the last frame in each one. Pass them out to students and have them complete the final frame by drawing a picture of what they think happened, accompanied by an appropriate caption.

Charting New Devices

To give students practice in comparing and contrasting between information they learn from reading with information learned through watching television, select a current topic such as the energy crisis or inflation. First, have students find articles from newspapers dealing with this topic and ask them to summarize the articles in chart form, point by point. Then ask them to watch the evening news broadcast on TV and gather any information heard on the same subject. Have them add this information to what they had already learned in the summary chart. Which source was more comprehensive? Were there any discrepancies?

Creating Situation

Write words expressing feelings or moods, such as jealousy, silliness, fear, etc., on index cards. Divide the class into groups of two or three and have each group pick a card. Each group should then prepare a short play or pantomime which illustrates the specified feeling or mood. Then have the rest of the class guess which feeling was portrayed.

Same or Different?

Explain to the students that sometimes two sentences can have similar meaning. Read the following pairs of sentences and tell students that one pair conveys similar meanings while the other does not.

1. Mrs. Donovan, our teacher, went to Spain last year.
   Mrs. Donovan is Spanish.

2. Louise had a big smile on her face because the dentist told her she had no cavities.
   Louise was happy because she had no cavities.

Ask students to tell you why one sentence pair (the second) conveys a similar meaning while the other does not. Then have each student write two sentences with similar meanings and another two sentences that use some of the same words but have vastly different meanings.

If It Happened

Read sentences such as the following to students and ask them to tell you how they would feel if they were in that particular situation.

1. If I heard a strange sound in the night, I would feel _____ .

2. If I received something I wanted for my birthday, I would feel _____.

3. If I tried and tried to do a new thing and still couldn't, I would feel _____.

Connected Events

Select two or three events from each of four stories the students have read recently. Write these events in mixed order on the board. Then say a story title to the students and ask them to pick the events that took place in that particular story. Repeat this process for the remaining three stories.

What's Missing?

Select three connected major events from a story recently read by the class. Read paragraphs about the first and third event, but not the second. Ask students to tell you the missing event. For example, you might read about Joe's cat climbing a tree and then about Joe happily hugging his cat again. Students would supply the part where the firemen came to rescue the cat.

Irony or Sarcasm?

Discuss the meaning of irony (expecting one thing and getting another) and sarcasm (saying one thing and meaning another). Put the following sentences on the board and ask children which quality each one conveys.

1. The first day Jill was able to go to the beach, it rained. (irony)

2. Thanks for the haircut—I always wanted to look like a monkey. (sarcasm)

3. The man who won the pie-eating contest was the author of a diet book. (irony)

4. Ted sacrificed a visit to the dentist in order to see the new Star Wars movie. (sarcasm)

Sign of the Zodiac

Gather information about horoscopes and discuss the qualities associated with people born under the different signs. Then have students list some of their favorite story characters and choose the sign they think each character was born under, based on the qualities the character displayed in the story. This will help students analyze the characters they read about.

Specific Sentences

Discuss with students the meaning of the term **specific**, then put the following sentences on the board:

1. There were a few children in the room.

2. There were ten children in the room.

Ask students to identify the sentence that is specific and tell why the other is not. Then ask them to orally construct sentences that are non-specific and change them to sentences that are more specific.

Cause and Effect

Explain that usually when something happens there is a cause for it. Put this sentence on the board: After the heavy snowstorm, the roof of the tool shed caved in. Choose a student to come to the board and draw one line under the cause and two lines under the effect. Do the same thing with other sentences to demonstrate cause and effect.

K6 Types of Reading Activities

1. Text

Comprehension Question Activities

A conventional type of reading activity or test consists of a text followed by comprehension questions. In this section, we shall look at some examples of this kind of material.

2. Task

Answering Comprehension Questions

Activity 1: Comprehension Text and Questions

Read the text below and answer the questions that follow.

Yesterday I saw the plagish flester gollining begrutnte h bruck. He seemed very chanderbil, so I did not jorter him, just deapled to him quistly. Perhaps later he will bsand dander, and I will be able to rangel to him.

1. What was the flester doing? Where was he doing this?
2. What sort of flester was he?
3. Why did the writer decide not to jorter him?
4. How did she deaple?
5. What did she hope would happen later?

You perhaps had no difficulty in answering the questions; however, answering the questions did not show that you understood the passage! In other words, you did not read the text successfully, in the sense that each word was understood in the passage. The conclusion is that answering comprehension questions, as such, may not encourage or provide proof of successful reading.

Question: What is it about these questions that makes them answerable, despite the incomprehensibility of the source text? Try to answer before reading on.

The answer, perhaps, is that their vocabulary simply echoes the text, while the grammar of both text and questions is fairly obvious and corresponds neatly, so that if you recognize the grammar context, you can simply slot in the appropriate vocabulary.

Activity 2: Comprehension Text and Questions

Read the text below and answer the questions that follow.

Yesterday I saw the new patient hurrying along the corridor. He seemed very upset, so I did not follow him, just called to him gently. Perhaps he will feel better, and I will be able to talk to him.

1. What is the problem described here?
2. Is this event taking place indoors or outdoors?
3. Did the writer try to get near the patient?
4. What do you think she said when she called to him?
5. What might the job of the writer be?
6. Why do you think she wants to talk to the patient?

Question: Here, the reader would have to understand the content of the passage in order to answer these questions (similar ones would be unanswerable if applied to the previous nonsense text). Can you put your finger on why this is so? In other words, in what ways—apart from the fact that they are in normal English—do these questions differ from those given in the first activity? Try answering before reading on. The questions here are different in that they do not quote verbatim from the text, but rather paraphrase it or request paraphrases. They invite some measure of interpretation and application of the reader's background knowledge. They demand real comprehension and encourage an interactive, personal engagement with the text, as well as being more interesting to answer. Interpretive questions often have more than one possible answer and can be used as a basis for discussion.

However, one disadvantage of the conventional text-plus-questions remains: the reader has no particular motive to read the text in the first place. If you are teaching a class that has a specific curriculum to adhere to, it may be difficult to choose an interesting text for reading. There is always room for extra reading for homework, or for a special Friday lesson.

K7 Reading Passages, Questions, and Answers

Long articles and reading passages are an excellent means to practice all three core reading skills: skimming, scanning, and intensive reading. Longer passages provide much more material for the teacher to work with and can introduce more complex topics for class discussion. As with any material, it is advisable for the teacher to pre-read the article and identify any potentially difficult terms or unfamiliar words.

It is also important to lead up to the article. Introduce the topic and try to warm up the class with some discussion. If there are any pictures accompanying the passage, or if there is a book cover or similar illustration, show these to the class and ask students to predict what the reading will be about. By having a lead-up discussion, you will help the students to activate any relevant vocabulary they already know and get them thinking about the topic.

For the first reading, it is often helpful for the teacher to read the article aloud to the students as they follow along in their books. This will help them to determine the flow of the article and to hear the correct pronunciation of new or unfamiliar words. Once you have read it to them, go around the room having each student read a segment or paragraph. After the class has finished reading the article aloud, ask them to take a few minutes and circle any vocabulary they did not understand. Take these up with the class. Also use this opportunity to explain any words that you think they may not have understood or any words that are used in a different context than the students may have seen before. A key component of any reading class is the introduction and explanation of new vocabulary. Be sure they understand what they have read before you have them proceed to any more in-depth questions.

K8 Article 1: Out to Lunch

A big meal and a long nap is still a way of life in Madrid.
Birds do it. Cats do it. And Spaniards most especially do it—every day, in broad daylight. They nap. Grown adults—executives, teachers, civil servants[1] wink off[2] in the middle of the workday. From 1 or 2:00 to 4:30 or so every afternoon, Spain stops the world for a stroll[3] home, a leisurely meal, and a few z's.[4] Common Market technocrats[5] have informed the Spanish that this is not the way things will
5 get done in a unified Europe.

At a time when productivity is the world's largest religion, the siesta tradition lives on.[6] In Spain, work operates under the command of life,[7] instead of the other way around. No task is so critical that it can't wait a couple of hours while you attend to[8] more important matters like eating, relaxing, or catching up on sleep. When the midday break hits, offices empty[9] and streets clear. Befuddled foreign-
10 ers quickly learn that they have entered a new circadian order.[10]

"At first, I kept looking for things to do in the afternoon, and I just couldn't believe that nothing was open," recalls Pier Roberts, an Oakland writer who lived in Spain for several years. "I walked the streets of Madrid looking for somewhere to go. It was a thousand degrees[11] outside, you could see the heat waves, and it was like a ghost town."[12]

15 Taking a long break in the middle of the day is not only healthier than the conventional lunch, it's apparently more natural. Sleep researchers have found that the Spanish biorhythm[13] may be tuned more closely to our biological clocks.[14] Studies suggest that humans are "biphasic" creatures, requiring days broken up by two periods of sleep instead of one "monophasic" shift. The drowsiness you feel after lunch comes not from the food but from the time of day.

20 "All animals, including humans, have a biological rhythm," explains Claudio Stampi, director of the Chronobiology Research Institute in Newton, Massachusetts. "One is a 24-hour rhythm—we get tired by the end of the day and go to sleep—and there is a secondary peak of sleepiness and a decrease in alertness in the early afternoon. Some people have difficulty remaining awake, doing any sort of task between one and four in the afternoon. For others it's less difficult, but it's there. So there is a biological reason for siestas."

25 Unlike the average lunch break, the siesta is a true break in the action because there is no choice but to come to a full and complete stop. You can't do errands; the shops are closed. You can't make business calls; nobody's at the office. Most people go home for lunch, or get together with family or friends for a glass of wine and nod out[15] afterwards.

The Spanish need their sleep. They've got a long night ahead of them because another key compo-
30 nent[16] of the siesta lifestyle is its nocturnal orbit.[17] After the afternoon work shift, from 4:30 to 8:00 p.m. or so, they may join friends for a drink. Dinner starts at 9:00 or 10:00 p.m., and from there it's out on the town[18] until one or two in the morning.

"It's a bad night in Madrid if you get home before six in the morning," laughs Roberts. The siesta's origins lie in climate and architecture. Like people in other places around the globe that blast furnaces[19]
35 much of the year, Spaniards turned to shade and stillness to avoid incineration[20] in the middle of the day. At night, packed, simmering dwellings drove people into the streets to cool down.

While climate is still a factor, the siesta lifestyle today is driven primarily by the social imperative[21] of Spanish life, which places an equal if not greater emphasis on life outside the office. "We are not so obsessed only with work," says Florentino Sotomayor of the Spanish Tourist Board. "We take a break
40 and have the opportunity of having coffee or beer with friends and thinking and talking about different issues, not only work."

1 government employees
2 go to sleep
3 a leisurely walk
4 a nap; a short sleep
5 government experts in science and technology
6 continues
7 working is less important than living
8 take care of; do
9 everyone leaves their office
10 a new way of organizing sleep and awake patterns

11 extremely hot
12 an empty town; a town without people
13 rhythm of life
14 natural body rhythms
15 go to sleep
16 important part
17 nighttime activity
18 having fun in town
19 very hot places
20 burning up
21 society's demands

After You Read

Understanding the Text

A) Multiple choice questions. For each item below, circle the answer that best completes each statement.

1. The main idea of this article is that _____.
    a) people everywhere should take naps
    b) napping is an important tradition in Spain
    c) it is important to have traditions
    d) the nightlife is exciting in Spain

2. During the midday break in Spain, people _____.
    a) go home for lunch
    b) do errands
    c) make business calls
    d) go shopping

3. The main idea of the fourth paragraph (lines 15–19) is that _____.
    a) the conventional lunch break is natural and healthy
    b) all animals have biological clocks
    c) food makes you feel drowsy
    d) it is natural for humans to nap

4. A biphasic creature needs _____.
    a) two sleep periods a day
    b) eight hours of sleep a day
    c) two days of sleep
    d) a long night of sleep

5. You can infer from the article that some businesspeople in other European countries _____.
    a) hope the siesta tradition will be introduced in their countries
    b) think the siesta tradition is impractical
    c) think that the siesta tradition will grow in popularity
    d) do not agree that napping is good for you

6. The overall tone of this article is _____.
    a) serious and academic
    b) light and silly
    c) light and informative
    d) scientific and technical

B) Consider the issues. Work with a partner to answer the questions below.

1. In line 6, the writer claims that "productivity is the world's largest religion." What do you think he means by this? Do you agree? Why or why not?

2. Each of the statements below is an exaggeration of the truth. Why do you think the author exaggerates the truth in these cases?
    *   "It was a thousand degrees outside ... "
    *   "It's a bad night in Madrid if you get home before six in the morning."

3. What do you think are the advantages and disadvantages of the siesta tradition? Add them to the chart below. Then decide if you think siestas are a good idea or not.

Advantages	Disadvantages
You have more time to spend with your family	

Building Reading Skills

Recognizing Supporting Details

Writers usually provide details and examples to support their ideas and opinions. Recognizing these supporting details will help you understand the writer's ideas.

Look back at the reading passage above and find at least one detail that supports each of the ideas below.

Important Ideas	Supporting Details
1. For the Spanish, life is as important—sometimes more important—than work.	1. Going home for lunch is the norm.
2. The siesta is healthier and more natural than the average lunch break.	2.
3. Nightlife is an important part of Spanish social life.	3.

Building Vocabulary

Word forms

When you learn a new word, it is useful to learn other forms of the same word. You can find these forms in a dictionary.

A) Complete the chart on the next page by adding the missing word forms. Then check your ideas by looking in a dictionary.

Noun	Adjective
1. productivity	
2. drowsiness	
3.	leisurely
4. tradition	
5.	biological
6. difficulty	

B) Choose words from the chart in Exercise A to complete the following sentences.

1. Some researchers think that people would be more _____ if they took a nap during the day.

2. Hot weather can make you _____.

3. Family life and _____ time are more important for many Spaniards than work.

4. A _____ lunch in Spain is long, relaxing, and delicious.

5. A reason for the siesta can be found in the science of _____.

6. It is _____ for many people to believe that in some countries, stores and businesses close for several hours during the middle of the day.

Language Focus
It is + adjective + infinitive

We often use it is + adjective + infinitive to give an opinion:

• Some people say it is healthy to take a nap in the afternoon.
• It is fun to go out on the town at night.
• It is hard for me to get up early in the morning.

A) What's your opinion? Add an adjective to each sentence below to state your opinion.

1. It is _____ to go home for lunch.

2. I think it is _____ to take a nap in the afternoon.

3. In my opinion, it is _____ to stay out until six in the morning.

4. I would say that it is _____ to eat a big meal in the middle of the day.

5. In my country, it is _____ for people to leave work for the afternoon.

B) Complete these sentences with your own ideas. Then share your ideas with a partner.

1. Today it is common for young people to _____.

2. I think it is easy to_____.

K

3. If you want to learn a language, it is important to _____.

4. In my opinion it is fun to_____.

5. I believe that it is wrong to_____.

Discussion and Writing

A) Group work. Your traditions give information about your values, or what you believe is important. What do you think these traditions say about values?

• In Spain, it is a tradition to take a long lunch break so you can have a leisurely lunch with your family and take a nap.

• In Japan, it is a custom to take your shoes off before you enter a house.

• In the United States and other countries, it is a tradition for men to give women flowers on birthdays, anniversaries, and other special occasions.

B) Work with several classmates to answer the questions below. Then share your group's answers with the class.

1. What is one of your culture's most important traditions? What does it say about your culture's values?

2. What is one of your favorite holiday traditions? Why do you like it?

3. What do these two quotations mean to you?

> A tradition without intelligence is not worth having.
>
> —T.S. Eliot (1888–1965)

> Tradition is a guide and not a jailer.
>
> —W. Somerset Maugham (1874–1965)

Crossword Puzzle

Use words from the reading to complete the crossword puzzle.

Across:

4 Water freezes at zero _____ Celsius. (line 13)

5 If you are _____ with something, you think about it all the time. (line 39)

7 _____, our; his, their

10 A _____ lunch break lasts about an hour. (line 15)

11 When you take a _____, you stop doing whatever you were doing.

12 Another word for sleepiness is _____. (line 18)

13 The opposite of old is _____.

14 In Spain, there are more hours of _____ in the summer than in the winter. (line 1)

16 The opposite of go is _____.

Down:

1 _____ means not rushed or hurried. (line 3)

2 The past tense of feed is _____.

3 hot, warm, _____, cold

6 A _____ town is completely empty. (line 14)

7 The _____ break in Spain is called the siesta. (line 9)

8 A _____ animal is active at night. (line 30)

9 For most people there is a decrease in _____ in the early afternoon. (line 22)

15 The opposite of out is _____.

Answer Key

After You Read

Understanding the Text

A)

1. The main idea of this article is that _____.
   b) napping is an important tradition in Spain

2. During the midday break in Spain, people _____.
   a) go home for lunch

3. The main idea of the fourth paragraph (lines 15–19) is that _____.
   d) it's natural for humans to nap

4. A biphasic creature needs _____.
   a) two sleep periods a day

5. You can infer from the article that some businesspeople in other European countries _____.
   b) think the siesta tradition is impractical

6. The overall tone of this article is _____.
   c) light and informative

B)

1. In line 8, the writer claims that "productivity is the world's largest religion." What do you think he means by this? Do you agree? Why or why not?

This means that the main focus of many people today is work; they will work long hours at the expense of other things, such as sleeping.

2. Each of the statements below is an exaggeration of the truth. Why do you think the author exaggerates the truth in these cases?

    •   "It was a thousand degrees outside … "

The author wants to emphasize the fact that it felt extremely hot, and the actual temperature would not convey just how oppressive the heat was.

    •   "It's a bad night in Madrid if you get home before six in the morning."

The author is trying to explain that Spaniards tend to stay out later than North Americans, and this is made clearer by exaggerating.

3. What do you think are the advantages and disadvantages of the siesta tradition? Add them to the chart below. Then decide if you think siestas are a good idea or not.

Answers will vary.

Building Reading Skills

Recognizing Supporting Details

Important Ideas	Supporting Details
1. For the Spanish, life is as important—sometimes more important—than work.	1. Going home for lunch is the norm.
2. The siesta is healthier and more natural than the average lunch break.	2. Humans are biphasic creatures, requiring days broken up by two periods of sleep instead of one monophasic shift.
3. Nightlife is an important part of Spanish social life.	3. After the afternoon work shift, they may join friends for a drink. Dinner starts at 9 or 10 p.m., and from there it's out on the town until one or two in the morning.

Building Vocabulary

Word forms

A)

Noun	Adjective
1. productivity	productive
2. drowsiness	drowsy
3. leisure	leisurely
4. tradition	traditional
5. biology	biological
6. difficulty	difficult

B)

1. Some researchers think that people would be more productive if they took a nap during the day.

2. Hot weather can make you drowsy.

3. Family life and leisure time are more important for many Spaniards than work.

4. A traditional lunch in Spain is long, relaxing, and delicious.

5. A reason for the siesta can be found in the science of biology.

6. It is difficult for many people to believe that in some countries, stores and businesses close for several hours during the middle of the day.

Language Focus
A) Answers will vary.
B) Answers will vary.

Discussion and Writing
A) Answers will vary.
B) Answers will vary.

K

Crossword Puzzle

Across:

4 Water freezes at zero <u>degrees</u> Celsius. (line 13)

5 If you are <u>obsessed</u> with something, you think about it all the time. (line 39)

7 <u>my</u>, our; his, their

10 A <u>conventional</u> lunch break lasts about an hour. (line 15)

11 When you take a <u>break</u>, you stop doing whatever you were doing.

12 Another word for sleepiness is <u>drowsiness</u>. (line 18)

13 The opposite of old is <u>new</u>.

14 In Spain, there are more hours of <u>daylight</u> in the summer than in the winter. (line 1)

16 The opposite of go is <u>stop</u>.

Down:

1 <u>Leisurely</u> means not rushed or hurried. (line 3)

2 The past tense of feed is <u>fed</u>.

3 hot, warm, <u>cool</u>, cold

6 A <u>ghost</u> town is completely empty. (line 14)

7 The <u>midday</u> break in Spain is called the siesta. (line 9)

8 A <u>nocturnal</u> animal is active at night. (line 30)

9 For most people there is a decrease in <u>alertness</u> in the early afternoon. (line 22)

15 The opposite of out is <u>in</u>.

K9 Article 2: Profits with Principles

An entrepreneur is a person who owns and runs a business. Entrepreneurs develop creative, new ideas and bring them to the marketplace. Anita Roddick was a successful entrepreneur who founded The Body Shop, a company that sells naturally based products for skin and hair. This company is the subject of the article that follows.

Pre-reading Questions

1. Do you know any successful entrepreneurs? Describe them to your classmates.
2. What qualities do you think make someone a successful entrepreneur? Make a list of those qualities. Share your list with your classmates.

Profits with Principles

Anita Roddick, founder of The Body Shop, was trained as a schoolteacher. She did not know anything about the cosmetics industry when she opened her first small shop in Brighton, England, in 1976. But she had good ideas, and people liked her products. Her business grew quickly. Because of her energy, determination, and vision, Anita Roddick became an international success story. At one time, she was one of the richest women in England. Today, there are over 2,000 branches of The Body Shop in 54 countries around the world.

The Body Shop manufactures and sells hundreds of naturally based products. Anita learned how people from traditional cultures use plants and herbs from their environment to take care of their bodies. In Sri Lanka, for example, she learned that women rub fresh pineapple on their skin to make it softer and smoother. With that knowledge she created a face product using pineapple. In Polynesia, she learned about many of the uses of cocoa butter. It makes the skin softer and the hair shinier. Cocoa Butter Hand and Body Lotion is one of The Body Shop's best-selling products.

The Body Shop does not believe in profits without principles. Respect for the environment is one of The Body Shop's most basic principles. The company uses as little packaging as possible to conserve natural resources and reduce waste. Customers are encouraged to bring their old containers to the shop to refill them. If they do this, they get a discount on their next purchase. The Body Shop is also strongly opposed to animal testing in the cosmetics industry. It never tests its products or ingredients on animals.

Helping communities in need is another principle. Anita encouraged all employees to do volunteer work with local groups. She gave employees four hours off each month to do their community work. Some projects included working with homeless people and AIDS victims. She also provided educational programs for her staff and customers. The Body Shop set up trade partnerships with communities in need around the world. Under Anita Roddick, "Trade Not Aid" was a cornerstone of the company. For example, The Body Shop made an agreement with the Kayapo Indians, who harvest Brazil nuts in the Amazon rainforest. The Body Shop used these nuts in one of its products, Brazil Oil Conditioner for hair. The agreement had several goals. One was to protect the plants the Kayapo Indians harvested from the rain forest. Another goal was to make sure that the Kayapo got the economic benefits from any commercial development in their area. Similar agreements were made with communities in India, Mexico, Nepal, Tanzania, and Zambia.

Although some of Anita Roddick's ideas for The Body Shop seemed unusual for the business world, she must have done something right. When L'Oréal purchased the Body Shop in 2006, it was a £652.3 million (967.2 million USD) deal, reportedly earning Anita £130 million (192.7 million USD).

After You Read

How Well Did You Read?

Read the following statements. If the statement is true, write the letter **T** on the line. If it is false, write the letter **F**.

_____ 1. Anita Roddick studied business in school.

_____ 2. The Body Shop is a very successful business.

_____ 3. Many of the ideas for The Body Shop's products come from traditional cultures around the world.

_____ 4. The philosophy of The Body Shop is similar to the philosophies of most other cosmetic companies.

_____ 5. One of The Body Shop's most important principles is respecting the environment.

Building Reading Skills

Scanning for Details

Read the following questions about The Body Shop. Then scan the article to find the answers. Work as quickly as possible. Do not read every word in the article. As soon as you find the answer to a question, move on to the next one.

1. When did the first Body Shop open?

2. How many branches of The Body Shop are there in the world today?

3. How many countries have branches of The Body Shop?

4. Where did Anita learn about the uses of cocoa butter?

5. Where do the Kayapo Indians live?

6. How much money did L'Oréal purchase the Body Shop for in 2006?

Discussion

1. Why do you think The Body Shop has become so successful?

2. How did Anita Roddick get ideas for The Body Shop's products? Do you think this is a good way? Why or why not?

3. How was Anita's philosophy for The Body Shop different from that of most other cosmetics companies? Do you agree with The Body Shop's philosophy? Why or why not?

4. In what ways did Anita show respect and concern for the environment?

5. What types of things did Anita do to help communities in need?

6. What do you think "Trade Not Aid" means?

K

Building Vocabulary

Circle the letter of the word that best completes each sentence.

1. The Body Shop is part of the _____ industry.
   a) traditional
   b) cosmetics
   c) environment

2. The company tries to _____ natural resources by using as little packaging as possible.
   a) conserve
   b) spend
   c) oppose

3. Many of the _____ for The Body Shop's products come from different countries around the world.
   a) goals
   b) cultures
   c) ingredients

4. The Body Shop _____ hundreds of skin and hair products.
   a) manufactures
   b) buys
   c) protects

5. The Body Shop _____ the use of animals for testing in the cosmetics industry.
   a) trains
   b) opposes
   c) believes in

6. Many of The Body Shop's employees do _____ work in their communities.
   a) commercial
   b) traditional
   c) volunteer

7. When customers bring in their old _____ to the shop for refills, they get a discount.
   a) products
   b) containers
   c) cosmetics

8. One goal of The Body Shop's trade partnerships was to _____ the Amazon rainforest.
   a) oppose
   b) manufacture
   c) protect

Answer Key—After You Read

How Well Did You Read?

__F__ 1. Anita Roddick studied business in school.

__T__ 2. The Body Shop is a very successful business.

__T__ 3. Many of the ideas for The Body Shop's products come from traditional cultures around the world.

__F__ 4. The philosophy of The Body Shop is similar to the philosophies of most other cosmetic companies.

__T__ 5. One of The Body Shop's most important principles is respecting the environment.

Building Reading Skills

Scanning for Details

1. When did the first Body Shop open?
   1976

2. How many branches of The Body Shop are there in the world today?
   Over 2,000

3. How many countries have branches of The Body Shop?
   54

4. Where did Anita learn about the uses of cocoa butter?
   Polynesia

5. Where do the Kayapo Indians live?
   Brazil

6. How much money did L'Oréal purchase the Body Shop for in 2006?
   £652.3 million/ $967.2 million

Discussion

1. Why do you think The Body Shop has become so successful?
   Answers will vary.

2. How did Anita Roddick get ideas for The Body Shop's products? Do you think this is a good way? Why or why not?
   Anita learned how people from traditional cultures use plants and herbs from their environment to take care of their bodies.

K

3. How was Anita's philosophy for The Body Shop different from that of most other cosmetics companies? Do you agree with The Body Shop's philosophy? Why or why not?

She focused on respecting the environment, she opposed testing on animals, and she gave her employees time off to volunteer in the community.

4. In what ways did Anita show respect and concern for the environment?

The company uses as little packaging as possible and encourages customers to refill their used containers for a discount.

5. What types of things did Anita do to help communities in need?

Anita encouraged her employees to volunteer in the community, provided educational programs for her staff and customers, and set up trade partnerships with communities in need around the world.

6. What do you think "Trade Not Aid" means?

This refers to establishing meaningful and sustainable trade partnerships with communities in need, rather than giving them money or other forms of assistance which will be depleted over time and leave the communities in need once again.

Building Vocabulary

1. The Body Shop is part of the _____ industry.
   b) cosmetics

2. The company tries to _____ natural resources by using as little packaging as possible.
   a) conserve

3. Many of the _____ for The Body Shop's products come from different countries around the world.
   c) ingredients

4. The Body Shop _____ hundreds of skin and hair products.
   a) manufactures

5. The Body Shop _____ the use of animals for testing in the cosmetics industry.
   b) opposes

6. Many of The Body Shop's employees do _____ work in their communities.
   c) volunteer

7. When customers bring in their old _____ to the shop for refills, they get a discount.
   b) containers

8. One goal of The Body Shop's trade partnerships was to _____ the Amazon rainforest.
   c) protect

K10 Using Newspapers in the ESL Classroom

Newspapers can be very inexpensive and compelling texts for literacy development. The newspaper provides an introduction to the political, social, and business aspects of the local community. The newspaper can assist in finding a job, buying a car, being made aware of sales, and choosing local entertainment. Incorporating newspapers into an ESL classroom offers the teacher authentic, practical, and easily accessible materials.

Newspaper Activities for Beginner Students

- Have students cut out pictures of items they like in the newspaper and then write sentences about the pictures.
- Read a few scores from the sports page and have students write them down.
- Find numbers in newspaper advertisements that deal with money and have students practice reading the prices aloud.
- Using pictures found in the newspaper, have students write sentences about the pictures using prepositions to describe the spatial relationships. (For example, "The man is standing **in front of** the house.")
- Discuss an issue found in an editorial that may be pertinent to students' lives.

Newspaper Activities for Intermediate Students

- Have students circle words they do not understand and ask them to try to figure out the meaning from the context or look up the definition in the dictionary.
- Cut out headlines from various articles and have students match the headlines with the appropriate stories.
- Cut photo captions from photographs and have students match the captions with the appropriate photos.
- Analyze advertisements to discuss the way prices vary from store to store. Students may report their findings by writing a paragraph.
- Collect newspaper photographs of people and have students make up stories about the people.

Newspaper Activities for Advanced Students

- Cut out several photographs of people and have students write descriptions of the people; let other students match the photographs with the corresponding descriptions.
- Work as a group to write a letter to the editor; more advanced students might write letters on their own.
- Follow a news item over a period of time and discuss the events that occur.
- Have students read an article that describes a problem and discuss the causes and effects of the problem.
- Have students work in pairs, interviewing each other about an article in the newspaper.

K11 Writing a Newspaper

Having your students create their own newspaper can be a challenging, yet a rewarding activity. They will be able to use specialized vocabulary and explore their more creative sides. The times given for each segment of the lesson are only approximate and, depending on the level of your class and the time available, can be expanded significantly.

The Pre-reading Activity: First 20 Minutes

After welcoming the students to the class, ask them if they read newspapers. This can be followed by a general discussion of the reasons for reading newspapers and how reading newspapers in English can be of benefit. Depending on their level, the students will negotiate English in different ways including using pocket dictionaries, writing down words, talking to their neighbors, and seeking clarification from the teacher. Possible reasons given for reading newspapers may be as follows:

• to keep up on current events
• to learn new words
• to learn new uses for old words
• to see difficult or unfamiliar words in context
• to improve reading and writing

The next step is to elicit from the class what topics and/or news are generally found in newspapers and list the responses on the board.

The Writing Activity: 30 Minutes

The class will write an English-language newspaper about their country or city. Put the students into groups and assign each group a section of the newspaper. The students will then collaborate on creating an article (or articles, depending on the size of the groups) for their section of the paper.

During the activity, urge the more proficient members of the group to encourage the less proficient ones to speak and help them to write their contribution. Go around the room and answer the various questions students might have.

Write the following instructions/reminders on the board:
• Consider the language (words, terms, and phrases) you typically see in a newspaper
• Look at the list of topics on the board
• Think of any interesting news about your country or city
• Think about advertising; something made in your country or some place of interest to tourists

Reading Aloud: 30 Minutes

Ask each group to read its newspaper section aloud. The students will find it easier to read their own contributions than the features written by others. Some of the groups may not have completed the task, but have them read what they have anyway.

Learning Outcomes

The results of these activities will vary depending on the language level of the students. Some groups may develop news items that focus on studies in their country, influenced by an education supplement they may have read. Other more organized groups may include news on a wider range of topics within their section, including advertising, editorials, and maybe even cartoons!

Newspapers can allow students to go beyond personal experiences by using the article, advertisement, and opinion formats as a source of ideas and language.

K12 Teaching the Class Novel

Below you will find suggested approaches to teaching the class novel.

Before you begin reading:

- Carry out prediction activities based on the cover, a blurb, or the title
- Use a picture(s) for a discussion of key ideas or themes in the novel
- Present theme-based scenario cards based on the key issues in the novel, e.g., What would you do if? or What advice would you give?

During reading:

- Create a mind map to collect details on a key character or theme; a more complex version of this for proficient students could show the links between characters or themes
- Set up a role description on the wall for a key character; keep adding notes as the novel progresses
- Create a flowchart of the plot; a more complex version could be used for multiple narratives
- Develop a tension graph by plotting key events in the novel against a scale (could be decided by the students) that measures tension, fear, self-esteem, etc.
- Make a family tree
- Carry out a hot-seating activity of characters at important points in the novel
- Do a glossary activity: collate words (with a particular focus, e.g., slang) as a class and find the definitions and keep this list on display during the unit
- Perform a role-play or freeze-frame activity of a key event; you might want to incorporate a hot-seating activity to reveal a character's motivation or feelings
- Rewrite an extract in a different form, or from a different viewpoint
- Keep a reading journal
- Execute a sequencing activity by cutting up a section of copies of the text which students then have to arrange in the correct order, focusing on the layout and structure of the text (paragraphs/connectives); students then give reasons why they chose that order
- Carry out close textual analysis which involves shared reading using a projector and teacher annotation; students then carry out their own text marking activities using a highlighter or scanning for a particular focus, e.g., verbs
- Do cloze activities or reverse cloze activities

After you have finished reading the novel:

- Make a ripple chart of the impact of a key character
- Do a You're the Witness role-play
- Do a quote search; provide quotes and students speculate who said it, when the character did it, and then find the answer
- Create a title for each chapter
- Summarize the plot/storyboard
- Cast the film of the novel
- Have a class debate; provide provocative statements about characters, events, and/or themes

Generic Starter or Recap Activities

Many of the following activities can be used as a starter activity to reinforce or revisit learning:
- Create mind maps or roles on the wall
- Add the theme just learned to the mind map using five key words
- Use your mind map to prepare two points on the characters that are important to the theme
- Prepare a sticky note to add to the role on the wall
- Do a card sort
- Rank or sort the characters or themes in answer to a question or statement about the novel
- Perform a statement and evidence/quote search
- Provide students with a list of statements to sort into true or false, or to rank; students then have to find evidence in the novel to support their judgment
- Provide students with a list of quotes to sort into true or false, or to rank; students then have to find evidence in the novel to support their answers

SECTION L
Teaching Writing

Content

L1 How to Help Students Develop Their Writing Skills

When you teach writing, you can use a genre-based writing approach or a process writing approach. Genre-based writing relates to a particular text type (e.g., a thank-you letter, a business report, or an article). Process writing focuses on the stages a writer goes through to produce text: brainstorming ideas, writing a draft, and editing.

Genre-Based Writing

When you teach students how to write a particular type of text, you can give them activities to practice accuracy, give them guidance in what to say and how to say it, or allow them to write completely freely. These three different types of activity can help students with their writing questions in different ways.

Accuracy Activities

Accuracy activities involve a range of writing exercises such as gap fill, reordering sentences, combining sentences with appropriate linking words, matching topic sentences and paragraphs, or rewriting texts. These exercises can help students develop the skills of linking ideas between sentences (cohesion), choosing suitable language (appropriacy), and organizing the structure of the text as a whole (coherence), as well as improving grammatical accuracy. The following exercise practices both coherence and cohesion.

 Reorder the following sentences to make the story clearer. Then combine some sentences to link the ideas. Use the words **and**, **so**, **as**.
Are there any other changes you need to make to avoid repeating words?

A dog stole a piece of meat. He wanted to eat it at home. He had to cross a river. He started to carry the meat home in his mouth. He went onto the bridge. He looked down into the water. He saw another dog in the river. The dog had a piece of meat. He wanted that piece of meat too. He opened his mouth. His piece of meat fell into the river. He tried to bite the dog. He went home with no meat.

The corrected version:

A dog stole a piece of meat. He wanted to eat it at home so he started to carry the meat home in his mouth. He had to cross a river and as he went onto the bridge he looked down into the water and saw another dog in the river, who had a piece of meat. He wanted that piece of meat too so he opened his mouth to bite the dog. His meat fell into the river, and so he went home with no meat.

Guided Writing

Guided writing involves giving students some help with the questions What have I got to say? and How can I organize my ideas? (coherence). You can do this by:

- presenting a series of pictures that tell a story and asking the students to write the story
- providing outline notes or key words
- handing out a model text so that students can see an example of the kind of writing they are expected to produce and use it as a pattern for their own text. You can help them by pointing out language that is commonly used in that type of text

Free Writing

Free writing is the most difficult task for students. A task like Write a story for homework or Write a letter to a newspaper gives them no help with any of their writing questions. However, there are some ways we can help them with free writing, while still leaving them the choice of what they write and how they express and structure their writing.

a) Provide a stimulus

- We can help them with the question of what to write by providing a stimulus. Pictures, music, and realia can help to stimulate the students' imagination. For example, pictures of people could provide inspiration for a character description; listening to a piece of music could inspire a story or a poem; and a collection of objects (such as a train ticket, a love letter, a ring, and a photo) could inspire a story.
- Listening or reading input before the writing activity can provide the students with ideas. For example, listening to a news broadcast could provide them with ideas for writing a newspaper article, or reading a letter from a magazine's advice column could provide a stimulus for writing a letter of advice.
- Holding a class or group discussion or a role play can help students develop ideas and rehearse them in speaking before they write them down. For example, a group discussion on climate change could generate ideas for an essay, or a role-play on a public meeting about plans for a new stadium could provide ideas for Letters to the Editor.

b) Work together

Cooperative writing where students brainstorm ideas together, or write in pairs or groups, can also help to generate ideas on the principle that sharing an idea can help to generate more ideas (two heads are better than one!).

c) Interactive writing activities

We can help students with the questions of Why am I writing? and Who am I writing to? by using interactive writing activities. Students can write letters which are then delivered by the teacher to another student, who writes a reply. You can then use the texts the students have written as a reading task. Making the writing activity into a game like this gives the students a sense of audience and a purpose.

Process Writing

Another way of helping students to express their ideas and organize them logically is through process writing. This means dividing the writing activity into several stages. Each stage practices a sub-skill important in the writing process. Below are examples of ways to practice sub-skills in process writing.

- brainstorm ideas about what to write
- choose ideas and group them under headings
- order the ideas and plan the structure, e.g., introduction, arguments for, arguments against, conclusion
- write rough notes to expand each idea
- write a rough version or draft
- pass it to another student for feedback
- edit: read through, rewrite, and correct

Correction and feedback

Looking at students' written work gives you an opportunity to assess their progress and to give them helpful feedback on their errors. However, be careful how you correct as it can be very discouraging to a student when a piece of work comes back covered in red ink. You will have to decide which errors are the most important, and mark these only. It is also valuable to the student to have to think out what the mistake was and correct it him or herself. For these reasons, it is useful to have a correction code. Underline the place where the error occurs and put a note or symbol in the margin saying what kind of error it is, e.g., a mistake in verb tense or a spelling mistake. Some commonly used symbols in correction codes are listed in the chart below.

T	tense
Pr	preposition
S	spelling
WO	word order
WF	word form (e.g., using a noun instead of a verb, as in **we have to analysis this)**
WW	wrong word or expression
A	article
Ag	agreement (e.g., subject and verb do not agree, as in **he go to town)**
P	punctuation
/	missing word

L2 Proofreaders' Marks

Below are some common proofreaders' marks that you may wish to use when correcting students' writing. You do not have to use these particular symbols, but they are some of the most common. Whatever symbols you use, be sure to teach them to your students so they understand what each means (even photocopy the list and give it as a handout on the first day of class), and most important of all, be consistent! The idea behind using symbols for proofreading is that you can quickly identify errors and your students can just as quickly see what they have done wrong. If the symbols are constantly changing, the whole purpose is defeated. Pick the method for marking that works best for you and stick with it.

Instruction	Marginal mark	Appearance in text
GENERAL		
Delete	ℓ	The dog is barking
Close up space	◡	The dog is ba rking
Delete and close up space	ℓ̃	The dog is barking
Let it stand; disregard change or deletion	stet	The naughty dog is barking
Insert letter or word	is	The dog barking
Substitute letter or word	ght	The dog is barking tonite
Insert space	#	the barkingdog
Insert hair space	hr#	the barking dog
Equalize word spacing	eq#	The dog is barking
Fix spacing on a loose line	fix#	The /dog /is /barking
Insert/indent one en space	⊡	⊡the barking dog
Insert/indent one em space	☐	☐the barking dog
Spell out	sp	I hear 2 dogs barking
New paragraph	¶	The dogs stopped barking. Later that night...
No new paragraph (run on)	no¶ run on	Two dogs were barking. I found it hard to sleep
New line	new line	The noisy dogs barked from 2:00 am until dawn
Transpose letters or words	tr	the dog barking
Move left	⊏	the dog was barking
Move right	⊐	the dog was barking
Flush left	fl	Population Figures (1996) Kamloops 76,394
Flush right	fr	Kelowna 89,442
Center	⊐⊏	The Barking Dog
Move up	⏜	the barking dog
Move down	⏝	the barking dog

L

Instruction	Marginal mark	Appearance in text
Align vertically	(align)	‖the barking ‖dog
Align horizontally	(align)	the dog barking

PUNCTUATION

Instruction	Marginal mark	Appearance in text
Insert period	⊙	The dog was barking
Insert question mark	?	Which dog was barking
Insert comma	⌃	The big scary, noisy dog was barking
Insert exclamation mark	!	Watch out for the scary dog
Insert semicolon	⌃;	The dog was barking was it ever loud!
Insert colon	⊙	I told you why I couldn't sleep that dog barked all night.
Insert apostrophe	⌄	the dogs favorite toy
Insert single/double quotation marks	⌄/⌄⌄	She said, I'm reading a story called The Green Canoe.
Insert hyphen	⹀	the game winning goal
Insert en dash	⫯N	Andrew Jackson (1767 1845)
Insert em dash	⫯M //	The third and most exciting game ended in a tie.
Insert parentheses	⟨/⟩	It weighs nearly 20 kg or 44 lbs

TYPOGRAPHIC STYLE

Instruction	Marginal mark	Appearance in text
Set in capital letters	(cap)	Have you seen rebecca today?
Set in lower case	(lc) //	I THINK she's with Emma.
Wrong font	(wf)	They went to the zoo.
Set in roman type	(rom)	But I love the zoo.
Set in italics	(ital)	I enjoy the dolce far niente atmosphere of the zoo
Set in light type	(lf)	I had to stay home with the baby
Set in bold type	(bf)	Pas, The see The Pas
Set in bold italic type	(bold ital)	A Study of Milton's Paradise Lost
Set in small caps	(SC) //	Ovid (43 BC-AD 17)
Set in subscript	⌃2	H2O
Set in superscript	⌄2	a^2 + b^2 = c2

L3 The Stages of a Writing Lesson

Before

Lead-in: In this stage, it is important to stimulate the students' interest and provide them with ideas. You can do this by beginning with a short listening or reading text, or a discussion on the topic they are going to write about. In the case of imaginative writing, you can begin with a stimulus, like pictures, music, or realia.

Language focus: You may wish to focus on some structures, vocabulary, or linking words that will be useful to the students as they write. If you have used a listening or reading text in the lead-in, you can take examples from this. If you are using a model text in a genre-based lesson, you can point out the way it is structured and elicit some useful language. If you are doing process writing you might like to do the language focus later in the lesson—perhaps after the students have done the first draft.

During

Writing task: Set the writing task or tasks. You may be doing a series of tasks, starting with accuracy exercises and progressing through guided to free writing, or you may be doing a series of sub-skills tasks in a process writing lesson. Circulate while the students are writing to offer help and check their work.

After

Transfer: You can use the texts that students have written as reading texts for other students to read, with a simple comprehension task.

Language focus: Collect students' texts and correct them using a correction code as above.

L4 Selecting Writing Tasks

The writing activities you choose should be interesting and motivating. Students will obviously be more motivated and have more ideas if the task engages their interest or seems relevant to their lives. The activities should also be appropriate to the students' level and ages.

Beginner and intermediate students will be able to write texts such as short passages about themselves, simple descriptions of people, an account of their daily routines, etc. As students progress, you can add a range of writing tasks from simple stories, different types of letters, diaries, newspaper articles, advertisements, simple poems, dialogues and plays, through to formal essays and reports.

Young students will enjoy writing simple stories. A group of newly arrived migrants will need writing related to their everyday lives such as form-filling, job applications, CVs, etc. Some groups may have specialized interests. A group of businessmen and women, for example, will need to learn to write business letters, emails, and reports. Students preparing to study abroad will need to practice academic essays.

If you have a general group, you can provide a range and variety of kinds of writing, including imaginative and creative writing like stories and poems, as well as more real-life writing like letters and emails. Imaginative writing can be a lot of fun for students and the sense of satisfaction and pride and creative buzz that comes from writing a simple story or poem in English will increase students' confidence and self-esteem.

L5 Sample Lessons: Focus on Writing

	Sample Lesson 1	Sample Lesson 2
Type of activity	Genre-based writing: guided for accuracy	Process writing: free
Lead-in	Using students' experience of giving and receiving presents to talk around the topic	Using realia to introduce the idea of an object having a history
Stimulus	Reading short notes and thank-you letters	Listening to a story, bag of realia
Task	Write a short message and a thank-you letter	Writing a story
Language focus	Letter-writing conventions Structure of a thank-you letter	Linking words for narrative Past passives
Transfer	Students' letters and replies become a Read-and-Complete task	Students' stories become a Listen-and-Guess task

L6 Writing a Children's Story

Work with a partner to write a short children's story of your own creation that includes an important life lesson. Your classmates will read your story and try to identify the life lesson.

Choose one of the following beginnings to your story:

1. Zoe and Peter Perfect had a perfect life. Zoe Perfect was beautiful, the perfect wife and mother, and a good friend to all. Peter Perfect was strong and handsome, a wonderful husband and father, and a leader in his community. Zoe and Peter were perfect in every way. The Perfects also had two perfect children: Ana and Stefan. Ana and Stefan honored their parents, studied hard at school, never fought, and always kept their rooms tidy. But then something unusual happened.

2. Once upon a time, in the land of Titanbury, there lived three ugly sisters and an ugly brother with their parents. The girls' names were Hurly, Burly, and Curly and the brother's name was Fluff. Other children in the land made fun of how the siblings looked. The children, however, did not know they were ugly because their parents always told them they were beautiful.

3. This is a story about two neighboring towns: Grosville and Kleinville. The people of Grosville were all very, very big. In fact, everything in Grosville was big. The people of Kleinville, on the other hand, were very, very small. Everything in Kleinville was small.

L7 Global Warming: A Cause-and-Effect Writing Lesson

Teaching Objective:
To practice cause-and-effect writing skills on environmental topics.

Materials:
You need to supply articles for students to read **before** beginning this lesson. The topic suggested here is global warming, but any topic can easily be substituted.

Skills:
Reading and speaking will be practiced, but the focus of this lesson is cause-and-effect writing practice.

Time:
At least one lesson needs to be devoted to reading, which will require one to two class periods.

Procedure:

1. Preparing to write: gathering information

You should provide students with several articles about global warming. (Articles can be found in English newspapers, textbooks, and on the Internet.) Included with these articles should be a note-taking worksheet to help students identify the main points and in particular, all causes and effects discussed in the articles. A sample format might include:

- a vocabulary list followed by a vocabulary exercise
- a paragraph-by-paragraph breakdown identifying the main point (guided by comprehension questions or key words)
- a chart or grid where students can write key words related to a) causes or b) effects (again guided by comprehension questions or key words)

The following worksheets will allow students to practice their cause-and-effect writing skills.

2. Preparing to write: making sentences

Cause and Effect Worksheet #1

Cause and effect shows the relationship between two things when one thing makes the other thing happen. If you can put the two things into a sentence using **if ... then ...**, then you have the requirements for cause and effect. For example, **if** you throw a ball up, **then** it will fall back down. In this case, throwing the ball up is the cause for it to fall down.

The following are some examples of cause and effect relationships:

- save money —> travel abroad
- eat too much —> get fat
- study politics —> become a lawyer
- stay out in the sun too long —> get a sunburn

Exercise One

Using your notes and worksheet from the reading(s), write as many cause and effect relationships as you can think of regarding global warming and the greenhouse effect.

—>

—>

—>

—>

—>

—>

—>

When we write cause and effect statements, we use words and phrases that are called connectors of result.

Connectors of result: so, therefore, consequently, as a result, for this (these) reason(s)

Examples:

She saved her money for more than one year, so now she is planning to travel abroad.

Last year, students in England ate too much greasy food. As a result, they got fat.

He studied politics; therefore, he became a lawyer.

Exercise Two

Connect your ideas from Exercise One with complete sentences. Use all the connectors of result at least once.

3. Preparing to write: brainstorming and organizing

Cause and Effect Worksheet #2

Organizing

There are two main ways to organize cause-and-effect compositions. One way is the group approach in which you first talk about all the causes together as a group, and then you talk about all the effects as a group. The other way is the alternating-chain approach in which you first discuss a cause, and then its effect. Then you discuss another cause and its effect, and so on.

Which is best?

At first, you might not know which approach is best for your topic. In general, if it is difficult to make a clear distinction between cause and effect, the group approach is probably best. On the other hand, if there is a direct relationship between cause and effect (each cause has a clear effect), then the alternating-chain approach might be better. In many cases, you might want to combine both types at different times. First you must get your ideas down on paper, and then you will see which approach seems best for you.

Exercise One: Brainstorming

Look again at your notes and sentences about global warming and the greenhouse effect. In Worksheet #1, you separated the causes and the effects of global warming. This time, we are going to group them so they are easier to work with. Using the group approach, first think of all the causes of global warming, and then think of the effects. To do this, ask yourself Why? as you list the causes. Then ask yourself What is the result of this? as you list the effects.

Global Warming and the Greenhouse Effect
A) Causes (Why is Earth getting warmer?)

1.

2.

3.

4.

B) Effects (What is the result of the above causes?)

1.

2.

3.

4.

Exercise Two: Organization
Group Approach

Look at the two lists above. Think about the relationship of the items in both lists and arrange them in a reasonable order. Do some causes or effects happen before others? Put each cause and each effect in some kind of order by replacing the numbers in the two lists.

Does each cause have a corresponding effect? If not, you should organize using the group approach. If so, then you are ready to begin thinking of the alternating-chain approach.

Alternating-Chain Approach

Match each cause with its coordinating effect. Again, arrange them in a reasonable order.

Exercise Three: Writing More Sentences

When you make a statement such as "If global temperatures rise, the level of the sea will rise and this will cause disaster," then you must include examples to support your claim. The connectors listed below will help you connect statements with supporting examples. Using your lists above, write cause-and-effect sentences supported by examples. Use as many of the following connectors as you can.

Connectors: for example, for instance, such as, one example of this is, as an illustration, take the case of

4. Writing: putting it all together

At this point, students should have enough ideas, words, and sentences listed on their worksheet and in their notes to begin writing well organized paragraphs. The teacher should remind them to include examples to support each of their cause and effect relationships. Once the first draft is completed, the teacher may opt to do peer editing in the next class before students rewrite their second drafts.

L8 The Essay

The Structure of an Essay

An essay consists of several paragraphs written about a central idea. There are different types of essays such as narrative, descriptive, expository, comparison and contrast, classification, process, cause and effect, and argumentative. The type of essay will depend on the purpose for writing the essay. There are a number of common features all essays have, no matter what kind they are. For example, every essay must have a title.

Although essays can have as few as three paragraphs, we will look at a basic five-paragraph essay. Each paragraph in the essay has a specific function.

Paragraph 1: The first paragraph serves as an introduction to the essay. It introduces the topic to be discussed, contains the thesis statement (the controlling idea of the essay), and gives some background information. In addition, it must attract the reader's attention.

Paragraphs 2–4: These are the developmental paragraphs. Depending on the type of essay being written, these main body paragraphs describe various aspects of the topic, outline causes or effects (or possibly both), indicate points of comparison or contrast, give examples, or describe processes. Each paragraph in the body has a topic sentence which clearly supports the thesis statement.

Paragraph 5: The final paragraph is the concluding paragraph. This paragraph restates or summarizes the main premise of the essay using different words than the introductory paragraph, and leaves the reader with a clear final thought.

Thesis Statement:

The thesis statement contains the controlling idea for the essay. It is a complete sentence and expresses a complete thought. It is similar to the topic sentence because it expresses an attitude, idea, or opinion about the topic that needs to be proved. The thesis statement is broader in scope than the topic sentence and expresses the controlling idea for the entire essay. The topic sentences contained in the body will all relate to the controlling idea in the thesis statement.

Steps to Writing an Effective Essay

Before attempting to write an essay, it is necessary to follow some basic steps.
- **Step 1:** Choose a topic and narrow it down.
- **Step 2:** Identify your target audience.
- **Step 3:** Write a thesis statement.
- **Step 4:** Brainstorm for ideas.
Note: If you are not sure what aspect of the topic you really want to write about, you will need to brainstorm before you produce your thesis statement.
- **Step 5:** Organize your ideas into related groups and discard any that do not relate to the thesis statement.
- **Step 6:** Write an outline for the essay.
- **Step 7:** Ensure that all points on the outline support the thesis.

L

- Step 8: Write the first draft of your essay.
- Step 9: Revise your essay.
- Step 10: Edit and give your essay a title if it does not already have one.
- Step 11: Write the second draft of your essay.
- Step 12: Proofread your essay.

The Outline

The outline, if done properly, may take you as much time to write as the actual essay; however, in the long run, it saves a lot of time and frustration. If you have carefully ensured that all your topic sentences support the thesis, that all the supporting details support the topic sentences, and that there are smooth transitions between the paragraphs, you will have an effective essay that is unified and coherent. Writing an essay without an outline is like building a house without a blueprint. You may know roughly how to build the house, but unless your foundations are extremely solid and your workmanship is superb, you will be stuck with a problem house that will need a lot of repair—that is, if it does not just collapse altogether!

A skeleton outline for a five-paragraph essay would be as follows:

A) Introductory Paragraph (1)

   i)   thesis statement
   ii) background information

B) Developmental (Body) Paragraphs (2–4)

Paragraph 2
   i)   topic sentence (a complete sentence supporting some aspect of the thesis)
   ii) supporting detail(s) (supports the topic sentence and is written in words or phrases)

Paragraph 3
   i)   topic sentence (a complete sentence supporting some aspect of the thesis)
   ii) supporting detail(s) (supports the topic sentence and is written in words or phrases)

Paragraph 4
   i)   topic sentence (a complete sentence supporting some aspect of the thesis)
   ii) supporting detail(s) (supports the topic sentence and is written in words or phrases)

C) Concluding Paragraph (5)

   i)   reference to, restatement of, or summary of the thesis
   ii) concluding comments

L9 Punctuation Rules

The Apostrophe (')

1. For plurals

An apostrophe and an **s** may be used to form the plural, but only of symbols, letters, and of words referred to as words.

- She knew her ABC's at the age of four.
- Study the three R's.
- Indent all ¶'s five spaces.
- Accommodate is spelled with two c's and two m's.
- There are four T's in my password.
- There are too many and's in that sentence.
- Between them they have three Ph.D.'s.

Note that when a word, letter, or figure is italicized, the apostrophe and the **s** are not.

Many people prefer to form such plurals without the apostrophe: Rs, ands. But this practice can be confusing, especially with lowercase letters and words, which may be misread. For example,

- How many ss are there in Nipissing?
- Too many thiss can spoil a good paragraph.

   In cases such as these, it is clearer and easier to use the apostrophe. Keep in mind that it is sometimes better to rephrase instances that are potentially awkward. For example,

- Accommodate is spelled with two c's and two m's. →Accommodate is spelled with a double-c and a double-m.
- There are too many and's in that sentence. →And is used too many times in that sentence.

2. To indicate omissions

Use apostrophes to indicate omitted letters in contractions and omitted (though obvious) numerals:

- aren't (are not)
- can't (cannot)
- doesn't (does not)
- don't (do not)
- isn't (is not)
- it's (it is)
- she's (she is)
- they're (they are)
- won't (will not)
- wouldn't (would not)
- goin' fishin' (going fishing) [informal]
- back in '83
- the crash of '29
- the summer of '96

Possessives

1. To form the possessive case of a singular or a plural noun that does not end in **s**, add **'s**. For example,
    *   the car's color
    *   children's books
    *   a day's work
    *   deer's hide
    *   Emil's briefcase
    *   Germany's capital
    *   the girl's teacher
    *   the women's jobs
    *   yesterday's news

2. To form the possessive of compound nouns, use **'s** after the last noun. For example,
    *   The Solicitor General's report is due tomorrow.
    *   Sally and Mike's dinner party was a huge success.

If the nouns do not actually form a compound, each will need the **'s**. For example,
    *   Sally's and Mike's versions of the dinner party were markedly different.

3. You may correctly add **'s** to form the possessive of singular nouns ending in **s** or an s-sound. For example,
    *   the class's achievement
    *   Congress's debates
    *   the cross's meaning
    *   an index's usefulness
    *   Keats's poems
    *   a platypus's bill

However, some writers prefer to add only an apostrophe if the pronunciation of an extra syllable would sound awkward. For example,
    *   Achilles' heel
    *   Bill Gates' Foundation
    *   Moses' miracles

But the **'s** is usually acceptable. For example,
    *   Achilles's heel
    *   Bill Gates's Foundation
    *   Moses's miracles

In any event, one can usually avoid possible awkwardness by showing possession with an of-phrase instead of **'s** (see number 5 below). For example,
    *   the miracles of Moses
    *   the poems of Keats
    *   the bill of a platypus

4. To indicate the possessive case of plural nouns ending in **s**, add only an apostrophe. For example,
    *   the cannons' roar
    *   the Chans' cottage
    *   the girls' sweaters
    *   the Joneses' garden

5. Possessive with 's or with of. Especially in formal writing, the 's form is more common with the names of living creatures, and the of-phrase with the names of inanimate things. For example,

- the cat's tail
- the girl's coat
- Sheldon's home town
- the contents of the report
- the leg of the chair
- the surface of the desk

But both are acceptable with either category. The 's form, for example, is common with nouns that refer to things thought of as being made up of people or animals or as extensions of them. For example,

- Florida's climate
- the city's bylaws
- the committee's decision
- the company's representative
- the factory's output
- the government's policy
- the heart's affections
- the law's delay
- the team's strategy

In addition, the 's form is used for things that are animate in the sense that they are part of nature. For example,

- the comet's tail
- the dawn's early light
- the plant's roots
- the sea's surface
- the sky's color
- the wind's velocity

Also, the 's form is used for periods of time. For example,

- today's paper
- a month's wages
- a day's work
- winter's storms

Beyond these common uses for 's, sometimes it is used to indicate a sense of personification. For example,

- at death's door
- beauty's ensign
- freedom's light
- *Love's Labour's Lost*
- the razor's edge
- the ship's helm
- time's fool

If it seems natural and appropriate to you, go ahead and speak or write of a car's engine, a book's contents, a rocket's trajectory, a poem's imagery, and so on.

Conversely, for the sake of emphasis or rhythm you will occasionally want to use an of-phrase where 's would be normal. For example, "the jury's verdict" lacks the punch of "the verdict of the jury." You can also use an of-phrase to avoid awkward pronunciations (see above). For example, those who do not like the sound of "Dickens's novels" can refer to the "novels of Dickens." For unwieldy constructions such as "the opinion of the minister of finance" it is preferable to write "the minister of finance's opinion." Further, whether you use **'s** or just **s** to form the plural of letters, figures, and so on, in order to avoid ambiguity, form possessives of abbreviations with **of** rather than with apostrophes. For example, the opinion of the MLA, the opinion of the MLA's, the opinion of the MLAs.

6. Double Possessives. There is nothing wrong with double possessives, showing possession with both an of-phrase and a possessive inflection. They are standard with possessive pronouns and can be used similarly with common and proper nouns. For example,

- a favorite of mine
- a friend of hers
- a friend of the family or of the family's
- a contemporary of Shakespeare or of Shakespeare's

And a sentence like **The story was based on an idea of Shakespeare** is at least potentially ambiguous, whereas **The story was based on an idea of Shakespeare's** is clear. But if you feel that this sort of construction is unpleasant to the ear, you can usually manage to revise it to something like **on one of Shakespeare's ideas**. Also, avoid such double possessives with a **that** construction. For example, His hat was just like that of Arthur's.

Brackets ([ ])

Brackets, or square brackets, are used primarily to enclose something inserted in a direct quotation, or if you need to put parentheses inside parentheses (as in a footnote or in a bibliographical entry).

When using square brackets in quoted material, keep changes to a minimum, but enclose any editorial addition or necessary change within square brackets. For example, you may want to clarify a fact or make a change in tense to make the quoted material fit the syntax of your sentence. For example,

- The author states that "the following year [2000] marked a turning point in [his] life."
- One of my friends wrote me that her "feelings about the subject [were] similar to" mine.

Use the word sic (Latin for thus) in square brackets to indicate that an error in the quotation occurs in the original. For example,

- One of my friends wrote me: "My feelings about the subject are similiar [sic] to yours."

Capitalization

Generally speaking, capitalize proper nouns, abbreviations of proper nouns, and words derived from proper nouns.

Names and Nicknames
Capitalize names and nicknames of real and fictional people and individual animals. For example,

- Nelson Mandela
- Clive Owen
- Cinderella
- King Kong
- Mark Twain
- Clarissa Dalloway
- Barack Obama
- Lassie Washoe

- Tiger Woods
- Rumpelstiltskin
- Michael Phelps

Professional and Honorific Titles

Capitalize professional and honorific titles when they directly precede and thus are parts of names. For example,

- Professor Tamara Jones (but Tamara Jones, professor at Columbia)
- Captain Janna Ting (but Janna Ting is a captain in the police force)
- Rabbi Samuel Singer (but Mr. Singer was rabbi of our synagogue)

Words Designating Family Relationships

Capitalize words designating family relationships when they are used as parts of proper names and also when they are used in place of proper names, except following a possessive. For example,

- Uncle Peter (but I have an uncle named Peter)
- There's my Uncle Peter (but There's my uncle, Peter)
- I told Father about it (but My father knows about it)
- I have always respected Grandmother (but Diana's grandmother is a lovely woman)

Place Names

Capitalize place names, including common nouns (river, street, park, etc.), when they are parts of proper nouns. For example,

- Active Pass
- Central Park
- the Amazon
- the Andes
- Asia
- Salt Lake City
- Buenos Aires
- Mt. Etna
- Hudson Bay
- Japan
- Lake Ladoga
- New York City
- Niagara Falls
- California
- Main Street
- the Gobi Desert
- the Hawaiian Islands
- the Mississippi River
- the Suez Canal
- Trafalgar Square
- Yellowstone National Park

Months, Days, Holidays

Capitalize the names of the months (January, February, etc.) and the days of the week (Monday, Tuesday, etc.), but not the seasons (spring, summer, autumn, fall, winter). Also capitalize holidays, holy days, and festivals (Christmas, St. Patrick's Day, Veterans Day, Hanukkah, Ramadan).

Religious Names

Capitalize names of deities and other religious names and terms. For example,

- God
- the Holy Ghost
- the Virgin Mary
- the Bible
- the Torah
- the Talmud
- the Dead Sea Scrolls
- Islam
- Allah
- the Prophet
- the Koran
- Apollo
- Jupiter
- Vishnu
- Taoism

Note: Some people capitalize pronouns referring to a deity; others prefer not to. Either practice is acceptable as long as you are consistent.

Names of Nationalities and Organizations

Capitalize names of nationalities and other groups and organizations and of their members. For example,

- American, Australian, Malaysian, Scandinavian, South American, Iraqi, Somalian, Texan
- Democrats, the Democratic Party
- Republicans, the Republican Party
- Roman Catholics, the Roman Catholic Church
- Lions, Kiwanis
- Teamsters
- the Miami Heat, the Toronto Blue Jays

Names of Institutions and Sections of Government, Historical Events, and Buildings

Capitalize names of institutions, sections of government, historical events and documents, and specific buildings. For example,

- Harvard University, The Mayo Clinic
- the Senate, the House of Representatives, Parliament
- the French Revolution, the Great War, World War I, the Gulf War
- the Cretaceous period, the Renaissance, the Ming Dynasty
- the Declaration of Independence, the Magna Carta, the Treaty of Versailles
- the British Museum, the Smithsonian Museum
- Westminster Abbey

Academic Courses and Languages

Capitalize specific academic courses, but not the subjects themselves (except for languages). For example,

- Philosophy 101, Fine Arts 300, Mathematics 204, English 112, Food Writing, Humanities 101
- an English course, a major in French (but a history course, an economics major, a degree in psychology)

Derivatives of Proper Nouns
Capitalize derivatives of proper nouns. For example,
- Haligonian, Celtic, Ethiopian, Kuwaiti
- Confucianism, Christian
- Shakespearean, Keynesian, Edwardian, Miltonic

Abbreviations of Proper Nouns
Capitalize abbreviations of proper nouns. For example,
- NBC
- IBT
- UN
- UAE
- D.C.
- GM

Note: abbreviations of agencies and organizations commonly known by their initials do not need periods, but non-postal abbreviations of geographical entities such as provinces or states usually do. When in doubt, consult your dictionary.

I and O
Capitalize the pronoun **I** and the vocative interjection **O**. For example,

O my people, what have I done unto thee? (Micah 6:3).

Do not capitalize the interjection **oh** unless it begins a sentence.

Titles of Written and Other Works
For titles of written and other works, use a capital letter to begin the first word, the last word, and all other important words. Leave articles (a, an, the) and any conjunctions and prepositions less than five letters long uncapitalized—unless one of these is the first or last word). For example,
- *The Blind Assassin*
- "Welcome to the Jungle"
- *Pan's Labyrinth*
- "O Canada"
- *The Metamorphosis*
- "Amazing Grace"
- *Huckleberry Finn*
- *Harry Potter and the Prisoner of Azkaban*
- *Roughing It in the Bush*

But there can be exceptions, for example, the conjunctions **nor** and **so** are usually capitalized; the relative pronoun **that** is sometimes not capitalized (*All's Well that Ends Well*); and in Ralph Ellison's *Tell It Like It Is, Baby* the preposition-conjunction **like** demands capitalization.

If a title includes a hyphenated word, capitalize the part after the hyphen only if it is a noun or adjective, or is otherwise an important word. For example,
- Self-Portrait
- *The Scorched-Wood People*
- *Murder Among the Well-to-do*

Capitalize the first word of a subtitle, even if it is an article. For example,
Beyond Remembering: The Collected Poems of Al Purdy

First Words of Sentences

Capitalize the first word of a major or minor sentence: anything that concludes with terminal punctuation. For example, Racial profiling. Now that's a controversial topic. Right?

First Words of Quotations That Are Sentences

Capitalize the first word of a quotation that is intended as a sentence or that is capitalized in the source—but not fragments from other than the beginning of such a sentence. For example, When he said, "Let me take the wheel for a while," I shuddered at the memory of what had happened the last time I had let him "take the wheel."

If something interrupts a single-quoted sentence, do not begin its second part with a capital. For example, "It was all I could do," she said, "to keep from laughing out loud."

First Words of Sentences within Parentheses

Capitalize the first word of an independent sentence in parentheses only if it stands by itself, apart from other sentences. If it is incorporated within another sentence, it is neither capitalized nor ended with a period (though it could end with a question mark or exclamation point). For example, She did as she was told (there was really nothing else for her to do), and the tension was relieved. (But of course she would never admit to herself that she had been manipulated.)

First Words of Sentences Following Colons

An incorporated sentence following a colon may be capitalized if it seems to stand as a separate statement, for example if it is itself long or requires emphasis, but the current trend is away from capitalization. For example,

- There was one thing, she said, which we must never forget: No one has the right to the kind of happiness that deprives someone else of deserved happiness.
- It was a splendid night: the sky was clear except for a few picturesque clouds, the moon was full, and even a few stars shone through. (The first **The** could be capitalized if the writer wanted particular emphasis on the details.)
- It was no time for petty quarrels: everything depended on unanimity.

With Personification and for Emphasis

Although it is risky and should not be done often, writers who have good control of tone can occasionally capitalize a personified abstraction or a word or phrase to which they want to impart a special importance of some kind. For example,

- In his quest to succeed, Greed and Power came to dominate his every waking thought.
- Only when it begins to fade does Youth appear so valuable.

Sometimes the slight emphasis of capitalization can be used for a humorous or ironic effect. For example, He insisted on driving His Beautiful Car: everyone else preferred to walk the two blocks without benefit of jerks and jolts and carbon monoxide fumes.

And occasionally, but rarely, you can capitalize whole words and phrases or even sentences for a special sort of graphic emphasis. For example,

- When we reached the excavation site, however, we were confronted by a sign warning us in no uncertain terms to KEEP OUT—TRESPASSERS WILL BE PROSECUTED.
- When she made the suggestion to the group, she was answered with a resounding YES.

Clearly in such instances, there is no need for further indications, such as quotation marks or underlining, though the last one could end with an exclamation point.

The Colon (:)

Colons are commonly used to introduce lists, examples, and long or formal quotations, but their possibilities in more everyday sentences are often overlooked. The reason a colon is useful is that it looks forward or anticipates: it gives readers a push toward the next part of the sentence. In the preceding sentence, for example, the colon sets up a sense of expectation about what is coming. It points out, even emphasizes, the relation between the two parts of the sentence (that is, a second part clarifies what the first part says). A semicolon in the same spot would bring readers to an abrupt halt, leaving it up to them to make the necessary connection between the two parts. In some of the following examples, the anticipatory function of the colon is perhaps less obvious, but it is there:

- **Vita's garden contained only white flowers: roses, primulas, and primroses.**
- **Let me add just this: anyone who expects to lose weight must be prepared to exercise.**
- **It was an unexpectedly lovely time of year: trees were in blossom, garden flowers bloomed all around, the sky was clear and bright, and the temperature was just right.**
- **The rain came down during the race: we soon started slipping on the slick pavement.**

Nevertheless, do not get carried away and overuse the colon: its effectiveness would wear off if it appeared more than once or twice a page.

The Comma (,)

The comma is a light or mild separator. It is the most neutral punctuation mark and the most used mark. A comma makes a reader pause slightly. Use it to separate words, phrases, and clauses from each other when no heavier or more expressive mark is required or desired.

Main Functions of Commas

Basically, commas are used in three ways; if you know these conventions, you should have little trouble with commas.

1. Use a comma between independent clauses joined by a coordinating conjunction (and, but, or, nor, for, yet, so). For example,
   - **We went to the National Gallery of Art, and then we walked to the White House.**
   - **Most of us went back to college in the fall, but Dorothy was tempted by an opportunity to travel, so she took off for Italy.**

2. Use commas to separate items in a series of three or more. For example,
   - **It is said that early to bed and early to rise will make one healthy, wealthy, and wise.**
   - **Michelangelo Buonarroti, Leonardo da Vinci, and Raphael Sanzio were three Italian painters.**

3. Use commas to set off parenthetical elements, such as interruptive or introductory words, phrases, and clauses, and nonrestrictive appositives or nonrestrictive relative clauses. For example,
   - **There are, however, some exceptions.**
   - **Grasping the remote control firmly, she walked away.**
   - **E.M. Forster's last novel, *A Passage to India*, is both serious and humorous.**
   - **Caffe latte, meaning coffee and milk in Italian, is a popular hot-coffee beverage in North America.**

Other conventional uses of the comma:

1. Use a comma between elements of an emphatic contrast. For example,
    This is a practical lesson, not a theoretical one.

2. Use a comma to indicate a pause where a word has been acceptably omitted. For example,
    *   Ron is a conservative; Sally, a radical.
    *   To err is human; to forgive, divine.

3. Use commas to set off a noun of address. For example,
    *   Simon, please write a thank-you note to your grandparents.
    *   Tell me, my darling, how you think I should handle this.

4. Use commas with a verb of speaking before or after a quotation. For example,
    *   Then Dora remarked, "That book gave me nightmares."
    *   "It doesn't matter to me," said Alain laughingly.

5. Use commas after the salutation of informal letters (Dear Gail,) and after the complimentary close of all letters (Yours truly,). In formal letters, a colon is conventional after the salutation (Dear Mr. Eng:).

6. Use commas with dates. Different forms are acceptable. For example,
    She left on January 11, 2003, and was gone a month.

(Note the comma after the year.) Or, you may also place the date before the month—a style preferred by some writers in Canada and Britain—in which case no comma is required. For example,
    She left on 11 January 2003 and was gone a month.

Whichever style you choose, make sure you use it consistently.

    When referring only to month and year, you may use a comma or not, but again, be consistent. For example,
    *   The book was published in March, 2007, in France.
    *   It was published here in March 2007.

7. Use commas to set off geographical names and addresses. For example,
    *   She left Glasgow, Scotland, and moved to London, England, in hopes of finding a better-paying job. (Note the commas after the names of the countries.)
    *   Their summer address will be 11 Bishop's Place, Lewes, Sussex, England.

The Dash (—)

The dash is a popular punctuation mark, especially in email and other informal communications. Hasty writers often use it as a substitute for a comma, or where a colon would be more emphatic. Use a dash only when you have a definite reason for doing so. Like the colon, the dash sets up expectations in a reader's mind. But, whereas the colon sets up an expectation that what follows will somehow explain, summarize, define, or otherwise comment on what has gone before, a dash suggests that what follows will be somehow surprising, involving some sort of twist, or at least a contrary idea. For example,
    The teacher praised my wit, my intelligence, my organization, and my research—and penalized the paper for its poor spelling and punctuation.

The dash adds punch to what follows it. A comma there would deprive the sentence of much of its force; it would even sound odd, since the resulting matter-of-fact tone would not be in harmony with what the sentence was saying. Only a dash can convey the appropriate tone. For example,

What he wanted—and he wanted it very badly indeed—was the last piece of chocolate cake.

To set off the interrupting clause with commas instead of dashes would not be incorrect, but the result would be weaker—for the content of the clause is clearly meant to be emphatic. Only dashes have the power to signal that emphasis; commas would diminish the force of the clause. The dash is also handy in some long and involved sentences; for example, after a long series before a summarizing clause, Our longing for the past, our hopes for the future and our neglect of the present moment—all these and more go to shape our everyday lives, often in ways unseen or little understood.

Even here, the emphatic quality of the dash serves the meaning, though its principal function in such a sentence is to mark the abrupt break. As with colons, do not overuse dashes. They are even stronger marks, but they lose effectiveness if used often.

The Dash and Coordinating Conjunctions

When you want a longer pause to create extra emphasis, a dash placed before a coordinating conjunction would produce a stronger effect than either a comma or a semicolon. For example,

Sameer protested that he was sorry for all his mistakes—but he went right on making them.

For a different rhetorical effect, change **but** to the more neutral **and**, then the dash takes over the contrasting function. For example,

Sameer protested that he was sorry for all his mistakes—and he went right on making them.

Similarly, consider the different effects of these two following versions of the same basic sentence:

- **It may not be the easiest way, but it's the only way we know.**
- **It may not be the easiest way—but it's the only way we know.**

Even a period could be used between such clauses, since there is nothing inherently wrong with beginning a sentence with **and** or **but**. Even as sentence openers, they are still doing their job of coordinating.

The Ellipse (…)

Ending a Sentence with Ellipsis

The three dots of an ellipsis are sometimes used at the end of a sentence, especially in dialogue or at the end of a paragraph or a chapter in order to indicate a fading away, or to create mild suspense.

Ellipses for Omissions

If, when quoting from a written source, you decide to omit one or more words from the middle of the passage you are quoting, indicate the omission with the three spaced periods of an ellipsis. For example, if you wanted to quote only part of the passage from Austen quoted at length on page 306, you might do the following:

As Jane Austen wryly observes, "a single man in possession of a . . . fortune must be in want of a wife."

Note: an ellipsis is not needed at the beginning of a quotation unless the quotation could be mistaken for a complete sentence—for example, if it began with **I** or some other capital letter.

Other punctuation may be included before or after the ellipsis if it makes the quoted material clearer. For example,

> **However little known the feelings or views of such a man may be . . . , this truth is so well fixed in the minds of the surrounding families.**

Three periods can also indicate the omission of one or more entire sentences, or even whole paragraphs.

The Exclamation Point (!)

Use an exclamation point after an emphatic statement or after an expression of emphatic surprise, emphatic query, or strong emotion. For example,

- He came in first; yet, it was only his second time in professional competition!
- What a loser!
- You don't say so!
- Isn't it beautiful today!
- Not again!
- Gosh!

Occasionally an exclamation point may be doubled or tripled for emphasis. It may even follow a question mark, to emphasize the writer's or speaker's disbelief. For example,

- She said what?!
- You bought what?! A giraffe?! What were you thinking?!

This device should not be used in formal and academic writing.

Hyphenation

To hyphenate or not to hyphenate? That is often the question. There are some firm rules; there are some sound guidelines; and there is a large territory where only common sense and a good dictionary can help you find your way. Since the conventions are constantly changing, sometimes rapidly, make a habit of checking your dictionary for current usage. The following are the main points to remember:

1. Use hyphens in compound numbers from twenty-one to ninety-nine.

2. Use hyphens with fractions used as adjectives: A two-thirds majority is required to defeat the amendment. When a fraction is used as a noun, you may use a hyphen, though many writers do not: One quarter of the audience was asleep.

3. Use hyphens with compounds indicating time, when these are written out: seven-thirty, nine-fifteen.

4. Use hyphens with prefixes before proper nouns. For example,
   - all-American, pan-Asian, pseudo-Modern
   - anti-Fascist, post-Victorian, semi-Gothic
   - ex-President, pre-Babylonian, trans-Siberian
   - non-Communist, pro-Democrat, un-American

But, there are well-established exceptions. For example,
- antichrist
- postcolonial
- postmodern
- transatlantic
- transpacific

5. Use hyphens with compounds beginning with the prefix **self**. For example,
- self-assured
- self-confidence
- self-deluded
- self-esteem
- self-made
- self-pity

Note: The words selfhood, selfish, selfless, and selfsame are not hyphenated, since **self** is the root, not a prefix.

Hyphens are conventionally used with certain other prefixes. For example,
- all-important
- ex-premier
- quasi-religious

Hyphens are conventionally used with most, but not all, compounds beginning with **vice** and **by**. For example,
- vice-chancellor
- vice-consul
- vice-regent (but viceregal, viceroy)
- by-election
- by-product (but bygone, bylaw, byroad, bystander, byword)

Check your dictionary.

6. Use hyphens with the suffixes **elect** and **designate**. For example,
- president-elect
- ambassador-designate

7. Use hyphens with **great** and **in-law** in compounds designating family relationships. For example,
- mother-in-law
- son-in-law
- great-grandfather
- great-aunt

8. Use hyphens to prevent a word being mistaken for an entirely different word. For example,
- He recounted what had happened after the ballots had been re-counted.
- If you're going to re-strain the juice, I'll restrain myself from drinking it now, seeds and all.
- Once at the resort after the bumpy ride, we sat down to re-sort our jumbled fishing gear.
- Check out the great sale prices of the goods at the check-out counter.

9. Use hyphens to prevent awkward or confusing combinations of letters and sounds. For example,
- anti-intellectual
- doll-like
- e-book
- e-learning

- photo-offset
- re-echo
- set-to

10. Hyphens are sometimes necessary to prevent ambiguity. For example,
- **ambiguous:** The ad offered six week old kittens for sale.
- **clear:** The ad offered six week-old kittens for sale.
- **clear:** The ad offered six-week-old kittens for sale.

Note the difference a hyphen makes to the meaning of the last two examples. In the following example, hyphenating **leveling out** removes the possibility of misreading the sentence:
To maintain social equality, we need a leveling-out of benefits.

Compound Nouns
Some nouns composed of two or more words are conventionally hyphenated. For example,
- free-for-all
- half-and-half
- jack-o-lantern
- merry-go-round
- rabble-rouser
- runner-up
- shut-in
- trade-in
- two-timer

But many compound nouns that one might think should be hyphenated are not, and others that may once have been hyphenated, or even two separate words, have become so familiar that they are now one unhyphenated word. Usage is constantly and rapidly changing, and even dictionaries do not always agree on what is standard at a given time. Some dictionaries still record such old fashioned forms as to-night and to-morrow as alternatives (use tonight and tomorrow). Clearly, it is best to consult a dictionary that is both comprehensive and up-to-date and use the form it lists first.

Compound Modifiers
When two or more words occur together in such a way that they act as a single adjective before a noun, they are usually hyphenated in order to prevent misreading. For example,
- a well-dressed man
- greenish-gray eyes
- middle-class values
- computer-ready forms
- a once-in-a-lifetime chance
- a three-day-old strike

When they occur after a noun, misreading is unlikely and no hyphen is needed. For example,
- The man was well dressed.
- Her eyes are greenish gray.

But many compound modifiers are already listed as hyphenated words. For example, Merriam-Webster's Collegiate Dictionary lists the following, among others:
- first-class
- fly-by-night
- good-looking

- habit-forming
- open-minded
- right-hand
- short-lived
- tongue-tied
- warm-blooded
- wide-eyed

Such modifiers retain their hyphens even when they follow the nouns they modify. For example, *The tone of the speech was quite matter-of-fact.*

Hyphenated Verbs

Verbs, too, are sometimes hyphenated. A dictionary will list most of the ones you might want to use. For example,

- double-check
- pole-vault
- second-guess
- sight-read
- soft-pedal
- two-time

But be aware that some two-part verbs can never be hyphenated. Resist the temptation to put a hyphen in two-part verbs that consist of a verb followed by a preposition. Be particularly careful with those that are hyphenated when they serve as other parts of speech. For example,

- I was asked to set up the display (but Many customers admired the set-up)
- Call up the next group of trainees (but The rookie awaited a call-up to the big leagues)

Suspension Hyphens

If you use two prefixes with one root, use what is called a suspension hyphen after the first prefix, even if it would not normally be hyphenated. For example,

- The audience was about equally divided between pro- and anti-Democrats.
- You may choose between the three- and the five-day excursions.
- You may either pre- or postdate the check.

Italics

Italics are a special kind of slanting type that contrasts with the surrounding type to draw attention to a word or a phrase, such as a title. The other main uses of italics are discussed below. In handwritten work, such as in an exam paper, represent italic type by underlining.

Names of Ships and Planes

Italicize names of individual ships, planes, trains, and so on. For example,

- *the Golden Hind*
- *the Spirit of St. Louis*
- *the St. Bonaventure*
- *Mariner IX*
- *the Lusitania*
- *the Columbia*
- *the Erebus and the Terror*
- *the Orient Express*

Non-English Words and Phrases

Italicize non-English words and phrases that are not yet sufficiently common to be entirely at home in English. English contains many terms that have come from other languages but that are no longer thought of as non-English and are therefore not italicized. For example,

- arroyo
- bamboo
- chutzpah
- corral
- eureka
- genre
- goulash
- hiatus
- litotes
- moccasin
- prairie
- sic
- spaghetti
- sushi
- tableau
- vacuum

There are also words that are sufficiently anglicized that do not require italicizing but that usually retain their original accents and diacritical marks. For example,

- cliché
- façade
- fête
- Götterdämmerung
- naïf

But English also makes use of many terms still felt by many writers to be sufficiently non-English to need italicizing. For example,

- *au courant*
- *Bildungsroman*
- *carpe diem*
- *chez*
- *coup d'état*
- *jihad*
- *joie de vivre*
- *raison d'être*
- *savoir faire*
- *schadenfreude*
- *verboten*
- *Weltanschauung*

Many such expressions are on their way to full acceptance in English. If you are unsure, consult a good up-to-date dictionary.

Words Referred to as Words

Italicize words, letters, numerals, and the like when you refer to them as such. For example,

- The word *helicopter* is formed from Greek roots.

- There are two *r*'s in embarrass. (Note that only the r is italicized; the **s** making it plural stays roman.)
- The number *13* is considered unlucky by many otherwise rational people.
- Do not use *&* as a substitute for *and*.

For Emphasis

On rare occasions, italicize words or phrases—or even whole sentences—that you want to emphasize. Perhaps as they might be stressed if spoken aloud. For example,

- One thing he was now sure of: *that* was no way to go about the task.
- Careful thought should lead one to the conclusion that *character*, not wealth nor connections, will be most important in the long run.
- If people try to tell you otherwise, *don't* listen to them.
- Remember that *Canberra*, not Sydney, is the capital of Australia.
- He gave up his ideas of fun and decided instead to finish his education. And it was the *most important* decision of his life.

Like other typographical devices for achieving emphasis (boldface, capitalization, underlining), italics is worth avoiding, or at least minimizing, in academic and other forms of writing. No typographical means of emphasis is, ultimately, as effective as punctuation, word order, and syntax. Easy methods often produce only a transitory effect, and repeated use soon reduces what effectiveness they have. Consider the following sentences and decide which of them you find most emphatic:

- Well, I felt just terrible when he told me that!
- I felt terrible, just terrible, when he told me that.
- I can think of only one way to describe how I felt when he told me that: I felt terrible.

Parentheses ( )

Parentheses have three principal functions in non-technical writing: (1) to set off certain kinds of interrupters; (2) to enclose cross-reference information within a sentence, as is done throughout a book; and (3) to enclose numerals or letters setting up a list or series, as we do in this sentence. Note that if a complete sentence is enclosed in parentheses within another sentence (here is an example of such an insertion), it needs neither an opening capital letter nor a closing period. Note also that if a comma or other mark is called for by the sentence (as in the preceding sentence, and in this one), it comes after the closing parenthesis, not before the opening one. Exclamation points and question marks go inside the parenthesis only if they are a part of what is enclosed. (When an entire sentence or more is enclosed, the terminal mark of course comes inside the parenthesis—as does this period.)

Interrupters Set Off with Parentheses

Use parentheses to set off abrupt interrupters or other interrupters that you wish to de-emphasize. Often interrupters that could be emphatic can be played down in order to emphasize the other parts of a sentence. For example,

- The stockholders who voted for him (quite a sizable group) were obviously dissatisfied with our recent conduct of the business.
- It is not possible at this time (it is far too early in the growing season) to predict with any confidence just what the crop yield will be.
- Speculation (I mean this in its pejorative sense) is not a safe foundation for a business enterprise.
- Some extreme sports (hang-gliding for example) involve unusually high insurance claims.

By de-emphasizing something striking, parentheses can also achieve an effect similar to that of dashes, though by an ironic tone rather than an insistent one.

The Period (.)

Use a period to mark the end of statements and neutral commands. For example,

- As of 2004, people in Japan use the Internet more than any other people in the world.
- Ezra Pound, the author of The Cantos, died in 1972.
- Don't let yourself be fooled by cheap imitations.

Use a period after most abbreviations. For example,

- abbr.
- Mr.
- Ms.
- Dr.
- Jr.
- Ph.D.
- B.A.
- St.
- Mt.
- etc.

Generally use a period in abbreviated place names. For example,

- B.C.
- N.D.
- N.Y.
- Mass.

But note that two-letter postal abbreviations do not require periods. For example,

- BC
- ND
- NY
- MA

Periods are not used after metric and other symbols (unless they occur at the end of a sentence). For example,

- km
- cm
- kg
- mc²
- ml
- kJ
- C
- Hz
- au
- Zr

Periods are often omitted with initials, especially of groups or organizations, and especially if the initials are acronyms—that is, words or names made up of initials (AIDS, NATO, UN). For example,

- AWOL
- UNICEF
- WHO

- CDC
- FBI
- TV
- APA
- MLA

When in doubt, consult a good dictionary. If there is more than one acceptable usage, be consistent.

Quotation Marks (" ")

There are two kinds of quotations: dialogue or direct speech (such as you might find in a story, novel, or nonfiction narrative or other essay) and verbatim quotation from a published work or other source (as in a research paper).

Direct Speech
Enclose all direct speech in quotation marks. For example,

> I remember hearing my mother say to my absentminded father, "Henry, why is the newspaper in the fridge?"

In written dialogue, it is conventional to begin a new paragraph each time the speaker changes. For example,

> "Henry," she said, a note of exasperation in her voice, "why is the newspaper in the fridge?"
> "Oh, yes," he replied. "The fish is wrapped in it."
> She examined it. "Well, there may have been a fish in it once, but there is no fish in it now."

Even when passages of direct speech are incomplete, the part that is verbatim should be enclosed in quotation marks. For example,

> After only two weeks, he said he was "fed up" and that he was "going to look for a more interesting job."

Single Quotation Marks (' ')
Put single quotation marks around a quotation that occurs within another quotation. This is the only standard use for single quotation marks. For example,

> In Joseph Conrad's *Heart of Darkness*, after a leisurely setting of the scene by the unnamed narrator, the drama begins when the character who is to be the principal narrator first speaks: "'And this also,' said Marlow suddenly, 'has been one of the dark places of the earth.'"

With Verbs of Speaking Before Quotations
When verbs of speaking precede a quotation, they are usually followed by commas. For example,

- Helen said, "There is something nasty growing in my fridge."
- Adriana fumbled around in the dark and asked, "Now where are the matches?"

Note that when a quotation ends a sentence, its own terminal punctuation serves also as that of the sentence.

> With short or emphatic quotations, commas often are not necessary. For example,

- He said "Hold your horses," so we waited a little longer.
- Someone shouted "Fire!" and we all headed for the exits.

Again, punctuate a sentence the way you want it to be heard; your sense of its rhythm should help you decide. On the other hand, if the quotation is long, especially if it consists of more than one sentence, or if the context is formal, a colon will probably be more appropriate than a comma to introduce it. For example,

> When the movie was over, Joanna turned to her companion and said: "We have wasted 90 minutes of our lives. The movie lacked an intelligent plot, sympathetic characters, and an interesting setting. Even the soundtrack was pathetic."

If the introductory element is itself an independent clause, then a colon or period must be used. For example,

> Joanna turned to her and spoke: "What a waste of time."

Spoke, unlike **said**, is an intransitive verb here.

If you work a quotation into your own syntax, do not use even a comma to introduce it. For example, when the word that follows a verb of speaking,

> It is often said that "[s]ticks and stones may break my bones, but words will never hurt me"—a singularly inaccurate notion.

With Verbs of Speaking After Quotations

If a verb of speaking or a subject–verb combination follows a quotation, it is usually set off by a comma placed inside the closing quotation mark. For example,

- "You attract what you manifest in your personality," said the speaker.
- "I think there's a fly in my soup," she muttered.

But if the quotation ends with a question mark or an exclamation point, no other punctuation is added. For example,

- "What time is it?" asked Francis, looking up.
- "I insist that I be heard!" he shouted.

If the clause containing the verb of speaking interrupts the quotation, it should be preceded by a comma and followed by whatever mark is called for by the syntax and the sense. For example,

- "Since it's such a long drive," he said, "we'd better get an early start."
- "It's a long drive," he argued; "therefore I think we should start early."
- "It's a very long way," he insisted. "We should start as early as possible."

Quotations Set Off by Indention

Colons are conventionally used to introduce block quotations. For example,

Jane Austen begins her novel *Pride and Prejudice* with the observation:

> It is a truth universally acknowledged, that a single man in possession of a good fortune must be in want of a wife. However little known the feelings or views of such a man may be on his first entering a neighborhood, this truth is so well fixed in the minds of the surrounding families, that he is considered as the rightful property of some one or other of their daughters.

Quotation Marks and Words Used in a Special Sense

As we do with block quotations outlined above, put quotation marks around words used in a special sense or words for which you wish to indicate some qualification. For example,

- What she calls a "ramble" I would call a 20-mile hike.
- He had been up in the woods so long he was "bushed," as lumberjacks put it.

Other Marks with Quotation Marks

Put periods and commas inside closing quotation marks, but put semicolons and colons outside them. For example,

> "Knowing how to write well," he said, "can be a source of great pleasure"; and then he added that it had "one other important quality": he identified it simply as "hard work."

The Semicolon (;)

The semicolon is a heavy separator, often almost equivalent to a period or a full stop. It forces a much longer pause than a comma does. And compared with the comma, it is used sparingly. Basically, semicolons have only two functions:

1. Use a semicolon between closely related independent clauses that are not joined by one of the coordinating conjunctions. For example,
   - Tap water often tastes of chemicals; spring water imported from France usually does not.
   - The lab had 20 new laptop computers; however, there were 25 students in the class.

2. Use a semicolon instead of a comma if a comma would not be heavy enough—if the clauses or the elements in a series have internal commas of their own. For example,

   > Their class presentation examined three novels written by American authors and set largely outside the United States: Norman Mailer's *The Naked and the Dead*, which is set in the South Pacific; Ernest Hemingway's *The Sun Also Rises*, which takes place primarily in Spain; and Mark Twain's *The Prince and the Pauper*, set in Tudor England.

The Slash (/)

When you run in more than one line of poetry, indicate the line-breaks with a slash with a space on each side. For example,

> Dante's spiritual journey begins in the woods: "Midway this way of life, we're bound upon / I woke to find myself in a dark wood / Where the right road was wholly lost and gone."

 # L10 Spelling Recommendations and Rules

For every spelling rule, inevitably there are exceptions. By applying the basic spelling rules and recognizing some of the exceptions explained here, your spelling will improve.

The following are some immediate recommendations you can offer to students:

1. When you speak, pronounce words carefully. The word **probably** will likely be misspelled if pronounced **probly**.

2. List your spelling enemies and attack them. Look at your past letters and papers. Then write or type out the words that have given you trouble in sentences and read them back. Soon the correct spelling will become second nature!

3. Make it a habit to look at words carefully. Practice seeing each letter in a word. Repeat it aloud if possible. It might help to pronounce difficult words the way they are spelled. A memory device (e.g., Eeee! I am seized! to remember the e-before-i reversal in **seizure**) may be used with some words.

4. Take time to proofread what you write. Experienced writers habitually reexamine their work for misspellings and punctuation errors.

5. Consult the dictionary for words you question, with the understanding that some words have multiple spellings or distinct foreign spellings.

6. Review the following spelling rules as necessary. Take a few minutes to put each rule in your own words for easier recall.

Spelling Rules

First Rule: Adding suffixes to one-syllable words

The word **pat** is a one-syllable word that ends in a single consonant preceded by a single vowel. In such words, double the last consonant when adding a suffix. For example,

- patted
- fattest
- shopper
- mapping
- bigger

If the word ends in two consonants, or if two vowels precede the final consonant, this rule does not apply. For example,

- climbed
- loaned
- meeting
- pulled,
- screamer
- sharper

Second Rule: Adding suffixes to words of two or more syllables

If the word is accented on the last syllable, like **prefer**, you may treat it as a one-syllable word. For example,

- preferring
- rebelling

Again, if the word ends in two consonants, or if two vowels precede the consonant, the rule does not apply. For example,

- alarmed
- ballooning
- reflection
- retained

Generally, if the last syllable is not accented, just add the suffix. For example,
- profitable
- rancorous
- showering

Third Rule: Adding suffixes beginning with vowels to words ending in silent **e**

A silent **e** is usually dropped from a word to add a suffix, if the suffix begins with a vowel. For example,
- advisor
- believable
- expensive
- finest
- sliding

Exceptions:

a) If the suffix **-able** or **-ous** is added to a word with a soft **g**- or **c**-sound, keep the **e**. For example,

    outrageous

b) Keep the **e** if the new word could be misunderstood or mistaken for another. For example,

    dyeing signifies dye not die

c) If the word ends in **ie**, drop the **e** and change the **i** to **y** before adding the suffix. For example,

    dying

Fourth Rule: Adding a suffix beginning with a consonant to a word ending in silent **e**

Keep the silent **e** on the end of words where the suffix begins with a consonant. For example,
- engagement
- extremely
- fateful
- sameness
- shoeless

Exceptions:
- argument
- awful
- judgment
- truly

Fifth Rule: Using **ie** and **ei**

Use the well-known saying "**i** before **e** except after **c**, or when it says **ay**" as in neighbor or sleigh. For example,
- believe
- ceiling
- chief
- conceited
- feign
- fierce
- piece

- pier
- reign
- receive
- sleigh

Exceptions:
- ancient
- either
- foreign
- forfeit
- height
- leisure
- neither
- seize
- sovereign
- weird

Sixth Rule: Adding suffixes to words ending in **y**

If a **y** is preceded by a vowel, leave it alone and add the suffix. For example,
- boyish
- displaying
- honeys
- playful
- preys
- stayed

If the **y** follows a consonant, change it to an **i** and add the suffix. For example,
- funniest
- happily
- penniless
- pitiful
- tried

Exceptions: To use certain suffixes, such as **-ing** keep the **y**. For example,
- babyhood
- denying
- ladylike
- partying
- worrying
- wryly

Seventh Rule: Making singular words plural

Add an **s** to most words. For example,
- books
- computers
- files

If a word ends in **s**, **ss**, **sh**, **ch**, or **x** always add **es**. For example,
- businesses
- dishes
- gases
- matches
- taxes

If a word ends in **y** preceded by a consonant, change the **y** to **ies**. For example,
- armies
- booties
- ladies
- libraries
- parties

If the **y** follows a vowel, just add **s**. For example,
- days
- joys
- says

Some words can be used as plurals without any changes. For example,
- antelope
- deer
- fish

Other words change their root spelling to form plurals. For example,
- goose/geese
- leaf/leaves
- tooth/teeth
- wolf/wolves

Changed word endings can also indicate a plural. For example,
- cactus/cacti
- octopus/octopi
- synopsis/synopses

L11 Teaching Spelling Strategies to ESL Students

Teaching spelling strategies to ESL students is challenging for instructors. Many of the inconsistencies of the English language with regards to word meaning and pronunciation are directly confronted by students when they begin to put words to paper. In addition, the homophonic, multi-syllabic nature of English can pose particular challenges to ESL students. However, there are many tips and tricks to help instructors and students sharpen their spelling skills.

Some Tricks for Teaching Spelling Strategies to ESL Students

ESL students benefit from many of the same spelling strategies that instructors use with native English-speaking populations. However, ESL students will inevitably require more time and practice when learning how to understand many of the spelling-related intricacies of the English language.

Using Memory Tricks or Mnemonics

Mnemonics are simple tricks students can use to help commit spelling words to memory. Associating the spelling of a word or part of a word with another word has proven to be a successful learning strategy. Providing students with some existing mnemonic examples will help them understand the concept, but students will be more successful if they create their own mnemonics for the words they have trouble spelling.

- My **secret**ary can't keep a secret.
- That is their **heir**loom.
- Add your **add**ress to your address book.
- That mos**quit**o better quit biting me.

Rhyming Helper

Rhyming is a classic spelling strategy for students of all ages. Rhyming a word or a part of a word with another word that is spelled the same is a great technique to help students learn. For example,

- fist, gist, mist
- mess, dress, unless, guess
- spell, smell, fell, tell, shell

These words are all spelled the same except for a different letter or two. Identifying how root sounds like this are spelled helps students quickly increase their spelling vocabularies.

Understanding Words That Sound Alike

For ESL students, spelling mistakes are often caused by a simple misunderstanding of word meaning. Some words in English are homophonic, meaning they sound exactly the same as another word but have a different meaning. Other words differ very subtly in how they are pronounced. While these words are not truly homophonic, they still pose challenges for ESL students. These similar sounding words are less problematic for ESL students in spoken conversation, but become a source of frustration for them when they construct written sentences. Calling attention to some of the most common similar sounding words can help demystify this confusing aspect of the English language. Consider the following examples:

- advise: Advise is a verb that means to counsel or suggest. (Would you advise me to go to graduate school?)
- advice: Advice is a noun that means a suggestion or an opinion about a matter at hand. (Ken gave me some good advice about going to graduate school.)

- conscious: Conscious is an adjective that means having knowledge of something or being aware or perceptive. (During that long meeting I was barely conscious.)
- conscience: Conscience is a noun and means to have an inner feeling to guide you through questions of right and wrong. (My conscience wouldn't let me take her money.)

- lead: Lead is a noun that refers to the dense, heavy metal. (This table feels like it's made of lead.)
- led: Led is the past participle form of the verb lead and means to guide or direct. (It was dark, but she led me across the field safely.)

L

Problem Parts of Words

Unfortunately, there are certain words that defy logic in English. While native speakers unconsciously accept that the words **good** and **food** can be spelled the same way yet pronounced differently, ESL students are understandably troubled by these illogical facets of their target language. Students should make a list of troublesome words and isolate exactly where the problem parts are within the words. These areas need to be studied diligently and committed to memory. For example,

- misspell
- privilege
- restaurant

Focusing on the specific letters and words that cause problems brings students' awareness to the source of the mistake and helps them to commit the proper spelling to memory.

Important Considerations for Students with Different Native Languages

Spelling is another area of ESL instruction where instructors run into the reality that there is no homogenized ESL student. Teaching spelling strategies to ESL students is complicated by the diversity of the demographic. Different students bring different native languages into the classroom. The interlanguages they create while they are in between their native language and their target language vary greatly depending on the phonetic, syntactic, semantic, and morphologic qualities of their native language.

A student whose native language is Spanish, for example, will face challenges with vowel sounds. Spanish uses a very static system with regards to how vowels are pronounced. The multitude of vowel sounds that English uses can cause particular spelling difficulties for native speakers of Spanish.

As an instructor, it is important to constantly be aware that the ESL experience varies greatly for every student, particularly when they speak different native languages.

 # L12 Mastering Spelling

English spelling is not only difficult, it can be downright frustrating because it is not consistent with the pronunciation of words. For instance, the **-ough** combination can have many different pronunciations, as seen in the words **cough**, **through**, and **although**. This does not mean students should just give up. English spelling does have patterns that can be learned, and there are tools to help students. Some words just have to be memorized.

Because English has absorbed so many words from different languages, it has also acquired spelling features of the words. Moreover, the Latin alphabet it uses is ill-suited to the sounds of a Germanic language like English. Some scientific and technical terms are based on Greek words—which has another alphabet. To make things more complicated, pronunciation has altered over the years, while spelling has not changed as much. For example, the silent **k** in words like **knight** used to be pronounced.

English spelling is an obvious target for reformers. They argue that it is chaotic and unnecessarily difficult to learn. Counter-arguments include the fact that a phonetically based spelling system (one based on sounds) would hide some semantic relationships (those based on meaning). For example, the words **sign** and **signify** are related (both come from the Latin **signus** for sign), but their kinship would not be as evident if **sign** were spelled **sine**.

Whether you are for or against English spelling reform, the fact remains that it is your responsibility to spell the words as they are currently accepted. In the world outside the classroom, spelling is also important. A misspelled document reflects badly on its author. Some people are poor spellers, and they have to work at it much harder than other people. Even avid readers can be bad at spelling.

Ideas for Learning to Spell New Words

Look, Cover, Write, Check, Look
Write a word clearly at the top of a piece of paper, then

Look: Look at the word. Say the word. Spell the word, using the letter names. Close your eyes and spell it. Open your eyes and check the spelling. If it is not the same, start again.

Cover: Fold over the top of the piece of paper so the word is hidden.

Write: Write the word from memory.

Check: Uncover the word. Check the spelling. Is it all right? If not, which parts are right?

Look: Look at the top word again.

Continue with the steps again until the word is written three times correctly.

Tracing
The word is written in large letters and the student traces over the word with their finger twice while saying the letters in the word. Using the letter names, A [ay], B [bee], C [cee], not the sounds. The student then writes it twice without looking at the word.

Saying the Letters Aloud
The student should write the word twice while saying the letters and then write it again without looking at the word. Use the letter names, A [ay], B [bee], C [cee], not the sounds.

Looking for the Words in Words
Students will find it easier to remember a word if you can encourage them to look for a word they know inside a word they do not know. You can help your students to come up with a sentence which draws attention to the embedded word.
- You hear with your ear
- What a hat!
- End is at the end in friend

Making Word Families
Students can be encouraged to relate a new word to others with some common features. For example,
- chat, chart, cheap
- main, gain, rain
- bush, rash, wish

Learning and Using Rules
Students can be helped to remember some spellings by learning spelling rules.

Memory Aids

Some words are difficult to remember, so it is useful to devise special ways of remembering them.

Using odd pronunciation:

- Saying **Wed-nes-day** for Wednesday
- Saying **bis-cu-it** for biscuit
- Saying **to-get-her** for together

Using sentences: Saying "big elephants can always upturn snake's eggs" to help spell **because**.

Reading and writing: Reading helps students to spell better.

Using the sounds in words: Students can be encouraged to sound out the word when spelling it. Many three-letter words can be sounded out, For example,

- big
- cat
- run

L13 Letter Formation

If your students are learning to print letters or are in need of improving their letter formation, you may find it useful to provide them with sheets of traceable letters. This will allow the students to practice the letters on their own time.

Traceable dotted letters are available online. Type **dotted print fonts** into a search engine to find printable worksheets.

Printing Upper-Case Letters

L

A   A   A   A   A   A   A   A   A   A   A

_____

B   B   B   B   B   B   B   B   B   B   B

_____

C   C   C   C   C   C   C   C   C   C   C

_____

D   D   D   D   D   D   D   D   D   D   D

_____

E   E   E   E   E   E   E   E   E   E   E

_____

F   F   F   F   F   F   F   F   F   F   F

_____

G   G   G   G   G   G   G   G   G   G   G

_____

H   H   H   H   H   H   H   H   H   H   H

_____

I   I   I   I   I   I   I   I   I   I   I

_____

J   J   J   J   J   J   J   J   J   J   J

_____

K   K   K   K   K   K   K   K   K   K   K

_____

L   L   L   L   L   L   L   L   L   L   L

M   M   M   M   M   M   M   M   M   M   M

N   N   N   N   N   N   N   N   N   N   N

O   O   O   O   O   O   O   O   O   O   O

P   P   P   P   P   P   P   P   P   P   P

Q   Q   Q   Q   Q   Q   Q   Q   Q   Q   Q

R   R   R   R   R   R   R   R   R   R   R

S   S   S   S   S   S   S   S   S   S   S

T   T   T   T   T   T   T   T   T   T   T

U   U   U   U   U   U   U   U   U   U   U

V   V   V   V   V   V   V   V   V   V   V

L

W   w   w   w   w   w   w   w   w   w   w

X   x   x   x   x   x   x   x   x   x   x

Y   Y   Y   Y   Y   Y   Y   Y   Y   Y   Y

Z   z   z   z   z   z   z   z   z   z   z

Printing Lower-Case Letters

a   a   a   a   a   a   a   a   a   a   a   a   a

b   b   b   b   b   b   b   b   b   b   b   b   b

c   c   c   c   c   c   c   c   c   c   c   c   c

d   d   d   d   d   d   d   d   d   d   d   d   d

e   e   e   e   e   e   e   e   e   e   e   e   e

f   f   f   f   f   f   f   f   f   f   f   f   f

g   g   g   g   g   g   g   g   g   g   g   g   g

h   h   h   h   h   h   h   h   h   h   h   h   h

i   i   i   i   i   i   i   i   i   i   i   i   i

j   j   j   j   j   j   j   j   j   j   j   j   j

k   k   k   k   k   k   k   k   k   k   k   k   k

l   l   l   l   l   l   l   l   l   l   l   l   l

m   m   m   m   m   m   m   m   m   m   m   m   m

n   n   n   n   n   n   n   n   n   n   n   n   n

o   o   o   o   o   o   o   o   o   o   o   o   o

p   p   p   p   p   p   p   p   p   p   p   p   p

q   q   q   q   q   q   q   q   q   q   q   q   q

r   r   r   r   r   r   r   r   r   r   r   r   r

L

s s s s s s s s s s s s s s

t t t t t t t t t t t t t t

u u u u u u u u u u u u u u

v v v v v v v v v v v v v v

w w w w w w w w w w w w w w

x x x x x x x x x x x x x x

y y y y y y y y y y y y y y

z z z z z z z z z z z z z z

SECTION M

Teaching Idioms

Content

M

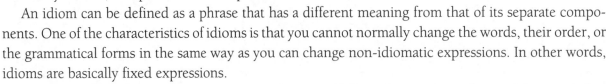
M1 What Is an Idiom?

Whenever you ask higher-level students what they would like to do more work on, the answer is invariably idioms, and phrasal verbs in particular.

An idiom can be defined as a phrase that has a different meaning from that of its separate components. One of the characteristics of idioms is that you cannot normally change the words, their order, or the grammatical forms in the same way as you can change non-idiomatic expressions. In other words, idioms are basically fixed expressions.

Sometimes the meaning of the idioms can be guessed from the meaning of one of the words but usually the meaning is completely different, which is why they are so tricky for students.

Care needs to be taken when writing idioms as many of them are only used in informal language. On the other hand, there are other expressions that are literary or old-fashioned and unsuitable for use in everyday language, except perhaps as a joke.

An appreciation of such expressions and a feeling for how and when they are used can certainly improve students' ability to read in the target language and to understand colloquial conversation. If the study of idioms is undertaken with the aim of improving receptive skills first, and then they are reinforced in daily conversations, the student will become more comfortable with them. This will help students to avoid problems with inappropriate use of idiomatic expressions. But how can students make sense of the plethora of idiomatic expressions that exist in everyday speech and writing? How can they even scratch the surface and approach this area of language in a systematic way?

One approach is to take certain basic key words in the target language and organize your notes selectively around them. For example, the English word **head** is the key word in a large number of idioms. The *Oxford Advanced Learner's Dictionary* lists (with definitions and notes on degree of formality) no fewer than 40 idioms in everyday use that contain this word. Other productive key words to look up in the dictionary for this purpose include colors, common animals, parts of the body, basic adjectives (e.g., long, fast), and natural phenomena (e.g., wind, sun). Use an up-to-date dictionary to refer to these terms, as opposed to a practice book devoted to idioms, because in these types of all-encompassing books, slightly obscure or old-fashioned expressions are often included.

Another approach is to compare idioms in L2 with idioms in the L1. This can be both an interesting exercise in itself and also a means for students to remember idioms more effectively. To illustrate the different meanings of an idiom, take the example **up to your eyes in work**. In French and Italian one is **submerged** in it, in German **suffocated** in it, in Spanish either **inundated** in it or **up to one's eyes** in it and in Serbian you have it **over your head**.

M2 Some Common Idioms

On the following pages you will find a number of common idioms. The idioms listed are organized in a few different ways: by key word (ball, way, word, etc.), by first word (in/out), or thematically (animals, body parts, foods, etc.).

Ball

a ball and chain

1. A problem that prevents you from doing what you would like to do: *The business never made any money and was regarded more as a ball and chain than anything else.*
2. [**humorous**] Somebody's husband or wife: *I must get home to the ball and chain!*

Origin: In the past, prisoners had to wear a heavy metal ball on a chain around one leg so that they could not escape.

the ball is in your/somebody's court

It is somebody's turn to speak, act, etc., next: *I've given them a list of the changes that I think are necessary, so the ball's in their court now.*

be on the ball

Be aware of what is happening and be able to react or deal with it quickly: *For the assistant manager's job we need someone who's really on the ball.*

get/keep/set/start the ball rolling

Begin/continue an activity, discussion, etc.: *I will start the ball rolling by introducing the first speaker.*

have (yourself) a ball [informal]

Enjoy yourself very much: *When these exams are finally over, we're going to have a ball.*

play ball (with somebody) [informal]

Be willing to work with other people in a helpful way, especially so that somebody can get what they want: *We need their help, but will they play ball?; So he won't play ball? He'll soon realize he can't manage without us.*

the whole ball of wax [informal]

The whole thing; everything: *I panicked, I cried—the whole ball of wax.*

Big

a big cheese/wheel [informal]

An important person with a lot of influence within an an organization, etc.: *His father's a big wheel in the industry.*

Origin: In this sense, **cheese** comes from the Urdu word **chiz**, meaning **thing**.

big deal (ironic) [informal]

Used for suggesting that something is not as important or impressive as somebody else thinks it is: *I've got tickets for next Saturday's football match. Big deal! Who's interested in football anyway?*

a big fish (in a little/small pond)

An important person but only in a small community, group, etc.: *I would rather stay here in the village and be a big fish in a little pond than go to the city where no one knows me; He thought he was important, but Harry was just a big fish in a very small pond.*

a big name/noise/shot [informal]

An important person: *What does Ian's dad do? Oh, he's a big shot in the city.*

the big picture [informal]

The situation as a whole: *Right now forget the details and take a look at the big picture.*

big time [informal]

1. (the big time) Great success in a profession, especially the entertainment business: *A bit-part actor who finally made the big time.*
2. On a large scale; to a great extent: *This time they've messed up big time!*

give somebody a big hand [informal]

Clap your hands loudly and enthusiastically: *Let's give a big hand, ladies and gentlemen, for our next performer...*

make it big

Be very successful: *He's hoping to make it big on television.*

me and my big mouth [spoken]

Used when you realize that you have said something that you should not have said: *I ruined the surprise, me and my big mouth!*

no big deal [spoken]

Used to say that something is not important or not a problem: *If I don't win, it's no big deal.*

one big happy family [informal]

A group of people who live or work together happily and without disagreements: *We were always together. We were like one big happy family;* (ironic) *Is your office a happy place to work in? Oh sure, we're just one big happy family. Everybody hates everybody else.*

too big for your boots [informal]

Thinking that you are more important than you really are: *His political rivals had decided that he was getting too big for his boots.*

Business

be (back) in business

Be working or operating (again) as normal: *Once the switch has been fixed, we will be back in business and we can use the machine again; It looks as though we're in business: she's agreed to lend us the money.*

be none of somebody's business; be no business of somebody's [informal]

No right to know something: *How much do you earn? That's none of your business; It's no business of yours who I go out with.*

the business end (of something) [informal]

The part of a tool, weapon, etc., that performs its particular function: *Never pick up a knife by the business end.*

business is business

A way of saying that financial and commercial matters are the important things to consider and that you should not be influenced by friendship, etc.: *He's a nice guy but business is business. He owes us money and he'll have to pay it back.*

get down to business

Start discussing or doing something seriously, especially after a time of social talk: *Well, it's getting late, perhaps we'd better get down to business.*

go about your business

Be busy with the things that you do every day: *He looked out onto the street and watched the people going about their daily business.*

have no business doing something/ to do something

Have no right to do something: *You have no business being here.*

it is business as usual

Things continue normally, despite difficulties or disturbances: *It was business as usual at the theater yesterday, despite all the renovations going on.*

like nobody's business [informal]

Very fast, very much, very hard, etc.: *He's been spending money like nobody's business recently.*

not be in the business of doing something

Not intending to do something (which it would be surprising for you to do): *I'm not in the business of getting other people to do my work for me.*

out of business

Having stopped operating as a business because there is no more money or work available: *The new regulations will put many small firms out of business; Some travel companies will probably go out of business this summer.*

Catch

be caught in the crossfire

Become involved in a situation where two people or groups of people are arguing, and suffer as a result: *When two industrial giants clash, small companies can get caught in the crossfire.*
Note: Crossfire is the firing of guns from two or more directions at the same time.

catch some rays [slang]

Sit or lie in the sun, especially in order to get a tan: *Let's go to the beach and catch some rays before the sun goes down.*

catch somebody's eye

Attract somebody's attention: *I liked all the paintings, but the one that really caught my eye was a Matisse; Can you try to catch the waiter's eye?*
eye-catching adj.: *an eye-catching advertisement*

catch somebody in the act (of doing something)

Find somebody while they are doing something they should not be doing: *She turned around to catch him in the act of trying to run upstairs.*
Note: This expression is often used in the passive: He was caught in the act of stealing a car.

catch somebody napping [informal]

Find somebody not prepared or not paying attention, and perhaps gain an advantage over them as a result: *Chelsea's defense was caught napping in the final moments of the game when Jones scored his second goal for Liverpool.*
Note: Nap means sleep, usually for a short time and especially during the day.

catch somebody off (their) guard

Happens when somebody is not prepared: *The question caught him off his guard and he couldn't answer; Businesses were caught off guard by the sudden rise in interest rates.*

catch somebody red-handed

Find somebody while they are doing something wrong, committing a crime, etc.: *The thief was caught red-handed as she was emptying the till.*
Origin: This originally referred to catching a person with blood still on their hands after killing somebody.

catch somebody with their pants down [informal]

Find or trap somebody when they are unprepared or not paying attention: *After the devastating attack on its military bases, the country was determined not to be caught with its pants down a second time.*

catch-22 (catch-22 + a catch-22 situation) [informal]

A difficult situation from which there is no escape because you need to do one thing before doing a second, and you cannot do the second thing before doing the first: *I can't get a job because I haven't got any experience, but I can't get experience until I get a job—it's a catch-22 situation.*

Origin: *Catch-22* is the title of a novel by Joseph Heller, in which the main character pretends to be crazy in order to avoid dangerous situations in war. The authorities say that he cannot be crazy if he is concerned about his own safety.

play catch-up

Try to equal somebody that you are competing against in a sport, competition, business, etc.: *The oil company has spent the last couple of years playing catch-up; We were forced to play catch-up after a bad start to the season.*

Change

change hands

Pass to a different owner: *The house has changed hands several times.*

change your mind

Change your decision or opinion: *He was intending to go to the party but now he's changed his mind and decided to stay in.*

a change of heart

A change in your attitude and feelings, especially by becoming kinder, more friendly, etc.: *The government has had a change of heart over the proposal to tax reforms and is now prepared to listen to public opinion.*

change the subject

Start to talk about something different, especially because what was being discussed was embarrassing or difficult to talk about: *I don't like talking about the war. Can't we change the subject?*

change your tune [informal]

Change your opinion about or your attitude to somebody/something: *Tom used to say that parents worry too much about their children, but he soon changed his tune when he became a parent himself!*

change your ways

Start to live or behave in a different way from before: *I've learned my lesson and I'm going to try to change my ways; It's unlikely your boss will change his ways.*

for a change

For variety; as an improvement on what usually happens: *We usually go to Cyprus for vacation but this year we've decided to stay at home for a change; Oh good! She's on time for a change.*

a wind/the winds of change

An event or a series of events that has started to happen and will cause important changes or results: *There's a wind of change in the attitude of voters; Winds of change were sweeping over the country.*

Origin: The former British prime minister Harold Macmillan used this phrase in a speech he made in 1960.

Dead

Dead and buried/gone

Dead, especially for a long time; long past and forgotten: *Long after I'm dead and gone, you'll still be carrying on the same as you ever were; Why bring up old disagreements that have been dead and buried for years?*

(as) dead as a/the dodo [informal]

No longer in existence; very old-fashioned: *Old business practices are as dead as a dodo in the computer age.*

Note: The dodo was a large bird that could not fly. It is now extinct (no longer exists).

(as) dead as a doornail [informal]

Completely dead: *This phone line is dead as a doornail.*

a dead duck [informal]

A plan, an idea, etc., that has failed or is certain to fail and that is therefore not worth discussing: *The new supermarket is going to be a dead duck—there's no demand for one in this area.*

a dead end [informal]

A point where no more progress can be made: *Lack of further clues meant that the murder investigation came to a dead end; He was in a dead-end job with no hope of a promotion.*

dead in the water

A person or plan that is dead in the water has failed and has little hope of succeeding in the future: *Now that the scandal is out, his leadership campaign is dead in the water.*

a dead letter/idea/proposal, etc.

Something that is no longer valid, useful, etc.: *The plans for a new school are a dead letter now that we know there will be no students for it.*

a dead loss

A person or thing that is useless or a complete failure: *This television is a dead loss—the picture fades completely after five minutes.*

dead meat [informal]

In serious trouble: *If anyone finds out, you're dead meat.*

(in) the dead of (the) night; at dead of night

In the quietest, darkest hours of the night: *She crept in at dead of night, while they were asleep.*

Opposite: in broad daylight

a dead ringer for somebody [informal]

A person who looks extremely like somebody else: *She's a dead ringer for her mother.*

Origin: A ringer was a person or thing that pretended to be another person or thing. In horse racing for example, a ringer was a horse that was substituted for another in order to cheat in a race.

dead wood [informal]

People or things that are no longer useful or necessary: *The management wants to cut costs by getting rid of all the dead wood in the factory. Fifty workers are to lose their jobs.*

Note: This refers to the parts of a tree or a branch that are dead and no longer produce fruit, etc.

dead to the world [informal]

Deeply asleep: *Within two minutes of getting into bed, I was dead to the world.*

over my dead body [spoken]

Used for saying that you will do everything possible to stop something from happening: *Mom, can I get a tattoo? Over my dead body!*

somebody wouldn't be seen/caught dead [spoken]

Used to say that you would not do a particular thing because you would feel stupid or embarrassed: *I wouldn't be seen dead in a hat like that; She wouldn't be caught dead in a place like this.*

Do

be/have to do with somebody/something

Be connected or concerned with somebody/something: *What do you want to see me about? It's to do with the letter you sent. I'm not sure what he does for a living but I know it's something to do with computers.*

could do with something [spoken]

Want or need something: *I could really do with a coffee; Her hair could have done with a wash; You look as if you could do with a good night's sleep.*

could/can do without something [spoken]

Not wanting something, for example criticism, advice, or complaints: *I could do without him telling me what to say all the time; I could have done without her calling me just as I was about to go out.*

do's and don'ts [informal]

What to do and what not to do; rules: *This book is a useful guide to the do's and don'ts of choosing and buying your first car.*

do something for somebody/something [informal]

Make somebody/something look better: *You know, that hat really does something for you!*

it/that (just) won't do; it/that will never do

Used to say that a situation is not satisfactory and should be changed or improved: *He's spending every afternoon in the park with his friends instead of going to school and that just won't do! I feel very upset but it would never do to show it.*

not do anything/a lot/much for somebody [informal]

Used to say that something does not make somebody look attractive: *That hairstyle doesn't do anything for her.*

that will do [informal]

Used to order somebody to stop doing or saying something that is sufficient or enough: *That'll do! I've heard enough of your complaints.*

what did you do with something?/where did you put, lose or hide something?

[usually in perfect and simple past tense] Used to ask what has been done with something or where something is: *What have you done with my scissors? They were on the kitchen table the last time I saw them.*

First

at first glance/sight

As things seem at first; judging by first appearances: *At first glance, the exam paper looked fairly difficult, but once I got started I found it quite easy.*

first of all

1. Before doing anything else; at the beginning: *First of all, let me ask you something.*
2. As the most important thing: *The content of any article needs, first of all, to be relevant.*

first among equals

The person or thing with the highest status in a group: *Our history classes were usually open discussion groups between us and our teacher, with the teacher as first among equals.*

first-come, first-served [saying]

People will be dealt with, seen, etc., strictly in the order in which they arrive, apply, etc: *We have 100 tickets for the performance, and they will be distributed on a first-come, first-served basis.*

first and foremost

Before everything else; most importantly: *First and foremost, we must ensure that the children are safe; Don't forget, he is first and foremost an actor, not a singer.*

(at) first hand

From your own experience or knowledge, rather than from somebody else; directly: *I know first hand what it is like to be poor—we always had very little money at home; We have a first-hand account of the raid from a witness.*

first off/up [informal]

Before anything else; to begin with: *First off, we will choose the teams, then we can start the game.*

first thing (tomorrow, in the morning, etc.)

At the beginning of the period of time mentioned, before doing anything else: *I always like a cup of tea first thing in the morning; Can you lend me some money? I'll pay you back first thing tomorrow.*

first things first [often humorous]

The most important or necessary duties, matters, etc., that must be dealt with before others: *First things first. We must make sure the electricity is turned off before we start repairing the stove; We have a lot to discuss, but, first things first, let's have a cup of coffee!*

(be) the first/last (person) to do something

Be very willing or likely/unwilling or unlikely to do something: *I'd be the first person to admit that I'm not perfect; Mary is the last person you'd see in a bar—she hates bars.*

from the (very) first

From the beginning: *They were attracted to each other from the very first.*

from first to last

From beginning to end; during the whole time: *It's a fine performance that commands attention from first to last.*

make the first move

Do something before somebody else, in order to end or to begin something: *If he wants to see me, he should make the first move.*

put somebody/something first

Treat somebody/something as the most important person or thing: *A politician should always put the needs of the country first and not his personal ambitions; He never put his family first.*

there's a first time for everything [saying, humorous]

The fact that something has not happened before does not mean that it will never happen: *The flood water has never reached the house before. Well, there's a first time for everything.*

Get

be getting on [informal]

1. People becoming old: *I'm getting on a bit now and I can't walk as well as I used to.*
2. The time becoming late: *It's getting on, so I'd better be off home.*

can't get over something [spoken]

Used to say that you are shocked, surprised, amused, etc., by something: *I can't get over how rude she was to me.*

get away from it all [informal]

Go away somewhere on holiday/vacation, etc., in order to escape from pressures at work, home, city life, etc.: *We went walking to get away from it all for a while; Why don't you get away from it all and spend a weekend in the mountains?*

get hold of somebody/something

Obtain something; reach or contact somebody: *Do you know where I can get hold of a telephone directory for Paris?; I spent all morning on the phone trying to get hold of the manager.*

get somebody nowhere/not get somebody anywhere

Not help somebody make progress: *His job is getting him nowhere. He ought to try and find another one; All these questions aren't getting us anywhere. We need to make a decision.*

get somewhere/anywhere/nowhere

Make some/no progress: *Now at last we're getting somewhere!; You'll get nowhere in life if you don't work harder; Are you getting anywhere with that new manager?*

get there [informal]

1. Finally achieve your aim or complete a task: *Peter is a slow learner, but he gets there in the end.*
2. [spoken] Used to express surprise or disapproval that somebody has been selfish, stupid, ungrateful, etc.: *I can't believe he didn't even say thank you. How ungrateful can you get?*

there's no getting away from it [informal]

Cannot ignore an important and possibly unpleasant fact: *There's no getting away from it. He's simply a better player than me.*

what are you, was he, etc., getting at? [spoken]

Used to ask, especially in an angry way, what somebody is/was suggesting: *I'm partly to blame? What exactly are you getting at?*

Give

don't give me that [spoken, informal]

Used to tell somebody that you do not accept what they say: *I didn't have time to do it. Oh, don't give me that!*

give as good as you get

Defend yourself very well when you fight or argue with somebody: *Don't worry about her. She can give as good as she gets.*

give it up (for somebody) [informal]

Show your approval of somebody by clapping your hands: *Give it up for Tommy!*

give me a break! [spoken]

Used when somebody wants somebody else to stop doing or saying something that is annoying, or to stop saying something that is not true: *I didn't mean it like that, so give me a break!*
Note: also used to express disbelief

give me something/ somebody (any day/ time) [spoken]

Used for saying you like something much more than the thing just mentioned: *I don't like the cafeteria. Give me a nice meal at a restaurant any day; I don't like baseball very much. Give me football any time.*

give somebody a break

Give somebody a chance; not judge somebody too harshly: *Give the lad a break—it's only his second day on the job.*

give it to somebody [spoken]

Punish somebody severely: *The manager will really give it to you when he finds out what you've done.*

give and take

Be willing to listen to other people's wishes and points of view and to change your demands, if necessary: *If we want this marriage to be successful, we both have to learn to give and take.*
Noun: *We can't all expect to have exactly what we want. There has to be some give and take.*

give or take (something)

Approximately correct: *It took us three hours, give or take a few minutes; It'll cost about $1,000, give or take.*

I/I'll give you that

Used when you are admitting that something is true: *I said an hour ago that we were going the wrong way, didn't I? Yes you did, I'll give you that.*

Have

and what have you [spoken]

Other things, people, etc., of the same kind: *He does all sorts of things—building, gardening, fencing, and what have you; If you add up the cost of gas, insurance, repairs and what have you, running a car certainly isn't cheap.*

have had it [informal]

1. Be in a very bad condition; be unable to be repaired: *This television's had it—we'll have to get a new one; The car had had it.*
2. Be extremely tired: *I've had it! I'm going to bed.*
3. Have lost all chance of surviving something: *When the truck smashed into me, I thought I'd had it.*
4. Be going to experience something unpleasant: *Dad saw you scratch the car— you've had it now!*
5. (also **have had it up to here [with somebody/ something]**) Be unable to accept a situation any longer: *I've had it with him— he's let me down once too often; I've had it up to here with these tax forms.*

have it (that ...)

Say that ... ; claim that ... : *Rumor has it that you're going to retire. Is that true?; She will have it that her brother is a better athlete than you, but I don't believe her.*

have it in for somebody [informal]

Want to harm or cause trouble for somebody because you have had a bad experience with them: *She's had it in for those boys ever since they damaged her roses; The government has had it in for the trade unions for years.*

have it in you

Have the unexpected ability, determination, courage, etc., to do something: *She managed to finish the crossword all on her own! I didn't know she had it in her!*

have it out with somebody

Have a serious discussion with somebody in order to end a disagreement, quarrel, etc.: *You must stop ignoring Fred because of what he said, and have it out with him once and for all!*

he, she, etc., isn't having any (of it) [informal]

Not willing to listen to or believe something: *I suggested sharing the cost, but he wasn't having any of it. I tried to persuade her to wait but she wasn't having any.*

Make

have the makings of something

(of a person) Have the necessary qualities or character to become something: *She's got the makings of a good tennis player, but she needs to practice much more.*

in the making

Developing into something or being made: *He's very good at public speaking—I think he's a politician in the making.*

make a break for it [informal]

Try to escape from prison, etc.: *Six prisoners shot a guard and made a break for it in a stolen car.*

make as if to do something [written]

Make a movement to seem as if you are about to do something: *He made as if to speak.*

make do (with something); make something do

Manage with something that is not really satisfactory: *I really need a large frying pan but if you haven't got one I'll have to make do with that small one; I didn't have time to go shopping today so we'll just have to make do.*

make a go of something [informal]

Be successful in something: *We've had quite a few problems in our marriage, but we're both determined to make a go of it.*

make good [informal]

Become rich and successful, especially when you have started your life poor and unknown: *He's a local boy made good.*

make good something

1. Pay for, replace or repair something that has been damaged or lost: *The suitcase went missing at the airport so the airline has agreed to make good the loss; The mechanic explained that they would have to make good the damage to the body of the car before they re-sprayed it.*

2. Do what you promised, threatened, intended, etc., to do: *When she became president she made good her promise to ensure equal pay for both men and women.*

make it

1. Be successful in your job: *She's a very good dancer but I'm not sure she'll make it as a professional; He wants to be a professor by the time he's 30. Do you think he'll make it?*

2. Succeed in reaching a place: *The train leaves in 10 minutes. Hurry up or we won't make it; I don't think we'll make it before dark.*

3. Survive after an illness, accident, etc.: *Do you think she's going to make it, doctor? It's really too soon to say.*

make like . . . [informal]

Pretend to be, know, or have something in order to impress people: *He makes like he's the greatest actor of all time.*

make the most of something

Get as much good as you can out of something: *The meeting finished early, so I decided to make the most of being in London and do some shopping; The opportunity won't come again, so make the most of it now.*

make nothing of something

1. Treat something as easy or unimportant: *What a hill! But even with her heavy bag, Amy made nothing of it and was moving at top speed.*
2. Not be able to understand or make sense of something: *He went to bed again and thought it over, but could make nothing of it. The more he thought about it, the less he understood.*

make-or-break [informal]

The thing which decides whether something succeeds or fails: *This movie is make-or-break for the production company; This is a make-or-break year for us.*

make something of yourself

Be successful in your life: *She has the education, the talent, and the brains to really make something of herself.*

of your own making

Used about a problem or difficulty caused by you rather than by somebody/something else: *The problem is of your own making, so don't try to blame anyone else.*

Take

be on the take [informal]

Accept money from somebody for helping them in a dishonest or illegal way: *It now seems that some of the officials were on the take, by accepting bribes and then issuing fake passports.*

be somebody's for the taking; be there for the taking

Easy to get: *With the team's closest rivals out of the championship, the title was theirs for the taking; She was surprised to find the money on the kitchen table, just there for the taking.*

have what it takes (to do something) [informal]

Have the qualities, ability, etc., needed to be successful: *He's certainly ambitious, but if you ask me he hasn't really got what it takes to be the best.*

I, you, etc., can't take somebody anywhere [informal, often humorous]

Used to say that you cannot trust somebody to behave well in public: *You've got soup all over your shirt—I can't take you anywhere, can I?*

take it [informal]

(often used with can/could) Be able to bear or tolerate something difficult or unpleasant such as stress, criticism, or pain: *They argued so much that finally he couldn't take it any more and he left her; People are rude to her in her job, and she feels she's taken it for long enough.*

take it (that...)

Think or suppose that something is true, will happen, etc.: *"I take it that you won't be back for lunch," she said as they left; You speak French, I take it?*

take it from here/there

1. Continue doing something that somebody else has started: *I explained how to start the machine, and let him take it from there; You work out who you want on your team and I'll take it from there.*
2. **They/we will take it from here/there**: they/we will do something and then decide what to do next: *We'll work out a business plan, see what the bank says, and then take it from there.*

take it from me (that...) [informal]

Believe me, because I have personal experience: *Take it from me—it's not easy to become a professional writer.*

take it on/upon yourself to do something

Decide to do something without asking anyone for permission (or being told to): *He took it upon himself to dismiss my secretary, which he had no right to do.*

take it out of somebody; take a lot out of somebody

Make somebody very tired or weak: *Driving all day really takes it out of you; That flu bug has really taken a lot out of her.*

take it out on somebody [informal]

Behave in an unpleasant way towards somebody because you feel angry, disappointed, etc., although it is not their fault: *I know you've had a bad day at work, but don't take it out on me.*

take something as it comes

Deal with difficulties as they happen, without worrying too much: *I don't plan for the future. I like to take life as it comes.*

Way

a lot, not much, etc., in the way of something

A lot, etc. of something: *We don't do a lot in the way of exercise; Is there much in the way of nightlife around here?*

across the way

On the other side of the street, etc.: *Music blared from the open window of the house across the way.*

all the way

1. **(also the whole way)** During the whole journey/period of time: *She didn't speak a word to me all the way back home.*
2. Completely; as much as it takes to achieve what you want: *I'm fighting him all the way; You can count on my support—I'm with you all the way.*

(that's/it's) always the way [spoken]

Used to say that things often happen in a particular way, especially when it is not convenient: *I was already late, and then I got stuck in a traffic jam. Yes, that's always the way, isn't it?*

any way you slice it (cut it) [informal]

However you choose to look at a situation: *Any way you slice it, consumers pay more for certain products in some countries than others.*

be born/be made that way

(of a person) Behave or do things in a particular manner because it is part of your character: *It's not his fault he's so sensitive—he was born that way.*

be in a bad way

Be very ill or in serious trouble: *He was attacked in the street last night and he's in quite a bad way, I understand; I hear the company's in a bad way. Yes, it's lost a lot of money.*

be on the way out/in

Be going out of/coming into fashion: *Short skirts are on the way out.*

be (well) on the/your way to/towards something

Be about to achieve something in the near future (usually something good): *We're on the way towards an election victory; He's well on the way to establishing himself among the top 10 players in the world.*

be set in your ways

Be unable or unwilling to change your behavior, habits or ideas, usually because you are old: *He's too set in his ways now to think about a career change.*

be under way

Have started and be now progressing or taking place: *A major search is under way to find the escaped prisoners; Negotiations are under way to resolve the dispute.*

by the way [spoken]

Used for introducing something you have just thought of, which may or may not be connected to what has just been said: *I had a meeting with Graham at work today ... by the way, I've invited him and his wife to lunch on Sunday.*

by way of something

1. **(of a journey)** Passing through a place: *They're going to Poland by way of France and Germany.*
2. As a kind of something; as something: *What are you thinking of doing by way of a vacation this year?; The flowers are by way of a thank-you for all her help.*

come your way

Happen to you or come into your possession, temporarily or permanently: *Some good luck came his way; When my grandmother dies, quite a lot of money will be coming my way.*

do something in a big/small way

Do something to a great/small extent; do something on a large/small scale: *He's got himself into debt in a big way; She collects antiques in a small way.*

do something on/along the way

1. Do something as you go somewhere: *Buy a burger and eat it on the way.*
2. Do something during the process of doing something else: *I've succeeded in this business, and met a lot of nice people along the way.*

either way; one way or the other

Used to say that it does not matter which one of two possibilities happens, is chosen or is true: *Was it his fault or not? Either way, an explanation is due; We could meet today or tomorrow. I don't mind one way or the other.*

every which way [informal]

In all directions: *Her hair was flying every which way.*

get in the way (of something)

Prevent somebody from doing something; prevent something from happening: *He wouldn't allow emotions to get in the way of him doing his job.*

get something out of the way

Deal with a task or difficulty so that it is no longer a problem or worry: *I'm glad I've got that visit to the dentist out of the way.*

get/have your (own) way (also have it/ things everything (all) your (own) way)

Get, believe, or do what you want, usually despite of the wishes or feelings of others: *She always gets her own way in the end; All right, have it your own way—I'm tired of arguing.*

give way (give in)

Break or fall down: *The bridge gave way under the weight of the large truck; I gave in to her demands so she got everything she wanted.*

give way (to somebody/something)

1. Allow somebody/something to go first: *Give way to traffic coming from the left.*
2. Feel and express a strong emotion, without trying to hide it or stop it: *She refused to give way to despair.*
3. Allow somebody to have what they want: *In arguments, I'm always the first to give way. We must not give way to their demands.*
4. Be replaced by something: *The storm gave way to bright sunshine.*

go a long/some way towards doing something

Help very much/a little in achieving something: *The new law goes a long way towards solving the problem.*

go out of your way (to do something)

Make a special effort to do something, usually to help or please somebody: *She went out of her way to cook a really nice meal.*

go somebody's way

1. Travel in the same direction as somebody: *I'm going your way. Do you want a lift?*
2. **(of events)** Be favorable to somebody: *Did you hear Alan got the job? It seems that things are going his way at last.*

go your own way

Do what you want, especially against the advice of others: *Teenagers always go their own way, and it's no use trying to stop them.*

have a way of doing something

Used to say that somebody often does something, or that something often happens in a particular way, especially when it is out of your control: *He has a way of arriving when you're least expecting him; Long-distance relationships have a way of not working out.*

have a way with somebody/something

Have a special ability to deal with somebody/something: *She's a very good teacher. She has a way with children; She's got a way with words (she is very good at expressing herself).*

in a way; in one way (also in some ways)

To a certain extent: *In a way, living in the town is better than the country, because there's much more to do; In one way, I'm sorry we didn't stay longer; I agree with you in some ways.*

in his, her, its, etc., (own) way

In a manner that is appropriate to or typical of a person or thing but that may seem unusual to other people: *I think she does love you in her own way.*

in more ways than one

Used to show that something that has been said has more than one meaning: *She's a big woman, in more ways than one (she is big in size, and also important or powerful).*

in the/somebody's way

Stopping somebody from moving or doing something: *You'll have to move—you're in my way; I left them alone, as I felt I was in the way.*

keep/stay out of somebody's way

Avoid somebody: *He's got a lot of work to do at the moment, so if I were you I'd stay out of his way until he's got it finished.*

look the other way

Ignore somebody/something deliberately: *We only had three tickets, but the woman at the door looked the other way and let all four of us in.*

lose your way

1. Become lost: *We lost our way in the dark.*
2. Forget or move away from the purpose or reason for something: *I feel that the project has lost its way.*

make way (for somebody/something)

Make enough space for somebody/something; allow somebody/something to pass: *Could you move your books to make way for the food?; People made way for my wheelchair.*

make your way (to/towards something)

Go to/towards something: *Would passengers please make their way to gate 15 for the flight to Paris; Don't worry, we can make our own way to the airport (get there without help, a ride, etc.).*

make your way in something

Succeed in something, especially a job: *She's trying to make her way in the fashion business; The time had come to leave home and start to make his way in the world.*

my way or the highway [informal]

Used to say that somebody else has either to agree with your opinion or leave: *Right now there is only one rule here. It's my way or the highway.*

no way [informal]

Definitely not; never: *Are you going to stay at school after you're 16? No way. I want to get a job; No way am I going to speak to him again!*

not stand in somebody's way

Not trying to stop somebody from doing something: *If you want to become a singer, we won't stand in your way.*

on your/the/its way

1. Coming; going: *If she phones again, tell her I'm on my way (coming to see her); I'd better be on my way soon (leave soon).*
2. During the journey: *I bought some bread on the way home.*
3. **(of a baby)** Not yet born: *She has two children and another one on the way.*

(in) one way and/or another/the other

In various different ways now considered together: *One way and another we had a very good time when we were students; In one way or another, we will finish the project.*

the other way around/round

1. In the opposite position, direction, or order: *I think it should go on the other way round.*
2. The opposite situation: *I didn't leave you. It was the other way around (you left me).*

out of the way

1. No longer stopping somebody from moving or doing something: *I moved my legs out of the way so that she could get past.*
2. Finished; dealt with: *Our region is poised for growth once the election is out of the way.*
3. Far from a town or city: *It's a lovely place, but it's a bit out of the way; A little out-of-the-way place on the coast.*

out of your way

Not on the route that you planned to take: *I'd love a ride home—if it's not out of your way.*

see which way the wind blows

See what most people think, or what is likely to happen before you decide how to act yourself: *Most politicians are careful to see which way the wind's blowing before they make up their minds.*

a/the/somebody's way of life

The typical pattern of behavior of a person or group: *the American way of life.*

that's the way [informal]

Used for showing pleasure or approval of what somebody is doing or has done: *That's the way. Just keep playing like that and you'll win.*

that's the way the cookie crumbles; that's the way it goes [informal]

A situation that cannot be changed, so it must be accepted: *She met somebody else and left me. That's the way the cookie crumbles, I suppose.*

there's more than one way to skin a cat [saying, humorous]

Many different ways to achieve something: *Have you thought about a different approach? There's more than one way to skin a cat.*

to my, your, etc., way of thinking

In my, etc., opinion: *To his way of thinking, cell phones should be banned on public transit.*

way back [informal]

A long time ago: *We've known each other since way back; I first met her way back in the fifties.*

the way of the world

What often happens; what is common: *Marriages don't always last for ever. That's the way of the world, I'm afraid.*

way to go! [informal, spoken]

Used to tell somebody that you are pleased about something they have done: *Good work, guys! Way to go!*

the way to somebody's heart

The way to make somebody like or love you: *The way to a man's heart is through his stomach (by giving him good food).*

work your way through college, etc.

Have a paid job while you are a student: *She had to work her way through law school.*

work, etc. your way through something

Read or do something from the beginning to the end of something: *He worked his way through the dictionary learning 10 new words every day; He's eating his way through all the restaurants that are recommended in the* Good Food Guide.

work your way up

Start with a badly paid, unimportant job and work hard until you get a well paid, important job: *He's worked his way up from an office junior to managing director.*

you, etc., can't have it both ways

You must choose between two things even though you would like both of them: *You want an interesting job that pays well and yet one where you don't have many responsibilities. Well, you can't have it both ways.*

Word

be as good as your word

Do what you have promised to do: *You'll find that she's as good as her word—she always comes if she says she will.*

be a man/woman of his/her word

Always do what he/she has promised to do: *If he said he'd help you, he will—he's a man of his word.*

by word of mouth

In spoken, not written, words: *The news spread by word of mouth.*

(right) from the word go [informal]

From the very beginning: *I knew from the word go that it would be difficult.*

(not) get a word in edgewise [informal]

(**usually used with can or could**) Not be able to say something, because somebody else is talking too much: *I tried to tell him what I thought, but I couldn't get a word in edgewise.*

give somebody your word (that ...); have somebody's word (that ....)

Promise somebody/be promised (that): *I give you my word that I'll pay you tomorrow; I've got his word that he'll fix the car by the weekend.*

go back on your word

Not do what you have promised; break a promise: *He said he wouldn't charge more than $100, but he went back on his word and gave me an invoice for $150.*

have a word (with somebody) (about something)

Have a short conversation about something, especially in private: *Can I have a word, Marie? It's about Jane.*

have/exchange words (with somebody) (about something)

Argue or quarrel with somebody because you do not like the way they have behaved: *I had to have words with him about his behavior; They both got angry and had words.*

in a word [spoken]

Used for giving a very short, usually negative, answer or comment: *In a word, stupid is how I'd describe him.*

in other words

Expressed in a different way; that is to say: *I don't think this is the right job for you, Pete. In other words, you want me to leave. Is that it?*

(not) in so/as many words

(Not) in exactly the same words that somebody says were used: *Did he actually say in so many words that there was no hope of a cure?*

keep/break your word

Do/fail to do what you have promised: *Do you think she'll break her word and tell everyone?*

leave word (with somebody)

Leave a message with somebody: *He left word with his secretary about where to contact him if necessary.*

not be the word for it

Used to say that a word or an expression does not describe something fully or strongly enough: *Unkind isn't the word for it! I've never seen anyone treat an animal so cruelly!*

not/never have a good word to say for/about somebody/something [informal]

Not/never have anything positive to say about somebody/something: *She rarely has a good word to say about her neighbors; Nobody has a good word to say about the new computer system.*

not a word (to somebody) (about something)

Do not say anything to somebody/anybody about something: *Not a word to Jean about the party—it's a surprise!; Remember, not a word about how much it cost.*

a play on words

A clever or amusing use of a word that has more than one meaning, or of words that have different meanings but sound similar; a pun: *When Elvis had his hair cut off in the army he said, "Hair today and gone tomorrow." It was a play on words—the usual expression is "here today and gone tomorrow."*

put in a (good) word (for somebody)

Say something good about somebody to somebody else in order to help them: *If you put in a good word for me, I might get the job.*

put words in/into somebody's mouth

Say or suggest that somebody has said something, when they have not: *You're putting words in my mouth. I didn't say the whole house was dirty, I just said the living room needed a clean.*

the spoken/written word

The language, in speaking/writing: *The spoken word is often very different from the written word.*

take somebody at their word

Believe exactly what somebody says or promises: *She said I could go and stay with her in London whenever I wanted, so I took her at her word.*

take somebody's word for it

Believe something that somebody has said: *You know more about cars than I do, so if you think it needs a new gearbox, I'll take your word for it; Can I take your word for it that the text has all been checked?*

take the words (right) out of somebody's mouth

Say exactly what another person was going to say: *The speed limit on highways should be raised. I agree completely! You've taken the words right out of my mouth!*

too funny, sad, etc., for words

Extremely funny, sad, etc.: *The comedian was too funny for words.*

words fail me

I cannot express how I feel (because I am too surprised, angry, etc.): *Words fail me! How could you have been so stupid?*

word for word

In exactly the same words; translated directly from another language: *I repeated what you said, word for word; a word-for-word account, translation, etc.*

a word to the wise

Used to introduce some advice, especially when only a few words are necessary: *The band is now touring America. A word to the wise—make sure you book tickets early.*

your, his, etc., word is law

Used to say that somebody has complete power and control: *Their father is very old-fashioned. His word is law in their house.*

your, his, etc., word is (as good as) your, his, etc., bond

Used to say that somebody always does what they promise to do: *Don't worry, you can trust my brother. His word's as good as his bond.*

your, his, etc., word of honor

Used to refer to somebody's sincere promise: *He gave me his word of honor that he'd never drink again.*

your/the last/final word (on/about something)

Your, etc., final decision or statement about something: *Will you take $900? No, $1,000 and that's my last word; Is that your final word on the matter?*

M3 Expressions with **In** and **Out**

Below are some common idioms beginning with either **in** or **out**. These, and other idioms, will be useful for more advanced students to fully understand the language and begin to sound like a native speaker.

Idioms with In

Idiom	Meaning	Example
in the nick of time	nearly too late; just in time; under the wire	They jumped from the burning boat in the nick of time—just before it sank.
in the nude	naked; in the buff	Sleeping in the nude has advantages and disadvantages.
in the offing	ready to happen, soon to be	A great event was in the offing: the discovery of penicillin.
in the picture	part of the scene; a factor	As Mr. Martin lost the election, he's not in the picture anymore.
in the poorhouse	poor; having little money	In 1936, they were in the poorhouse. They couldn't grow crops, and nobody had a job.
in the red	showing a financial loss; losing money	Last year our business was still in the red—still showing a loss.
in the road	blocking the way; preventing movement	We'll have to move the table. It's in the road.
in the running	competitive; could win	With ten games remaining, the Cubs are still in the running. They have a chance to win.

Idioms with **Out**

Idiom	Meaning	Example
out loud	loud enough to hear; spoken clearly	Dad was very angry, but he didn't swear out loud.
out of	have no more; have none; run out	Stop at the bakery, please. We're out of bread.
out of bounds	off the playing field; across boundary lines	Ramon kicked the soccer ball over my head and out of bounds.
out of breath	short of breath; puffing; out of breath	She was out of breath after climbing the stairs.
out of commission	not operating; out of order	My brain is out of commission. I can't think today.
out of context	taken out of the sentence; missing important words	Brian's comment, "Roll of the dice," was taken out of context.
out of control	not managed; wild; not under control	The crowd was out of control. People were fighting and looting.
out of hand	not controlled; disciplined	The children got out of hand. I couldn't control them.
out of harm's way	out of danger; in a safe place	Jerry parked the car off the road—out of harm's way.

M4 Animal Idioms

Choose the correct meaning of each idiom.

1. Wow! **It's raining cats and dogs** today! I wish I'd brought my umbrella to school!
    a) I forgot my umbrella today.
    b) It's raining heavily.
    c) Cats and dogs are falling from the sky.

2. When I told my mom I would be home around 2 a.m. **she had a cow**!
    a) My mom bought a baby cow.
    b) My mom is really strange.
    c) My mom was really upset.

3. Jean: How did you know it was my birthday today?
    Susan: Oh, **a little birdie told me!**
    a) Jean told Susan it was her birthday.
    b) An unnamed person told Susan about Jean's birthday.
    c) Susan told Jean it was her birthday.

4. Frank: Why didn't your brother ride the roller coaster with us?
    Sam: Oh, he's such a **scaredy cat**! He won't get on any fast ride.
    a) Sam's brother is afraid to ride the roller coaster.
    b) Sam's brother is a cat.
    c) Sam's brother didn't go on the roller coaster.

5. When the telemarketer told me I could buy some concert tickets for only $10.00 if I gave him my credit card number, **it seemed a little fishy** to me, so I hung up the phone.
    a) I thought the telemarketer smelled like a fish and I didn't like that.
    b) I thought the telemarketer was a dangerous fish and he scared me.
    c) I thought the telemarketer was dishonest and I felt suspicious of him.

6. I never learned how to use a computer, so I lost my job to a new employee. **It's a dog-eat-dog world**.
    a) Only the strong or the best survive.
    b) Dogs are eating dogs at the office.
    c) Dogs like to eat dogs for lunch.

M5 Idioms with Body Parts

Match the equivalent or near-equivalent sentences.

_____ 1. You did it. You **have to face the music.**

_____ 2. Yes, you **hit the nail on the head**!

_____ 3. You two don't **see eye to eye**.

_____ 4. You have to **learn it by heart**.

_____ 5. You are **an old hand** at teaching.

_____ 6. That's great! You have everything **under your thumb**.

_____ 7. You don't want to **stick your neck out**, do you?

   a) You have to memorize it.
   b) You're experienced.
   c) You have control of the situation.
   d) You don't want to take the risk.
   e) You have to accept the consequences of your actions.
   f) You don't agree with each other.
   g) You're absolutely right.

M6 Food Idioms

Complete each sentence with the appropriate word or phrase.

1. The **cream of the crop** means it is _____.
   a) the worst
   b) the best

2. To **egg on** means to _____.
   a) encourage
   b) discourage

3. If it's **just your cup of tea**, it is _____.
   a) perfect
   b) all wrong

4. If you are **cool as a cucumber**, you are _____.
   a) panicked
   b) calm

5. If you **have a finger in the pie**, you are _____ in something.
   a) involved
   b) disinterested

6. **Use your noodle** means _____.
   a) to act
   b) to think

7. **In a nutshell** means _____.
   a) concisely
   b) it is finished

8. **In the soup** means _____.
   a) in serious trouble
   b) having a good time

9. A **hot potato** is a question which _____.
   a) answers itself
   b) is difficult to settle

10. If you **eat humble pie** you _____.
    a) accept shame
    b) are defensive

M7 Change Idioms into Everyday English

One helpful way to test students' understanding of idioms is to have them translate idiomatic expressions into everyday English. Students must assess the context and the intended meaning and explain what the idiom is saying.

1. He was **all ears** when his boss talked.

_____.

2. He is a **chip off the old block**.

_____.

3. He is **thick in the head**.

_____.

4. The bank robbers were **armed to the teeth**.

_____.

5. His comments **threw a wet blanket** on the discussion.

_____.

6. They were **beat** after three days of hard work.

_____.

7. Jack **was hard up** to pay his rent.

_____.

8. The storm left them **all in the same boat**.

_____.

9. The house fire meant we had to **start from scratch**.

_____.

M8 Idioms Lesson Plan

Idioms

Proficiency/Grade level: Intermediate and above

Objectives:
* Students will be able to identify what idiomatic language is and be able to give examples.
* Students will communicate effectively with others.

Materials:
* Index cards with an idiomatic expression written on one side and the definition written on the other (one card per pair of students)
* One sheet of white paper per pair of students
* Pencils, colored pencils, markers for each pair of students
* Nine game cards

Procedure

Pre Lesson: (5 minutes)

Begin by saying that idioms are words, phrases, or expressions that cannot be taken literally and every language has them. Learning them makes understanding and using a language a lot easier and more fun!

Provide the example **raining cats and dogs**. Ask students to describe what they visualize when they hear the expression and ask if anyone knows what the expression means. Ask someone to share what he or she visualized and draw a picture to go along with it on the board. Then explain to the students that they will be getting into groups and discussing and illustrating different idioms that they will be given.

Learning Activity: (10 minutes)

Divide students into pairs and give them an index card. The pairs will discuss their idiomatic expression and share it with the rest of the students at their table and discuss possible situations when they would use it. Each pair will then illustrate the literal meaning of the expression itself, just as they did in the opening activity with **raining cats and dogs**. Students will use a pencil to write the idiomatic expression on the reverse side of the paper.

Practice: (10-15 minutes)

Once the students are done illustrating their expression, they will give it to the teacher to display on the board. Next to these illustrations, there will be game cards (one for each illustration that the students have drawn) that are numbered on one side and have one of the idiomatic expressions written on the other side. As a class, students will match the appropriate expression with the literal illustration that describes it. They must pick a number, read the expression written on the back of it, and then choose an illustration that depicts it. Once a match is made, the teacher will ask the group that had the phrase to share what it means. The teacher will give an example of when it would be used.

Closure/Extension: (2 minutes)

After the activity, the teacher will ask the students to share any experience they have had with idioms. For the remainder of the week, students will be encouraged to pay specific attention to idiomatic phrases, or any phrases they do not understand, and write them down so they can bring them to class for further discussion.

M9 Idioms Review

In pairs, take turns asking each other the following questions. Discuss the meanings of any idioms you are unfamiliar with.

1. Do you know any songs or poems **by heart**?

2. Do you **take after** your mother or your father?

3. Do you **have a crush on** anyone right now?

4. Have you ever seen anything **blow up**?

5. What's the difference between **on sale** and **for sale**?

6. Is there anything your **heart is set on** getting for your next birthday?

7. Have you ever **put your foot in your mouth**?

8. What was the last thing you did that **took a lot of guts**?

9. How long does it take you to **go back and forth** to school every day?

10. Are you getting **fed up with** studying idioms?

M10 Idiom Games

Idioms are common, everyday expressions with figurative meanings. When taken literally, idioms do not make much sense, but they do offer great opportunities for creative thinking, humor, and word play. Get your students' study of idioms soaring with these classroom games. To play, give groups of three or four students cards with unfamiliar idioms.

Idiom Bluffs: Each group writes the real definition and two false definitions on the back of each idiom card. Later, give the group a chance to read its cards and have the rest of the class guess the true definition.

Idiom Pictionary: Each student takes one idiom card. If the idiom is not well-known, the student can check the meaning. He or she draws a quick picture of the literal meaning and invites the group to guess the idiom.

Eat Your Idioms: Give your students some food for thought as they create a plateful of idiom snacks. Brainstorm a list of idioms having to do with food and eating, such as **apple of your eye** and **go bananas**. Invite students to make idiom snacks by cutting food shapes out of construction paper and writing the idiom on the shape. Then have them use glue sticks to attach the shapes to paper plates. Display these full plates with the title **Eat Your Idioms**.

The Idiom Times: Give your class a chance to participate in a group project by hitting the stands with an issue of *The Idiom Times*. Begin by brainstorming popular idioms that are related to school activities, such as **hitting the books**, **buckling down**, or **saved by the bell**. Invite individual students or small groups of students to write funny and quick newspaper-style stories that play on the literal meaning of idioms. For example, Students Buckle Down! Several students were found buckled to their chairs in the library. Teachers are attempting to solve this problem … Collect articles and combine them into a class newsletter issue of *The Idiom Times* or post the stories on a bulletin board. Students may wish to create illustrations to accompany their articles.

M11 Getting to Know Some Idioms Better

A) Guessing the Meaning from Context

Guess the meaning of each idiom as it is used in the following sentences. Provide either a synonym or a definition. Underline the context clues which help you to guess the meaning.

1. Joe has borrowed money three times without paying me back, and now he wants $50! That's the **last straw**! _____

2. I had a **close call** when a big truck nearly hit me as I was crossing the street. _____ _____

3. He thinks and talks as if he knows everything, but he really doesn't; he's full of **hot air**. _____ _____

4. My friend thinks he's a **big shot** because he has some responsibilities in the city mayor's office. _____

5. When I said I liked her dinner, which really was terrible, I told a **white lie** because I didn't want to hurt her feelings. _____

6. At first Mary agreed to marry John, but soon she was having **second thoughts**. _____ _____

7. Because Mr. Smith knows the ins and outs of plumbing, he's an **old hand** at it. _____ _____

8. Joe puts his heart and soul into his work, so that everyone thinks he's a real **eager beaver**. _____ _____

9. I'm afraid that there's no way we can fix your old car; you'd better get rid of it because it's a **lost cause**. _____

10. At most parties, people socialize by engaging in a lot of informal **small talk**. _____ _____

Class discussion:
Decide which idioms were easy to guess and which were not. Consider the importance of context clues in your decisions.

B) Checking Your Guesses

Using Exercise A to help you, check your guesses by choosing the correct idiom which corresponds with the description you see underneath each line. Be sure to use context clues and to use the correct grammar forms.

last straw	white lie	eager beaver
close call	small talk	lost cause
hot air	second thoughts	
big shots	old hand	

1. Some police officers think they are _____ because of the legal power they have.
   (important person)

2. An employee may be considered an _____ if he works very hard in order to please his boss. (enthusiastic worker)

3. When the baby started crying again for the fourth time, that was the _____.
   (final annoyance)

4. Some people like to contact each other on the telephone for some _____.
   (informal conversation)

5. Because I really didn't like his new suit at all, I told him a little _____.
   (kind untruth)

6. Mike is an _____ at fixing cars; he has repaired hundreds of them
   (experienced worker)
   with no complaints from his customers.

7. The two airplanes had a _____ when they almost hit each other in the sky over San Francisco. (narrow escape)

8. We tried to save the damaged boat from sinking in the sea, but it was a _____.
   (hopeless situation)

9. The criminal had _____ about robbing the bank after he saw the new security guard. (reconsideration)

10. Big shots often are people who think they are wise but who really are full of _____.
    (exaggerated talk)

C) Explanation of the Idioms

last straw
1. Final annoyance which results in a loss of patience
2. Final trouble which results in defeat

This idiom is always used with a definite article; it usually is preceded by **that was**.
• First Tom, Dick, and Mary refused to help me; when my best friend, Joe, also refused, that was the last straw.
• Last week my car's door broke, and yesterday the radio stopped working. When the engine failed today, that was the last straw!
• After losing three difficult soccer games, our team lost to a very easy team; that was the last straw!

close call
Narrow escape (from danger); a situation where someone was almost seriously hurt
This idiom may be used in the plural.
• The motorcyclist had a close call when he fell off his bike; fortunately, he only received several small cuts.
• A thief attacked Jim with a knife, but was scared off by a police siren. That was a close call for Jim!
• A soldier in war can expect to face many close calls.

hot air
Exaggerated talk; unproven ideas
This idiom is often preceded by **a lot of** or **full of**, plus the verb **be**. No article is used.
• No one likes a person who thinks very highly of his own opinions but is really full of hot air.
• John's speech was just a lot of hot air because he didn't really know what he was talking about.

big shot
Important person
This idiom is considered informal, even slang; it is often used when a person is really less important than he thinks he is.
• The politician knew a lot of big shots in business who donated a great deal of money to his campaign.
• The world is full of people who think that they are big shots, but few ever get into the history books.
• The students who are active in government and sports on our campus think they are big shots, but I don't think so.

white lie
Kind untruth; small lie
This idiom is often used when the truth may hurt someone's feelings.
• I told a white lie when I told him that I liked his poor painting.
• A little white lie can save you from embarrassment.

small talk

Informal conversation; idle chitchat

No article can be used with this idiom, but quantity words often are.

- Some people are bothered by small talk because it's usually boring.
- A little small talk between strangers can sometimes lead to a long-lasting relationship.

second thoughts

Reconsideration; change of mind or opinion

The idiom is usually used as the object of the verb **have**. No article is used, and the singular form cannot be used.

- Tom had second thoughts about joining the military after high-school graduation.
- The brave soldier had no second thoughts as he attacked the enemy.

old hand

Experienced worker; very knowledgeable person

The preposition **at** usually follows the idiom; a plural form may be used.

- In the Old West, cowboys were old hands at controlling cattle.
- The veteran yachtsman was an old hand at sailing boats.

eager beaver

Enthusiastic worker; industrious person

This idiom is often used when someone is trying to impress his boss or superiors.

- Eager beavers are often resented by other workers in an office.
- If you really want to get ahead, it's better to be an eager beaver.

lost cause

Hopeless situation; a situation which is a complete failure

This idiom usually requires the verb **be** and an indefinite article.

- I think that your desire for give and take with that stubborn man is a lost cause; he rarely changes his mind.
- If a marriage has too many ups and downs, it may be a lost cause.

Class discussion:

Now that you have learned the meanings of the idioms and how to use them in sentences, go back to Exercise A and Exercise B and check your answers. As you do this, consider the following questions:

1. How many idioms did you guess correctly in Exercise A?

2. How much better did you do in Exercise B?

3. Are there any idiom meanings which are still not clear to you?

4. Is there anything you have noticed about the grammatical usage of these idioms?

D) Learning the Grammar Rules

Part I

The nominal idioms in this chapter are composed of various **adjective + noun** combinations. These combinations can be used as subjects, objects, or as noun phrases after prepositions.

Examples:

White lies are never good.
  subject

That was a very **close call**!
              object

I'm tired of **small talk**.
        noun phrase

1. What is the difference between the first idiom above and the last two idioms?

2. Do you think that the idioms could change form?

Part II

Look carefully at the following sets of sentences. Some sentences are correct and some are incorrect (indicated by *). Answer the questions by comparing the sentences.

Set A

1. I had second thoughts about marriage.

2. *I had a second thought about marriage.

3. Joe's actually full of hot air.

4. *Joe's actually full of hot airs.

a) How does sentence #2 differ from #1?
b) How does sentence #4 differ from #3?
c) What can you conclude about the nouns in these sentences?

Because the noun phrases in this chapter are idioms, certain unexplainable rules are used, just as was the case with all previous idioms in this book. One rule is that some of the nouns must be used in the plural, while others must be singular, and still others may vary in form.

I had second thoughts about marriage.	(plural form)
*I had a second thought about marriage.	(singular form incorrect)
Joe's actually full of hot air.	(singular form)
*Joe's actually full of hot airs.	(plural form incorrect)
I had a close call.	(both singular and plural forms are correct)
I've had many close calls.	

M

Set B
1. The race-car driver had many close calls.

2. *The race-car driver had many closer calls.

3. He's really an eager beaver about work.

4. *He's really a beaver about work.

a) What is the difference between sentences #1 and #2?
b) What is the difference between sentences #3 and #4?
c) What do these sentences tell you about the adjectives in these idioms?

The adjectives in these idioms are restricted in form. In general, only one particular adjective can be used with any noun form to create a special idiom, and this form usually cannot be deleted or altered in any way.

The race-car driver had many close calls.	(correct form)
*The race-car driver had many closer calls.	(no alteration possible)
He's really an eager beaver about work.	(correct form)
*He's really a beaver about work.	(no deletion possible)

There are no easy ways for learning the special rules which are used—only hard work, practice, and memorization will reward you the most.

E) Multiple-Choice Exercise

Choose the idiom which has the best meaning in the context below. No idiom is used twice as a correct answer. Be careful about the grammar rules which you have learned.

1. The sixth time he called me at midnight was the _____.
   a) lost cause
   b) last straw
   c) hot air

2. It feels good to relax after you accomplish some necessary _____.
   a) eager beavers
   b) odds and ends
   c) part and parcel

3. Having _____ with him is no fun because he does all the talking!
   a) small talk
   b) ups and downs
   c) hot air

4. Because he never stops talking, most of what he says is full of _____.
   a) small talk
   b) ups and downs
   c) hot air

5. Most of the _____ in this country work very seriously or productively.
   a) old hand
   b) rank and file
   c) eager beavers

6. The criminal was ignored completely by his own _____.
   a) big shot
   b) flesh and blood
   c) old hand

7. When I make a final decision, I never have any _____.
   a) close calls
   b) pins and needles
   c) second thoughts

8. When it's a matter of _____, I'm usually the one who has to compromise.
   a) ins and outs
   b) give and take
   c) white lie

F) Writing Exercise

Answer each question or statement by using each idiom in a meaningful, grammatically correct sentence.

1. If you had some small troubles on a car trip, what would be the last straw?

2. What was the last close call that you had?

3. Why do some people think that politicians are full of hot air?

4. How could a big shot become a small fry (an unimportant person)?

5. Have you ever told a white lie to anyone? Why or why not?

6. When did you have second thoughts about something?

7. Are you an old hand at anything? What?

8. Why do eager beavers annoy lazy workers?

9. When, if ever, do you enjoy small talk?

10. Do you think that the world situation is a lost cause? Why or why not? (You might want to write a small paragraph on this topic.)

M12 Matching Idioms

Mouth Idioms

Match the idioms on the left with the explanations on the right. There are more explanations than you need so make sure you select the right ones!

1. You took the words right out of my mouth.	a) I felt anxious.
2. Why are you so down in the mouth today?	b) It made me feel hungry.
3. I was born with a silver spoon in my mouth.	c) I felt passionate.
4. I had my heart in my mouth.	d) I felt thirsty.
5. It left a nasty taste in my mouth.	e) It created a bad impression.
6. It made my mouth water.	f) It gave me an upset stomach.
7. Stop putting words in my mouth.	g) I was born into a rich family.
8. Since I came to New York, I've been living from hand to mouth.	h) I was born with a speech impediment.
	i) Life has been a struggle.
	j) Life has been easy.
	k) Somehow you knew what I was going to say.
	l) Stop misquoting me.
	m) Support your words with actions.
	n) You're ruled by your heart, not your head.
	o) You're very miserable.

Answers: 1. k), 2. o), 3. g), 4. a), 5. e), 6. b), 7. l), 8. i)

Heaven and Hell Idioms

Match the idioms on the left with the explanations on the right. There are more explanations than you need so make sure you select the correct ones!

1. Living with you is heaven on earth.	a) Having good intentions isn't enough.
2. I'd move heaven and earth to get that job.	b) I'm not going to let anything stand in my way.
3. I'm determined to succeed come hell or high water.	c) I don't care what happens to you.
4. As far as I'm concerned, you can go to hell.	d) I think you've got a really good chance.
5. You haven't got a hope in hell.	e) It's going to cost a great deal of money.
6. The road to hell is paved with good intentions.	f) Living with you is everything I've always wanted.
7. I'm afraid there's going to be hell to pay!	g) Living with you is unbearable.

8. You scared the hell out of me.	h) There's going to be a lot of trouble.
9. What you're asking for is pennies from heaven.	i) Whatever happens, I won't give up.
	j) What you're asking for is a miracle.
	k) What you're doing is begging.
	l) You gave me an awful fright.
	m) You've got no chance at all.
	n) You helped me to overcome my fear.

Answers: 1. f), 2. b), 3. i), 4. c), 5. m), 6. a), 7. h), 8. l), 9. j)

Black and White Idioms

Match the idioms on the left with the explanations on the right. There are more explanations than you need so make sure you select the correct ones!

1. I want your promise in black and white.	a) Don't be so pessimistic!
2. Why are you giving me such black looks?	b) Fortunately I'm no longer in debt.
3. Why do you always look on the black side (or dark side)?	c) I'm different from all the rest and they disapprove of me.
4. You're the kind of person who'll swear black is white to get what you want!	d) I'm happy to say that I've found another job and that I'm no longer unemployed.
5. I'm the black sheep of my family.	e) I didn't tell you the truth but for a good reason.
6. It's time you waved the white flag.	f) I think you'd better admit defeat.
7. It was only a white lie so I hope you'll forgive me.	g) It's time you stood up for yourself.
8. Thankfully I'm now in the black again.	h) Please put it in writing.
	i) What on earth have I done to upset you?
	j) Why are you always criticizing me?
	k) You're constantly insulting me and I've had enough.
	l) You're prepared to use any means possible to achieve your ends.

Answers: 1. h), 2. i), 3. a), 4. l), 5. c), 6. f), 7. e), 8. b)

SECTION N
Culture Shock

Content

N1 Opportunity for the Teacher

The teacher who goes overseas has a unique opportunity to be immersed in the host culture. As long as the experience, including all the stages of culture shock, is seen as a unique opportunity, the experience will be a positive one.

What Is Culture Shock?

Living in a foreign culture is an experience many people look forward to. However, we are often unprepared for the extent of the cultural dissimilarity we encounter. Culture shock is a very real phenomenon, and all travelers entering a foreign culture are affected by it in some way.

> Culture shock is the term used to describe the more pronounced reactions to the psychological disorientation most people experience when they move for an extended period of time into a culture markedly different from their own. For some people, the bout with culture shock is brief and hardly noticeable. For others, it can cause intense discomfort, often accompanied by hyperirritability, bitterness, resentment, homesickness, and depression. In some individuals, culture shock may be accompanied by distinct physical symptoms of illness.
>
> —R.L. Kohls

Culture shock is the feeling of not knowing what to do or how to do things in a new environment and not knowing what is appropriate and inappropriate. It is the physical and emotional discomfort one suffers when living in another country or region and is precipitated by the anxiety that results from losing all familiar signs and symbols of social interaction.

Where Does Culture Shock Come From?

Culture shock is not the result of a specific event. It does not strike suddenly or have a single common cause. Instead, it comes from the experience of encountering ways of doing, organizing, perceiving, or valuing things that are different from your own. This may threaten your basic unconscious belief that the customs, assumptions, values, and behaviors of your culture are right.

Culture shock acts cumulatively. It builds up slowly from a series of small events that are difficult to identify.

N2 Symptoms of Culture Shock

The symptoms of culture shock can appear at any time while you are in a new culture. Although one can experience pain from culture shock, it is also an opportunity for learning and acquiring new perspectives. Some symptoms of culture shock are as follows:

* Sadness, loneliness, melancholy
* Preoccupation with health
* Aches, pains, allergies
* Insomnia, desire to sleep too much or too little
* Changes in temperament, depression, feeling vulnerable, feeling powerless
* Anger, irritability, resentment, unwillingness to interact with others

- Identifying with the home culture or idealizing the home country
- Loss of identity
- Trying too hard to absorb everything in the host culture or country
- Inability to solve simple problems
- Lack of confidence
- Feelings of inadequacy or insecurity
- Developing stereotypes about the host culture
- Developing obsessions such as overcleanliness
- Longing for family
- Feelings of being lost, overlooked, exploited, abused

 ## N3 Stages of Culture Shock

Culture shock has many stages. Each stage may be ongoing or may appear only at certain times. The first stage is the incubation stage. In this stage, the teacher entering the host country may feel euphoric and be pleased by all of the new things encountered. This period is called the honeymoon stage, as everything encountered is new and exciting.

In the second stage, the teacher may encounter some difficult times and crises in daily life. For example, communication difficulties may occur, such as not being understood when speaking. The teacher may experience feelings of discontent, impatience, anger, sadness, and incompetence. This occurs because she is trying to adapt to a culture that is very different from her culture of origin. Adapting to the ways of the host country is a difficult process and takes time to complete. During the transition, there can be strong feelings of dissatisfaction.

In the third stage, the teacher gains some understanding of the host culture and experiences new feelings of humor, satisfaction, and psychological balance. She may not feel as lost and will start to have a feeling of direction as the environment becomes more familiar and the desire to belong becomes stronger. This allows the teacher to evaluate the ways of the home culture versus those of the host culture.

In the fourth stage, the teacher realizes that the host culture has good and bad things to offer. This integration stage is accompanied by a more solid feeling of belonging. The teacher starts to define herself and establish goals for living.

The fifth stage is called reentry shock. This occurs when a return to one's place of origin is made. The teacher may find that things at home are no longer the same as they were when she left. Also, some newly acquired customs will not be in use in the home culture.

These stages may occur at different times for each person and each individual has her own way of reacting during each stage of culture shock. As a consequence, some stages will be longer and more difficult than others. Many factors contribute to the duration and effects of culture shock, such as the individual's mental health, personality, previous experiences, socioeconomic conditions, familiarity with the language, family and/or social support systems, and level of education.

How to Fight Culture Shock

The majority of individuals and families who immigrate to a new country have the ability to positively confront the obstacles of a new environment. The following are some ways to combat stress produced by culture shock:

- Develop a hobby.
- Do not forget the good things you already have!
- Remember that there are always social resources that you can make use of.
- Be patient. Adjusting to a new environment will take time.
- Learn to be constructive. If you encounter an unfavorable environment, do not put yourself in that position again. Be easy on yourself.
- Do not try too hard.
- Learn to include a form of physical activity in your routine. This will help combat sadness and loneliness in a constructive manner. Exercise, swim, take an aerobics class, etc.
- Relaxation and meditation are proven to be very helpful for people who are going through stressful periods.
- Maintain contact with people from your home country. This will give you a feeling of belonging and will reduce your feelings of loneliness and alienation.
- Maintain contact with the host culture. Learn the language. Volunteer in community activities that allow you to practice the language that you are learning. This will help you feel less stress about language and feel useful at the same time.
- Allow yourself to feel sad about the things that you have left behind, such as your friends and family.
- Acknowledge the sorrow of leaving your home country, but accept your new surroundings. Focus your power on getting through the transition.
- Pay attention to relationships with your family, friends, and co-workers. They will serve as support for you in difficult times.
- Establish simple goals and evaluate your progress.
- Find ways to live with the things that do not fully satisfy you.
- Maintain confidence in yourself. Follow your ambitions and continue your plans for the future.

N4 Important Factors for Successful Cultural Adaptation

Researchers have proven that the factors below are indicative of a person who is able to deal with living in a foreign culture and the associated culture shock in a healthy manner. Possessing these character traits means that you will be able to handle the uncertainty of living in another culture. How many traits describe you?

- **Open-mindedness:** the ability to keep one's opinions flexible and receptive to new stimuli
- **Sense of humor**: the ability to laugh things off will help guard against despair
- **Ability to cope with failure:** this ability is critical because everyone fails at something overseas!
- **Communicativeness:** the ability to communicate one's feelings and thoughts to others, verbally or non-verbally
- **Flexibility and adaptability:** the ability to respond to or tolerate the ambiguity of new situations, keep options open, and avoid judgmental behavior

- **Curiosity:** the desire to know about other people, places, ideas, etc.
- **Positive and realistic expectations:** a positive mind frame
- **Tolerance for differences and ambiguities:** a sympathetic understanding for beliefs or practices differing from one's own
- **Positive regard for others:** the ability to express warmth, empathy, and respect for others
- **A strong sense of self:** individuals who have a clear, secure feeling about themselves are neither weak nor overbearing in their relations with others

 ## N5 How to Prepare to Teach English Abroad

Teaching English abroad can be a great learning opportunity and a lot of fun, but if you do not prepare ahead at least a little, it could turn into a stressful nightmare. By preparing for both teaching and living in another culture, you can prevent most of the unpleasant moments that can happen to teachers overseas. If you are wondering how to prepare to teach English abroad, here are some tips.

- Connect with other teachers. If you are in negotiations with a school, ask to talk with some other teachers who are working there. Visit online forums for ESL teachers and look for teachers who have worked in the country you will be going to. Ask about the local lifestyle and get tips for teaching, such as which topics are good for sparking discussion and which you should avoid.
- Gather teaching material. The school you teach for will most likely have a library for teachers, but it is better to be prepared before you leave. Look at the ESL teaching material you can get in your area. Try to find at least a basic book of grammar exercises to take with you. Also gather some interesting reading like comics, travel brochures, and even grocery store flyers.
- Brush up on English grammar and other varieties of English (e.g., British English). Even though you just finished an ESL teaching course, it would not hurt to dig a little deeper into the nuances of English grammar. It is not enough to say a phrase is incorrect because it sounds wrong—you will need to clearly explain the rules behind it. Why is it **A little red rubber ball** and not **A rubber red little ball**? Likewise, you will need to know the differences between British, American, and other varieties of English so you do not assume a student has made a mistake when they are just using a different variety of English.
- Learn about your host culture's beliefs about education. Ideas about what makes a good teacher vary widely by culture. People in some cultures like teachers who are lively and like to joke around, while others expect teachers to be serious. In some cultures, students prefer to listen to a lecture and take notes, while in others, students want to interact with each other.
- Build your language-teacher vocabulary. Teaching will be a lot easier if you know the local language's words for things like **verb** and **present continuous**. If you are studying the local language, finding translations for potentially confusing English phrases will help both you and your students. A construction like **All that glitters is not gold** can be very hard to explain without a translation.
- Establish a backup plan. Do not expect your employer to get you settled in the country or your students to build your social life. Before you go, consider how you will meet the locals, improve your language skills, and learn your way around town. Prepare ahead for problems, too. What will you do if you cannot stand the accommodations the school provides, you lose your job, or you get sick?

Tips and Warnings

If you are leaving soon and do not have time to do all this, do not panic. Once you arrive, you can work on learning more about English grammar and local learning preferences. Just make sure you have a lesson plan for the first day of class because some schools may throw you right into a class the day you arrive. It is a good idea to prepare some biographical information about yourself and trivia about your country to share with the students. Showing pictures of your family or your favorite meal can also spur some interesting discussion and help your students to get to know you.

Learn something about the culture before you arrive. At the very least, spend some time online reading about the culture's views on etiquette, gender roles, and general social rules. The more you know about the culture of the country where you will be teaching, the more enjoyable the first few weeks will be and the less culture shock you will experience.

N6 Host Culture Questionnaire

Before packing up your life and moving to a new country for an extended period of time, it is probably a good idea to learn a little bit about the host culture to help with your adjustment and to make the transition as smooth as possible. Every country has its own unique history and heritage as well as its own quirks and customs. While you will not be expected to recount a detailed chronology of the nation's history, it never hurts to familiarize yourself with some of the factors that influence the way the people live and the events that have shaped their national identity. Researching in books and online can give you a detailed understanding but can also be very time consuming. If possible, try to find someone who was born in the country you are moving to or who lived there for a time (perhaps as a fellow English teacher), and ask her some of the questions listed below.

History

- Outline the major events in the country's history.
- Who are the national heroes? Explain why they are considered heroes/heroines.
- What is the history of this country's relationship with the US?
- What are the national holidays?

Politics

- What is the current political structure of the country?
- Who are the major current leaders?
- Is military service compulsory?

Religion

- What is/are the dominant religion(s)?
- Is there an official state religion?
- What are the sacred writings of the dominant religions?

Female/Male Relationships

- Are there separate societal roles for men and women?
- What are the rules or norms for romantic relationships within this country?
- Do young people date? If so, do they date in groups or in couples? Do they need a chaperone? Are such relationships formal or informal?
- Can unmarried men and women have a romantic relationship?
- What is the norm regarding premarital sex?
- Is it acceptable to hold hands and kiss in public?

Family

- Describe a typical marriage ceremony and celebration.
- What are the attitudes toward divorce? Family planning? Contraception? Abortion?
- What is seen as the ideal family size? Is the typical family nuclear or extended?

Social Etiquette

- What are the special privileges of age or gender?
- When is one expected to present or accept gifts? What kinds of gifts are appropriate?
- How do people greet each other and how do they take leave of each other? Are there differences based on social status, age, and gender?

Dress

- Is there customary attire for men, women, and children? Is there a traditional or an indigenous style of dress?
- What is the appropriate dress for a foreigner in this country?
- Are there special dress customs? What type of clothing might be taboo?
- What types of clothing might be required for various occasions?

Food

- What foods are most popular? How are they prepared?
- What are the dining customs (e.g., what utensils are used, if any)?
- Are there taboo foods that are not considered edible or are not permitted for religious or traditional reasons?

Leisure

- What are the favorite leisure activities of adults and young people?
- What are the favorite sports? Is there a national sport?
- How available are televisions and radios?

Health

- What kinds of health services are available? Where are they located?
- Are there common home remedies for minor ailments? What are the attitudes toward traditional medicines? Is traditional medicine commonly practiced?
- Is the water potable?
- Which immunizations are required in order to enter the country? Which are advisable?

Values

- What things are taboo in this culture? What things are taboo to talk about in everyday conversation?
- What type of moral code is followed? How does this moral code influence attitudes toward drinking alcohol, drug taking, gambling, and premarital or extramarital sex?

Education

- Is education free? Is it compulsory and to what age? Is it available to everyone?
- In schools, are students separated by age, gender, race, caste, or class?
- What kinds of schools are considered best: private, public, or religious?
- What style of teaching prevails in schools?
- What is the school year calendar?
- Describe the university system and how it differs from the system in the US.

Daily Life

- Are the prices marked on merchandise or are you expected to bargain? How is bargaining conducted?
- Are you allowed to touch merchandise for sale? Does touching indicate a desire to buy?
- When does the normal workday and school day begin and end? Is there a siesta time?
- What is the customary time to visit friends?
- What is the currency? What is the current value to the dollar? Is it stable? Will you be permitted to carry it out of the country?

On Being a Foreigner in This Country

- How does the financial position and social status of an ESL teacher compare with the majority of people living in this country?
- Do these people generally like Americans and other foreigners?
- Upon arriving in the country, must foreigners register with city officials? The police? The American embassy?
- Is a visa required in order to enter the country? Any sort of registration for longer stays? What regulations apply to foreigners?
- Is a visa needed to travel to neighboring countries?
- What should you do if you find yourself in legal trouble?
- Are there special laws governing the activities of foreigners?

N7 Teaching Abroad Information

Preparing Yourself for Culture Shock

Perhaps the greatest strategy for successful cultural adaptation is the maintenance of a strong sense of personal identity.

Ask yourself these questions:
- Am I aware of the cultural norms and values of my host country? What are the host country's expectations of me?
- Why am I going overseas (e.g., learning, growth, language acquisition or improvement, interest in the host country, self-motivation)?
- What am I willing to attempt? How will I respond to language barriers and unfamiliar non-verbal cues?
- How do my personal beliefs and values influence my lifestyle and behavior?

Think seriously about your motives for going abroad and entering another culture. Be confident in your decision and realize that despite the difficulties you may encounter, your trip overseas will ultimately be rewarding and fulfilling. Also understand that this may not be the right time for you to be traveling abroad. Deciding not to teach abroad is all right—you have a whole lifetime ahead of you.

Responding to Culture Shock

Even with all the preparation you have done, you will still experience some culture shock. Here are some points to remember:
- Realize that culture shock is normal.
- Accept the lesson that culture shock imparts—one's own culture does not possess the single right way or best way of providing for human needs and enjoyment.
- Select a few topics about your host country that you are interested in and investigate them thoroughly (e.g., music, art, the environment, women's issues).
- Look consciously for logical reasons behind everything that seems strange, difficult, confusing, or threatening. Examine your experiences from the host culture's perspective.
- Make a list of all the positive aspects of your present situation. Put the list in a place where you can see it throughout the day. Keep a journal so that you can look back on your progress. Keep yourself busy and active; keep your mind occupied. Do not sit around feeling sorry for yourself.
- During your most difficult times, take a trip—get away to a scenic spot or a nearby country. When you return, be open to having good "coming back home" feelings.
- Even during the worst times (especially at the worst times), have faith that you will work your way through culture shock to the brighter days that lie ahead—even if you do nothing but wait. An open mind and these tips will help guide you safely through your experience of culture shock.
- Avoid the temptation to spend all your time with expatriates, especially if they belittle the host culture. Resist making jokes or disparaging comments—these can be offensive and will slow down the process of adaptation.
- Maintain a healthy sense of humor. Make sure that you can laugh at yourself and the mistakes you make.
- Talk to someone who has been through the cultural adaptation process. This person can probably give you a positive perspective on the experience you are having.

Stages of Cultural Adjustment

This roller-coaster ride is a natural pattern of valleys and peaks, where excitement and interest are succeeded by depression, disorientation, or frustration. The intensity of the ups and downs depends upon the individual, as does the length of time an individual experiences each stage. It is important to realize that this process is both natural and necessary for the sojourner's optimum adjustment to the new culture.

N8 Predeparture Checklist

The following is a suggested list of activities to complete before you leave. You will need to add to the list and prioritize accordingly. Use a journal to set out a plan to deal with the logistics of predeparture preparation. If you are prepared before you go overseas, you will find adapting to your new culture less stressful and your culture shock will be less intense.

Citizenship

- Apply for a passport. Ensure that you have a passport that is valid until at least one month after your return date. Allow three to four weeks for the application process.
- Arrange for appropriate visas. This may take several months. Work visas are available through the appropriate embassy.
- Obtain the address of the American embassy or consulate closest to your residence overseas.
- What do you know about the US? Review your current affairs and be prepared to be a cultural ambassador.

Financial

- Clear any debts (e.g., loans).
- Ensure you know the payback plan for any student loans.
- Cancel automatic withdrawals from your bank account if necessary.
- Be sure to plan ahead for filing your income tax.
- Arrange a power of attorney or for someone you trust to make bank deposits and transfers, pay credit card bills, and carry out other legal matters.
- Bring cash (in both American and local currencies), traveler's checks, and credit cards (optional).

Health

- What are you covered for in terms of health and accident insurance? What additional coverage is required? Baggage and trip cancellation insurance is often a wise precaution.
- Begin your immunization schedule up to three months in advance if you are going to a tropical region of Asia, Africa, or Latin America. Consult your doctor about which immunizations are necessary/recommended.
- Think about prescription medications that you may need while you are away.
- Carry spare glasses and a lens prescription.
- Go to the doctor and dentist for checkups.
- Find out the laws regarding the consumption of alcohol.
- Ensure your emergency contact information is accessible, reliable, and well documented.

Travel

*   Find out your overseas mailing address before leaving.
*   Research the best airplane ticket deals. Discounts are often available early. Do you want an open-ended ticket giving you a flexible return date?
*   Will your driver's license expire while you are away? If you are planning to drive while abroad, check whether you should obtain an international driver's license before you leave.
*   If you are going to call the US a lot, you may want to purchase an international phone card. Check with various long distance companies.
*   Find out the luggage weight restrictions for the airline you are flying with. Will your school pay for the cost of transporting extra belongings?
*   Look into the voltages in your host country before carrying electrical devices with you.
*   Take some small gifts for your host school and photos of your friends and family.
*   Brush up on your foreign language skills and/or buy a phrase book.

N9 Information for Gay, Lesbian, Bisexual, and Transgendered (GLBT) Teachers

Below are some tips to help you prepare for your time abroad and your transition back into American life when you return. Before you go, it is important to reflect on the culturally based ideas and definitions of sexual identity and consider how your identity as a GLBT person may affect your relationship with host nationals, your cultural adjustment, and your overall experience abroad.

Considerations before Leaving

*   Cultures vary in terms of what is considered appropriate behavior and how sexual identities are defined and understood.
*   Behavioral signals mean different things in different cultures. For example, hand holding among males in some countries is a custom of special friendship and respect, and may be common among heterosexual men.
*   In some countries, sexual orientation can be a basis for persecution under the law. In such places, personal safety considerations may influence you to hide your sexual identity. If this is the case in your situation, try to remind yourself that you still have a strong, healthy personal identity, but that you may not be sharing all of it with others because you realize that your safety is paramount.

Suggestions on Preparing to Go Abroad

*   If you are "out" in the US, reflect on what it means to leave behind a support system of friends and family. Being GLBT abroad has been described by some as a second coming out. Consider how you will re-establish your identity overseas.
*   Before you leave, learn as much as possible about your host country's norms on friendship and dating, expected social behavior, and general attitudes toward sexual matters.
*   If possible, contact other GLBT people in your host country and ask them questions.

- Obtain information on the support systems such as meeting places and organizations available in your host country. Find out if these systems will be useful to you.
- Ask yourself the following questions: What role, as a visitor, do you/should you have in the host culture? Does your right to be GLBT in America conflict with your host country's religious or cultural values and traditions? How will you reconcile your human rights with the cultural values of your host society? Are there any safety considerations that you should be aware of?

Considerations upon Reentry

If you chose to come out while abroad, it may be helpful to reflect on the following:
- How will your coming out affect your return to friends and family? Will you be able to reintegrate into these relationships upon your return or will you need to find a different supportive community?
- Some family and friends may want to dismiss your sexual orientation as temporary, due to the experience abroad, rather than acknowledge it as a lifelong identity.
- Consider the ways in which your identity may have changed, both independently of and as a result of your coming out.

SECTION O

Resources

Content

O1 General Teaching Resources

Tried and Tested ESL Books to Help You in Your Classroom Abroad

Adelson-Goldstein, Jayme, and Norma Shapiro. *Oxford Picture Dictionary* **(2nd Edition). Oxford University Press, 2008. (ISBN: 978-0-19-436976-3)**

This book's theme-based units are filled with colorful, detailed illustrations which help explain any new vocabulary. Workbooks are also available.

Frauman-Prickel, Maxine, and Noriko Takahashi. *Action English Pictures.* **Alta Book Center, 1999. (ISBN: 978-1-882483-71-6)**

This book contains hundreds of illustrations on a variety of subject matters. All of the pictures are photo-copiable and are a great addition to any classroom using the Total Physical Response method. The illustrations and picture sequences are grouped into units and contain sample lessons and exercise sheets.

Gaetz, Lynne. *Open Book English Skills.* **Longman, 2007. (ISBN: 978-276131907-2)**

This book presents relatable, interesting readings on international artists and humanitarians. Intended for intermediate level and above, it contains vocabulary and slang isolations accompanied by a DVD and CD.

MacAndrew, Richard, and Ron Martinez. *Taboos and Issues.* **Language Teaching Publications, 2002. (ISBN: 978-1-899396-41-2)**

A high-intermediate to advanced conversation book. *Taboos and Issues* contains controversial and unusual conversation topics. Care should be taken to ensure that students are comfortable discussing some of the topics, but the possibilities for great and engaging class discussion make this book a worthwhile resource for any teacher looking to spice up his or her conversation class.

Parrett, Martin. *Grammar for English Language Teachers.* **Cambridge University Press, 2007. (ISBN: 978-0-521-47797-0)**

This book helps explain and teach grammar concepts. It provides an accessible reference for planning lessons. Each chapter includes a section that outlines some typical difficulties students may encounter and offers ways of overcoming them.

Swan, Michael. *Practical English Usage.* **Oxford University Press, 2005. (ISBN: 978-0-19-442098-3)**

This grammar resource book has answers to many grammar questions that could come up in class. It is arranged like a dictionary and gives usable examples.

Zelman, Nancy Ellen, and Patrick R. Moran. *Conversation Inspirations.* **Pro Lingua, 2005. (ISBN: 978-0-86647-195-4)**

Filled with debate, interview, discussion, and role-playing ideas, this book contains a broad selection of conversational topics, from specific situations such as interactions in a restaurant or job interview, to broader topics such as politics, sports, and technology. It is a useful resource for any speaking class.

More Useful Books for ESL Teachers

Andrew, M. *Words with Wings: Ideas for writing in different forms and contexts for infants and juniors*. Belair Publications, 1991. (ISBN: 978-0-947882-15-0)

Ashworth, M. *The First Step on the Longer Path to Becoming an ESL Teacher*. Pippin Publishing, 1992. (ISBN: 978-0-88751-054-0)

Azar, B. *Understanding and Using English Grammar*, 3rd Edition. Pearson Education, 2002. (ISBN: 978-0-13-097605-5)

Azar, B., and S. Hagan. *Basic English Grammar*, 3rd Edition. Pearson Longman, 2006. (ISBN: 978-0-13-184412-4)

Azar, B. *Fundamentals of English Grammar*, 3rd Edition. Pearson PTR Interactive, 2007. (ISBN: 978-0-13-235335-9)

Briggs, S. *Grammar: Strategies and Practice*. Scott Foresman, 1997. (ISBNs: Beginner 978-0-673-19599-9, Intermediate 978-0-673-19604-0, Advanced 978-0-673-19605-7)

Broukal, Milada. *Idioms for Everyday Use*. National Textbook Company, 1994. (ISBN: 978-0-8442-0748-3)

Brown, H. Douglas. *Teaching by Principles: An Interactive Approach to Language Pedagogy*, 3rd Edition. Pearson ESL, 2007. (ISBN: 978-0-13-612711-6)

Brown, H. Douglas. *Principles of Language Learning and Teaching*, 5th Edition. Pearson-Longman, 2006. (ISBN: 978-0-13-199128-6)

Gray, Loretta S. *Practice Makes Perfect: Idiomatic English*. McGraw Hill, 2000. (ISBN: 978-0-8442-2394-0)

Gray, Loretta S. *Practice Makes Perfect: English Verbs*. McGraw Hill, 2004. (ISBN: 978-0-07-142646-6)

Gruber, B. *Writing Ideas Ready to Use*. Frank Schaffer Publications, 1983. (ISBN: 978-0-86734-050-1)

Gunderson, L. *ESL Literacy Instruction: A Guidebook to Theory and Practice*. Routledge, 2008. (ISBN: 978-0-415-98972-5)

Hornby A.S., Ed. *Oxford Advanced Learner's Dictionary*, 7th Edition. Oxford University Press, 2008. (ISBN: 978-0-19-400116-8)

Huizenga, J. *Can You Believe It? Book 1: Stories and Idioms from Real Life*. Oxford University Press, 2000. (ISBN: 978-0-19-437279-4)

Huizenga, J. *Can You Believe it? Book 2: Stories and Idioms from Real Life*. Oxford University Press, 2000. (ISBN: 978-0-19-437275-6)

Huizenga, J. *Can You Believe It? Book 3: Stories and Idioms from Real Life*. Oxford University Press, 2000. (ISBN: 978-0-19-437276-3)

Irving, N. *Test Your Punctuation*. Usborne Publishing, 1995. (ISBN: 978-0-88110-766-1)

Irving, N. *Test Your Grammar*. Usborne Publishing, 1995. (ISBN: 978-0-7460-1723-4)

Johnson, D., R. Johnson, and E. Holubec. *Cooperation in the Classroom*. Interaction Book Company, 1998. (ISBN: 978-0-939603-04-6)

Kohls, R.L. *Survival Kit for Overseas Living*. Intercultural Press Inc., 2001. (ISBN: 978-1-85788-292-6)

Langan, J. *Sentence Skills: A Workbook for Writers: Form B*. McGraw-Hill, 2003. (ISBN: 978-0-07-282087-4)

Meyers, M. *Teaching to Diversity: Teaching and Learning in the Multi-Ethnic Classroom*. Irwin Publishing, 1994. (ISBN: 978-0-201-55547-9)

Molinsky, Steven J., and Bill Bliss. *Side by Side*, 3rd Edition w/CD. Pearson-Longman, 2001. (Book 1 ISBN: 978-0-13-111959-8; Book 2 ISBN: 978-0-13-111960-4)

Really Learn 100 Phrasal Verbs, 2nd Edition. Oxford University Press, 2007. (ISBN: 978-0-19-431744-3)

Pratt, D. *Curriculum Planning: A Handbook for Professionals*. Harcourt, 1994. (ISBN: 978-0-15-501098-7)

Write Source Series. The Write Source Educational Publishing House. (Multiple titles and ISBNs)

Yagoda, Ben. *When You Catch an Adjective, Kill It!* Broadway Books, 2007. (ISBN: 9780767920780)

O2 Games for the Classroom

Clark, Raymond C. *Index Card Games for ESL*. Pro Lingua, 2002. (ISBN: 978-0-86647-158-9)

This book contains seven game techniques plus sample games that are easy to prepare and play using standard index cards. Student-centered activities provide practice in vocabulary building, sentence and paragraph structure, pronunciation and spelling, questioning, and conversation. Includes games for students of Beginner, Intermediate, and Advanced level.

Clark, Raymond C. *More Index Card Games and Activities for English*. Pro Lingua, 1993. (ISBN: 978-0-86647-075-9)

This presents more index card games which practice skills similar to those in *Index Card Games for ESL*.

Hadfield, Jill. *Elementary Communication Games*. Addison Wesley Longman, 1996. (ISBN: 978-0-17-555695-3)

This book contains 96 pages of beginner games designed to encourage and facilitate communication in an ESL classroom.

Hadfield, Jill. *Intermediate Communication Games*. Longman, 2001. (ISBN: 978-0-17-555872-8)

This book builds upon *Elementary Communication Games* and contains 128 pages of communication games designed for intermediate level students.

Hadfield, Jill. *Advanced Communication Games*. Longman, 2000. (ISBN: 978-0-17-555693-9)

Continuing the series, *Advanced Communication Games* contains 128 pages of games to get advanced students talking.

Hadfield, Jill, and Charles Hadfield. *Reading Games*. Nelson, 1995. (ISBN: 978-0-17-556891-8)

This book contains 144 pages of reading games for intermediate to advanced students.

Hadfield, Jill, and Charles Hadfield. *Writing Games*. **Longman Nelson ELT, 1990.**
   (ISBN: 978-0-17-555898-8)

This book contains 116 pages of writing games for intermediate to advanced students.

Kealy, James, and Donna Inness. *Shenanigames*. **Pro Lingua, 1997. (ISBN: 978-0-86647-100-8)**

Shenanigames contains 49 games for practicing specific grammar in an ESL classroom, with clear instructions for all games. There are a total of 96 photocopiable pages of games to teach grammar including adjectives, adverbs, clauses, comparatives, modals, conditional sentences, gerunds and infinitives, nouns, verbs, participles, and prepositions.

Steinberg, Jerry. *Games Language People Play*, **2nd Edition. Dominie Press: Pippin Pub., 1991.**
   (ISBN: 978-0-88751-017-5)

Covering levels from beginner to advanced, this book offers 110 games in all. Each game carries an indication of the language skill or combination of skills being employed (reading, writing, listening, speaking) and the optimal group size, from as few as 10 students to games suitable for classes of unlimited size. The game's instructional objective (for example, vocabulary expansion) the materials needed, a full description, and additional suggestions are all provided.

 # O3 Online Resources

ESL Directory

For an up-to-date listing of over nineteen thousand schools worldwide, broken down by continent, country, and region, log in to www.oxfordseminars.com/esl-schools-directory/

   Once you have logged in with your username and password, you will have access to contact information (website/phone/email/fax), specific job postings, average salary compensation, required qualifications, and other pertinent information such as flight or accommodation provisions. The site is updated regularly with new schools around the world. Consider it your portal to ESL teaching!

General ESL Information

Oxford Seminars	http://www.oxfordseminars.com
Dave's ESL Café	http://www.eslcafe.com
The English Zone	http://www.english-zone.com
Resources for TESL Instructors	http://www.englishlearner.com/teachers/index.html
Linguistic Funland	http://www.linguistic-funland.com
About.com ESL Page	http://esl.about.com
English Club	http://www.englishclub.com
TEFL.net	http://www.tefl.net
ESL Lounge	http://www.esl-lounge.com
ELT Web	http://www.eltweb.com
WWW ESL Resources	http://www.catesol.org/resource.html
ESL/EFL World	http://www.esl-eflworld.com
ESLoop	http://tesol.net/esloop
English Teachers Network	http://www.etni.org
One Stop English	http://www.onestopenglish.com

Professional Development

TESOL Association	http://www.tesol.org
International Association of TEFL	http://www.iatefl.org
TEFL Professional Network	http://www.tefl.com
ELT Network	http://www.eltnewsletter.com
TESL Canada	http://www.tesl.ca
Developing Teachers	http://www.developingteachers.com
Japan Association for Language Teachers	http://www.jalt.org
EnglishTeachers.net	http://englishteachers.net
ELT Calendar of Events—Japan	http://eltcalendar.com

Lesson Plan Ideas

Everything ESL Lesson Ideas	http://www.everythingesl.net/lessons
English-To-Go Reuters Lessons	http://www.english-to-go.com
Englishpage.com	http://www.englishpage.com
About.com ESL Lessons	http://esl.about.com/education/esl/bllessonplans.htm
EFL4U Lesson Worksheets	http://www.efl4u.com
ESL Lesson Plans for Teachers	http://www.eslflow.com
Churchill House English Lessons	http://www.churchillhouse.com/english/downloads.html
EFL/ESL Lesson Plans	http://iteslj.org/Lessons
Teach-nology Lesson Plans	http://www.teach-nology.com/teachers/lesson_plans/esl
Rong Chang ESL	http://www.rong-chang.com
Business English Links and Ideas	http://www.geocities.com/kurtracy
ESL Kid	http://www.eslkid.com

ESL Games and Activities

Online Study Site for ESL Students	http://www.manythings.org/e/grammar.html
Discovery Kids Puzzlemaker	http://puzzlemaker.discoveryeducation.com
Games and Activities	http://iteslj.org/c/games.html
John and Sarah's TEFL Pit Stop	http://lingolex.com/jstefl.htm
Teaching Children	http://www.genkienglish.net/games.htm
Many Things	http://www.manythings.org
Crayola	http://www.crayola.com
ESL Kid Stuff	http://www.eslkidstuff.com
ESL & English Games	http://www.shambles.net/pages/learning/EnglishP/eslgames
MES English	http://www.mes-english.com
TEFL Games	http://www.teflgames.com
Fun with Words	http://www.fun-with-words.com
Activities for ESL Students	http://a4esl.org

Classroom Resources

Randall's ESL Cyber Listening Lab   http://www.esl-lab.com
Wordsmyth (Requires membership)   http://www.wordsmyth.net
English Learner Online Tests   http://www.englishlearner.com/tests/index.shtml
Worksheets for Students and Teachers   http://www.bradleys-english-school.com/worksheets/
                                          index.html
ESL Teacher Resources   http://bogglesworldesl.com
Printable Pages and Worksheets   http://abcteach.com
Online Quizzes, Songs, and Stories   http://www.eflclub.com
Language Impact Conversation Starters   http://www.languageimpact.com/articles/rw/conv_starters.htm
Holiday Zone, Worldwide Holiday Info   http://www.theholidayzone.com/
Ready-to-Print TEFL Handouts   http://www.handoutsonline.com/
Printable Play Money   http://www.donnayoung.org/math/money.htm
                                          http://www.moneyinstructor.com/wsp/playmoney.asp
English Resource   http://www.englishresource.com

Teaching Tips

Hands-On English, 40 Hints & Tips   http://www.handsonenglish.com/40tips.html
Dave's ESL Café Ideas   http://www.eslcafe.com/ideas
Community ESOL   http://www.communityesol.org.uk
ESL/EFL Hints and Pointers   http://genkienglish.net/general.htm
Tips for Teaching Grammar   http://www.ateg.org/grammar/tips.php

Communities and Forums

EnglishTeachers.net   http://englishteachers.net
ESL/EFL Teachers' Chatboard   http://teachers.net/mentors/esl_language
ESL Partyland Discussion Forums   http://www.eslpartyland.com/tdisc.htm
ESL Café Teacher Forums   http://forums.eslcafe.com/teacher
English Teachers in Germany   http://elt.yuku.com

Grammar Help

English Grammar and Writing   http://www.edufind.com/english/grammar
Write ELT Grammar Help   http://www.writeit.fi/ruth/writeit-resources-grammar
English Zone Grammar   http://english-zone.com/index.php?ID=1
Guide to Grammar and Writing   http://grammar.ccc.commnet.edu/grammar
English the Easy Way   http://www.english-the-easy-way.com

Writing and Vocabulary Ideas

200 Vocabulary Exercises	http://web2.uvcs.uvic.ca/elc/studyzone/200/vocab
English Vocabulary	http://eleaston.com/vocabulary.html
English Page Vocabulary	http://www.englishpage.com/vocabulary/vocabulary.html
Purdue Online Writing Lab	http://owl.english.purdue.edu
English Works! Writing Index	http://depts.gallaudet.edu/englishworks/writing/main/index.htm
Writing Tips Essay Builder	http://www2.actden.com/writ_den/tips/essay/index.htm
IT Journal ESL Writing	http://iteslj.org/links/ESL/Writing
Mark's ESL World's Writing Center	http://marksesl.com/writing_center.html
Learning Vocabulary Fun	http://www.vocabulary.co.il
The Write Source	http://www.thewritesource.com/

ESL Magazines

EL Gazette	http://www.elgazette.com
English Teaching Professional	http://www.etprofessional.com
ESL Magazine	http://www.eslmag.com
Hands-on English	http://www.handsonenglish.com
Mary Glasgow Magazines	http://www.link2english.com
Modern English Digest	http://www.modernenglishdigest.net
Modern English Teacher	http://www.onlinemet.com
TESOL Quarterly	http://www.tesol.org/tq

International Bookstores

SBS (Argentina)	http://www.sbs.com.ar
Disal (Brazil)	http://www.disal.com.br
Liv. Martins Fontes (Brazil)	http://www.martinsfontes.com.br
Special Book Services (Brazil)	http://www.sbs.com.br
Chapters/Indigo (Canada)	http://www.chapters.indigo.ca
The English Centre (Canada)	http://www.theenglishcentre.ca
Equilibrium Bookstore (Canada)	http://www.equilibrium.ab.ca/bookstore.htm
Sophia Books (Canada)	http://www.sophiabooks.com/
Vancouver Community College Campus Bookstore (Canada)	http://www.bookstore.vcc.ca/booksesl.html
SBS (Chile)	http://www.sbs.cl
Algoritam (Croatia)	http://www.algoritam.hr
Bohemian Ventures (Czech Rep.)	http://www.venturesbooks.com
Mega Books International (Czech Rep.)	http://www.megabooks.cz
Nakladatelstvi Fraus (Czech Rep.)	http://www.fraus.cz
English Center (Denmark)	http://www.englishcenter.dk
Allecto Bookshop (Estonia)	http://www.allecto.ee
The Academic Bookstore (Finland)	http://www.akateeminen.com
Bookshop Staheli Ltd. (Germany)	http://www.staehelibooks.ch
Kosmos Floras Bookshops (Greece)	http://www.floras.gr

Sanseido Bookstore (Japan)   http://www.books-sanseido.co.jp
Kyobo Book Centre (Korea)   http://www.kyobobook.co.kr
CenterCom (Russia)   http://www.centercom.ru
Slovak Ventures (Slovakia)   http://www.venturesbooks.com
DZS (Slovenia)   http://www.dzs.si
The Uppsala English Bookshop (Sweden)   http://www.ueb.se
Bergli Books (Switzerland)   http://www.bergli.ch
Staeheli (Switzerland)   http://www.staehelibooks.ch
Hans Stauffacher (Switzerland)   http://www.stauffacher.ch
BEBC (UK)   http://www.bebc.co.uk
Alta Book Center Publishers (USA)   http://www.altaesl.com
Delta Systems Co. Inc. (USA)   http://www.delta-systems.com
ESL Games Bookstore (USA)   http://www.eslgames.com/Bookstore.asp
World of Reading, Ltd. (USA)   http://www.wor.com

ESL Publishers

ABAX EL T Publishers   http://www.abax.co.jp
Adams & Austen Press Publishers   http://www.aapress.com.au
Barron's   http://www.barronseduc.com/english-Ianguage-arts.html
Cambridge University Press   http://www.cup.cam.ac.uk
Dymon Publications   http://www.dymonbooks.com
EFL Press   http://www.EFLPress.com
Encomium Publications, Inc.   http://www.encomium.com
Express Publishing EL T Books   http://www.expresspublishing.co.uk
Full Blast Productions   http://www.fullblastproductions.com
Garnet Education   http://www.garneteducation.com
HarperCollins Publishers   http://www.harpercollins.com
Hachette Livre   http://www.madaboutbooks.com
Houghton Mifflin   http://www.hmco.com
JAG Publications   http://www.jagpublications-esl.com
John Benjamins Publishing   http://www.benjamins.com/cgi-bin/welcome.cgi
Keyways Publishing   http://www.keywayspublishing.com
Longman English language Teaching   http://www.longman-elt.com
Marshall Cavendish EL T   http://www.mcelt.com
Oxford University Press   http://www.oup.com
Pro Lingua Associates   http://www.ProLinguaAssociates.com
Richmond Publishing   http://www.richmondelt.com
Summertown Publishing   http://www.summertown.co.uk
The McGraw-Hill Companies   http://www.mhhe.com/catalogs/hss/esl
Heinle Cengage Learning   http://www.heinle.com
Pearson Longman   http://www.pearsonlongman.com

Travel and Health Information

Fodor's Travel Guides	http://www.fodors.com
Frommer's Travel Guides	http://www.frommers.com
Let's Go Travel Guides	http://www.letsgo.com
Lonely Planet	http://www.lonelyplanet.com
Rough Guides	http://www.roughguides.com
1000 Travel Tips	http://1000traveltips.org
GapYear.com	http://www.gapyear.com
Canuck Abroad	http://www.canuckabroad.com
The Globetrotters Club	http://www.globetrotters.co.uk
Time Out	http://www.timeout.com
Virtual Tourist	http://www.virtualtourist.com
Directory of Travel	http://travel.org
Tour2Korea	http://www.tour2korea.co.kr
Travel South America	http://www.travel-amazing-southamerica.com
Journey Woman	http://www.journeywoman.com
Centers for Disease Control and Prevention	http://www.cdc.gov/travel
Travel Medicine & Vaccination Centre	http://www.tmvc.com
Travel Health Online	http://www.tripprep.com
World Health Organization—Travel	http://www.who.int/topics/travel/en

Information for Gay, Lesbian, Bisexual, and Transgender Teachers and Travelers

Planet Out	http://www.planetout.com
International Gay and Lesbian HRC	http://www.iglhrc.org
Amnesty International	http://www.ai-lgbt.org
International Lesbian and Gay Association	http://www.ilga.org
Rainbow Special Interest Group	http://www.indiana.edu/~overseas/lesbigay

Other Useful Links

The World Time Server	http://www.worldtimeserver.com
Online Currency Converter	http://www.xe.com
Western Union Money Transfer	http://www.westernunion.com
Cybercafés Around the World	http://cybercafes.com
CIA World Factbook	https://www.cia.gov/library/publications/the-world-factbook
Online Encyclopedias	http://www.encyclopedia.com http://www.wikipedia.org
Online Dictionaries and Thesauri	http://www.merriam-webster.com http://www.dictionary.com

SECTION P
Games and Activities

Content

P1 Icebreaker Games

The Name Game

Goals
- Learning classmates' names
- Getting to know classmates better

How to play

To begin playing the Name Game (also known as the Adjective Game), have one person in the room choose a word that describes him- or herself as a person. The catch is that the word must start with the first letter of his or her first name. For example, if a student is named Veronica, she would say "Hello! My name is Vivacious Veronica." The person after her must say her adjective and name before saying his own. So the second person might say, "Hello, Vivacious Veronica, my name is Silly Sam." Then the third person might say, "Hello, Vivacious Veronica and Silly Sam, my name is Easy-going Edwin." This continues on until all of the students have taken a turn. The last student will have quite a challenge in this game, having to remember everyone's name and adjective before stating his or her own.

Human Knot Game

Goals
- Team building and communication
- Problem solving
- Getting to know classmates better

Setup

Have students form groups of about 10 people each. The students in each group should stand in a circle, facing toward each other, shoulder-to-shoulder with the person to their right and the person to their left. First, instruct the students to lift their left hands and reach across to take the hand of someone standing across the circle from them. Next, have them lift their right hands and reach across to take the hand of another person standing across the circle. Make sure that no two people standing directly beside each other are holding hands.

How to Play

To play, the group must communicate and figure out how to untangle the knot (forming a circle of people) without ever letting go of any hands. If you wish, this icebreaker can be played competitively. In this case, at least two groups will form human knots, and when the teacher says, "Ready... Set... Go!" the groups race to become the first one to untangle. If any group member lets go of a hand (breaks the chain), then his group must start again from the beginning, or you could impose a penalty/punishment for that person (e.g., wearing a blindfold).

The length of time needed to play this game will vary. You can impose a time limit if you wish to make the game more challenging. When you are done with the Human Knot Game, you can ask some debriefing questions, such as How well did your group work together?; What strategies did your group adopt?; or How did it feel to solve the game?

Two Truths and a Lie

Goals
- Improving questioning skills
- Getting to know classmates better

Setup
Have everyone sit in a circle. Each student prepares three statements, two of which are true and one of which is a lie.

How to Play
In any order, each student shares his or her three statements with the entire class. The object of the game is to figure out which statement is a lie. The other students may ask a predetermined number of questions in order to gather information about the statements. The class then votes on each statement, and the student reveals which one is the lie.

Variation: Two Truths and a Dream Wish
As an interesting variation to this game, you can play a version called Two Truths and a Dream Wish. Instead of just stating a lie, students say something that is not true, but that they wish to be true. For example, someone who has never been to Hawaii might say, "I visited Hawaii when I was young." This interesting spin often leads to unexpected, fascinating results as people share touching wishes about their lives.

P

Sorts and Mingle

Goals
- Improving conversation skills
- Getting to know classmates better

Setup
Tape a sign to each of the classroom's walls, labeling the walls North, East, South, and West.

How to Play
The first step to Sorts and Mingle is the Sorts game. Call out a question presenting two contrasting choices and have the students move to either the East or West of the room (e.g., "Do you prefer soccer or baseball?"). Then, call out two more choices and have students move South or North. This way, all the students have to move somewhere and can't get lost in the crowd. Sorts that work well include movie/book; salty/sweet; dress up/casual; inside/outside; be on the stage performing/in the audience watching; etc.

The second step, the Mingle game, is also interesting and effective as an ice breaker. Call out a general category and have the students mingle around to find others who have the same answer and form groups based on these common answers. After about 30 seconds to one minute, have each group call out its answer. It is okay if someone does not have anyone else who has the same answer. Just try to avoid two groups with the same answer (this means they didn't mingle very well!). Some examples of questions to prompt mingling are What is your favorite dessert?; What type of toothpaste do you use?; If you could attend one huge event what would you choose? (the Olympics, World Cup, Academy Awards, etc.); What is your least favorite chore?; If you could be the very best at something, what would it be?

Human Sculptures Game

There are two variations of this game—one version is a competitive guessing game, while the other version is based on creative interpretations of various topics. The instructions for both versions are below.

Goals
• Getting to know classmates better
• Improving cooperative skills

Setup
Have students position their desks and chairs around the perimeter of the room so there is plenty of room for moving around in the center of the classroom.

How to Play
Human Sculptures: Guessing Game Version

Announce a category (e.g., famous movies or famous songs—the more specific, the better). Then divide the class into small groups (about three to five students). Each group has to brainstorm an idea that goes along with the topic and then the team's leader must write down the idea on a sheet of paper and turn it in to you, to check that the idea is appropriate for use. Each group then creates a sculpture using their bodies. Every member of the group should make up some part of the entire sculpture. After a predetermined time limit (for example, five minutes), the students look at the other teams' sculptures. Each team is allowed two guesses to figure out what the other team has formed. Whichever group guesses correctly (or the closest) is the winner.

How to Play
Human Sculptures: Noncompetitive Version

Announce that the class will participate in a human clay activity. Ask the students to provide their own interpretations or illustrations of some category of events or other topics (prepared in advance by you).
   Some examples of categories that you could use are:
• A topic related to specific subject matter learned in the classroom
• An important event or experience
• An important event in history
• A famous scene from a movie
• A line from a famous song

Demonstrate an example before the students are asked for their interpretations (to help put them at ease, especially those who might be reluctant to act in front of the class). This noncompetitive version can be a good way to see how people illustrate content learned in class, or something personally meaningful to them.

I Have Never _____

Goals
- Getting to know classmates better
- Practicing speaking skills
- Practicing listening skills

Setup
Have students arrange their desks in a circle so that they are able to see everyone else.

How to Play
While seated in a circle, the students should hold out all 10 fingers and place them on their desks for the others to see. One by one, each student announces something that he or she has never done; for example, I have never been to Ireland. For each statement, all the other students remove a finger if they have done what the speaker has not. So, if three other students have been to Ireland before, those three people must put down a finger, leaving them with nine fingers. The goal is to stay in the game the longest (to have fingers remaining). Thus, it is a good strategy for students to make statements about things that most people have done, but they haven't. This can be humorous (e.g., I have never skipped a class in school or I have never soiled my pants). The game provides a good way to find out unique experiences and facts about classmates.

Celebrity ID Game

Goals
- Getting to know classmates better
- Practicing questioning skills

Setup
Prepare nametags with the names of well-known people or characters (e.g., Tiger Woods, Michael Jordan, Harry Potter, Mickey Mouse)

How to Play
Affix a label to each student's back. Then announce that it is time for the game to begin. At this point, students should mingle and introduce themselves to each other and ask their classmates yes or no questions to gain clues about their own identities. When a student correctly identifies his or her celebrity identity, that student removes the nametag and continues to mingle until a predetermined amount of time has elapsed.

P2 Have You Ever ... Game

This activity is a modification of a few different activities. This is a game for students to practice asking Have you ever ... questions and responding to them. Divide students into groups of four to ten. Distribute play money equally to each student. You can find play money in some toy stores or you can print your own from a website that provides sheets of play money (refer to Section O: Resources for suggested websites). Cut out and shuffle the Tell the Truth or Tell a Lie cards from page 384 and place them in one pile at the center of the table. Model Have you ever ... + past participle questions for your students, as well as ways to respond to Have you ever ... questions.

Example

Have you ever sung in public?

Yes, I have. or No, I haven't.

Remind students that they will have to change the simple present to a past participle. The first student starts and asks someone else in his group a Have you ever ... question. The student who is asked the question should draw a card from the pile of Tell the Truth or Tell a Lie cards and answer according to the card. The rest of the students are allowed to ask three follow-up questions to try to determine whether the person answering is telling the truth or lying. Then all of the students, except for the student who answered, bet on whether the student is telling the truth or lying. The student answering the question must pay the bets. It's a good idea to set a maximum bet so one student doesn't go completely bankrupt on one question.

Example

In a group of six students (made up of Chandler, Joey, Monica, Phoebe, Rachel, and Ross), Ross starts and decides to ask Monica, "Have you ever stayed up all night?" Monica, who has never stayed up all night, draws a Tell a Lie card and answers, "Yes, I have." Since three follow-up questions are allowed, Joey begins and asks "When?" Monica replies, "Last summer." Phoebe then asks Monica, "Who were you with?" Monica replies, "My cousin." Chandler asks Monica, "Where were you?" Monica replies, "In our cabin." Rachel then asks, "What did you do all night?" Ross steps in and says, "Three questions are up. It's time to bet."

Ross: "Three dollars it's a lie"
Phoebe: "Two dollars. Truth"
Chandler: "uh ... one dollar, lie"
Joey: "Two dollars she's lying"
Rachel: "Three dollars says she's telling the truth"

Monica then shows her Tell a Lie card. She collects Phoebe's and Rachel's money, since they were wrong, but has to pay Ross three dollars, Joey two dollars, and Chandler a dollar. Overall, she lost one dollar. Play proceeds for a set time period. This activity can also be used to practice When was the last time you ...

Here are some topic suggestions for questions.

Have you ever … (you will have to change the verb tense)

sing/in public

think/out loud

find/money

be/hang out to dry

tell/gossip

stick/with the bill

shake hands/someone famous

hit/a baseball

meet/someone famous

make up/after an argument

begin/book/never finish

lead/an expedition

drink/yak's milk

pay/someone else's dinner

ring/a church bell

say/something you regret

run/students' council

sell/a car

come home/past your curfew

shoot/a goal

go/Europe

sit in a waiting room/more than three hours

beat up/someone at school

stand in line/more than three hours

blow up/at a friend

tell/a secret to a friend

decide/to break up with someone

win/the lottery

choose/a team

build/a model

draw/a cartoon

burn/yourself

drive/for more than eight hours

feel/an earthquake

eat/alligator

keep/diary

fall/more than 10 feet

break/promise

fly/to Hong Kong

leave a class/early

forget to do something important

lose/something valuable

get/ripped off

oversleep

give/as well as you got

sleep in

grow/your own vegetables

spend/more than 1,000 dollars at once

hide/from someone

be/in Paris

know/a politician

bring a pet/school

lie down on a straw bed

buy/anything expensive

see/the sunrise

catch/a fish

show someone around your town

fight/a cause

steal/gum

seek/someone in the want ads

take/a computer course

teach/anything

throw/a party

Tell the Truth	Tell a Lie
Tell the Truth	Tell a Lie
Tell the Truth	Tell a Lie
Tell the Truth	Tell a Lie
Tell the Truth	Tell a Lie
Tell the Truth	Tell a Lie
Tell the Truth	Tell a Lie
Tell the Truth	Tell a Lie
Tell the Truth	Tell a Lie
Tell the Truth	Tell a Lie
Tell the Truth	Tell a Lie
Tell the Truth	Tell a Lie
Tell the Truth	Tell a Lie
Tell the Truth	Tell a Lie
Tell the Truth	Tell a Lie

P3 Word Searches

Word searches are a good activity to teach vocabulary recognition. Many students enjoy the puzzle-solving aspect of word searches, but they can also serve an educational purpose. You can use them to introduce new vocabulary or reinforce previously learned words. Although not as useful as more detailed readings and definitions, repeated exposure to new words is still beneficial for ESL students. Beyond any direct learning aspect, word searches can be used as a fun reward for students who finish an in-class assignment before the rest of the class. You can also extend the activity and have the students work alone or in groups to create their own word searches. As another alternative, rather than giving your students the list of words to find, you can have them answer questions or correctly conjugate verbs to come up with the words in the puzzle.

Animals

Word List	p	y	m	z	l	a	a	d	r	a	z	i	l	d	g
giraffe	t	e	s	s	q	u	i	r	r	e	l	j	l	j	w
moose	j	i	c	c	q	v	p	g	j	p	b	p	g	l	k
pig	b	w	g	t	s	n	a	k	e	o	c	z	e	q	n
cat	u	n	b	e	j	y	j	m	o	h	l	a	v	z	u
elephant	f	r	q	v	r	z	z	p	y	r	t	y	t	z	m
tiger	f	a	q	p	m	d	p	r	v	t	j	j	w	a	p
lizard	a	b	q	t	j	t	n	a	h	p	e	l	e	e	i
deer	l	b	e	g	y	o	t	b	m	e	h	c	j	p	h
bear	o	i	s	z	n	m	c	r	b	d	s	p	t	o	c
squirrel	h	t	a	l	n	o	g	z	a	q	b	o	s	s	g
buffalo	r	o	p	i	g	m	i	o	a	e	e	e	o	p	s
rabbit	e	g	t	e	b	a	v	l	q	t	b	q	d	m	c
snake	e	q	n	n	v	m	r	q	c	w	p	h	d	r	l
lion	d	e	h	q	j	e	f	f	a	r	i	g	d	r	n
chipmunk															

Eating

Word List	j	y	v	g	h	t	s	a	f	k	a	e	r	b	e
delicious	j	s	n	c	k	e	c	a	n	c	w	d	h	g	l
hungry	b	e	w	v	l	n	c	a	b	r	e	p	p	u	s
sweet	h	q	m	e	l	h	i	w	h	d	r	v	b	a	o
sour	h	c	v	t	e	b	a	r	y	d	m	p	s	q	s
lunch	w	g	n	d	c	t	s	l	d	c	e	r	m	e	t
breakfast	h	y	p	u	t	z	m	b	n	z	a	l	j	h	a
eat	j	r	t	r	r	z	m	h	m	j	l	g	o	b	r
supper	p	g	z	t	m	b	c	r	s	m	j	t	r	l	v
drink	v	n	m	g	q	n	d	p	h	h	s	l	u	c	i
starving	b	u	r	t	u	b	r	t	a	e	j	j	o	g	n
full	y	h	z	l	y	r	e	n	n	i	d	b	s	n	g
meal	t	g	s	g	a	b	l	v	z	c	m	a	w	d	a
dinner	p	z	d	e	l	i	c	i	o	u	s	z	l	h	n
brunch	g	w	w	s	t	r	a	y	h	b	l	l	u	f	p

Family members

Word List	p	t	b	j	g	s	y	d	d	n	a	b	s	u	h
brother	c	r	m	b	e	r	l	o	r	e	h	t	o	m	j
sister	b	e	p	t	c	j	a	s	w	o	y	g	p	z	m
mother	j	h	q	o	s	g	v	n	p	o	e	c	e	i	n
aunt	e	t	y	u	n	c	l	e	d	h	e	o	o	p	z
uncle	p	a	l	q	w	j	b	t	d	m	p	f	v	v	e
cousin	b	f	c	t	n	u	a	m	w	d	o	p	i	p	n
grandmother	h	d	r	o	a	p	y	n	r	e	p	t	e	w	n
grandfather	m	n	e	e	u	m	m	w	r	e	h	w	h	c	c
son	h	a	h	t	h	s	m	g	j	e	t	p	b	e	v
daughter	w	r	t	d	h	t	i	p	j	j	t	s	e	s	r
niece	g	g	o	l	r	h	v	n	n	o	e	z	i	n	s
nephew	s	b	r	g	r	e	t	h	g	u	a	d	o	s	q
husband	j	j	b	c	q	b	s	o	n	z	t	n	n	t	t
wife

See Section O: Resources for websites that allow you to create your own word searches and puzzles.

P

P4 Twenty Questions

Level: Pre-intermediate to Advanced
Skills Practiced: Asking and answering Yes or No questions
Time: Flexible (usually four to six minutes per round with as many rounds as you like)

Setup
Print out the topic cards below or make your own set of cards. Make sure each player has a piece of paper on which to record his or her points.

Animals	Countries
Sports	Foods
Singers	Bands
Actors	Actresses
Jobs	T.V. Shows

How to Play
This game is a variation on the traditional Twenty Questions, with players asking questions requiring a Yes or No answer to discover whatever the question-master is thinking. Unlike the traditional game, which starts with the question, Is it an animal, vegetable, or mineral? this version starts with the question-master stating the general topic of whatever he is thinking of. This could be one of the topics found on the topic cards provided (animals, countries, foods, sports, actors, actresses, singers, bands, movies, T.V. shows) or another topic related to whatever your students have recently studied. Players may earn points in a variety of ways, with each keeping a record of his or her score.

Place the topic cards face down in a pile on a table at the front of the classroom and put a pen and piece of paper next to the pile. After explaining the game, ask for a student to volunteer to be the first question-master. This student then comes forward and takes the top card and thinks of something relevant to the card's topic. After writing this on the piece of paper provided, he or she then states the topic.

Players begin asking Yes or No questions, with the first player raising his or her hand to ask the first question. If the question is grammatically correct, this player earns a point and the question-master answers it. If the question is not grammatically correct, another player may try to ask the same question correctly, again after raising a hand. If correct, this player earns a point. If it is still not correct, ask the question again yourself and have the question-master answer it. (If the question-master isn't sure of an answer, he or she should say so.)

The game continues with players asking questions in the same manner. If any player thinks he or she knows what the question-master is thinking of, that student should say so. If the guess is not correct, the question-master earns one point and play continues as before. If it is correct, the player guessing earns three points and becomes the next question-master. This player then comes forward, picks up the next topic card, and play continues as before.

If no one has guessed what the question-master is thinking of after 20 questions have been asked, the question-master states what it is and earns one point. Another student then volunteers to be the next question-master.

After you have finished playing, add up the points to determine the winner.

Tips
- It might be best to keep a record on the board of the number of questions asked during each round.
- If your students are having trouble thinking of questions, you can help out by asking some yourself.
- If a beginner or lower-intermediate class is playing, you might want to write some model questions on the board before play begins.

 # P5 Hot Seat

Level: Beginner to Advanced
Skills Practiced: Speaking and listening
Time: Flexible

Setup
Prepare a list of five to nine words your class has recently learned.
Draw a scoring table on the board, such as this one:

Team A	Team B

How to Play
Ask your students to form two teams and have them move their chairs forward to form two groups facing the board. After explaining the rules of the game, ask for one player from each team to move his or her chair forward again and turn it to face the group. These players then sit in their chairs (now **hot seats**) with their backs to the board.

Write the first word on the board, making sure the players in the hot seats cannot see it. After you say "Go!" the members of each team try to elicit this word from their team-member in the hot seat without saying the word or giving any clues as to its spelling. For example, if the word is **vitamins**, players could make statements such as We need lots of these in our food, or ask leading questions such as What does fruit have a lot of? The team whose hot-seat player first says the target word wins a point.

The two players in the hot seats then swap seats with other members of their respective teams. After writing the second word on the board, say "Go!" again, and so on. The game continues until all the words have been used, and the team with the most points at the end of the game wins.

Tips
- If neither of the players in the hot seats has stated the word within a reasonable length of time, move on to the next word without having the players swap seats.
- It is a good idea to tell the players the total number of words you intend to write on the board before play begins. This allows players to gauge their team's chances of winning as the game progresses.
- There are many possible variations on this game. Instead of recently learned words, you could write the names of famous people, movie titles, song titles, countries, famous places, etc.
- For a small class (three to six students), set up just one hot seat and have a player write any word on the board. The other players try to elicit this word from the player in the hot seat. After the student in the hot seat has had a chance to guess two or three different words, players alternate roles as they wish. This variation does not have to involve scoring.

P6 What's the Word? (Beginner)

Level: Beginner
Skills Practiced: Vocabulary recall and sentence construction
Time: Flexible

In this game players take turns miming in order to elicit a word or verb phrase. Other players call out words or phrases until someone calls out the correct one. This player earns a point for his or her team and the chance to earn another point by correctly using the word or phrase in a sentence.

Setup
Print out the set of cards below or make your own set using recently taught vocabulary.

Actor	Barber
Construction worker	Doctor
Lawyer	Librarian
Pilot	Police officer
Scientist	Teacher

Draw a scoring table on the board, such as this one:

Team Awesome!	Team Genius!

How to Play

After explaining the game and modeling the roles, divide the class into two teams and have each team choose a name. Then place the cards face down in a pile at the front of the classroom.

Ask for any member of the first team to come forward. This player then takes the top card and acts in such a way as to suggest (without speaking) whatever is written on the card.

If any member of either team thinks he or she knows what is written, that student calls it out. The first player to call it out correctly earns a point for his or her team. This player can then earn another point by correctly using the word or words in a sentence.

A player from the second team then comes forward and picks up the next card and mimes whatever is written on it, and so on. Play continues until all the cards have been used, with the team that earns the most points winning.

Tips

• If no one has guessed what is written on the card within a reasonable length of time, ask for the student who is acting it out to state it before continuing the game as usual.

• To play a shorter game, either set a time limit for the game as a whole or use just a few of the cards.

 # P7 What's the Word? (Intermediate)

Level: Intermediate
Skills Practiced: Vocabulary recall and sentence construction
Time: Flexible

Setup

Make a set of cards similar to those on page 390 using recently taught vocabulary.
Draw a scoring table on the board, such as this one:

Team Wolf	Team Tiger

How to Play

In this game, students take turns eliciting compound nouns by miming each of the constituent words. To begin, a player indicates **first word** by raising one finger and then acts in such a way as to suggest this word. Those watching call out words they believe the student may be acting out until someone calls out the correct one. The player miming then nods, holds up two fingers, and begins miming the second constituent word. For example, if the word is **basketball**, the player tries to elicit **basket**, and then **ball**. The player must not, however, mime the word **basketball** itself by running around as if playing the game.

Explain the game and model if necessary (emphasize that the players must not try to mime the target word itself, but each part of the word in turn). Then divide the class into two teams and have each team choose a name. Next, place the cards face down in a pile at the front of the classroom.

Ask for any member of the first team to come forward. This player takes the top card and tries to elicit each part of the word as explained above. If another student correctly guesses the first part, the player miming nods and then continues by trying to elicit the second part.

If any member of either team thinks he or she knows the complete word, that student raises a hand. If correct, his or her team wins a point. The player stating the correct word can then earn the team another point by correctly using the word in a sentence.

A player from the second team then comes forward to elicit whatever is written on the next card, and so on. Play continues until all the cards have been used, with the team that earns the most points winning.

Tips

- If no one has guessed the word within a reasonable length of time, ask the student who is miming to state it. A player from the other team then comes forward to continue play.
- To play a shorter game, either set a time limit for the game as a whole or use just a few of the cards.

P8 Time Bomb

Skills Practiced: Counting in English
Level: Beginner
Time: Flexible

This is a great game that really makes students think. It sounds simple, but try it out and see how tough, and fun, it really is!

How to Play

Put the students into groups of two to ten. The first person says either "1," "1, 2" or "1, 2, 3."

The next student continues on and can say an additional one, two, or three numbers. For example, if the first person said "1, 2," the second person can say either "3" or "3, 4" or "3, 4, 5."

Continue around the group until one person is forced to say "12." He or she is now out.

Start again from "2."

Tips

- This game is really addictive, and great for motivation. But remember the golden rule: losing does not mean losing, it just means you get another chance to try again!
- If you want to teach a bit of culture as well, try making 13 the number and explain that 13 is often considered unlucky in Western countries.

P9 The "What did you say?" Game

Level: High Beginner to Advanced
Skills Practiced: Questioning skills plus "Sorry," "Again, please," and "What did you say?"
Time: Flexible

The beauty of this game is that it seems really easy at first, but soon turns out to be quite chaotic! It is great for getting your students used to important phrases and it gets them in the habit of asking when they have not understood something. It is a review game so you have to make sure your students have practiced questioning beforehand.

How to Play
Introduce and explain the phrases **Sorry**, **Again, please**, and **What did you say?** to your class. Ensure that everyone understands how these phrases are used.

Divide the students into two groups. Secretly give each team five different questions to ask, such as What is your name?, How old are you?, What is your favorite color?, What is your favorite animal?, and What is your favorite food? Make sure the students know how to answer. It might be a good idea to let them choose a set of questions beforehand to review, and then choose which ones you give to each team. If they are having difficulty understanding a question, explain it to them using words, pictures, or some combination of both.

Have the teams face each other in two lines. The students will then ask the student who is standing opposite from them the question, and then write down the answer. Of course, everyone is doing this simultaneously.

This sounds simple, but there is a twist … the two lines of students have to be 10 feet apart! This results in a lot of shouting and I'm sorry, what did you say?–type questions. Make sure you enforce proper questioning when students are asking the speaker to repeat what was said; otherwise the game can degenerate into unproductive chaos.

Content

Q1 Introduction to the United States of America

Background

Britain's American colonies broke with the mother country in 1776 and were recognized as the new nation of the United States of America following the Treaty of Paris in 1783. During the 19th and 20th centuries, 37 new states were added to the original 13 as the nation expanded across the North American continent and acquired a number of overseas possessions. The two most traumatic experiences in the nation's history were the Civil War (1861–1865), in which a northern union of states defeated a secessionist confederacy of 11 southern slave states, and the Great Depression of the 1930s, an economic downturn during which about a quarter of the labor force lost its jobs. Buoyed by victories in World Wars I and II and the end of the Cold War in 1991, the US remains the world's most powerful nation state.

Location

- continent of North America
- borders both the North Atlantic Ocean and the North Pacific Ocean
- between Canada and Mexico

Climate

- mostly temperate
- tropical in Hawaii and Florida
- arctic in Alaska
- semiarid in the great plains west of the Mississippi River
- arid in the Great Basin of the southwest
- low winter temperatures in the northwest are ameliorated occasionally in January and February by warm chinook winds from the eastern slopes of the Rocky Mountains

Natural Resources

- coal
- copper
- lead
- molybdenum
- phosphates
- uranium
- bauxite
- gold
- iron
- mercury
- nickel
- potash
- silver
- tungsten
- zinc
- petroleum
- natural gas
- timber

Geography Note

- world's third-largest country by size (after Russia and Canada) and by population (after China and India)
- Mt. McKinley, Alaska, is the highest point in North America
- Death Valley, California, is the lowest point in North America

Population

308,745,538 (April 2011)

Languages (2011 census)

- English 74%
- Spanish 11.5%
- other Indo-European 0.15%
- Asian and Pacific island 2.8%
- other 0.04%

Note: Hawaiian is an official language in the state of Hawaii

Capital

Washington, D.C.

Administrative Divisions

50 states and 1 district*:

- Alabama
- Alaska
- Arizona
- Arkansas
- California
- Colorado
- Connecticut
- Delaware
- District of Columbia*
- Florida
- Georgia
- Hawaii
- Idaho
- Illinois
- Indiana
- Iowa
- Kansas
- Kentucky
- Louisiana
- Maine
- Maryland
- Massachusetts
- Michigan
- Minnesota
- Mississippi
- Missouri
- Montana
- Nebraska
- Nevada
- New Hampshire
- New Jersey
- New Mexico
- New York
- North Carolina
- North Dakota
- Ohio
- Oklahoma
- Oregon
- Pennsylvania
- Rhode Island
- South Carolina
- South Dakota
- Tennessee
- Texas
- Utah
- Vermont
- Virginia
- Washington
- West Virginia
- Wisconsin
- Wyoming

National Holiday

Independence Day, 4 July (1776)

Executive Government

chief of state: president; vice president
Note: the president is both the chief of state and head of government

head of government: president; vice president

cabinet: cabinet appointed by the president with senate approval

elections: president and vice president elected on the same ticket by a college of representatives who are elected directly from each state; president and vice president serve four-year terms (eligible for a second term)

Agriculture (products)

- wheat
- corn
- other grains
- fruits
- vegetables
- cotton
- beef
- pork
- poultry
- dairy products
- fish
- forest products

Industries

- leading industrial power in the world
- highly diversified and technologically advanced
- petroleum
- steel
- motor vehicles
- aerospace
- telecommunications
- chemicals
- electronics
- food processing
- consumer goods
- lumber
- mining

Exports—commodities (2009)

- agricultural products (soybeans, fruit, corn) 9.2%
- industrial supplies (organic chemicals) 26.8%
- capital goods (transistors, aircraft, motor vehicle parts, computers, telecommunications equipment) 49.0%
- consumer goods (automobiles, medicines) 15.0%

Imports—commodities (2009)

- agricultural products 4.9%
- industrial supplies 32.9% (crude oil 8.2%)
- capital goods (computers, telecommunications equipment, motor vehicle parts, office machines, electric power machinery) 30.4%
- consumer goods (automobiles, clothing, medicines, furniture, toys) 31.8%

 ## Q2 The National Flag

- On January 1, 1776, the Continental Army was reorganized in accordance with a Congressional resolution which placed American forces under George Washington's control. On that New Year's Day, the Continental Army was laying siege to Boston which had been taken over by the British Army. Washington ordered the Grand Union flag hoisted above his base at Prospect Hill. It had 13 alternate red and white stripes and the British Union Jack in the upper left-hand corner (the canton).

In May of 1776, Betsy Ross reported that she sewed the first American flag.

On June 14, 1777, in order to establish an official flag for the new nation, the Continental Congress passed the first Flag Act: "Resolved, That the flag of the United States be made of thirteen stripes, alternate red and white; that the union be thirteen stars, white in a blue field, representing a new Constellation."

Between 1777 and 1960, Congress passed the following acts that changed the shape, design, and arrangement of the flag and allowed for additional stars and stripes to be added to reflect the admission of each new state:

- Act of January 13, 1794: provided for 15 stripes and 15 stars after May 1795.
- Act of April 4, 1818: provided for 13 stripes and one star for each state, to be added to the flag on the 4th of July following the admission of each new state, signed by President Monroe.
- Executive Order of President Taft dated June 24, 1912: established proportions of the flag and provided for arrangement of the stars in six horizontal rows of eight each, a single point of each star to be upward.
- Executive Order of President Eisenhower dated January 3, 1959: provided for the arrangement of the stars in seven rows of seven stars each, staggered horizontally and vertically.
- Executive Order of President Eisenhower dated August 21, 1959: provided for the arrangement of the stars in nine rows of stars staggered horizontally and 11 rows of stars staggered vertically.

Q

Today the flag consists of 13 horizontal stripes, 7 red alternating with 6 white. The stripes represent the original 13 colonies, the stars represent the 50 states of the Union. The colors of the flag are symbolic as well: red symbolizes hardiness and valor; white symbolizes purity and innocence; and blue represents vigilance, perseverance, and justice.

Q3 The National Anthem

Oh, say, can you see, by the dawn's early light,
What so proudly we hailed at the twilight's last gleaming?
Whose broad stripes and bright stars, thro' the perilous fight;
O'er the ramparts we watched, were so gallantly streaming.
And the rockets' red glare, the bombs bursting in air,
Gave proof through the night that our flag was still there.
Oh, say, does that star-spangled banner yet wave
O'er the land of the free and the home of the brave?

On the shore dimly seen, thro' the mists of the deep,
Where the foe's haughty host in dread silence reposes,
What is that which the breeze, o'er the towering steep,
As it fitfully blows, half conceals, half discloses?
Now it catches the gleam of the morning's first beam,
In full glory reflected, now shines on the stream;
'Tis the star-spangled banner: oh, long may it wave
O'er the land of the free and the home of the brave!

And where is that band who so vauntingly swore
That the havoc of war and the battle's confusion
A home and a country should leave us no more?
Their blood has wash'd out their foul footstep's pollution.
No refuge could save the hireling and slave
From the terror of flight or the gloom of the grave,
And the star-spangled banner in triumph doth wave
O'er the land of the free and the home of the brave.

Oh, thus be it ever when free men shall stand,
Between their loved homes and the war's desolation;
Blest with vict'ry and peace, may the heav'n-rescued land
Praise the Power that has made and preserved us as a nation.
Then conquer we must, when our cause is just,
And this be our motto: "In God is our trust";
And the star-spangled banner in triumph shall wave
O'er the land of the free and the home of the brave!

Q4 The History of the "Star-Spangled Banner"

If there is anything taken more seriously than the US flag, it is possibly the national anthem. The "Star-Spangled Banner" accompanies just about every major American function and major sporting event. A significant honor is bestowed on those asked to sing what is probably the best known national anthem in the world.

The lyrics illustrate a moment in US history during the war with the British and one man's relief in seeing the US flag still flying after a vicious bombardment.

Before the Battle

The War of 1812 had been a particularly brutal conflict with the British. The British had burned down the Capitol building and the White House in Washington, and were set on taking the port of Baltimore, which was protected in part by Fort McHenry. After an initial land attack had been blocked, 16 ships of the British fleet positioned themselves for a massive attack on the fort.

Before the fleet came within canon range, two Americans, Colonel John Skinner and a lawyer and part-time poet by the name of Francis Scott Key, had gone out to one of the British ships. They had come to negotiate the release of Dr. William Beanes, a friend of Key's who had been seized following the attack on Washington. The British agreed, but all three had learned too much about the forthcoming attack and were detained by the British on board the frigate *Surprise* until it was over.

The "Defense of Fort McHenry"

The attack started on September 12, 1814, and continued for the next two days. Skinner, Key, and Beane watched much of the bombardment from the deck and, through the nights of the 12th and 13th they caught glimpses of the star-shaped fort with its huge flag—42 feet long, with 8 red stripes, 7 white stripes, and 15 white stars—that had been specially commissioned to be big enough so that the British could not possibly fail to see it from a distance.

In the dark of the night of the 13th, the shelling suddenly stopped, and through the darkness the Americans could not tell whether the British forces had been defeated, or whether the fort had fallen.

As the sun began to rise, Key peered through the lifting darkness, anxious to see if the flag they had seen the night before was still flying. He then scribbled on the back of an envelope the first lines of a poem he called "Defense of Fort McHenry":

> O, say can you see, by the dawn's early light,
> What so proudly we hail'd at the twilight's last gleaming

As the mist started to clear, he was aware that there was a flag flying—but was it the British flag? It was difficult to tell:

> What is that which the breeze o'er the towering steep,
> As it fitfully blows, half conceals, half discloses?

But finally the sun rose, and with intense relief and pride he saw that the fort had withstood the onslaught:

> 'Tis the star-spangled banner—O long may it wave
> O'er the land of the free and the home of the brave.

In the third verse of the poem, Key expresses his particular bitterness towards the British:

> Their blood has washed out their foul footsteps' pollution.
> No refuge could save the hireling and slave
> From the terror of flight or the gloom of the grave,

An understandable feeling of the time, but as the two nations came closer, such sentiments were not considered appropriate, and as a result, this third verse is usually omitted.

The Poem Becomes an Anthem

On the way back to shore, and later in his lodgings, Key completed all four verses of the poem, and the following morning he took it to his brother-in-law, a local judge, who thought it so good that he arranged to have it printed as a pamphlet.

It is very likely that Key only ever intended this as a poem. However, there was a very popular song of the time which had the same form and meter, and there can be no doubt that Key was heavily influenced by it—ironically, this was the tune of a British drinking song!

When the pamphlets were printed, they included the name of this song to which the poem should be sung: "Anacreon in Heaven." Nobody is sure whether this was Key's idea, or whether his brother-in-law had made the connection, but to this day, the American national anthem is sung to the tune of a British drinking song.

At one time, the English composer Dr. Thomas Arnold was thought to be its composer as it was used as the constitutional song of the Anacreonic Society—a drinking club based in a pub in the Strand, London—for which Arnold had written numerous songs. However, it is now accepted that the song was actually written by John Stafford Smith for the same society, probably in 1771.

Key made a number of handwritten copies of his original poem, introducing the occasional change. But it was not just Key who made alterations, as various editors along the way have also had a hand in altering spelling, punctuation, and even the words. The original text of the poem has therefore varied depending on what version was read. One of the original copies that Key wrote was sold to the Maryland Historical Society for $26,400 in 1953, and the actual flag that he saw is preserved in the Smithsonian Institution.

In 1916, President Woodrow Wilson ordered that it should become the national anthem to be played by the military and naval services, but it was not until March 3, 1931, that it was officially designated as the national anthem by an act of Congress:

> "Be it enacted by the Senate and House of Representatives of the United States of America in Congress assembled, that the composition known as The Star-Spangled Banner is designated as the National Anthem of the United States of America."

Q5 Map of the USA

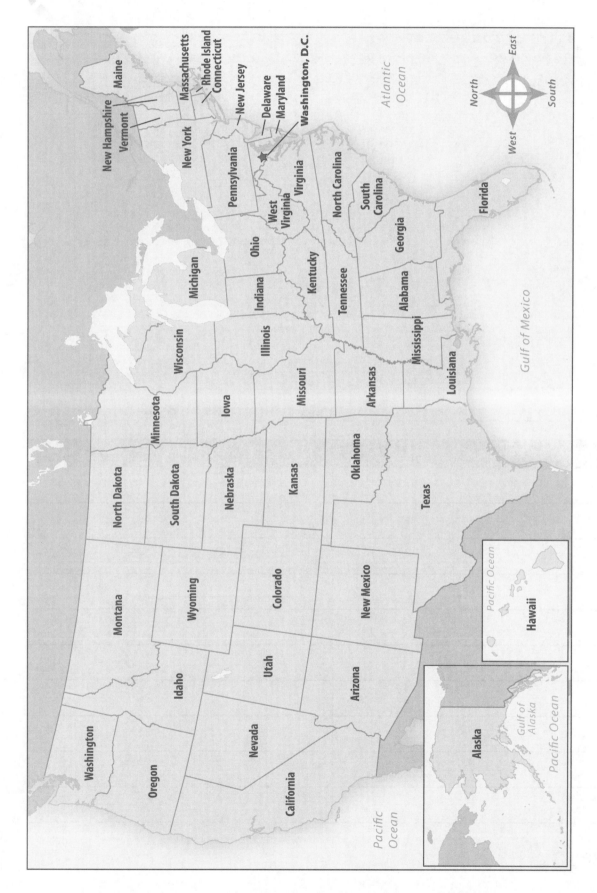

Q6 Map Quiz

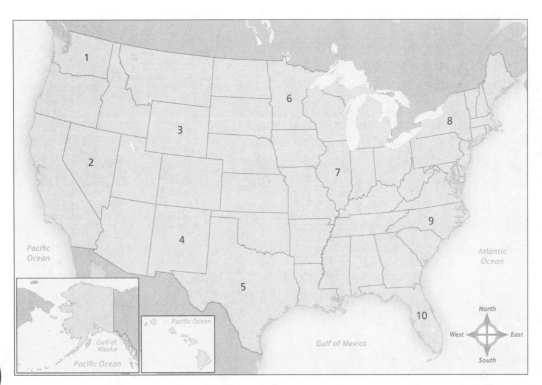

Name: _____ **Class:** _____ **Date:** _____

STATE	CAPITAL
1.	
2.	
3.	
4.	
5.	
6.	
7.	
8.	
9.	
10.	

SCORE: _____

Q7 Population Distribution Worksheet

Name: _____ Class: _____ Date: _____

1. Using an atlas or a reliable website, complete the table below:

Five Most Populous States	Five Largest States	Five Most Populous Capital Cities

Five Least Populous States	Five Smallest States	Five Least Populous Capital Cities

Q

2. Look at the states with the largest populations. Are these the same states that have the largest areas?

_____

3. Why—other than its size—might a state have a large population?

_____

_____

4. In which state is the most populous capital city located?

_____

5. Which state has the smallest population?

_____

6. Why do you think its population may be so low?

_____

_____

7. Which state has the smallest area?

_____

8. Look at a map of the population distribution of the United States to figure out where the capital cities with the largest populations are located. Are these cities near each other?

_____

_____

Q

9. Do these cities have anything else in common, in terms of their location?

_____

_____

_____

_____

10. List as many reasons as possible why someone might want to live in one of the least populous capital cities.

_____

_____

_____

_____

_____

SECTION R
Sample Planning

Content

This section contains sample lesson and unit plans, as well as ideas for evaluation and skill progression. Each of the samples can be modified to suit your individual class and teaching style. It is recommended that you approach this section as simply a guide; it is always best for the teacher to create his or her own lessons to ensure that the material is covered in the way most applicable to the specific course curriculum and the needs of the class.

R1 Conversation Skills Syllabus

Before planning a speaking or listening lesson, it is important to consider what level your students are and what they should be able to do at that level. There will be specific goals for the course (often set by the school or academy where you are teaching), as well as certain conversational and social competencies that will be expected of students of a given level. It is your job as the teacher to ensure that your students are performing with a competency appropriate for their level and to facilitate their progression to higher levels of proficiency.

Course Goals

- Develop students' oral/aural fluency in the four main areas of competence: social interaction, following and giving instructions, exchanging information, and persuasion
- Offer authentic, meaningful conversation practice in a non-threatening environment
- Empower students to speak English outside of the classroom

Specific Conversation Skills

WEEK	TOPIC
1	Asking and responding to questions
2	Small talk
3	Body language
4 and 5	Giving/asking for directions
6 and 7	Expressing an opinion
8	Presentation skills
9	Interviewing
10	Problem Solving

Oral/Aural Competencies

Research on second-language learning has identified four areas for oral/aural competence for students of all levels and ages:
1. Social interaction (e.g., inviting/refusing an invitation, social etiquette)
2. Following and giving instructions (e.g., how to get to school, to the library)
3. Exchange of information (e.g., giving personal information at a bank)
4. Forms of persuasion (e.g., suggesting, arguing, negotiating, recommending, debating, warning)

1. Social Interaction
a) Beginner-level students should be able to:
- Use basic courtesy formulas (thank you, please, etc.)
- Express satisfaction/dissatisfaction ("Dinner was delicious, thank you.")
- Greet, introduce others and self, and ask questions ("Hello, my name is…", "This is Kathy…", "What do you do?")
- Ask permission ("May I open the window?")
- Open, respond to, and close a short, casual exchange and engage in small talk ("It's a beautiful day.")

b) Intermediate-level students should be able to:
- Give and respond to compliments ("I love your sweater.")
- Express worry ("I think the weather is too bad to drive to the city tonight.")
- Give and get permission ("Could I borrow your pen?")
- Apologize/make excuses ("I am very sorry I was late. There was an accident on the highway.")
- Express and respond to disappointment ("That's too bad, I wanted to see that movie.")
- Offer something and accept an offer ("Would you like me to drive you to work tomorrow?")
- Express hope, regret, and gratitude ("Thank you for the wonderful time yesterday.")
- Use courtesy levels according to the formality of the situation
- Greet and identify self clearly on the phone ("Hi, this is Roger speaking. How may I help you?")
- Express sympathy ("I am very sorry to hear that your cat is sick.")

c) Advanced-level students should be able to:
- Express indifference ("It doesn't matter to me. I will watch either movie.")
- Approve/disapprove ("I don't think it was a good idea to bring your dog to the meeting.")
- Express intentions ("My sister and I are planning a trip for our parents.")
- Express value judgments ("Hondas are nice cars, but I would prefer a Lexus.")
- Use rhetorical questions, tag questions, and exclamations ("That wasn't a good idea, was it?")
- Use interpersonal skills in social exchanges for greater effectiveness

2. Following and Giving Instructions
a) Beginner-level students should be able to:
- Understand positive/negative commands and requests
- Understand and give simple sets of instructions and directions

b) Intermediate-level students should be able to:
- Understand instructions for simple technical and non-technical tasks
- Give spoken instructions and directions
- Understand directions and instructions by phone

c) Advanced-level students should be able to:
- Understand and give instructions on technical and non-technical tasks of medium to high complexity in person or by phone

3. Exchange of Information

a) Beginner-level students should be able to:
- Provide basic personal information related to the context
- Express ability/inability
- Indicate problems in communication—check, clarify, ask for repetition, and request confirmation
- Identify, demonstrate, and describe
- Ask for information
- Express needs, wants, and preferences in the present and for the future
- Express satisfaction/dissatisfaction

b) Intermediate-level students should be able to:
- Ask for and provide more detailed information related to appropriate contexts
- Express agreement/disagreement
- Deal with problems in communication
- Express obligation, ability, inability, certainty, and possibility
- Discuss options
- Engage in conversation on a general topic of interest
- Express and analyze opinions on a familiar topic
- Conclude and summarize
- Take turns effectively and change topics smoothly

c) Advanced-level students should be able to:
- Obtain, organize, and present information
- Give definitions and detailed descriptions of objects, ideas, states, and processes
- Obtain information by interviewing/surveying
- Explain reasons and use cause-and-effect constructions
- Respond to feedback
- Represent and defend opinion/point of view
- Discuss pros and cons
- Support own view with facts, experience, and opinions of others
- Maintain conversation

4. Forms of Persuasion

a) Beginner-level students should be able to:
- Request service or assistance
- Attract attention
- Agree, compromise, accept, and reject
- Respond to warnings

b) Intermediate-level students should be able to:
- Request assistance, attract attention, and invite
- Use polite formulaic expressions with instructions, suggestions, and requests
- Give and ask for suggestions or advice
- Predict consequences
- Indicate solutions to problems

c) Advanced-level students should be able to:
- Attract attention, express concern, and seek advice
- Argue a point
- Ask for and suggest sources of information
- Negotiate a solution/compromise
- Suggest solutions to problems
- Complain and demand/invite cooperation from others
- Request feedback

R2 Sample Lesson Format

Activity	Approximate Time
Warm-up	10 minutes
Process	40–50 minutes
Conclusion	15 minutes

This lesson plan format will allow for the following:
- A lot of practice time for students
- A standard daily structure or routine
- A variety of activities within a single lesson

Variations on the Lesson Plan Format Theme

In order to keep this standard lesson plan format from becoming boring, it is important to remember that there are a number of variations that can be applied within the various segments of the lesson plan format.

Warm-up

Students might arrive at your class late, tired, stressed, or otherwise distracted. In order to get their attention, it is best to open with a warm-up activity. The warm-up can be as simple as telling a short story or asking students questions. The warm-up can also be a more thought-out activity such as playing a song in the background or drawing an elaborate picture on the board. While it is possible to start a lesson with a simple How are you?, it is much better to tie your warm-up to the theme of the lesson.

Process

The body of the lesson can take a variety of forms:
- Reading selection
- Soliciting students' knowledge about a specific point
- Teacher-centered explanation
- Listening selection
- Short video
- Student presentation

This should include the main "meat" of the lesson. For example, if you are working on phrasal verbs, you can provide a short reading extract peppered with phrasal verbs.

As students practice the new skill, you can give them feedback on their progress. This practice may be very structured or more free-flowing and may include discussions, writing activities, or games.

Conclusion

It is important to wrap up any lesson upon its completion. Use this opportunity to check students' understanding of what was taught, discuss and address any difficulties, assign homework, and briefly show how the lesson ties in to the rest of the course or unit.

 # R3 Methodological Suggestions for the Classroom

Delivery Method	Suggestion
1. Pairs and small groups	If you wish to vary speaking activities that are normally done in pairs, make them small-group activities instead. Rather than performing a simple dialogue, students will have to interact with multiple students in a more meaningful way.
2. Dialogues and conversations	Incorporating structured dialogues and conversations into classroom activities is a great low-pressure way to encourage students to practice speaking. For beginner classes, provide students with a complete script. As they progress, you can provide scripts for some students, while the others must produce their parts spontaneously based on the framework of the conversation.
3. Role-plays and simulations	Both of these can be good speaking and listening exercises. For a role-play, give students an imaginary situation and have them act as a character in that situation (e.g., a police officer writing a ticket or a librarian giving a book to a patron). For a simulation, give the students a situation and have them respond as themselves in that situation (e.g., they are at a restaurant or train station, or they are lost and must ask for directions).
4. Discussions	Classroom discussions are a great way to get students to speak without being overly concerned with producing perfectly grammatical sentences. They also give you a chance to learn more about your students' thoughts and opinions.
5. Chain responses	In a chain response, someone (such as the instructor) will pose a question or make a statement and a student will respond. The next student will respond to the first student's response, and so on, until everyone has had an opportunity to speak.

6. Room and student configurations	If you are able to move the desks or tables in your classroom, it can be beneficial to do so for certain activities. You may want to move desks into a circle for class discussions, out of the way for role-plays, etc.
7. Mime and drama	Miming can be a fun way to get students to practice new vocabulary; one student can act out a recently learned word or phrase while the others guess the answer. The student who guesses correctly then acts out the next word or phrase, and so on.

R4 Evaluation Suggestions

Whether you will be assessing students during their ongoing activities or in a quiz or test situation, there are broader organizational decisions to be made. You should determine the best match between the organizational method and the type of student information to be gathered. Organizational methods are listed below.

Assessment Stations

Assessment stations refer to areas designated by the teacher that are used specifically for assessment purposes. These areas may be located inside or outside the classroom.

A teacher may decide to use assessment stations to have students demonstrate a skill, make observations, or manipulate materials. The teacher may observe and keep records of student performance, or students may work through assessment stations, recording their work in a written format.

Individual Assessments

Individual assessments focus on individual student progress. Assessment activities constructed by the teacher are completed individually by the students. Teachers may wish to have students work individually on written assignments, presentations, or performance assessment tasks in order to evaluate individual progress.

Group Assessments

Group assessments focus on the progress a group of students has made by allowing them to cooperate and collaborate to complete assessment activities organized by the teacher. In order to assess social skills and cooperative learning processes, teachers may decide to have students complete written assignments or presentations, or demonstrate their new skills while in groups.

Contracts

A contract refers to an agreement between a student, or a group of students, and a teacher regarding what activity will be undertaken, who will do it, how it will be done, when it will be completed, and how it will be evaluated according to the criteria established.

Contracts may specify any written assignments, presentations, or performance of skills that are to be demonstrated by the student. Students may fulfill some of the requirements of their contracts by assessing their own work.

R

Self- and Peer-Assessments

Self-assessment refers to the students' own assessment of their progress in knowledge, skills, processes, or attitudes. Peer-assessment refers to students' assessment of other students. Peer-assessments may be conducted either individually or collaboratively in groups.

Students may participate in a variety of self- and peer-assessment activities involving their written assignments and presentations, or their performance of skills and processes. Students may also assess their efforts on quizzes and tests. Contracts frequently have a self- or peer-assessment component.

Portfolios

A portfolio is a collection of student work that assists the student and teacher in making judgments about the student's learning progress. Samples of work to be included may be selected by the student, by the teacher, or by both in consultation with each other.

Copies of tests, quizzes, contracts, and assignments, and assessments of presentations and of skills are examples of items that may be included in portfolios. In addition, samples of students' day-to-day work completed on an individual basis or in groups may be added to the portfolios. Copies of self-assessment and peer-assessment instruments may also be included in the portfolio.

Informal Assessments

Ongoing, informal assessments can be useful. For example, a teacher's log book can provide valuable insight into a student's progress.

R5 Asking and Responding to Questions

Asking questions in an ESL classroom is important, no matter what level the students are. Always make sure that you ask questions that are appropriate for your students' learning levels.

During the first few days of class, ask students a lot of getting-to-know-you questions. These are generally very simple and straightforward, such as When is your birthday? or How long have you been studying English? and they will allow you to learn about everyone in the classroom. Beginner students can also respond easily to Yes or No questions and questions requiring simple answers. At this stage, you could also have students interact with each other by playing Twenty Questions, where each question requires a Yes or No answer.

As students progress, you can start introducing open-ended questions. Encourage students to engage in conversations, using open-ended questions to elicit increasingly more detailed responses. You may also want to introduce tag questions, such as It's a nice day, isn't it? so that students become comfortable with this common style of speech.

Useful Vocabulary

Question Words
- Who? What? Where? When? Why?
- How? (… much?, … far?, … long?)

Sample Questions
- Is this your first time at the American Language School?
- What are your hobbies?
- Why do you want to learn English?
- Where can you get a haircut?
- How much does it cost to go out for dinner?

Expressions to Extend or Encourage Conversation
- Really!
- What happened next?
- That's interesting …
- Why do you think so?
- Oh?
- I see …

At all levels, it is important to check that learners can ask questions as well as answer them—asking and answering questions being the two most basic functions necessary for survival in a foreign language.

—Nic Underhill

On the following pages, you will find some sample lessons and activities that you can use in an ESL classroom. Some of them are full lessons that may span multiple-class sessions, while others are shorter activities that can be incorporated into a larger lesson plan. As with all lessons, it is important to consider the activities carefully and to properly lead up to and follow up on any skills introduced or developed during the course of the lesson. It is advisable to consider your own manner of teaching and comfort level with the material before using the samples provided. You should also modify them to suit your class and teaching style as needed.

 ## R6 Reintroducing Phrasal Verbs to ESL Students

Teaching phrasal verbs requires extra attention, as students find phrasal verbs rather difficult to learn. Learning phrasal verbs out of a dictionary can help, but students really need to read and hear phrasal verbs in context to be able to truly understand their correct usage. This lesson takes a two-pronged approach to helping students learn phrasal verbs. It begins with a reading comprehension which can also serve to introduce some interesting student stories for discussion. This comprehension is peppered with phrasal verbs which can then be discussed as a class. The second part of the lesson includes a brainstorming session for students to create lists of phrasal verbs to share with one another.

Aim: Improve phrasal verb vocabulary

Activity: Reading comprehension followed by brainstorming session and discussion

Level: Intermediate to high intermediate

Outline

Tell the students a little bit about what you have done that teaching day (e.g., I got up at seven this morning. After I had breakfast, I put together tonight's lesson plan and came to school. I got onto the bus at X and got off at Y....).

Ask students which of the verbs you used were phrasal verbs and ask them to repeat those verbs. At this point, you might want to ask them if they have ever looked up **get** in a dictionary. Ask them what they discovered.

Explain that phrasal verbs are very important in English—especially for native speakers of the language. You can point out that it might not be important for them to be able to use a lot of phrasal verbs if they use their English with non-native speakers. However, it is important that they have a passive knowledge of phrasal verbs, as they will need to understand more and more phrasal verbs as they become used to reading, exploring, and listening to materials in English. If they are going to communicate in English with native speakers, they will really need to use and understand phrasal verbs.

Have the students read the short story "Adventures Growing Up," (on the following page) which is full of phrasal verbs. Ask the students some general comprehension questions about the text. Then, ask them to tell a story of their own from their youth.

Now that you have discussed the text, ask the students to look at the phrasal verbs list and find these verbs, which are interspersed throughout the reading selection. Once the students have found these phrasal verbs, ask them to provide synonyms for each one.

Write a list of common verbs that can be combined with prepositions to make phrasal verbs. The following list is a good starting point:

- take
- get
- make
- put
- bring
- turn
- be
- carry

Divide students into groups of three or four each. Then, ask students to choose three of the verbs from the list and brainstorm to come up with as many phrasal verbs as they can, using each of the three verbs. They should also write sentences for each of the phrasal verbs.

As a class, ask students to take notes while you write down the phrasal verbs that each group provides. You should then give a spoken example or two for each of the phrasal verbs so that students can understand the phrasal verbs from the context of your examples.

Once you have provided the students with examples, ask them to read their own examples and check to make sure that they have used the phrasal verbs correctly. Do not introduce the idea of separable and inseparable phrasal verbs at this point. The students will already be dealing with a lot of new information. Save that for a future lesson!

Identifying Phrasal Verbs

Read the following text and try to find the phrasal verbs.

Adventures Growing Up

I was brought up in a small town in the countryside. Growing up in the countryside offered lots of advantages for young people. The only problem was that we often got into trouble because we made up stories that we acted out around town. I can remember one adventure in particular: one day as we were coming back from school, we came up with the brilliant idea to make out that we were pirates looking for treasure. My best friend Tom said that he made out an enemy ship in the distance. We all ran for cover and picked up a number of rocks to use for ammunition against the ship as we got ready to put together our plan of action. When we were ready to set off on our attack, we slowly went along the path until we were face-to-face with our enemy—the postman's truck! The postman was dropping off a package at Mrs. Brown's house, so we got into his truck. At that point, we really didn't have any idea about what we were going to do next. The radio was playing so we turned down the volume to discuss what we would do. Jack was all for switching on the motor and getting away with the stolen mail! We were just children, but the idea of actually making off with a truck was too much for us to believe. We all broke out in nervous laughter at the thought of us driving down the road in this stolen postal truck. Luckily for us, the postman came running towards us shouting, "What are you kids up to?!" Of course, we all got out of that truck as quickly as we could and took off down the road.

Phrasal Verbs

to make out	to get ready	to set off
to make off with	to be up to	to turn down
to drop off	to take off	to get into
to set off	to grow up	to bring up
to get out of	to make up	to break out
to get into		

How many other phrasal verbs can you find in the text?

R7 Listening in Color

Level: Beginner to advanced
Time: 15 minutes
Objective: To learn vocabulary through specific visual associations
Materials: A large, colorful picture

Preparation
Choose a brightly colored picture (e.g., a painting or poster) in which there is plenty of action. It should not be too complicated. Prepare to describe the picture without mentioning any color.

Procedure
1. Put the picture in a place where the class will not be able to see it. Tell them that the picture is very colorful but that they will have to imagine the colors for themselves. Then describe the picture in full detail, but do not mention any colors.

2. Ask the students to tell the class which colors they imagined. They should be as specific as possible.

3. Show the class the picture and have a class discussion about it. The following points may come up in the discussion:
    *   how the painter felt when he or she painted it
    *   what kind of painter he or she was/is
    *   what kind of room it would suit
    *   would you like it in your house?

Variation
Instead of using a picture, you can tell a story, taking care not to use any reference to color in your descriptions. Then ask the students to retell the story in color (e.g., The dark-eyed girl put on her blue coat…).

Comments
Our visual perception is very complicated, and even those of us who are highly visual may differ markedly in how we visualize. Color, for example, may be vitally important for some; for others, line, shape, or proportion may dominate.

R8 Senses and Expression

Level: Lower-intermediate to advanced
Time: 25–40 minutes
Objective: To make students aware of their sensory preferences through the words they choose and the texts they respond most strongly to
Materials: A copy of the sample sheet on page 419 for each student

Preparation
Make copies of the sample sheet below, which consists of three descriptions of the same car accident, each written from a different sensory perspective.

Procedure
1. Read the three descriptions aloud to your class and ask them what differences they notice between them.

2. Read the descriptions again and repeat your question.

3. Hand out copies of the sample sheets and have students read the descriptions themselves.

4. Ask students to work on their own and weave the bits they like from each description into a new one. They should make some additions of their own to the new description.

5. Tell them to pass around what they have written. Alternatively, students can put their descriptions up on the walls and then go around and read what the other students have written.

Comments
The language that we use often reflects the way in which particular senses dominate our perceptions and thoughts: those of us who are primarily auditory, for example, may use a high proportion of sound words and metaphors. Similarly, we may respond better to language that matches our sensory preferences. (Skilled interviewers and counselors often use this approach to encourage people to talk.) In this activity, students are led to become aware of their sensory preferences and to use them creatively.

Sample Sheet

An Accident

1. Swooping down to the right. Air rushing in through the windshield. Back onto the highway surface—grinding, shuddering along the central barrier. Over on two wheels. I am high, high. We are tipping? We sway for hours. Oomph, oomph, down on four wheels and amazingly I am in control again. Veer over onto the hard shoulder and find I have stopped. A tingling of fine glass on top of my skin.

2. I see the phone as it goes. Then there is a blank, like I'm not there, until I see cars coming the other way close, over the barrier. Everything looks tipped over—we are on two wheels. Now that I can see everything clearly and the fog in my head has cleared, I steer us over to the hard shoulder. In the mirror I see cars pulling up. How must all that have looked to the people behind us?

3. A sharp crack. Metal on metal. The muffled shattering of the windshield powdering. Normal tire roar and thud, thud, thud—we are back on the highway. Screeching, scratching, scraping along the steel barrier. Bang, bang, back on four wheels. And now, stillness all around me.

R9 Debating

Debating offers a great opportunity for students to practice analytical, persuasive, and argumentative language. Although challenging for lower-level students, debates can be an interesting and lively activity for a speaking class. To assist students in structuring their opinions and arguments, the debate topics may be given in advance to allow them to prepare some notes. However, it is not necessary to always provide the topics in advance. It is beneficial for students to have an opportunity to practice thinking on the spot and structuring their arguments at a moment's notice. Some relevant vocabulary, such as leading phrases and rebuttals, and the nature of persuasive speech should be introduced beforehand. Below are some examples of debate vocabulary that you may wish to teach your students before attempting a debate as a class lesson.

Useful Vocabulary for Debating

Agreement
- Uh-huh
- Yes
- Right
- Sure
- I know
- I see
- I agree

Expressing an Opinion
- In my opinion …
- I believe that …
- What I mean is …
- Personally, I think …

Delight
- Interesting
- Great
- Terrific
- Wonderful
- Fantastic

Surprise
- Oh really!
- My goodness!
- No kidding!
- Wow!

Disagreement
- Oh no!
- Impossible!
- Oh, come on!
- No way!

Asking for an Opinion
- Well, what do you think?
- Do you agree?
- Let's have your opinion.
- What would you say?

Doubt
- Maybe…
- Well…

Disagreeing
- I don't agree with you…
- Yes, but don't you think…
- I'm afraid I have to disagree…

Agreeing
- That's a good point.
- So do I./Neither do I.
- I feel the same way.
- That's just what I think.
- You are absolutely right.
- I agree with …

Interrupting
- Excuse me, did you say that … ?
- So what you are saying is that …
- Could you repeat that?

Continuing
- And then?
- Go on.
- What else?

Clarifying
- Let me repeat what I said.
- What I said was …
- I'm not saying that. What I'm saying is …
- What I meant to say was …

Below you will find some topics for debating, which are divided into two levels of proficiency. First, the students should be divided into teams (each team may contain as few as one student or as many as half the class) and the teams should be paired up to oppose one another. Then each pair of teams should decide which team will choose a topic. Once a topic is chosen, the opposing team will decide which side of the debate they wish to take—agreement or disagreement. Note that each topic is a statement that can be argued as being true or false. Make sure to tell the students that their personal beliefs are not at issue. In fact, they may have to make arguments in favor of a side they completely disagree with. The purpose of the exercise is to build conversational and persuasive skill rather than to air personal opinions.

Before presenting lists of debate topics in your classroom, be sure to consider the students' religious and ethnic backgrounds. Do not offer topics that will make any of the students feel uncomfortable or singled out in any way.

Elementary Topics

1. Watching television is bad for young children.

2. It is better to live in the city than in the country.

3. All criminals should go to prison.

4. Everybody should play a sport even if they are not very good at it.

5. It is better to have a brother or sister than to be an only child.

6. You should always obey your parents, even if you do not agree with them.

7. Every country should have the same laws.

8. You can learn important things by playing computer games.

9. Everybody should learn how to cook.

10. Parents should give their children lots of help with homework.

Intermediate and Advanced Topics

1. Democracy is the best form of government.

2. Capital punishment should be prohibited regardless of the crime.

3. Professional athletes deserve the high salaries they receive.

4. Parents should not use physical punishment to discipline their children.

5. We should only consume organic food.

6. Violence in the media causes violence in our society.

7. The effects of global warming can be reversed.

8. Health care should be paid for by the government.

9. Assisting someone to commit suicide should be legal.

10. All problems can be resolved without violence.

SECTION S
Homework

Content

Focused Reading

This chapter corresponds with *How to Teach English*, by Jeremy Harmer, chapters 1 through 8.

    The following questions are arranged according to chapter. Before reading a chapter, read the questions corresponding to it. Answer the questions after you have finished reading the chapter.

S1   Chapter 1: Learners

1. Why do students learn English? List reasons covered in *How to Teach English* and brainstorm three new ideas.

2. Name one of the main tasks for teachers. How can teachers accomplish this task?

3. What is the philosophy behind self-access centers?

4. List three characteristics of good classroom learners.

5. Name two differences among adults, adolescents, and children as learners.

6. List the key differences between the broad language levels (beginner, intermediate, and advanced).

7. What is the plateau effect?

 ## S2 Chapter 2: Teachers

1. Name five qualities that good teachers possess.

2. What is rough-tuning? Give an example of when rough-tuning is used.

3. What are the different roles a teacher may have in the classroom?

4. Why is it important to offer a variety of activities and topics?

5. Why is flexibility important in teaching? Give a clear example.

S

S3 Chapter 3: Managing the Classroom

1. What are the four key elements of teacher presence in the classroom? Briefly describe each.

2. What are three important vocal factors for teachers to keep in mind while teaching? Why are they important?

3. Describe three different classroom seating arrangements. Which do you think you would prefer in your classroom and why?

4. What are the three different types of student groupings? Explain both a positive and a negative aspect of each (based on your own opinion).

 ## S4 Chapter 4: Describing Learning and Teaching

1. What is the difference between acquisition and learning?

2. Define and explain ESA.

3. What are the three lesson sequences presented (pp. 54–57)? Which do you think you would be most comfortable using to present classroom lessons and why?

4. What are the five main teaching models? Which do you prefer and why?

S5 Chapter 5: Describing Language

1. What are transitive and intransitive verbs? Give two examples of each.

2. What are direct and indirect objects? Give an example of each.

3. What is a simple sentence?

4. What is the difference between countable and uncountable nouns? Give three examples of each.

5. What is an auxiliary verb? Give an example.

S

6. What are three types of pronouns? Give an example of each.

7. What is the difference between a definite and an indefinite article?

8. What do conjunctions do? Give an example of each type of conjunction.

9. What ultimately determines which one of several meanings applies to a word?

10. What is a language function? Give two examples of functions.

11. What are the three key areas of focus in pronunciation? Briefly describe each one.

S6 Chapter 6: Teaching the Language System

1. Explain the difference between mistakes, slips, errors, and attempts.

2. What are three easy ways to help students understand the meaning of new words?

3. What are developmental errors and false friends?

 ## S7 Chapter 7: Teaching Reading

1. What are two benefits of authentic reading texts?

2. Which three reading skills should students acquire?

3. Name and describe three of the six principles behind the teaching of reading.

S8 Chapter 8: Teaching Writing

1. How does writing provide reinforcement of language learned?

2. How does writing aid in language development?

3. Which two activities from the writing suggestions on pages 118-120 of *How to Teach English* do you like best? Why?

S

SECTION T
Practicum Guidelines

Content

T1 Preparing for Your Practicum

The following are some questions to consider before preparing your practicum lesson. There are answers below each question, but it is always a good idea to consult your instructor before moving forward. Your instructor will not simply be evaluating your practicum lesson; she is also there as a guide to assist you in preparing your lesson. Think of your instructor not as a judge, but as a mentor—as someone who will help you bring together all of the knowledge you have gained during the course and put it to use in a practical lesson.

What approach should I use in my practicum and future classroom lessons?

You have learned about several approaches to teaching language throughout your TESOL/TEFL Teacher Training Certification Course. It is a good idea to consider the merits of each and to build your own personal approach as you develop your teaching style. See Section A for an overview of the various teaching models.

The Oxford Seminars TESOL/TEFL Teacher Training Certification Course is focused primarily on the Communicative Approach to language teaching because this is the approach that many international language schools are looking for from teacher candidates. In some two-day interviews, you may be asked to design and teach a lesson on the second day of the interview process. Most schools will be looking for candidates who are able to use a highly interactive and engaging approach, such as that used in Communicative Language Teaching, because it gives students a more stimulating learning experience. Learning best occurs when students are engaged and when they are gaining knowledge that is immediately applicable and useful.

How does ESA apply to my practicum?

ESA stands for Engage, Study, and Activate. ESA is a breakdown of the elements that should be included in a lesson that follows the Communicative Approach. The following is a review of ESA.

Engage

Students tend to tune out when they are not emotionally engaged. The teacher should start the lesson in a way that amuses, motivates, moves, or stimulates students. Some engaging activities include games, music, discussion, interesting pictures, dramatic stories, and amusing anecdotes. Remember this rule of thumb: the more engaged the students, the more effective the lesson.

Study

This is the component of the lesson in which students are asked to focus on a specific aspect of language and how it is constructed. The lesson could be a grammar point taught by the teacher or discovered by the students, or it could focus on new vocabulary or phrases, specific communicative tasks, or other aspects of language or vocabulary. Study work can take the form of direct teacher instruction, group work, independent learning, or class discussion, to give a few examples.

Activate

This element describes exercises and activities that are designed to get students to use language as freely and communicatively as possible. The objective is for students to use any and all language that may be appropriate for a given situation or topic and to practice any new language learned during the study element of the lesson. Some typical exercises include role-playing, simulations, debates and discussions, and story and poem writing.

All of these elements should be used in your lesson. It is most likely that the lesson will be made up of several short activities or components; ensure that each of these components fits under one or another ESA category. The order of ESA may be changed to suit your teaching style and comfort level, as well as the needs of the particular lesson. Some lesson activities are more suited to an EAS format, where the learning item is practiced first (e.g., a dialogue or an interview) and then the results are studied. Usually this is followed by a second activation phase where the students put to practice what they learned from their earlier mistakes.

How should I focus my lesson?

Your lesson should have a clear objective, and every aspect of the lesson should work toward meeting that objective. If you cannot justify how an activity helps to meet your objective, you should take that activity out of your lesson plan. More information on lesson planning can be found in Section D.

What steps should I take when starting to plan my lesson?

- Write down your objective. Make sure it is something achievable in the time you have for the lesson. Teach English grammar is not a good example of an achievable lesson objective!
- Write down the age and level your lesson is designed for.
- Keep in mind any cultural or linguistic considerations that may affect your lesson.
- Brainstorm ways of engaging your students in the lesson.
- Brainstorm a list of activities that will help you meet your objective.
- Note how long you will spend on each activity. Consider setup time for any materials or student movement (e.g., getting into groups or pairs, moving from one station to another).

How long should my lesson be?

You are required to create a plan for a 60-minute lesson even though the actual practicum may be shorter (depending on the specification from your instructor). This is because most language classes will be about one hour in duration and you will be giving copies of your lesson plan and handouts to all of the other students in your TESOL/TEFL class for their future use.

What sorts of activities should I include in my lesson?

Remember your objective. Try to incorporate as many of the core language skills as possible into your lesson (speaking, listening, reading, and writing), but stay focused on the narrow objective you are trying to achieve. A lesson on paragraph writing would not necessarily be well spent if most of the class time is taken up with listening and role-playing activities. However, it is also important to integrate the specific focus of the lesson into the language as a whole.

Even if your presentation will be less than 60 minutes, try to include all of the activities you would do in a full hour class to meet your objective. If time is a concern, introduce the activity and explain the process, but skip the actual work element during your practicum. It is not necessary to have your classmates spend 10 minutes converting present tense verbs to the past tense; however, if that is a core element in the activation component of your lesson, then you must include it in your plan and materials.

Try to pique your students' curiosity and creativity. You will want to engage them in what they are learning and give them an opportunity to explore the language and to try new things. You also don't want to bore them with too many mundane tasks or rote memorization. Consider your strengths, interests, and talents and make the best use of them. Anything you can do to enhance your lesson will be appreciated by your students (and instructor!).

What if my lesson seems repetitive or redundant?

That is okay. Unless you are teaching advanced students, your lesson may seem a little repetitive. A lot of language learning comes through practice, and practice means a lot of repetition. Most of the time your objective will be to teach one particular skill or point, but you will find many different ways of meeting this objective that appeal to the different types of learners in your class (e.g., auditory, visual, tactile).

What are some helpful tips for my presentation?

- Plan out the presentation in advance. Rehearse what you will say; imagine potential questions or difficulties; and have a backup plan in case a key element goes wrong (e.g., the CD player doesn't work).
- Create props and other visuals to increase student interest.
- Develop a lesson that will actively involve and engage students.
- Keep in mind the 80:20 ratio of student talking time (STT) to teacher talking time (TTT). Do not skip key instructions or explanations for the sake of maintaining the ratio, but use it as a guide. The idea is to ensure that students will have sufficient time to practice communicating in English.
- Bring any materials that the students might need (e.g., handouts, markers, glue, props).
- Elicit as much information as possible from the students. Ask them open-ended questions and let them come up with the answers on their own, but be prepared to lead them in the right direction if necessary.
- Have the students figure out the topic rather than saying, "Today we are going to talk about … "
- While they do have their place in an ESL lesson, try to keep photocopied grammar worksheets to a minimum.
- Review the Practicum Assessment Rubric in your Welcome Package. While planning and envisioning your lesson, you should have an idea of what the course instructor will be looking for while watching your presentation. Make eye contact with the students; have a logical flow from each stage of the lesson to the next; and be confident and animated in front of the class.
- Try to relax—nobody expects a perfect presentation. The point is that you learn something in the process of planning and delivering a lesson.
- Most importantly, have fun! Your enjoyment and enthusiasm will spill over to your students and make the lesson more engaging for everyone.

T2 Final Word

The practicum is your opportunity to show what you have learned in the Oxford Seminars TESOL/ TEFL Teacher Training Certification Course. It is not just a final assignment that you need to complete in order to get your certificate; it is an opportunity for you to put into practice the various theories and methods that have been discussed during the course. Approach it as if it were a real lesson with real students. The more authentic you imagine the scenario, the better your lesson will be and the more effective it will be as practice for your future teaching endeavors.

The lessons you learn and the skills you practice are not just for this course; they are things you will use and develop as you embark on your ESL teaching career. Your instructor is an experienced ESL teacher and is there to help you with your planning and to offer feedback on your lesson delivery, so take advantage of this opportunity, ask questions, and get as many teaching tips as possible. Accept any feedback or constructive criticism as an opportunity for improvement. Consider the practicum a way for you to demonstrate what you have learned and to improve your future lessons to help you become the best teacher you can be.

SECTION U
English-Language Teaching

Content

U1 English-Language Teaching

Once you have completed your TESOL/TEFL certification, opportunities for teaching ESL the world over will be open to you. You can teach adults or children, university students or professionals. You can teach in small private settings, or in large academies and public schools. You can tutor one-on-one, facilitate online Q & A sessions, grade computer-based language proficiency tests, or engage in a variety of other options. There are people from all walks of life and in every corner of the globe who have an interest in learning English.

Take advantage of the Graduate Placement Service included with your Oxford Seminars course, and if teaching ESL is something you are considering as a long-term career, explore some of the many enhancements and specializations that are open to you as a trained and certified ESL teacher. Most importantly, go overseas and live the adventure that first inspired you to consider teaching English as a second language.

What Next?

Once you have a couple of years of ESL teaching experience, you may decide that you could benefit from further training. If you have an undergraduate degree, you may consider undertaking a TESOL/TEFL graduate degree program. Or, if you have become interested in a particular aspect of ESL teaching, you may seek out a training program that focuses on your area of interest.

This section provides further information relating to ongoing training, as well as other avenues you may wish to pursue such as managing an ESL school or publishing.

U2 Career Development for ESL Teachers

As a new ESL teacher, while you gain experience, you will discover that there is still much to learn. The first few years on the job will be an intense experience that will open your eyes to new possibilities. There are several paths outlined below and explained in greater detail further on. Take some time to consider which of these may be best suited to your particular skills and ambitions.

Training as a Specialist

If you have expertise or interest in a specialized area such as business, technology, law, engineering, or medicine, you can undertake training in teaching English for Specific Purposes (ESP). The growth of English as a worldwide language for business, technical, and academic communication among speakers of other languages is fueling the demand for ESP teachers.

Teaching with Technology

The field of Computer Assisted Language Learning (CALL) focuses on the use of computer technology for ESL teaching. If you have good computer skills, you can combine these with your TESOL/TEFL skills to become qualified in this high-demand area.

Master's Degree Courses

Pursuing a Master's degree will give you a chance to focus on your particular area of interest or to discover new aspects of the TESOL/TEFL field. Master's programs vary in their emphasis on theory versus application. Some careful research will be necessary to ensure that you select a program that is right for you. Some programs may require ESL teaching experience as a prerequisite for entry.

Doctorate Degrees

Doctorate programs offer both PhD and EdD degrees, with the former emphasizing research, and the latter focusing on application to education or to administration. These programs may be offered by linguistics or English departments, or by faculties of education.

Publishing

Teachers who have developed teaching materials have an opportunity to publish these either as books or on the Internet. Alternatively, if you have a research background, you may wish to publish articles in journals, many of which are available online.

The Business of ESL—Managing or Owning an ESL School

If you have become an experienced ESL teacher and have an entrepreneurial inclination, you may aspire to a management position or even to owning your own ESL school. You could begin down this path by taking a teaching position in an ESL school to acquire experience teaching the prospective teachers of ESL. The next step would be to apply for a position in management, which would allow you to find out first-hand how such a business works.

 ## U3 English for Specific Purposes (ESP)

ESP is based on the needs of the students, and generally focuses on their job-specific or academic language needs. The most common ESP subject is business English, although many students study English specific to their careers in law, pharmaceuticals, tourism, hospitality, and so on.

The methodology used to teach specialized English will vary depending on the discipline of the students and the environment in which they will use the language. Most students are adults, either in post-secondary programs or in the workplace, who have at least an intermediate level of proficiency in English.

Securing a job teaching ESP will often require a specialized knowledge of the subject matter, or at least the relevant and appropriate vocabulary. If you have a degree, diploma, or work experience in a field that currently employs a lot of individuals from abroad, you could find your expertise in high demand. You may, however, need to be creative in your job search when seeking an ESP teaching position. While some schools employ teachers for specialized fields, it is often companies themselves that will directly hire teachers to instruct their employees. Contact the human resources departments of any companies in your field that you believe employ or should employ ESP instructors for their staff, and find out what the hiring process is.

Many individuals will also hire ESP tutors to help them study one-on-one. Private tutoring can be a very rewarding and lucrative opportunity for ESP instructors. You can post your résumé in a local paper or an online job bank to advertise your services, or keep your eyes open for ads requesting an ESP tutor.

Business English

Business English is one of the most in-demand types of ESP (although many schools will classify it as a discipline separate from ESP). More and more resources are being produced to aid business English instructors, so you should not have much difficulty finding business English books or Internet-based materials.

Teachers' qualifications to teach business English are dependent on their general TESOL/TEFL training and their background knowledge of the subject area. Oxford Seminars Teaching Business English specialization module is a 40-hour enhancement for your TESOL/TEFL certification that will prepare you to plan and develop lessons for teaching English to adults in the business community.

English for Academic Purposes (EAP)

ESL students who plan to enter an English-language post-secondary institution often enroll in EAP courses. These classes are generally for more advanced students who need to improve their language skills to the level required in college or university.

Very often, the aim of these courses is to prepare students to write the TOEFL (Test of English as a Foreign Language). Many non-native English speakers are required to write this test and achieve a minimum score in order to gain admission to higher education programs in North America. Because of the high number of students who are required to take the TOEFL, gaining a solid understanding of how to prepare students to take the test will offer you a wealth of teaching and tutoring opportunities. Oxford Seminars offers a Teaching TOEFL Preparation specialization module that provides teachers with the necessary background and strategies to help students successfully prepare for the TOEFL test. The specialization module is a 40-hour enhancement for your TESOL/TEFL certification.

Children

There is always a high demand for teachers who are experienced in teaching children. This can be quite different from teaching adults, and can require a lot of energy and innovation on the part of the instructor. If you have an interest in working with young students, you will find no shortage of employment opportunities available. Oxford Seminars offers a specialization module in Teaching English to Children. This specialization module is a 40-hour enhancement for your TESOL/TEFL certification that expands upon philosophies examined in the course and delves further into such topics as language acquisition, child development, and ways of fostering phonemic awareness. The module prepares teachers to design and implement a creative and interactive curriculum specifically geared for young students.

U4 Learning to Teach with CALL

Computer technology is now playing an increasingly influential role in education. Language education has been no exception to this trend, and in recent years growing numbers of teachers are taking graduate-level courses in the field of computer assisted language learning (CALL). There are a number of reasons for this trend. The possibilities for self-directed learning through computer programs open up many opportunities for students who lack access to English language schools or lack the means and time to enroll in an ESL program. Computers are also of valuable assistance in more traditional language learning environments. Computer-assisted learning is growing in influence in many different fields, of which language teaching is just one. CALL programs are generally quite intensive and are often full university degree programs. It is important to consider your goals before committing to such an ambitious undertaking.

List of CALL Degree Programs in the US

Iowa State University
Ames, Iowa
Website: http://www.iastate.edu/
Telephone: Graduate Studies 515-294-2477
Degree: MA in Teaching English as a Second Language/Applied Linguistics with CALL specialization
http://www.grad-college.iastate.edu/programs/APresults3.php?apnumber=97

Monterey Institute of International Studies
Monterey, California
Website: http://www.miis.edu/
Telephone: Graduate School of Language and Educational Linguistics 831-647-4185
Degree: Graduate Certificate in Computer-Assisted Language Learning (CALL)
http://language.miis.edu/tdc/call.html

Northern Arizona University
Flagstaff, Arizona
Website: http://home.nau.edu/
Telephone: Department of English 928-523-4911
Degree: PhD in Applied Linguistics
http://www.cal.nau.edu/english/phd_program.asp

Ohio University
Athens, Ohio
Website: http://www.ohio.edu/
Telephone: Department of Linguistics 740-593-4564
Degree: MA in Applied Linguistics with CALL courses
http://www.ohiou.edu/linguistics/graduate/index.html

 # U5   Master's Degree Programs

After considering where you would like your career path to take you, you may decide to enroll in a Master's program. Factors influencing this decision may include the desire to earn a higher salary, to secure a more senior teaching or managing position, or simply to deepen your knowledge of teaching English as a second language.

There is not one standard TESOL program that is offered by all schools. Graduate courses will vary from school to school, and the program related to TESOL at a given school may be a Master of Arts, Master of Science, Master of Teaching, or Master of Education. In addition, depending on where you study, the end result may be a Master's degree with one of a number of names, including TESL, TEFL, TESOL, Second Language Education, or Applied Linguistics.

Admission to a Master's program normally requires an undergraduate degree, possibly in a specified discipline. You may also need to have a teaching certificate or documented experience teaching ESL. Each university will outline its full admission requirements in its course calendar and on its website.

Before applying to any program, you will want to do some research on the school offering the program. You should find out about the following:

- the type of degree offered
- the specific courses offered
- the focus of the program (practical versus theoretical)
- the areas of specialization of the faculty members
- whether the credentials earned through the program are recognized by the public school system (if that is where you want to teach)

Once you have researched this information, you will probably have a fairly clear idea of which school and program are right for you.

Keep in mind that if your plan is to teach after you graduate, you should seek out a school that stresses a practical approach. If, however, you are planning to continue your studies and pursue a PhD, you should find a program with a more theoretical approach.

List of Master's Degree Programs

Many universities in the United States and Canada offer Master's degrees specializing in teaching English as a second language. A list of universities is provided here as a starting point for researching these numerous and evolving programs.

US

Arizona State University
Phoenix, Arizona
Website: http://www.asu.edu/
Telephone: School of Educational Innovation and Teacher Preparation 480-727-1103
Degree: MEd in English as a Second Language (ESL)
https://webapp4.asu.edu/programs/t5/majorinfo/ASU00/EDESLMA/graduate/false

Ball State University
Muncie, Indiana
Website: http://cms.bsu.edu/
Telephone: Department of English, Graduate Programs 765-285-8415
Degree: MA in TESOL
http://cms.bsu.edu/Academics/CollegesandDepartments/English/Academics/Programs/Masters/TESOL.aspx

California State University
various cities, California
Website: http://www.calstate.edu/
Telephone: 562-951-4000
Degree: MA in TESOL
http://www.calstate.edu/gradprograms/

Central Michigan University
Mount Pleasant, Michigan
Website: http://www.cmich.edu/
Telephone: English Graduate Program 989-774-3574
Degree: MA in TESOL
http://cmich.edu/chsbs/x23522.xml

Columbia University, Teachers College
New York, New York
Website: http://www.tc.edu/
Telephone: TESOL Program, Teachers College 212-678-3795
Degrees: MA, EdM in TESOL
http://www.tc.edu/TesolAl/index.asp?Id=Programs&Info=TESOL

Eastern Michigan University
Ypsilanti, Michigan
Website: http://www.emich.edu/
Telephone: Department of Foreign Languages and Bilingual Studies 734-487-0130
Degree: MA in TESOL
http://www.emich.edu/public/foreignlanguages/

Florida State University
Tallahassee, Florida
Website: http://www.fsu.edu/
Telephone: College of Education 850-644-6885
Degrees: MA, MS in English Education
http://www.coe.fsu.edu/Academic-Programs/Departments/School-of-Teacher-Education-STE/
Degree-Programs/English-Education

Georgetown University
Washington, DC
Website: http://www.georgetown.edu/
Telephone: Department of Linguistics 202-687-5956
Degree: Master of Arts in Teaching English as a Second Language (MAT)
http://www1.georgetown.edu/departments/linguistics/programs/graduate/masters/

Georgia State University
Atlanta, Georgia
Website: http://www.gsu.edu/
Telephone: Office of Academic Assistance and Graduate Admissions 404-413-8000
Degree: Master of Arts in Teaching (MAT)
http://msit.gsu.edu/4801.html

Indiana University at Bloomington
Bloomington, Indiana
Website: http://www.iub.edu/
Telephone: Department of Second Language Studies 812-855-7951
Degree: MA in TESOL and Applied Linguistics
http://www.indiana.edu/~dsls/degrees/master.shtml

Indiana University of Pennsylvania
Indiana, Pennsylvania
Website: http://www.iup.edu/
Telephone: Graduate English Admissions Office 724-357-2263
Degree: MA in TESOL
http://www.iup.edu/upper.aspx?id=91110

Iowa State University
Ames, Iowa
Website: http://www.iastate.edu/
Telephone: Graduate English Office 515-294-2477
Degree: MA in TESL/Applied Linguistics
http://www.grad-college.iastate.edu/programs/APresults3.php?apnumber=97

Monterey Institute of International Studies
Monterey, California
Website: http://www.miis.edu/
Telephone: Graduate School of Language and Educational Linguistics 831-647-4185
Degree: MA in TESOL
http://language.miis.edu/tdc/matesol.html

New York University
New York, New York
Website: http://www.nyu.edu/
Telephone: TESOL program 212-998-5494
Degree: MA in TESOL
http://steinhardt.nyu.edu/teachlearn/mms/ma/tesol

Northeastern Illinois University
Chicago, Illinois
Website: http://www.neiu.edu/
Telephone: Graduate College 773-442-6000
Degree: MA in Linguistics with TESL concentration
http://www.neiu.edu/~tesl/index.htm

Northern Arizona University
Flagstaff, Arizona
Website: http://home.nau.edu/
Telephone: Department of English 928-523-4911
Degree: MA in TESL
http://www.cal.nau.edu/english/tesl_ma.asp

Northern Illinois University
DeKalb, Illinois
Website: http://www.niu.edu/
Telephone: Department of English 815-753-6622
Degree: MA in TESOL
http://www.engl.niu.edu/graduate/MA_programs/tesol.shtml

Ohio State University
Columbus, Ohio
Website: http://www.osu.edu/
Telephone: Office of Academic Services 614-292-2332
Degree: MA in Foreign and Second Language Education (FSLED)—includes TESOL
http://ehe.osu.edu/edtl/academics/ma/fsl/

Ohio University
Athens, Ohio
Website: http://www.ohio.edu/
Telephone: Department of Linguistics 740-593-4564
Degree: MA in Linguistics with TESOL concentration
http://www.ohio.edu/graduate/deptfactsheets/linguistics.cfm

Pennsylvania State University
various cities, Pennsylvania
Website: http://www.psu.edu/
Telephone: Department of Applied Linguistics 814-865-7365
Degree: MA in TESL
http://aplng.la.psu.edu/academicPrograms/maTesl.shtml

Portland State University
Portland, Oregon
Website: http://www.pdx.edu/
Telephone: Department of Applied Linguistics 503-725-4088
Degree: MA in TESOL
http://www.ling.pdx.edu/degrees_MA_TESOL.html

Purdue University
West Lafayette, Indiana
Website: http://www.purdue.edu/
Telephone: Director, English as a Second Language 765-494-3769
Degree: MA in English as a Second Language
http://www.cla.purdue.edu/english/esl/ma.html

Queens College of CUNY
New York, New York
Website: http://www.qc.cuny.edu/
Telephone: Department of Linguistics and Communication Disorders 718-997-2870
Degree: MS in Education: TESOL
http://qcpages.qc.edu/LCD/programs/LING/ms_tesol.htm

Southern Illinois University
Carbondale, Illinois
Website: http://www.siu.edu/
Telephone: Department of Linguistics 618-536-3385
Degree: MA in TESOL
http://www.linguistics.siuc.edu/graduate/tesol.html

Syracuse University
Syracuse, New York
Website: http://www.syr.edu/
Telephone: Linguistic Studies, Concentration Advisor 315-443-2244
Degree: MA in Linguistic Studies, TESOL Concentration
http://lang.syr.edu/academics/Linguistics/MA-Linguistics-LanguageTeaching.html

University at Albany, State University of New York
Albany, New York
Website: http://www.albany.edu/
Telephone: Educational Theory and Practice Department 518-442-5020
Degree: MS in TESOL
http://www.albany.edu/etap/graduate_programs/masters/ms_tesol.htm

University of Alabama
Tuscaloosa, Alabama
Website: http://www.ua.edu/
Telephone: Department of English 205-348-5065
Degree: MA in Applied Linguistics/TESOL
http://graduate.ua.edu/catalog/15900.html

University of Arizona
Tucson, Arizona
Website: http://www.arizona.edu/
Telephone: Department of English 520-621-1836
Degree: MA in English as a Second Language
http://grad.arizona.edu/live/programs/description/61

University of California, Davis
Davis, California
Website: http://www.ucdavis.edu/
Telephone: School of Education 530-752-0757
Degree: Education (Credential with MA)
http://www.gradstudies.ucdavis.edu/programs/program_detail.cfm?id=33

University of California, Los Angeles
Los Angeles, California
Website: http://www.ucla.edu/
Telephone: Department of Applied Linguistics & TESL 310-825-4631
Degree: MA in Applied Linguistics & TESL
http://www.appling.ucla.edu/index.php?option=com_content&task=view&id=12&Itemid=41

University of Cincinnati
Cincinnati, Ohio
Website: http://www.uc.edu/
Telephone: Division of Teacher Education 513-556-3600
Degree: MEd in Literacy & Second Language Studies
https://webapps.uc.edu/DegreePrograms/Program.aspx?ProgramQuickFactsID=1634&ProgramOutlineID=584

University of Georgia
Athens, Georgia
Website: http://www.uga.edu/
Telephone: The Department of Language and Literacy Education 706-542-4526
Degree: MEd in TESOL & World Language Education with specialization option in Teaching English to
Speakers of Other Languages (TESOL)
http://www.coe.uga.edu/lle/academic-programs/masters-programs/tesol-world-language-education-
programs/teaching-english-to-speakers-of-other-languages-tesol/m-ed/

University of Hawai'i at Mānoa
Honolulu, Hawaii
Website: http://www.uhm.hawaii.edu/
Telephone: Department of Second Language Studies 808-956-8610
Degree: MA in Second Language Studies
http://www.hawaii.edu/sls/

University of Illinois at Urbana-Champaign
Urbana and Champaign, Illinois
Website: http://illinois.edu/
Telephone: Division of English as an International Language 217-333-1506
Degree: Master of Arts in the Teaching of English as a Second Language (MATESL)
http://www.deil.uiuc.edu/

University of Iowa
Iowa City, Iowa
Website: http://www.uiowa.edu/
Telephone: Foreign Language and ESL Education 319-335-5324
Degrees: MAT, MA—Foreign Language and ESL Education
http://www.education.uiowa.edu/teach/flesled/default.aspx

University of Kansas
Lawrence, Kansas
Website: http://www.ku.edu/
Telephone: School of Education, Curriculum and Teaching, Graduate Admissions 785-864-4435
Degrees: MA, MS in Curriculum and Instruction (emphasis in TESL)
http://www.soe.ku.edu/ct/academics/endorsements/esl/

University of Maryland, College Park
College Park, Maryland
Website: http://www.umd.edu/
Telephone: College of Education, Department of Curriculum & Instruction, TESOL Coordinator 301-405-4157
Degrees: MEd in TESOL, Master's Certification Program (MCERT) with a specialization on TESOL
http://www.education.umd.edu/EDCI/SLEC/masters.html

University of Massachusetts Amherst
Amherst, Massachusetts
Website: http://www.umass.edu/
Telephone: School of Education, Graduate Admissions Office 413-545-0721
Degree: MEd with a concentration in Bilingual, English as a Second Language, and Multicultural Education
http://www.umass.edu/education/academics/med_concentrations.shtml

University of Oregon
Eugene, Oregon
Website: http://www.uoregon.edu/
Telephone: Department of Linguistics, Graduate Admissions 541-346-3901
Degree: MA in Linguistics with a Language Teaching Specialization (LTS)
http://logos.uoregon.edu/programs/graduate/masters.shtml

University of Pennsylvania
Philadelphia, Pennsylvania
Website: http://www.upenn.edu/
Telephone: Graduate School of Education, Office of Admissions 877-736-6473
Degree: Master of Science in Education (MSEd)
http://www.gse.upenn.edu/degrees_programs/

University of Pittsburgh
Pittsburgh, Pennsylvania
Website: http://www.pitt.edu/
Telephone: School of Education Office of Admissions 412-648-2230
Degree: MEd TESOL with Specialization in Foreign Language Education
http://www.education.pitt.edu/foreignlanguage/

University of Southern California
Los Angeles, California
Website: http://www.usc.edu/
Telephone: USC Rossier School of Education 213-740-0224
Degrees: Master of Science in Teaching English to Speakers of Other Languages (MS TESOL), Master
of Education in Teaching English as a Foreign Language (ME TEFL)
http://rossier.usc.edu/academic/

University of Texas at Austin
Austin, Texas
Website: http://www.utexas.edu/
Telephone: College of Education, Foreign Language Education 512-232-4080
Degree: MA with English as a Foreign/Second Language specialization
http://www.edb.utexas.edu/education/programs/fle/

University of Utah
Salt Lake City, Utah
Website: http://www.utah.edu/
Telephone: Department of Linguistics 801-581-8047
Degrees: MA TEFL Program
http://www.hum.utah.edu/linguistics/?&pageId=6112

University of Wisconsin-Madison
Madison, Wisconsin
Website: http://www.wisc.edu/
Telephone: School of Education, Department of Curriculum and Instruction, Graduate Office
608-263-7466
Degree: MS in Curriculum and Instruction with ESL and/or Bilingual Education as the area of
concentration
http://www.education.wisc.edu/ci/esl/eslprograms/default.asp

Canada

McGill University
Montreal, Quebec
Website: http://www.mcgill.ca/
Telephone: Integrated Studies in Education 514-398-4525
Degree: MA in Second Language Education
http://www.mcgill.ca/edu-integrated/graduate/

University of Alberta
Edmonton, Alberta
Website: http://www.ualberta.ca/
Telephone: Faculty of Education, Department of Educational Psychology 780-492-5245
Degree: MEd in Teaching English as a Second Language
http://www.edpsychology.ualberta.ca/GraduatePrograms/TeachingEnglishAsASecondLanguage/
MastersProgram.aspx

University of Calgary
Calgary, Alberta
Website: http://www.ucalgary.ca/
Telephone: Graduate Programs in Education 403-220-5675
Degrees: MEd, MA, Graduate Diploma, Graduate Certificate—Second Language Teaching (SLT)
Specialization
http://www.ucalgary.ca/gpe/teaching-english-additional-language

University of Toronto: Ontario Institute for Studies in Education
Toronto, Ontario
Website: http://www.oise.utoronto.ca/oise
Telephone: Graduate Admissions & Registration 416-978-1682
Degrees: MEd, MA in Studies in Second Language Education (SLE)
http://www.oise.utoronto.ca/ctl/Prospective_Students/CTL_Graduate_Programs/
Second_Language_Education_%28SLE%29/index.html

York University
Toronto, Ontario
Website: http://www.yorku.ca/
Telephone: Graduate Program in Linguistics and Applied Linguistics 416-650-8046
Degree: MA in Applied Linguistics
http://www.yorku.ca/gradling/about.html

U6 Doctoral Study

After completing a Master's degree, you may wish to continue your studies in TESOL/TEFL. Some schools offer PhD programs that will prepare you for a career in instructing students up to the Master's or doctoral level, designing postsecondary programs, or conducting research. If you think you may want to apply to a doctoral program, discuss this with an academic advisor at your school; he can let you know which path of study would be best while you are completing your Master's degree.

Studying for a Doctorate

As with Master's degrees in TESOL/TEFL, doctoral programs are becoming more common. As this trend continues, employers at respected post-secondary institutions can demand an increasingly higher level of education from the English teachers and researchers they employ.

If you decide that this direction of study is for you, be sure to do some research similar to what was suggested before embarking on a Master's program, including inquiring about the exact degree that will be conferred upon you, and specifics about the faculty's areas of research.

List of Doctorate Degree Programs

Many universities in the US and Canada offer doctorate degrees specializing in TESOL/TEFL. A list of universities is provided here as a starting point for researching these numerous and evolving programs. This list is by no means comprehensive and it should be viewed merely as a starting point. If your alma mater is not listed and you know they offer a PhD program in teaching ESL, then by all means contact them for further information.

US

Columbia University, Teachers College
New York, New York
Website: http://www.tc.edu/
Telephone: TESOL, Teachers College 212-678-3795
Degree: EdD in TESOL
http://www.tc.edu/TesolAl/

Florida State University
Tallahassee, Florida
Website: http://www.fsu.edu/
Telephone: College of Education 850-644-6885
Degree: PhD in English Education
http://www.coe.fsu.edu/Academic-Programs/Departments/School-of-Teacher-Education-STE/
Degree-Programs/English-Education/Doctoral

Georgia State University
Atlanta, Georgia
Website: http://www.gsu.edu/
Telephone: Office of Academic Assistance and Graduate Admissions 404-413-8000
Degrees: EdS, PhD in Teaching and Learning
http://msit.gsu.edu/index.htm

Indiana University at Bloomington
Bloomington, Indiana
Website: http://www.iub.edu/
Telephone: Department of Second Language Studies 812-855-7951
Degree: PhD in Second Language Studies
http://www.indiana.edu/~dsls/degrees/phdSLS.shtml

Indiana University of Pennsylvania
Indiana, Pennsylvania
Website: http://www.iup.edu/
Telephone: Graduate English Office 724-357-2263
Degree: PhD in Composition and TESOL
http://www.english.iup.edu/graduate/phd-ct/default.htm

New York University
New York, New York
Website: http://www.nyu.edu/
Telephone: TESOL program 212-998-5494
Degree: PhD in TESOL
http://steinhardt.nyu.edu/teachlearn/tesol/phd/

Northern Arizona University
Flagstaff, Arizona
Website: http://home.nau.edu/
Telephone: Department of English 928-523-4911
Degree: PhD in Applied Linguistics
http://www.cal.nau.edu/english/phd_program.asp

Ohio State University
Columbus, Ohio
Website: http://www.osu.edu/
Telephone: Office of Academic Services 614-292-2332
Degree: PhD in Foreign, Second, and Multilingual Language Education
http://ehe.osu.edu/edtl/academics/phd/fsmle/

Purdue University
West Lafayette, Indiana
Website: http://www.purdue.edu/
Telephone: Director, English as a Second Language 765-494-3769
Degree: PhD in ESL
http://www.cla.purdue.edu/english/esl/phd.html

University at Albany, State University of New York
Albany, New York
Website: http://www.albany.edu/
Telephone: Educational Theory and Practice Department 518-442-5020
Degree: PhD in Curriculum and Instruction
http://www.albany.edu/etap/graduate_programs/doctoral/doctoral_programs.htm

University of California at Los Angeles
Los Angeles, California
Website: http://www.ucla.edu/
Telephone: UCLA Applied Linguistics & TESL 310-825-4631
Degree: PhD in Applied Linguistics
http://www.appling.ucla.edu/index.php?option=com_content&task=view&id=12&Itemid=41

University of Cincinnati
Cincinnati, Ohio
Website: http://www.uc.edu/
Telephone: Division of Teacher Education 513-556-3600
Degree: EdD in Literacy & Second Language Studies
https://webapps.uc.edu/DegreePrograms/Program.aspx?ProgramQuickFactsID=1635&ProgramOutlineID=585

University of Georgia
Athens, Georgia
Website: http://www.uga.edu/
Telephone: Department of Language and Literacy Education 706-542-4526
Degrees: PhD in Language and Literacy Education, EdS in TESOL
http://www.coe.uga.edu/lle/academic-programs/doctoral-program/language-literacy-education/
teaching-english-to-speakers-of-other-languages-tesol/

University of Hawai'i at Mānoa
Honolulu, Hawaii
Website: http://www.uhm.hawaii.edu/
Telephone: Department of Second Language Studies 808-956-8610
Degree: PhD in Second Language Studies
http://www.hawaii.edu/sls/

University of Illinois at Urbana-Champaign
Urbana and Champaign, Illinois
Website: http://illinois.edu/
Telephone: Division of English as an International Language 217-333-1506
Degree: PhD in Second Language Studies
http://www.deil.uiuc.edu/

University of Iowa
Iowa City, Iowa
Website: http://www.uiowa.edu/
Telephone: Foreign Languages and ESL Education 319-335-5324
Degree: PhD in Foreign Language and ESL Education
http://www.education.uiowa.edu/teach/flesled/default.aspx

University of Kansas
Lawrence, Kansas
Website: http://www.ku.edu/
Telephone: School of Education, Curriculum and Teaching, Graduate Admissions 785-864-4435
Degrees: EdD, PhD in Curriculum and Instruction (emphasis in TESL)
http://soe.ku.edu/ct/

University of Maryland, College Park
College Park, Maryland
Website: http://www.umd.edu/
Telephone: College of Education, Department of Curriculum & Instruction, TESOL Coordinator 301-405-4157
Degree: PhD in Second Language Education and Culture
http://www.education.umd.edu/EDCI/SLEC/doc.html

University of Massachusetts Amherst
Amherst, Massachusetts
Website: http://www.umass.edu/
Telephone: School of Education, Graduate Admissions Office 413-545-0721
Degrees: EdD, PhD in Language, Literacy and Culture
http://www.umass.edu/education/academics/phd_concentrations.shtml

University of Oregon
Eugene, Oregon
Website: http://www.uoregon.edu/
Telephone: Department of Linguistics, Graduate Admissions 541-346-3901
Degrees: PhD in Linguistics
http://logos.uoregon.edu/programs/graduate/phd.shtml

University of Pittsburgh
Pittsburgh, Pennsylvania
Website: http://www.pitt.edu/
Telephone: School of Education Office of Admissions 412-648-2230
Degrees: EdD, PhD in Foreign Language Education
http://www.education.pitt.edu/foreignlanguage/

University of Texas at Austin
Austin, Texas
Website: http://www.utexas.edu/
Telephone: College of Education, Foreign Language Education 512-232-4080
Degree: PhD in Teaching English as a Second/Foreign Language
http://www.edb.utexas.edu/education/programs/fle/

University of Wisconsin-Madison
Madison, Wisconsin
Website: http://www.wisc.edu/
Telephone: School of Education, Department of Curriculum and Instruction, Graduate Office
608-263-7466
Degree: PhD in Curriculum and Instruction with ESL and/or Bilingual Education as the area of concentration
http://www.education.wisc.edu/ci/esl/eslprograms/default.asp

Canada

McGill University
Montreal, Quebec
Website: http://www.mcgill.ca/
Telephone: Integrated Studies in Education 514-398-4525
Degree: PhD in Educational Studies
http://www.mcgill.ca/edu-integrated/graduate/

University of Alberta
Edmonton, Alberta
Website: http://www.ualberta.ca/
Telephone: Faculty of Education, Department of Educational Psychology 780-492-5245
Degree: PhD in Studies in Teaching and Learning English as a Second Language
http://www.edpsychology.ualberta.ca/GraduatePrograms/TeachingEnglishAsASecondLanguage/
DoctoralProgram.aspx

University of Calgary
Calgary, Alberta
Website: http://www.ucalgary.ca/
Telephone: Graduate Programs in Education 403-220-5675
Degrees: PhD of Philosophy in Languages and Diversity
http://ucalgary.ca/gpe/programs/doctor-philosophy-phd-language-and-diversity

University of Toronto, Ontario Institute for Studies in Education
Toronto, Ontario
Website: http://www.oise.utoronto.ca/oise
Telephone: Graduate Admissions & Registration: 416-978-1682
Degrees: PhD, and EdD—Studies in Second Language Education (SLE)
http://www.oise.utoronto.ca/ctl/Prospective_Students/CTL_Graduate_Programs/
Second_Language_Education_%28SLE%29/index.html

York University
Toronto, Ontario
Website: http://www.yorku.ca/
Telephone: Graduate Program in Linguistics and Applied Linguistics 416-650-8046
Degree: PhD in Applied Linguistics
http://www.yorku.ca/gradling/about.html

U7 Getting Published

Some teachers may find that they have a penchant for devising unique lesson plans or teaching methods that work particularly well in ESL classrooms. If you are one such teacher, you might consider writing your own book for use in English language classrooms. Although the publishing process can be a little different for every author, here are the general steps toward seeing your words in print.

The Idea

Before you approach any publisher with a book proposal, make sure you know exactly what makes your idea special. There are a lot of books for ESL students already—why will yours stand out? Maybe you have a unique way of focusing on the various skill areas, or your subject matter is particularly groundbreaking. Whatever your secret weapon is, make sure that you can explain it to others, both clearly and succinctly. If other teachers get excited about your book idea when you mention it to them, you just might have a winner.

Contacting a Publisher

Once you have a clear, concise summary of your book proposal, you will need to locate a publisher who is interested in producing your book. A good first step is to look under "Publishers" in Section O: Resources. Take a look at the types of books published by various companies to figure out where your idea might fit in. For example, if your book is geared toward Business English students, you should avoid pitching your idea to a publisher specializing in children's ESL books.

When you have found a publisher who you believe would want to publish your book, contact the acquisitions editor and request a few minutes of his time to discuss your ideas. The editor may ask you to send more information about your proposal, or direct you toward another publisher who may be a better fit for your book.

The Submission

If a publisher is interested in your proposal, you will probably be asked to submit a formal book proposal which includes the following information:

The Book
- A synopsis and description of the book
- A detailed table of contents
- A brief outline of the book's distinctive or innovative features, with a more detailed description of the two or three most important ones
- A brief outline of the characteristics of the book (end-of-chapter summaries, checklists, exercises, etc.)
- The length and format of the book
- A description of the look of the book (pictures, inserts, charts, etc.)
- The pedagogical approach the book takes and the reasoning behind it
- Supplements that are intended to go with the book (e.g., instructor's manual, exercise book, etc.)
- Report on how much of the book is currently completed
- Estimate of the time required to complete the manuscript

The Author
- An explanation of why you are writing the book
- Your résumé
- A note about any other experience that qualifies you in the ESL field
- A note about any sales avenues that you may have access to
- Other interesting facts about you that may be influential in the selling or marketing of the book

The Market
- Is the book for the classroom or independent learners?
- Is there a specific program, class, or level for which it is intended?
- What is the approximate size of the market for this book? How was this number reached?
- What books would be in competition with this book?
- How will this book set itself apart from the competition?

Sample Chapter
- A sample chapter, or chapters, that highlights the writing style, pedagogical approach, and prominent features of your book

Compiling the information required for this submission and writing a sample chapter can be quite a time-consuming process, so be prepared for some hard work before a publisher even agrees to produce your book. If you believe that your book should be in the hands of future students, however, the effort will be well worth it.

Writing the Book

Congratulations—once you have reached this point, you are on your way to being a published author! You will work with an editor who will give you feedback throughout the writing process. The editor may also distribute your manuscript to other teachers who will test it out in their classrooms to give you practical feedback before your book is published. Based on this feedback, you may want to revise some portions of your manuscript to appeal to a larger number of teachers.

Between the time that you complete your manuscript and the time that your book is published, your work will be minimal, although you may be waiting for something to happen for months. No need to worry—during this time, your work is being copyedited and formatted to look like a professional publication. You will be amazed to see the finished product.

Your Published Book

Seeing your completed book in a bookstore can be very validating. It means that other people admire your work and want to learn something from you. Being able to tell your friends that you are a published author and collecting royalties can be pretty rewarding as well. Keep in mind that your work does not end at the time of publication. You may be asked to speak to other teachers at conferences or other events, and you may even be asked to write another book. Be prepared for anything!

U8 School Management

Some schools offer diplomas or degree programs in ESL Teaching Management. Taking one of these programs is a good step toward securing a management position at a language school, but is not the only way to pursue this career path.

Many teachers find that over the course of their teaching experience, they are given more and more responsibility in terms of school administration, the purchasing of resources, or curriculum development. These all place managerial responsibilities on the teachers, and can be a way of training them for a more senior position. In small companies, this progression may happen quickly, so if you find yourself being given additional duties beyond your job description as a teacher, be sure that you are comfortable taking them on. You may also want to ask whether accepting extra responsibility will in fact lead you toward a more lucrative school management position.

How to Get There

If running a language school is your long-term goal, you can work toward this from the beginning of your career. One key to doing this is to show your employer that you are willing and able to do the job. Teachers who turn out to be successful administrators tend to be very focused in their work while also being able to easily adapt to unfamiliar situations. You will need to show your employer that you are enthusiastic about teaching and learning, that you are reliable in your lesson planning and your availability to your students, and that you have the initiative to direct yourself and others.

Let your boss know about your desire to manage a school; he or she may otherwise not know about your career goals. While it is a great idea to have this discussion early on in your employment so that you are not passed over for positions you may have wanted, give yourself some time to explore your role as a teacher first. Coordinating other instructors will be difficult if you yourself do not have a firm grasp of what does and what should happen in an ESL classroom. Take some time to learn what works well in the classroom, both from the teacher's and the students' points of view. Explore the strategies and techniques introduced throughout this manual, experiment with your own ideas, and do not be afraid of making mistakes—this is often the best way to learn.

Try not to become so focused on your own career goals that you ignore those of the teachers around you. Your colleagues may have similar aspirations, and perhaps more experience than you do. Take the time to observe their classes and try to understand which teaching strategies work well in their classrooms. Listen to their advice. Introduce new ideas that you have learned from them into your classroom. All of this can help you carve out your own niche in the world of English-language teaching.

Working for Yourself

While managing a language school may appeal to you, working to achieve someone else's vision for the school may not. Establishing your own language school is an option, if you have the resources to do so. Starting up a school in a foreign country may sound like a great idea for you, but be sure to look into local employment and business laws before doing anything else. Also be sure to research the market well to find out about the demand for English language instruction and any existing competition.

If you decide to go ahead with your business plan, you may want to take some courses in accounting or business management if you do not already have a strong background in these areas.

With the right experience, attitude, and skills, running your own school can be very financially and personally rewarding. There is nothing quite like the feeling of being your own boss, but coupled with that feeling is the pressure to perform and succeed. Running a business is not for everyone, but for those of an entrepreneurial bent, it can be not just the end-goal of their teaching experience, but the starting point of a new endeavor.

U9 Teacher Associations

Teacher associations provide valuable networking opportunities for all ESL teachers and are of particular importance to new teachers who are establishing themselves in the field.

International Associations

Computer Assisted Language Instruction Consortium (CALICO)
Texas State University
214 Centennial Hall
San Marcos, TX 78666 US
Telephone: 512-245-1417
Website: https://www.calico.org/

CALICO is a professional organization that serves a membership involved in both education and technology. CALICO has an emphasis on language teaching and learning but reaches out to all areas that employ the languages of the world to instruct and to learn. CALICO is a recognized international clearinghouse and leader in computer assisted learning and instruction. It is a global association dedicated to computer assisted language learning (CALL).

International Association of Teachers of English as a Foreign Language (IATEFL)
Darwin College, University of Kent
Canterbury, Kent, CT2 7NY UK.
Telephone: 0044 1227 824430
Website: http://www.iatefl.org/

IATEFL is the International Association of Teachers of English as a Foreign Language. Founded in the UK in 1967, it now has over 3,500 members in 100 different countries throughout the world. IATEFL's mission is to link, develop, and support English language teaching professionals throughout the world. It provides a range of regular publications and holds an Annual International Conference with an extensive program of talks and workshops.

Modern Language Association of America (MLA)
26 Broadway, 3rd floor
New York, NY 10004-1789 US
Telephone: 646-576-5000
Website: http://www.mla.org/

Founded in 1883, the Modern Language Association of America provides opportunities for its members to share their scholarly findings and teaching experiences with colleagues and to discuss trends in the academy.

NAFSA: Association of International Educators
1307 New York Avenue, NW, 8th floor
Washington, DC 20005-4701 US
Telephone: 202-737-3699
Website: http://www.nafsa.org/

NAFSA: Association of International Educators is a member organization promoting international education and providing professional development opportunities to educators in the field. Hundreds of NAFSA members volunteer to serve the association and thousands advocate for international education.

Teachers of English to Speakers of Other Languages, Inc. (TESOL)
700 South Washington Street, Suite 200
Alexandria, Virginia 22314 US
Telephone: 703-836-0774
Website: http://www.tesol.org/

Incorporated in 1966, TESOL is a global association for English-language teaching professionals headquartered in Alexandria, Virginia, in the US TESOL encompasses a wide network of educators worldwide. TESOL offers members serial publications, books, and electronic resources on current issues, ideas, and opportunities in the field of English-language teaching. TESOL also conducts a variety of workshops and symposia, including an annual convention.

American Associations

American Council on the Teaching of Foreign Languages (ACTFL)
1001 N. Fairfax St., Suite 200
Alexandria, VA 22314
Telephone: 703-894-2900
Website: http://www.actfl.org/

ACTFL is a national organization dedicated to the improvement and expansion of the teaching and learning of all languages at all levels of instruction. ACTFL is an individual membership organization made up of more than 9,000 foreign language educators and administrators as well as government and industry.

Association for the Advancement of Computing in Education (AACE)
P.O. Box 1545
Chesapeake, VA 23327-1545
Telephone: 757-366-5606
Website: http://www.aace.org/

AACE, founded in 1981, is an international, not-for-profit educational organization with the mission of advancing information technology in education and e-learning research, development, learning, and its practical application. AACE serves the profession with its international conferences, publications, digital library, career center, and other opportunities for professional growth.

National Association for Bilingual Education (NABE)
1313 L Street N.W. Suite 210
Washington, D.C. 20005-4100
Telephone: 202-898-1829
Website: http://www.nabe.org/

NABE is a professional organization at the national level, devoted to representing both English-language learners and bilingual education professionals. NABE represents a combined membership of more than 20,000 bilingual and ESL teachers, administrators, paraprofessionals, university professors and students, researchers, advocates, policy makers, and parents.

TESOL Affiliates

The following is a list of American regional or state-based affiliates of Teachers of English to Speakers of Other Languages, Inc. (TESOL). As this is a growing list, consult the TESOL website at www.tesol.org for up-to-date information.

Alabama-Mississippi TESOL (AMTESOL), http://www.amtesol.org
Alaska Association of Bilingual Education (AKABE), http://www.ankn.uaf.edu/NPE/ANEA/AKABE/
Arizona TESOL (AZ-TESOL), http://www.az-tesol.org/
Arkansas TESOL (ARKTESOL), http://arktesol.org/
California and Nevada TESOL (CATESOL), http://www.catesol.org/
Carolina TESOL, North and South Carolina, http://www.carolinatesol.org/
Colorado TESOL (CoTESOL), http://www.colorado.edu/iec/cotesol/
Connecticut TESOL (ConnTESOL), http://www.conntesol.net/

Georgia TESOL (GATESOL), http://www.gatesol.org/

Hawai'i TESOL, http://www.hawaiitesol.org/

Illinois TESOL-BE (ITBE), http://www.itbe.org/

Indiana TESOL (INTESOL), http://www.intesol.org/

Intermountain TESOL (ITESOL); Utah, Idaho, and Wyoming; http://www.itesol.org/

Kansas TESOL (KATESOL), http://katesol.org/

Kentucky TESOL (KYTESOL), http://www.kytesol.org

Louisiana TESOL (LaTESOL), http://latesol.org/

Maryland TESOL (MDTESOL), http://www.marylandtesol.org/

Massachusetts Association of Teachers of Speakers of Other Languages (MATSOL), http://www.matsol.org/

Michigan TESOL (MITESOL), http://www.mitesol.org/

Mid-America TESOL (MIDTESOL); Kansas, Iowa, Nebraska, Missouri; http://www.midtesol.org/

Minnesota TESOL (MinneTESOL), http://www.minnetesol.org/

New Jersey TESOL/New Jersey Bilingual Educators (NJTESOL/NJBE), http://www.njtesol-njbe.org/

New York State TESOL (NYS TESOL), http://www.nystesol.org/

Northern New England TESOL (NNETESOL); Maine, New Hampshire, Vermont; http://www.nnetesol.org/

Ohio TESOL, http://www.ohiotesol.org/

Oklahoma TESOL (OKTESOL), http://www.oktesol.com/

Oregon TESOL (ORTESOL), http://www.ortesol.org/

PennTESOL-East; Pennsylvania (Eastern), Southern New Jersey, and Delaware; http://www.penntesoleast.org/

Sunshine State TESOL of Florida (SSTESOL), http://www.sunshine-tesol.org/

Tennessee TESOL (TNTESOL), http://www.tntesol.org/

TexTESOL-I, El Paso, Texas; http://www.textesol.org/

TexTESOL II; San Antonio, Texas; http://www.textesoltwo.org/

TexTESOL III; Austin, Texas; http://www.textesol.org/region3/

TexTESOL IV; Houston, Texas; http://www.textesoliv.org/

TexTESOL V; Dallas, Texas; http://www.textesolv.org/

Three Rivers TESOL (3R TESOL); Western Pennsylvania and West Virginia; http://3riverstesol.org/index.html

Virginia TESOL (VATESOL), http://www.vatesol.cloverpad.org/

Washington Area TESOL (WATESOL); Washington DC, Delaware, Maryland, Virginia;
     http://www.watesol.org/

Washington Association for the Education of Speakers of Other Languages (WAESOL),
     Washington State, http://www.waesol.org/

West Virginia TESOL (WVTESOL), http://tesolwv.org/

Wisconsin TESOL (WITESOL), http://www.witesol.org/

Canadian Associations

British Columbia Teachers of English as an Additional Language (B.C. TEAL)
206-640 West Broadway
Vancouver, BC V5Z 1G4
Telephone: 604-736-6330
Website: http://www.bcteal.org/

B.C. TEAL is an organization of educators dedicated to the growth and development of the profession of English-language teaching so that English-language learners from diverse cultures can work toward achieving their goals.

Canadian Association of Second Language Teachers (CASLT)
CASLT National Office
300-950 Gladstone Avenue
Ottawa, ON K1Y 3E6
Telephone: 1-877-727-0994
Website: http://www.caslt.org/

CASLT was established in 1970, and has evolved from a small organization of volunteers dedicated to supporting second-language teachers into a multi-level organization. These second languages encompass both official and international languages.

Teaching English as a Second Language in Canada (TESL Canada)
104-8557 Government Street
Burnaby, BC V3N 4S9
Telephone: 604-298-0312
Website: http://www.tesl.ca/

TESL Canada is a national organization dedicated to advancing communication and coordinating awareness of issues for those concerned with English as a second language and English skills development. The organization promotes advocacy for ESL learners, unifies teachers and learners by providing a forum and network capabilities, supports the sharing of knowledge and experiences across Canada, and represents diverse needs and interests in TESL nationally and internationally.

Teachers of English as a Second Language of Ontario (TESL Ontario)
405-27 Carlton St.
Toronto, ON M5B 1L2
Telephone: 416-593-4243
Website: http://www.teslontario.org/

Established in 1972, TESL Ontario is a nonprofit organization serving the needs of teachers of English as a Second Language (ESL) and English Literacy Development (ELD). In its commitment to professional development and advocacy, TESL Ontario addresses the range of competencies, experiences, and issues which influence the success of immigrants, refugees, visa students, and others who are learning English.

 # U10 Volunteer Programs

The worldwide need for ESL teachers outstrips the funding available to hire them. To fill the gap, nonprofit organizations seek out volunteers with the relevant training and skills to fill ESL teaching positions in developing countries as well as in Canada and the US. With a credential from a TESOL/TEFL certification course, you will be well positioned for placement in a position of your choosing. In exchange for going without financial benefit, you will be well rewarded with the experience that you need to obtain a paid position and with the satisfaction of helping to fill a crucial need.

Some of the organizations listed below place American and Canadian volunteer ESL teachers directly in ESL teaching positions either at home or abroad. Others are a source of information about such organizations. A few websites are listed that cater to students planning a gap year, or a break from formal education often involving volunteering abroad; this practice, which is common in the United Kingdom, is beginning to take hold in North America.

If you are contemplating a position abroad with a particular organization, be sure to research the level of assistance you will receive for arranging travel, visas, and accommodation. Training may also be offered—ideally, this should be tailored to help you to meet the specific needs of those served by the organization. Your ability to succeed in the field will be enhanced by an organization that provides good support.

AmeriCorps
http://www.americorps.org/

AmeriCorps offers opportunities for adults of all ages and backgrounds to serve in the US through a network of partnerships with local and national nonprofit groups. AmeriCorps members address critical needs, including improving literacy, in communities all across America.

Amerispan Study Abroad
http://www.amerispan.com/

AmeriSpan has evolved from offering three Spanish schools in Latin America to offering numerous language schools which teach over 15 languages in more than 45 countries throughout the Americas, Europe, Asia, the Middle East, Australia, and Africa.

Center for Interim Programs
http://www.interimprograms.com/

The Center for Interim Programs is a consulting service that helps young people in the US find meaningful gap-year placements. Since its inception in 1980 as the first organization of its kind in the US, Interim has designed creative gap-year opportunities for over 5,000 young people.

Christians Abroad
http://www.cabroad.org.uk/

Christians Abroad places volunteer teachers in schools in communities in the developing world, such as in Africa, Asia, and the Middle East.

Colorado China Council (CCC)
http://www.asiacouncil.org/

CCC is a non-political, educational outreach organization dedicated to developing programs to deepen the American public's understanding and appreciation of China's history, culture, and contemporary life. CCC does this by sending people from North America to China for either a month in the summer or a full year to teach English, as well as other subjects, at Chinese universities.

Cross-Cultural Solutions (CCS)
http://www.crossculturalsolutions.org/

CCS is an international not-for-profit organization in the field of international volunteering. CCS provides opportunities for volunteers to teach English in low-income communities. Both inexperienced and experienced volunteers can teach vocabulary, assist with pronunciation, and support students as they practice speaking English. CCS has a worldwide staff of over 300 people and operates in 12 countries, with administrative offices located in the US, the UK, Canada, and Australia. CCS has no political or religious affiliations.

Dave's ESL Cafe

http://www.eslcafe.com/

Dave's ESL Cafe provides a list of organizations that recruit volunteer ELS teachers at http://www.esl-cafe.com/search/Jobs/Volunteer/.

Friends of World Teaching-Nursing (FOWT)

http://www.fowt.com/

FOWT helps American and Canadian educators locate employment at English-speaking schools and colleges throughout the world.

Gap Year Abroad—Travel CUTS

http://www.gapyearabroad.ca/

Travel CUTS, Canada's leading, student-owned travel company brings to bear its 35 years of expertise in travel with Gap Year Abroad. Participants may include students taking a break after high school or after completing an undergraduate degree, professionals taking a sabbatical, or retirees. Volunteering opportunities include teaching English abroad.

Global Routes

http://www.globalroutes.org/

Global Routes offers summer community service programs for high-school students and gap year and college semester teaching internships for students 18 years of age and older in Belize, China, Costa Rica, the Dominican Republic, Ecuador, Ghana, India, Kenya, Mexico, Nepal, Peru, Tanzania, Thailand, and Vietnam.

India Literacy Project (ILP)

http://www.ilpnet.org/

ILP is a developmental support organization that works in partnership with local nongovernmental organizations (NGOs) and networks in India to play the role of a catalyst for literacy. ILP's main role is to enable and support its NGO partners. ILP's website provides information about these NGOs and their literacy programs.

International Foundation for Education and Self-Help (IFESH)

http://www.ifesh.org/

IFESH is a nongovernmental, nonprofit, charitable organization aiming to reduce hunger and poverty; empower the local community by raising the standard of literacy; and foster cultural, social, and economic relations between Americans and Africans, particularly those Americans who are of African descent. The organization focuses on programs in the areas of literacy, education, vocational training, agriculture, nutrition, and health care. IFESH's primary area of concern is sub-Saharan Africa.

National Adult Literacy Database (NALD)

http://www.nald.ca/

NALD, a Canadian organization, provides an online digital library that links the diverse players in the literacy community. NALD provides complete, full text documents and books, as well as a resource catalog; researches and organizes educational material found elsewhere on the web; connects partners with experts in the field; and publicizes literacy-related activities and events. NALD is based in Fredericton, New Brunswick.

Peace Corps

http://www.peacecorps.gov/

The Peace Corps is an agency of the US federal government devoted to world peace and friendship. More than 200,000 Peace Corps volunteers have served in 139 host countries to work on issues ranging from AIDS education to information technology and environmental preservation. Education is the Peace Corps' largest program area, with volunteers serving as teachers of English, math, science, and business. Volunteers have to be at least 18 years old and US citizens.

Planet Gap Year

http://www.planetgapyear.com/

Planet Gap Year aims to create the first interactive online community for US high-school graduates and college students to plan a productive gap year.

ProLiteracy Worldwide

http://www.proliteracy.org/

ProLiteracy Worldwide is a nonprofit international literacy organization based in Syracuse, New York, that was formed by the 2002 merger of Laubach Literacy International and Literacy Volunteers of America, Inc. It sponsors educational programs that help adults and their families acquire the literacy practices and skills they need to function more effectively in their daily lives. ProLiteracy America, the United States Programs Division of ProLiteracy Worldwide, represents 1,200 community-based volunteer and adult basic education members in the United States. ProLiteracy's International Programs Division works with grassroots partner programs in 65 developing countries around the world.

Tie Online

http://www.tieonline.com/

The TIE online newspaper and interactive website posts ads for international teaching job vacancies in top American and British schools abroad. Positions are for teachers, interns, and administrators.

VIA

http://www.viaprograms.org/

VIA (formerly Volunteers in Asia) is a private, non-profit, non-religious organization dedicated to increasing understanding between the United States and Asia through service and education. Since 1963, the Asia Programs have provided US Residents with an opportunity to work and live within an Asian culture while meeting the needs of Asian host institutions. Current long-term and summer programs exist in Cambodia, China, Indonesia, Myanmar, Thailand, and Vietnam. Their Stanford Programs offer a wide range of short-term, international study programs between the US and Asia and among various Asian nations. Short-term spring and summer programs for students focus on a variety of themes, including language and culture, service learning, and healthcare.

VolunteerMatch

http://www.volunteermatch.org/

VolunteerMatch, a nonprofit organization, is dedicated to helping everyone find a great place to volunteer. The organization offers a variety of online services to individuals, nonprofit organizations, and corporations. The VolunteerMatch service is the preferred internet recruiting tool for more than 60,000 nonprofit organizations.

VSO (Voluntary Service Overseas)

http://www.vso.org.uk/

VSO is the world's leading independent international development charity that works through volunteers to fight poverty in developing countries. Some VSO placements are for English-language teaching positions. VSO recruits volunteers who live in the EU, Canada, the US, and a number of other countries.

VSO Canada (Voluntary Service Overseas Canada)

http://www.vsocan.org/

VSO Canada is the Canadian partner of Voluntary Service Overseas (VSO).

WorldTeach

http://www.worldteach.org/

WorldTeach is a nonprofit, nongovernmental organization based at the Center for International Development at Harvard University. WorldTeach provides opportunities for individuals to make a meaningful contribution to international education by living and working as volunteer teachers in developing countries. Volunteers receive training, language preparation, and field support. WorldTeach programs are open to native speakers of English; volunteers do not have to be US citizens.

World University Service of Canada (WUSC)

http://www.wusc.ca/

WUSC recruits Canadian university students and professionals for various volunteer assignments in the developing world.

SECTION V

The Oxford Seminars Online Component

Content

V1 Goals of the Online Component

The online component is an important part of your education as an ESL teacher. Completing the course will help you do the following:

✓ Reinforce the fundamentals of TESOL/TEFL/TESL, so you'll feel more confident in the classroom
✓ Build on what you learned in class, so you'll be a better teacher
✓ Get ahead of the competition by being more qualified, making you more employable
✓ Feel more motivated and excited about teaching, by giving you new ideas and strategies for helping your students

The online component covers topics that you need in order to teach ESL successfully.

It covers areas such as the following:

• English grammar (simple and complex grammatical structures, the twelve tenses of the English language, the parts of speech, as well as common grammatical errors and misconceptions)
• The role of the teacher within a communicative language classroom
• Effective and engaging lesson planning
• Analyzing communicative teaching methodologies
• The fundamentals of language acquisition, learning, and teaching
• How to teach grammar through stimulating and engaging lessons, with a focus on the role of grammar in facilitating communication
• Analyzing ESL case studies and teaching scenarios
• Reviewing and applying ESL teaching theories and concepts

V2 How to Access the Online Component

Check your email on Monday morning, after you complete the in-class component, for an email from Oxford Seminars detailing how to set up your *My Oxford Seminars* account. This email address is your login email for your account. Refer to Section Three of the *100-Hour Course Handbook* for complete details.

V3 Timing and Structure of the Online Component

Time Frame

- You have 105 days from the last day of the in-class portion of the course to complete the online component.
- The upper right-hand corner of your screen will show you the number of days you have remaining.

Topics and Organization

- The online component is divided into 16 topics. Topics 3–12 contain readings, activities, and quizzes.
- You are required to complete these topics in the order they are presented.
- You need to complete all readings, activities, and quizzes in each topic in order to unlock the next topic.
- Topics that you have not unlocked will appear grayed out on the Course Homepage, and will have the word "locked" with a small image of a lock displayed in the "Status" column of the page.
- You can begin the Final Assignment once all previous topics have been completed.

Need Help?

Take advantage of our Frequently Asked Questions (FAQs) section. Answers to the most frequently asked questions can be found easily on any page of the online component. The link can be found on the top navigation bar.

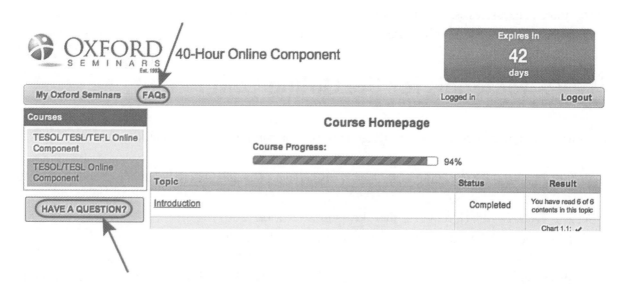

If your question is not answered in the FAQs, click on the "Have a Question?" link in the left-hand navigation column.

Please be as specific in your question as possible, so we can provide the answers you need. We will respond as quickly as possible, usually within 1–3 business days.

V4 Tracking Your Progress

The Course Homepage tracks your progress as you complete the online component.

The Course Progress bar shows you the percentage of the online component you have already completed, and the Status and Result sections give you further information to chart your progress. (See the image below.)

Course Homepage

Course Progress:

[progress bar] 15%

Topic	Status	Result
Introduction	Completed	You have read 6 of 6 contents in this topic
Topic 1: Getting Comfortable with Grammar	Completed	Chart 1.1: ✔ Chart 1.2: ✔ Chart 1.3: ✔
Topic 2: Unit and Lesson Planning	Completed	You have read 5 of 5 contents in this topic

- When you have completed all the readings, activities, and quizzes in Topics 1–15, you will gain access to Topic 16: Final Assignment.
- After you pass the Final Assignment, you will still have access to Topics 1–15 for future reference when you are teaching abroad.

Please note: The quizzes assist you in measuring your progress, but are not counted in the final score. The Final Assignment is the only score that is counted.

V5 Materials for the Online Component

The online component uses materials provided in the online component itself, as well as the following texts:

1. Oxford Seminars' *TESOL/TEFL Certification Course Training Manual* (Oxford Seminars, Oxford University Press, 2014).
2. *How to Teach English* (Jeremy Harmer, Pearson Education, 2007).
3. *Grammar Sense 2*, Second Edition (Oxford University Press, 2012).

As you progress through each of the topics, you will be directed to readings and tables within the online content, as well as within each of the three texts listed above.

Questions in the Final Assignment are drawn from all of these resources.

V6 Navigating the Online Component

When you log in to the online component you will see the Course Homepage.

This page shows all 16 topics to be completed, as well as your progress to date. You need to complete each topic in order from 1–15, working through all the activities and tasks.

Once you complete a topic, it will unlock your access to the next topic. You can see your progress in the "Status" column to the right of each topic and in the Course Progress bar on the Course Homepage. (See the image below.)

Course Homepage

Course Progress: 94%

Topic	Status	Result
Introduction	Completed	You have read 6 of 6 contents in this topic
Topic 1: Getting Comfortable with Grammar	Completed	Chart 1.1: ✔ Chart 1.2: ✔ Chart 1.3: ✔
Topic 2: Unit and Lesson Planning	Completed	You have read 5 of 5 contents in this topic
Topic 3: The Present	Completed	Intro Quiz: 0/8 TR Quiz: 0/10
Topic 4: The Past	Completed	Intro Quiz: 0/8 TR Quiz: 0/10
Topic 5: The Future	Completed	Intro Quiz: 0/8 TR Quiz: 0/10

When you click on a topic link from the Course Homepage, you are taken to an introduction page with information on the content of that topic.

You can navigate back to the Course Homepage at any time by clicking on the Course Homepage link at the top of the left-hand navigation column.

Left-hand Navigation Column

The left-hand navigation column indicates where you are within each topic. When you click on a topic, it will be highlighted so you can easily identify your current location.

Quiz Review Page

After you complete the Intro Quiz and the Topic Review Quiz, your score will be visible on the quiz pages and also on the Course Homepage.

V7 Navigating the Topics

Once you have completed all parts of a topic, you will be directed back to the Course Homepage to begin the next topic.

Topic 1: Getting Comfortable with Grammar
Topic 1 encourages you to think about English grammar. The activities in Topic 1 assess your grammar knowledge and challenge you to determine common errors made by English speakers, both native and non-native.

Topic 2: Unit and Lesson Planning
Topic 2 introduces you to your texts through discussion on long-term unit planning, with a focus on how to structure units and use teaching resources.

Topics 3–12: Grammar Guide with Five Elements
Topics 3–12 guide your progress through the *Grammar Sense 2* text and also draw from material covered in Oxford Seminars' *TESOL/TEFL Certification Course Training Manual* and Jeremy Harmer's *How to Teach English*. Each of these topics consists of the following five elements:

- **Intro Quiz:** The Intro Quiz assesses your previous knowledge of the topic material and introduces concepts that will be covered in the topic. After completing the Intro Quiz, you will be able to view the correct answers and receive suggestions for review, if needed. The Intro Quiz **does not** affect your final score.
- **Essential Reading:** This section directs you through the material in *Grammar Sense 2*. The questions will guide your reading and assist you in thinking critically about the material being covered. These questions **are not** graded.
- **Grammar Tables and Timelines:** This section assembles all the grammar tables and timelines relevant to the topic. You can view them for quick reference, or print them and use them to present grammar material in your own ESL classroom. (Note: Within the *Grammar Sense 2* text, grammar tables are referred to as "Form Charts".)
- **How to Teach…:** This section discusses communicative approaches and activities that you can use in future lesson planning.
- **Topic Review Quiz:** The Topic Review Quiz is the final activity in each topic and is used to evaluate your understanding. As well as reviewing grammar concepts from the topic, the quiz also presents related teaching scenarios that may arise in an ESL classroom. These quizzes **do not** affect your final score; they are used for you to measure your progress and to prepare you for the Final Assignment.

Topic 13: Communicative Grammar Teaching
Topic 13 reviews communicative approaches to language teaching and explores how these approaches can be applied to teaching grammar. In this topic, you will review a series of questions regarding approaches to grammar instruction and consider each in detail.

Topic 14: Teaching Resources, Lesson Starters, and Grammar Games
Topic 14 provides a variety of teaching resources and lesson plan ideas to assist you in your future classroom. Once you have read all the pages of this topic, you will be directed back to the Course Homepage to begin the next topic.

Topic 15: Online Component Summary

Topic 15 is a summary of all the material studied in the online component. You will be asked to re-attempt the same charts you completed in Topic 1 in order to self-assess your development throughout the online component. Completing this topic will provide access to Topic 16: Final Assignment.

 # V8 About the Final Assignment

Before You Begin the Final Assignment

- Topics 1–15 must be completed before you can begin the Final Assignment.
- The Final Assignment consists of 100 questions.
- The questions will draw from the following:
    - Material covered in the in-class component
    - Material provided in the online component
    - Oxford Seminars' *TESOL/TEFL Certification Course Training Manual*
    - *How to Teach English* by Jeremy Harmer
    - *Grammar Sense 2*

The Final Assignment **does not need to be completed in one sitting**. You can save your progress, click on the logout button, and return as many times as necessary (within the deadline) to complete all questions.

The questions will be in a similar format as in the Intro and Topic Review Quizzes.

Your 100-hour certificate will be mailed to the US address we have on file. If you need to update your address, click on the "Update contact information" button in the left-hand navigation bar, **before** submitting the Final Assignment.

While Writing the Final Assignment

- Your answers are automatically saved when you hit "Next" after each question. You may return and change your answers; you may also skip questions and return to them later.
- The Final Assignment is open-book; you may refer to your notes and the materials included with the course.
- Once you submit the Final Assignment, you will be unable to change your answers.

After You Complete the Final Assignment

- After submitting your Final Assignment, your course score will be displayed immediately on your *My Oxford Seminars* homepage.
- A score of 65 percent or higher is required to pass the Final Assignment and complete the course. If you do not meet the minimum passing score of 65 percent, you can choose to retake the Final Assignment for a fee.
- You will retain access to the material covered in Topics 1–15, but **will not** be able to retake the Final Assignment or quizzes, once you have submitted your Final Assignment and successfully passed the course.

Credits

Section A

16 Noam Chomsky. Lecture, January 1970, delivered at Loyola University, Chicago. "Language and Freedom," published in *For Reasons of State* (1973)

Section B

18/25 http://www.funderstanding.com/content/about-learning; 23/27 De La Cruz, Y. and S. Armstrong. A volunteer literacy tutor training model for teaching adults with or without learning disabilities. Pottsdown YWCA Adult Literacy Centre, 1995; 29 *Multiple Intelligences in the Classroom* (p.41) by Thomas Armstrong. — Alexandria, VA: ASCD. © 2000 by ASCD. Used with permission. Learn more about ASCD at www.ascd.org; http://www.workshoppersonline.com/davidlazear.htm; 33 *Multiple Intelligences in the Classroom* (p.45) by Thomas Armstrong. — Alexandria, VA: ASCD. © 2000 by ASCD. Used with permission. Learn more about ASCD at www.ascd.org; 34 *Multiple Intelligences in the Classroom* (p.2) by Thomas Armstrong. — Alexandria, VA: ASCD. © 2000 by ASCD. Used with permission. Learn more about ASCD at www.ascd.org; 35 http://behaviourinterventions.com/Documents/Stages_of_Development.pdf; 37 Stephen Lieb, from VISION, Fall 1991; 39 This material appears courtesy of Frontier College. www.frontiercollege.ca

Section C

48 http://writing.colostate.edu/guides/teaching/esl/start.cfm; 50 Alan Hofmeister; 52 Bhola, H. S. 1990. Evaluating "Literacy for development" projects, programs and campaigns: Evaluation planning, design and implementation, and utilization of evaluation results. Hamburg, Germany: UNESCO Institute for Education; DSE; 53 based on Chamberlain, P. and Medeiros-Landurand, P. (1991). Practical considerations for the assessment of LEP students with special needs. In E. Hamayan & J. Damico (eds.), *Limiting Bias in the Assessment of Bilingual Students.* (p 112-156). Austin, Texas: Pro-ed; 54 Developed for United States Department of Education. Copyright © 2000 RMC Research Corporation; 56 http://www.squires.fayette.k12.ky.us/

Section D

60 http://www.teflteachthai.com/First_Day_of_Class.html; 61 "12 Steps to Clearer Instructions" by Jaimie Scanlon. Used with permission; 63 Rochelle Keogh; 71 Elspeth Deir, Joan McDuff, Queen's University Faculty of Education

Section E

78 Copyright © Performance Learning Systems, Inc. ® . Performance Learning Systems, Inc. is an educational services company located in Allentown, Pa. and on the World Wide Web at www.plsweb.com. Used with permission. All rights reserved; 79 Joseph F. Zisk, Ed.D; 79 Copyright 2008 Inspiring Teachers Publishing, Inc; 80 Reprinted with the permission of Thomas R. McDaniel and Phi Delta Kappan; 82 *Back off, Cool down, Try again: Teaching Students How to Control Aggressive Behavior* by Sylvia Rockwell. Publisher: Reston, Va: Council for Exceptional Children, ©1995; 83 Barrie Bennett; 85 Kizlik, R.J. (2008, August 29) An Effective Classroom Management Context [Online ADPRIMA.COM Retrieved, (2008, August 28) from http://www.adprima.com/managing.htm; 88 Adapted from the East Bay AIDS Education and Training Center, Oakland, CA; 91 Adapted from an article in *Individuals*, a publication of the Temperament Project, Spring, 1994; 92 http://everything2.com/index.pl?node_id=774827; 95 ©2008 by Sue Watson (http://specialed.about.com/library/templates/contract5.doc). Used with permission of About, Inc. which can be found online at www.about.com. All rights reserved.

Section F

98 *Alpha to Omega*, Hornsby, Shear, & Pool; 98/101 WRITINGENGLISH.COM helps to make your writing excel; 113 *Understanding and Using English Grammar*, Betty Azar, Copyright 1999. Reprinted by permission of Pearson Education, Inc; 116 http://www.gallaudet.edu/CLAST/Tutorial_and_Instructional_Programs/English_Works.html; 118 Copyright © Language Dynamics, http://www.englishpage.com/irregularverbs/irregularverbs.html; 128 Dennis Oliver http://www.eslcafe.com/pv/pv-list.html; 129 www.language.ca; 132 Brown, H. *Principles of Language Learning and Teaching.* New York: Longman, 2000; 133/135/139 *Introduction to Teaching English*, Jill Hadfield & Charles Hadfield, Oxford University Press; 134 *Grammar*, Scott Thornbury, Oxford University Press; 143 From *For the Love of Language: Poetry for every learner*, by Nancy Lee Cecil. © 1993. Reprinted by permission of Portage & Main Press. www.portageandmainpress.com; 144 Stephen S. Pickering

Section G

146 T. Iveson (2006); 148 Reprinted by permission of rhlschool.com, Copyright RHL 1999; 150 Vocabulary 2nd ed, Morgan & Rinvolucri Oxford University Press; 157 *English Know How Book 1*, Blackwell, Naber, Manin, & Dubofsky, Oxford University Press

Section H

161 *The Cambridge Guide to Teaching English to Speakers of other Languages*, David Nunan & Ronald Carter; p. 56-65 Cambridge University Press, 2001. Reprinted with the permission of Cambridge University Press; 171 From the *Canadian Oxford Dictionary*, 2nd Edition. Edited by Katherine Barber. Copyright © Oxford University Press Canada 2004. Reprinted by permision of the publisher; Alex Case has published hundreds of reviews, articles, lesson plans, worksheets, and tips in TEFL magazines and online; 176 Sony/ATV Tunes; 177 **Friday I'm In Love**. Words and Music by Robert Smith, Simon Gallup, Paul S. Thompson, Boris Williams and Perry Bamonte. Copyright © 1992 by Fiction Songs Ltd. All Rights for the world Administered by Universal Music Publishing MGB Ltd. All Rights for the U.S. Administered by Universal Music - MGB Songs. International Copyright Secured All Rights Reserved. *Reprinted by Permission of Hal Leonard Corporation*; 179 http://www.yourdictionary.com/library/mispron.html

Section I

186 Penny Ur, Cambridge University Press, 1996 *A Course in Language Teaching—Practice and Theory*. Reprinted with the permission of Cambridge University Press; 188/213 Barrie Bennett, based on *Cooperative Learning* by Spencer Kagan; 190 Rules for the Game of Charades is from http://www.cs.umd.edu/~nau/misc/charades.html; 191 Ray Graham and Mark Walsh; 196/198/205/207/208/210/211/212 From *Have Your Say!* by Irene McKay. Copyright © Oxford University Press Canada 1999. Reprinted by permission of the publisher; 199 ©2008 by Kenneth Beare (http://esl.about.com/library/lessons/blfriend.htm) Used with permission of About, Inc. which can be found online at www.about.com. All rights

reserved; 201 http://www.eastsideliteracy.org/tutorsupport/ESL/ESL_Messages.htm; 215 Daniel J. Deal (New York, NY); 215 http://www.eslcafe.com/idea/index.cgi?display:1143745570-21575.txt; 216 http://iteslj.org/games/9966.html; 217 http://iteslj.org/Lessons/Counihan-Activities/Intonation.html; 220 Copyright Meridian International Center, Washington, DC, USA; 220 *Oxford ESL Dictionary*, Oxford University Press

Section J

222 Fifty Ideas to Improve Listening, Pearson Education, Pearson Education Limited. Copyright © Pearson Education Ltd 2006. Publishing as Pearson Longman. All rights reserved; 223/224/226 *Young Learners*, Sarah Phillips, Oxford University Press 1993; 228 http://hungary.usembassy.gov/uploads/images/6AZDMEFOw_f1g59zdHYGaw/unit_5_listening.pdf; 233 **IF I HAD $1000000**. Words and Music by STEVEN PAGE and ED ROBERTSON © 1994 WB MUSIC CORP., FRESH BAKED GOODS and TREAT BAKER MUSIC. All Rights Administered by WB MUSIC CORP. All Rights Reserved; 235 Used with the permission of Wilkins Management; 236 ©2008 by Kenneth Beare (http://esl.about.com/od/teachingadvancedlevel/a/tvlesson.htm.) Used with permission of About, Inc. which can be found online at www.about.com. All rights reserved; 236 Chris Cotter juggles English teaching and curriculum design in Japan. He also runs Heads Up English, a site devoted to producing real and relevant materials, ideas, and advice for both teachers and students. You can see more of his work at www.headsupenglish.com

Section K

240 ©2008 by Kenneth Beare (http://esl.about.com/od/englishreadingskills/a/readingskills.htm.) Used with permission of About, Inc. which can be found online at www.about.com. All rights reserved; 241 *Skillful Reading: A Text and Workbook for Students of English as a Second Language*, by Sonka & Whalley, Prentice-Hall 1981; 244 Thank you to Ted Power for permission to use "Teaching L2 reading: Classroom activities: skills needed for reading different texts-types" from English Language Learning and Teaching at http://www.btinternet.com/~ted.power/esl1108.html; 246 Nicholas Criscuolo; 251 Penny Ur, Cambridge University Press, 1996 *A Course in Language Teaching—Practice and Theory*. Reprinted with the permission of Cambridge University Press; 253 Select Readings Intermediate, Lee & Gundersen, Oxford University Press 2001; 263 *Companies with a Conscience*, Carol Pub. Group 1992; 263 ERIC Digests; 264 Nitya Rani & Prof. Premakumari Dheram, School of English Language Education, EFL University (formerly CIEFL), Hyderabad, India; 270 http://www.thegrid.org.uk/learning/english/14-19/resources/writing/documents/TeachingtheclassnovelSuggestedapproaches.doc

Section L

274 *Introduction to Teaching English*, Jill Hadfield & Charles Hadfield, Oxford University Press; 277 From Canadian Oxford Spelling Dictionary. Edited by Robert Pontisso & Eric Sinkins. Copyright © Oxford University Press Canada 1999. Reprinted by permission of the publisher; 280; From Breakthroughs, 2nd edn, by Marina Engelking and Gloria McPherson-Ramirez. Copyright © Oxford University Press Canada 2008. Reprinted by permission of the publisher; 281 http://iteslj.org/Lessons/Ogasawara-Warming.html; 285 From Breakthroughs Workbook, 2nd edn, by Marina Engelking and Gloria McPherson-Ramirez. From Breakthroughs, 2nd edn, by Marina Engelking and Gloria McPherson-Ramirez. Copyright © Oxford University Press Canada 2008. Reprinted by permission of the publisher; 287 From The Canadian Writer's Handbook, 5th edn, by William E. Messenger, Jan de Bruyn, Judy Brown, and Ramona Montagnes. Copyright © Oxford University Press Canada 2008. Reprinted by permission of the publisher; 307 http://www.ritro.com/sections/tips/story.bv?storyid=77; 311 http://www.yourdictionary.com/esl/Teaching-Spelling-Strategies-to-ESL-Students.html; 314 Surrey County Council (Services for Schools and Learning); 313 From *Skill Set: Strategies for Reading and Writing* by Lucia Engkent. Copyright © Oxford University Press Canada 2007. Reprinted by permission of the publisher.

Section M

322/357 Michael Berman is a teacher, writer and Core Shamanic Counsellor. Other ELT publications by Michael include "A Multiple Intelligences Road to an ELT Classroom" (Crown House), and "Tell Us A Story" (Brain Friendly Publications). For further information, please visit www.Thestoryteller.org.uk; *Oxford Idioms: Dictionary for Learners of English*, Oxford University Press; 338 Permission from Wayne Magnuson, author, ENGLISH IDIOMS, Sayings & Slang; 339 http://a4esl.org/q/h/9807/km-animalidioms.html; 340 http://a4esl.org/q/h/vm/m-body.html; 342 http://a4esl.org/q/h/9801/lk-idiomsp.html; 343 Megan Thompson & Kimberly E. Day-Hoenisch; 344 © 1999 Scholastic, Inc. This material is published under license from the publisher through the Gale Group, Farmington Hills, Michigan; 345 *Practice with Idioms*, Oxford University Press

Section N

356/362 With thanks to Queen's University International Centre, Kingston, Canada, for supplying material for students going abroad; http://edweb.sdsu.edu/people/cguanipa/cultshok.htm; 358 Factors Important to Successful Intercultural Adjustments. Online 17 November 2004 (http://www.worldwide.edu/travel_planner/culture_adjusting.jsp); 359 http://www.ehow.com/how_2170747_prepare-teach-english-abroad.html; 360 http://ancillaries.dal.ca/images/ises/Preparing_for_Departure_Mar07.pdf; 368 http://www.research.uwaterloo.ca/international/predeparture/checklist-printable.html; 365 http://studyabroad.isp.msu.edu/forms/glbt.html

Section P

378 http://www.group-games.com; 381 www.Canada-ESL.com — Online ESL Lessons, Resources, Study English in Canada, Teach English Abroad; 388/389/390 Matthew Errey (teflgames.com); 392/393 www.GenkiEnglish.com

Section Q

396 The World Factbook at www.cia.gov; 399 http://www.usa-flag-site.org/history.shtml; 401 http://www.gbjann.com/anthem/history.htm; 403 *Step Forward 1*, Jane Spigarelli, Oxford University Press 2007

Section R

408 http://www.language.ca/pdfs/clb_adults.pdf; 411/415 ©2008 by Kenneth Beare (http://esl.about.com/od/esleflteachingtechnique/a/lesson_format.htm) Used with permission of About, Inc. which can be found online at www.about.com. All rights reserved; 413 Saskatchewan Ministry of Education, Regina, Canada; 415 *Testing Spoken Language*, Nic Underhill, Cambridge University Press 1987; 418 *Vocabulary* 2nd ed, Morgan & Rinvolucri Oxford University Press

Oxford Seminars' TESOL/TEFL Certification Course Locations

Arizona
Phoenix
Tucson

California
Berkeley
Fullerton
Irvine
Los Angeles
Northridge
Riverside
Sacramento
San Diego
San Francisco
San Jose
Santa Barbara
Santa Cruz

Colorado
Boulder
Denver

Connecticut
Hartford
New Haven

District of Columbia
Washington, D.C.

Florida
Jacksonville
Miami
Orlando
St. Petersburg

Georgia
Atlanta

Hawaii
Honolulu

Illinois
Chicago
Evanston

Indiana
Bloomington
Indianapolis

Iowa
Des Moines
Iowa City

Kentucky
Lexington
Louisville

Louisiana
Baton Rouge
New Orleans

Maryland
Baltimore
College Park

Massachusetts
Amherst
Boston

Michigan
Ann Arbor
Detroit
East Lansing

Minnesota
Minneapolis
St. Cloud

Missouri
Kansas City
St. Louis

Nevada
Las Vegas
Reno

New Jersey
New Brunswick
Newark

New York
Albany
Buffalo
Manhattan
Queens
Rochester
Stony Brook
Syracuse

North Carolina
Chapel Hill
Charlotte
Winston-Salem

Ohio
Cincinnati
Cleveland
Columbus

Oklahoma
Norman
Oklahoma City

Oregon
Eugene
Portland

Pennsylvania
Philadelphia
Pittsburgh

Rhode Island
Providence

South Carolina
Columbia
Greenville

Tennessee
Memphis
Nashville

Texas
Austin
Dallas
Houston
San Antonio

Utah
Salt Lake City

Virginia
Norfolk
Richmond

Washington
Seattle
Tacoma

Wisconsin
Madison
Milwaukee

Canada
Burnaby
Calgary
Edmonton
Halifax
Hamilton

London
Montreal
North York
Ottawa
Regina

Saskatoon
St. John's
Toronto
Vancouver
Victoria

Waterloo
Windsor
Winnipeg

INDEX